THE PLATFORM

ITS RISE AND PROGRESS

THE PLATFORM

ITS RISE AND PROGRESS

BY

HENRY JEPHSON

IN TWO VOLUMES

VOL. II

New York
MACMILLAN AND CO.
AND LONDON
1892

TYPOGRAPHY BY J. S. CUSHING & CO., BOSTON, U.S.A.

PRESSWORK BY BERWICK & SMITH, BOSTON, U.S.A.

CONTENTS

VOLUME II

PART III

PART IV

PART V

PART VI

PART III

CHAPTER XIV

The Roman Catholic Emancipation Agitation

CHAPTER XV

The First Reform Act Agitation

CHAPTER XVI

The Platform after the Reform Act

PART IV

CHAPTER XVII

The First Crisis of Chartism

CHAPTER XVIII

The Anti-Corn-Law Agitation

CHAPTER XIX

The Second Crisis of Chartism

PART V

CHAPTER XX

The Second Reform Act Agitation

CHAPTER XXI

The Bulgarian Atrocity Agitation

CHAPTER XXII

The Platform at the General Election of 1880

CHAPTER XXIII

The Third Reform Act Agitation

PART VI

CHAPTER XXIV

Concluding Considerations

CHAPTER XIV

THE ROMAN CATHOLIC EMANCIPATION AGITATION

WHILE the Platform, under the soothing influence of the material prosperity of the country, was still in a quiescent state, and before any endeavour was made to turn to account the freedom that had been secured, the English people were to have exhibited to them the instructive example of how the Platform could be made a great political power—they were to be shown what really might be made of the privilege of free meeting and free speaking.

Hitherto the champions and votaries of the Platform had been hampered by the restrictions on the right of meeting and on the expression of opinion, but part of their weakness was due to a defect of their own, and not to the oppression of the Government. Hitherto the Platform had been devoid of such organisation as would make it really powerful, and that was a matter which concerned them to supply. Neither such organisation as the leaders of the Economy Agitation adopted, nor that of the London Corresponding Society, nor yet that of Major Cartwright and his Hampden Clubs, had added much to its efficiency. There had been no general organisation, no central directing body, no controlling power.

In the more recent agitations the men whose names have become familiar to us as the most prominent public speakers, never had either the means or the ability to give it any real form of organisation, or to give its spasmodic and isolated acts any cohesion. There was no union among them; each of them went pretty much his own way, and they appear to have been unwilling or unable to co-operate, or to undertake the building up and conducting of an organisation. It was easy enough for men like them to assemble large meetings, and to secure listeners. As Hooker wrote many years before: "He that goes about to persuade a multitude that they are not so well governed as they ought to be, shall never want attentive and favourable hearers." But they do not seem to have been able to get further than speaking at meetings. They went to a place, made a speech, and came away again; but beyond exciting, or instructing, or encouraging the people, or giving voice to their thoughts, they did little more.

How long a period might have elapsed before the advantages of organisation would have been brought home to the English people, had they been left to their own resources, it is impossible to say, for the instruction suddenly came from outside, and Ireland afforded to England not mere theoretic instruction in the matter, but an actual visible example of the power of the Platform when backed by organisation of a complete and thorough character. As the lesson was not lost on the English people, it is desirable to give a somewhat detailed account of the celebrated Irish organisation which succeeded in forcing from a reluctant English Government the emancipation of Roman Catholics. The narrative, moreover, illustrates under a strong light some of the most interesting features connected with the Platform.

It has been unnecessary so far to refer to the Platform in Ireland. Ireland had not joined nor participated in any of the Platform agitations which I have described. Until the end of the eighteenth century she had a separate Parliament of her own, and she had had agitations of her own, and the Platform had been freely used, but success or failure there had no bearing on the Platform in England. Nor had she participated either up to this in the Platform agitations in England after the Union. The civic industrial population of Great Britain were set on their own particular objects. The vast majority of the population of Ireland had their particular desires and ambitions, and there was no bond of alliance whatever for joint agitation—nothing whatever in common between them.

Mr. Wyse, in his history of the Catholic Association, which was written very shortly after the events which it chronicles, has drawn an elaborate contrast between the action of public opinion in the two countries.

"Public opinion in Ireland," he says, "and public opinion

in England, are not to be measured by the same standard. In England it is, like its civilisation, the slow but robust growth of many centuries; it has risen out of the cool study of great political and commercial questions; out of the slow comparison of their principles, with their exemplifications in existing government; out of a tranquil and persevering observation of the influence of both on all classes of society in the neighbouring countries, particularly in France and America, and a keen and often an involuntary application of the common sense conclusions drawn from such comparison to their own. In Ireland everything is partial, everything is momentary, everything is impulse—there is no standard, or the standard changes every day. Upon the great middle layer of English society no question falls without leaving its lasting impression. Upon a corresponding, though by no means a similar class in Ireland, the utmost which can be expected is a strong but transient sentiment, ruffling for a moment the surface, but then leaving the depths as dead and as sluggish as before.

"In a word, the Irish act on belief, the English on conviction—one *feels*, the other *knows;* reason in general is the guide of one nation, passion of the other, and one impression lasts, and the other passes away."[1]

There is much that is true in this description, but there were some impressions among the Irish which did not pass away. They may have been active at one time, and dormant at another, but they were held as tenaciously as any martyr ever held his faith, and the subject of the Irish agitation, which was to afford so much instruction to the people of England, was one of these—namely, the civil position of the Roman Catholics in the State. For long had this question agitated Ireland, and many efforts had been made to obtain a removal of the disabilities imposed by law on Catholics. It is unnecessary for us to go back further than the year 1823. Sheil, one of the great workers for the cause, and one of the most brilliant speakers, has given us the following description of the state of the question in that year:—"An entire cessation of Catholic meetings," he says, "had taken place. We had virtually abandoned the question. Not only was it not

[1] See *Historical Sketch of the late Catholic Association of Ireland*, by Thomas Wyse, Esq., jun., vol. i. p. 189.

debated in Parliament, but in Ireland there was neither committee, board, nor association. The result was, that a total stagnation of public feeling took place, and I do not exaggerate when I say that the Catholic question was nearly forgotten; all public meetings had ceased; no angry resolutions issued from public bodies; no exciting speeches appeared in the public papers. . . . A general stagnation diffused itself over the national feelings. The public pulse had stopped, the circulation of all generous sentiment had been arrested, and the country was palsied to the heart."[1]

It was in this state of stagnation that the Catholic Association came into existence, with the object of obtaining from the British Parliament the removal of the disqualifications under which Roman Catholics suffered. Mr. Wyse has given a description of its origin: "Mr. O'Connell and Mr. Sheil," he says, "met by accident in the year 1823 at the house of a common friend in the mountains of Wicklow; and, after mutually lamenting the degraded and torpid state of their Catholic countrymen, agreed to sign an Address, and enclose it without delay to the most influential gentlemen of their body. This was the first foundation of the Association. The summons was at first treated by some with scorn, with indignation by others, with neglect by all. . . . A few newspaper rencontres succeeded; the old war of recrimination recommenced; it attracted the public attention; it excited the public feeling; an interest was created, and from that moment everything was success."[2] And then he describes the formation of the Association: "The first seeds of the Catholic Association," he says, "were scarcely perceptible; ten or twenty individuals met in a retired room at a tavern in Sackville Street and resolved boldly to commence.[3] The nucleus was formed; it increased; every day presented an accession of new and enthusiastic members. . . . A new principle, that of an open club, without canvass or ballot, the members admissible on the *viva voce* proposition of a friend, and the subscription of £1 was adopted. . . . The Association gained daily in strength;

[1] *Memoirs of the Right Hon. R. L. Sheil*, by W. T. M'Cullagh, vol. i. p. 183.

[2] Wyse, vol. i. p. 198.

[3] On the 10th May 1823 the meeting was held at which the resolution was adopted for the appointment of a Catholic Association.—See *Select Speeches of Daniel O'Connell, Esq., M.P.*, by his son.

it soon embraced all classes in the roll of its members. The aristocracy joined it. . . . Behind them came the almost entire body of the gentry. . . . The (Catholic) clergy, too, had sent in from time to time their adhesion. The recruits from the younger clergy were numerous beyond precedent; they advocated its principles and executed its measures, not merely with the fidelity of a tried friend, but with the zeal and enthusiasm of a proselyte."

The central Association sat in Dublin. It was composed of the ablest Catholics of the time, foremost among them being the greatest of Irish popular orators—Daniel O'Connell and Richard Lalor Sheil. It held weekly meetings, at which thrilling speeches were delivered advocating the cause of the Catholics. The speeches were fully reported in the daily Press, and thus obtained a very large circulation. But the Association did not confine its labours to the capital, nor to speeches. Every device which ingenuity could suggest for awakening the people and winning their active support was put into operation. To obtain the necessary funds for carrying on the agitation, and with the object of giving the people a continued interest in the matter, the "Catholic Rent," or the offering of one penny a month for the furtherance of the cause, was proposed and adopted. This step in itself entailed a great use of the Platform; for when the inhabitants of a parish wished to contribute to the "rent," a meeting of the parish was summoned. At the meeting a chairman was appointed, "frequently, though not always, the priest." Resolutions were proposed approving of the collecting of the rent, and a Committee appointed, with a secretary and a treasurer to manage the collections. Rent collectors were then appointed, and correspondence with the Central Association opened, and thus the Central body became possessed of a local parish organisation throughout Ireland of the most powerful character. "The rent collection soon settled into a system; the collectors became the disciplined, as the rent contributors were the irregular troops of the Association;" and, as Wyse said, "The Association engrossed the attention of multitudes. The entire country formed but one Association."

From the debates in the House of Commons further information can be gathered as to the power of the Association.

It was pointed out there that the Association, "though a public body, differed from most public meetings in this point —that they were all of one mind. There was no competition of opinion; no opposing voice was heard. Every speech was previously arranged, and every decision was unanimous. . . . The Association appointed their Committees of Grievances, of Education, and of Finance. They had almost copied verbatim the sessional orders of the House.[1] They met when they pleased; and, in point of fact, they were in the habit of sitting from January to December, and of exercising their powers with as much strictness and severity as any absolute monarch could do."[2]

Another forcible description of the Association is given by Canning. He described it as "Self-elected, self-constructed, self-assembled, self-adjourned; acknowledging no superior, tolerating no equal; interfering in all stages with the administration of justice; denouncing publicly before trial individuals against whom it institutes prosecutions, and rejudging and condemning those whom the law has acquitted; menacing the free Press with punishment, and openly declaring its intention to corrupt that part of it which it cannot intimidate; and lastly, for these and other purposes, levying contributions on the people of Ireland."[3]

The power of the Association became at last so great that an outcry was raised by a large part of the public in Great Britain against it, and the Government felt impelled to take action to curtail its influence.

The King, in his speech opening the Session of Parliament in February 1825, condemned it. He said: "There never was a period in the history of this country when all the great interests of the nation were at the same time in so thriving a condition. . . . It is the more to be regretted that Associations should exist in Ireland which have adopted proceedings irreconcilable with the spirit of the Constitution, and calculated, by exciting alarm, and by exasperating animosities, to endanger the peace of society, and to retard the course of national improvement."[4]

Immediately after the opening of the Session a Bill was

[1] Speech of Mr. Goulbourn, 10th February 1825.—Hansard, vol. xii. p. 168.
[2] See Plunket's *Speech*, p. 317. [3] Hansard, vol. xii. p. 465. [4] *Ibid.* p. 1.

introduced for the Suppression of Unlawful Societies in Ireland, in which category the Catholic Association was included.

Peel, who was then Home Secretary, "conceived Parliament to be the sole constitutional judge of such matters (as Catholic disabilities), and if Parliament thought a law ought to be continued, those who fancied themselves aggrieved by it must not resort to unconstitutional measures to procure its abolition. They might petition, they might represent their grievances to Parliament, and their petitions and representations would be taken into consideration; but Parliament would abandon its duty, if it allowed any body of men to act independently of its authority, and only according to their own free pleasures. He claimed the right of Parliament to act as it should think fit, if it should deem the Catholic Association, or any other of the same sort, at variance with the principles of the Constitution."[1] The Act made every Society illegal which was constituted for the redress of grievances either in Church or State, renewing its meetings for more than fourteen days or collecting or receiving money.

In the course of the debate on the Bill, Canning raised even a more important question than the one under discussion, more important as being a question possibly affecting the whole of the kingdom and not merely part of it—namely, the compatibility of any such body existing side by side with Parliament. It is one of the gravest political questions in connection with the Platform, and will hereafter have to be again referred to. He said: "When I speak of the representative character of the Catholic Association, I do not mean to assert that it has ever affirmed itself to be the representative of the people of Ireland. No such thing; it is too wise in its generation to hazard so impolitic a declaration. If it had done so, it would have been unnecessary to argue the present question; for no new Act of Parliament would in that case have been necessary to enable the law to deal with it. . . . A representative character has, however, been attributed to it by others. The repeated statements which have been made in this debate, that this Association is, and is held to be, the virtual representative of the people of Ireland, call

[1] Hansard, vol. xii. p. 248, 1825.

upon the House to consider whether such an Association can coexist with the House of Commons. Can there, I ask, coexist in this kingdom, without imminent hazard to its peace, an assembly constituted as the House of Commons is, and another assembly invested with a representative character, as complete as that of the House of Commons itself, though not conferred by the same process? Does not the very proposition that such is the character, and such the attributes of the Catholic Association, even if not actually true at the present time, warn us at least what the Association, if unchecked, may become? And if the Catholic Association, with the full strength and maturity of the representative character, could not (as assuredly it could not) coexist with the House of Commons, shall we not check the Association in time, before it has acquired that strength and maturity?"[1]

The Act promptly proved to be a dead letter. The Association, it is true, came to an end, but a new Catholic Association was at once formed, which evaded the prohibition of the Act, and which proceeded with increased vigour to improve the organisation, and to evoke greater manifestations than ever of public opinion.

Meetings were held in the provinces, in one or other of the counties by rotation, and the leaders of the Association went down to them and addressed the people. O'Connell's fame as an orator is so well known that it is needless to give details of his speeches, or the occasions on which he spoke. His place was the Platform. It was there that the power of his oratory was most displayed, and there that he won one oratorical triumph after another. He was supported by many other forcible and eloquent speakers, foremost among them being Sheil.

Monsieur Duvergier, in his *Lettres sur les Elections Anglaises*, 1827, has described the fascination of Sheil's oratory: "In a word I was seduced, I was dazzled, and together with me the whole assembly. During an entire hour one single soul, that of the orator, seemed to animate the living mass; and from time to time you would have said that an electric shock completely convulsed them. I never before assisted at so absolute a triumph."[2]

[1] Hansard, vol. xii. p. 470, 1825. [2] See M'Cullagh's *Sheil*, vol. i. p. 311.

One of the plans of the Association for impressing the public mind was that of holding a number of meetings simultaneously.

"On a specified day," said Sheil, "let simultaneous meetings be held in every chapel in Ireland. Upon the same day 2500 meetings will be held—thus an enormous movement of the population will be produced. Hitherto the giant has raised but a single limb, henceforth the whole frame of the public mind shall be put at once into motion. Briareus should arise and lift up his hundred arms together." [1]

Another proposal was the taking a census of the Roman Catholic population of Ireland, and the formation of a register of the names and addresses of all the parish priests in Ireland, with the view to its being taken.

The advantages of such a proceeding were pointed out by Sheil,[2] who said: "Thus an individual intercourse with every parish priest would be established. They would thereby obtain a series of conductors, through which the feeling they were solicitous to circulate might be readily conveyed. From one extremity of the land to the other a regular and uniform communication would be set on foot, and a great national agency would be established. This being once effected, the general census might be taken in a week, and, what was still more important, that population might be organised into supplication, and disciplined in what might be called the tactics of petitioning."

The most important stimulus to the agitation was given by the Platform at the provincial meetings or conventions.[3] Wyse has given us a description of their effects on the people: "Such a convention," he says, "was really a series of impressive political lectures to the people on their grievances and their rights, which left behind them thoughts which burned for many months afterwards in the hearts of the peasantry, gave them a visible and sensible connection with the leading classes of their countrymen, and taught them that upon the co-operation and union of all orders depended mainly

[1] See M'Cullagh's *Sheil*, vol. i. p. 253. [2] *Ibid.* p. 262.

[3] Sheil once said to Moore: "There was but little public spirit in Ireland—they wanted continually lashing up; the priests were the only lever by which they could raise the people, and they had now brought them fully into play."—M'Cullagh's *Sheil*, vol. i. p. 275.

the chance which all orders might have of a future restoration to their rights. The provincial meeting travelled round the entire province in four or five years, and each town, and each succeeding year, vied in the numbers it could assemble, in the magnificence of its preparations, in the boldness of its resolutions, in the spirit which it generated, with its predecessors. The clergy of the entire neighbourhood assisted . . . and the eloquence of the demagogue came mended from the tongue of the ecclesiastic, and fell with a more persuasive force upon the willing attention of the people. A sort of religious sanction was thus communicated imperceptibly to a cause which, to those not immediately engaged in its promotion, appeared purely and altogether political.[1]

"In the country such an event (as a provincial meeting) is an epoch which fills a great portion of the peasant's existence; it is the hope of his entire family for months before, and the boast for months after; the speeches are read and re-read with the utmost assiduity, learned by heart, discussed and cited with an earnestness and sympathy unintelligible to a mere citizen."[2]

A description of one of these provincial meetings enables us to realise their general character. The meeting which immediately followed the successful contested election at Waterford —the first in which a candidate favourable to the Catholics had triumphed—may be taken as a good illustration.

It took place in the month of August, "while," as Wyse says, "the public heart was still burning with exultation, and heaving with the throes of the late unparalleled victory.

"The meeting was held in the Catholic Church of the city. The whole of the great area of the building was densely crowded with the population from the country. Immediately before the altar rose the Platform, on which were assembled Catholic and Protestant indiscriminately around the chair.

"It was a glorious morning—and the spirit of the people in full unison with the joyousness of the season, and still fresh with the late triumph, burst forth in a tumult of enthusiasm, which soon spread its contagion to the most indifferent heart in that vast assembly.

"Several speeches had been heard with more than ordinary

[1] Wyse, vol. i. p. 226. [2] *Ibid.* p. 241.

marks of approbation, when Mr. O'Connell at last appeared on the Platform. It is on such occasions that Mr. O'Connell is truly eloquent; but on this occasion he far exceeded himself. There broke out a clamour of joy which had no words, but escaped in rude gestures from every man below him, when appealing in bold and awful language to the young blood of Ireland on the one side, and to the infatuated Government of the country on the other, he threw himself as a mediator between both, and implored them, ere another generation, rushing impetuously into the ranks of present men, should render negotiation, as in America, impossible, to rouse from their slumber in haste, to extend the hand ere it was too late, and to save rather than have to rescue, through carnage, perhaps, and conflagration, their common country."[1]

This Waterford election had been a memorable one in the annals of the agitation. The leaders had divined or discerned the great truth, that the most effective way in which the Platform could be made to influence the Government was through its action on the House of Commons, and the General Election of 1826 offered a tempting opportunity to the Association to wrest the representation of certain counties in Ireland from the great landed proprietors. In Ireland the county franchise was very low—a nominal 40s. freehold, but in reality a household, or rather a cabinhold suffrage—and there were very large numbers of electors. It was hoped that in some cases at least they might be induced, in the interest of their religion, to vote against their landlords, whose obedient slaves they hitherto had been. The first victory was in the County Waterford, the 40s. freeholders revolting there; and in Louth the Association also triumphed. These were great and encouraging victories, and gave fresh stimulus to the cause.

Time crept on, changes taking place in the Administration in England—Lord Liverpool's health broke down, and he became too ill to continue in office. Canning succeeded him as Prime Minister, and after a few months died; then Lord Goderich became Prime Minister, and then the Duke of Wellington. But the changes scarcely affected the course of the agitation. Regardless of them it sped its way, nor did the leaders relax their energy for one moment. To what position

[1] Wyse, vol. i. p. 242.

it had reached in the summer of 1828 Sheil's speech of the 14th June bears testimony.[1] "So far from denying that this Association (which, in truth, represents Ireland) governs the people, through the power of public opinion, I proclaim it. We are endowed with great authority. It is but needful that we should lift the signal, and 7,000,000, as if by the power of enchantment, start up at our command.[2] If so much has been already done, is opportunity not to be afforded for effecting still more? Do they think that nothing more can be effected? Do they think that no further consolidation can take place? Do they think that our materials for excitement are exhausted, and that, from this crater of the public passions, no more lava can be poured out?"

One would have thought that the resources of organisation had been already exhausted; but, at O'Connell's suggestion, "Churchwardens" were appointed for each parish, to furnish monthly reports of the progress of the rent, and the census, and other matters, and also were employed as vehicles for the circulation of the public papers which were sent down to them containing full reports of the speeches at the meetings of the Association in Dublin.

Not yet content with their organisation the Association improved it, and it was settled "That the Association should continue the head club, committee, or association; that in each county there should be established a similar association or club under the immediate control of the Association; that in each parish there should be formed a similar club or association under the immediate control of the County Club." This was very generally carried into effect; and at last "The nation had become a nation of politicians, not a single chapel which had not its lecturer, not a single lecturer which had not thousands for his audience."[3]

Just as Ireland had reached this high level of political

1 M'Cullagh's *Sheil*, vol. ii. p. 10.

2 This part of his statement was slightly exaggerated. The population of Ireland at this time was under 7,750,000; of these probably 1,750,000 were Protestants; of the 6,000,000 remaining, over 3,000,000 were females; of the remaining 3,000,000 about one-third were under fifteen years of age. See, however, Sir R. Peel's Speech of 5th March 1829, *Parliamentary Debates*, vol. xii. p. 747.

3 Wyse, vol. i. p. 340.

organisation, certain changes in the Cabinet led to a vacancy in the representation of the County Clare, and the Association determined to contest the seat. O'Connell undertook to stand, though as a Roman Catholic he was disqualified from being a member of Parliament. The election took place in the latter end of June and beginning of July 1828. Often has it been described, for it was the decisive battle in the prolonged struggle for emancipation.

The phase of it on which we need to dwell is the part played in it by the Platform, and never in the history of the Platform have the circumstances under which it has been used been so striking. An alliance of religious passions and national enthusiasm, in a highly impulsive and excitable people, was worked on by powerful speakers in the most impressive surroundings, and the effect was overwhelming.

"From the moment that Mr. O'Connell's intention of opposing Mr. Fitzgerald was announced, the county of Clare was traversed in every direction by the orators of the Association and the parish priests. With unwearied activity they hurried from parish to parish, assembling and haranguing the squalid electors. The places which they chose for their convocations were the popish chapels, partly from convenience, and partly to aid the religious character which their mission instantly assumed. As Mr. Sheil afterwards said, 'Every altar became a tribune.'"[1]

Vesey Fitzgerald, the Government candidate, writing to Peel on the 17th June, says: "On Sunday I am informed that exhortations were addressed to the congregations, and a circular letter is to be read at all the altars on next Sunday."[2]

But these exhortations must have been cold and commonplace in comparison with others which were addressed to them.

"When we roused them at midnight," said Steele, one of the workers of the Association, "and called them to their illuminated altars, and stood with their priests, and told them he summoned them to vote for O'Connell, for their religion, and their country, it is not within the power of language to convey any conception of the scene."

Macnevin, too, gives a description of another meeting of the election: "Mass being finished, Father Murphy threw his

[1] *Annual Register*, 1828, p. 124.

[2] Peel's *Memoirs*, vol. i. p. 107.

vestments off, and without laying down the priest, assumed the politician. He addressed the people in Irish, and called upon them to vote for O'Connell in the name of their country and of their religion. . . . The close of his speech was peculiarly effective. He became inflamed by the power of his emotions, and while he raised himself into the loftiest attitude to which he could ascend, he laid one hand on the altar, and shook the other in the spirit of almost prophetic admonition; and while his eyes blazed and seemed to start from his forehead, thick drops fell down his face, and his voice rolled through lips livid with passion and covered with foam. It is almost unnecessary to say that such an appeal was irresistible. The multitude burst into shouts of acclamation, and would have been ready to mount a battery roaring with cannon at his command."[1]

O'Connell was returned by a triumphant majority of more than two to one. "Let men declaim for a century," said Sheil at the election; "and if they have no real grievance, their harangues will be empty sound and idle air. But when what they tell the people is true, when they are sustained by substantial facts, effects are produced of which what has taken place at this election is only an example."

Just after O'Connell's return, as if to emphasise its import, "the period, for which the abortive statute of 1825 had been enacted, expired," the old Catholic Association was at once resuscitated, and the pledge was renewed "to contest the return to Parliament of every man who would not declare himself an opponent to the Duke of Wellington's administration."

The position which the Association had reached is thus summarised in a letter from the Lord Lieutenant of Ireland, dated 2d July 1828: "Such is the extraordinary power of the Association, or rather of the agitators, of whom there are many of high ability, of ardent mind, of great daring, that I am quite certain they could lead on the people to open rebellion at a moment's notice."[2]

To this pitch of excitement and resolution had the Platform, in the hands of great popular orators, backed by a

[1] *The Speeches of the Right Honourable Richard Lalor Sheil, M.P.*, by Thomas Macnevin, p. 53.

[2] Peel's *Memoirs*, vol. i. p. 147.

powerful, widespreading organisation, brought a highly excitable and impressionable people.

It remains to trace the effect of all this agitation on the Government, and, owing to the very full information given in Sir Robert Peel's *Memoirs*,[1] we are able to trace the effect even minutely. Peel, the principal member of the Ministry, early addressed himself to considering the new phase of the question brought about by the result of the Clare election. He wrote: "In this case of the Clare election, and of its natural consequences, what was the evil to be apprehended? Not force, not violence, not any act of which law could take cognisance. The real danger was in the peaceable and legitimate exercise of a franchise according to the will and conscience of the holder. In such an exercise of that franchise, not merely permitted, but encouraged and approved by constitutional law, was involved a revolution in the electoral system of Ireland—the transfer of political power, so far as it was connected with representation, from one party to another."

The summer of 1828 found the Government still all at sea on the Catholic question. Peel had, however, come to recognise the necessity of considering "whether it might not be better to encounter every eventual risk of concession than to submit to the certain continuance, or rather, perhaps, the certain aggravation of existing evils;"[2] and on the 11th August he wrote to the Duke of Wellington: "Take what view we may of the Catholic question, we must admit that we labour under this extreme and overwhelming embarrassment with reference to the present condition of Ireland; that the Protestant mind is divided and very nearly balanced upon the most important question relating to Ireland. We cannot escape from the discussion of that question, and we cannot meet it without being in a minority in one branch of the Legislature. In the House of Commons in 1827 there was a majority of four against concession; in 1828 there was a majority of six in its favour. The change certainly was not effected by any other cause than the progress of uninfluenced opinion. The actual number therefore in the House of Commons in favour

[1] See *Memoirs of Sir Robert Peel, Bart., M.P.*, p. 117, published by the Trustees of his Papers—Lord Mahon and Sir Edward Cardwell, M.P.

[2] Peel's *Memoirs*, vol. i. p. 182.

of the measure is on the increase. The House of Commons of the last Parliament, and the House of Commons of this Parliament, have each decided in favour of the principle of concession. The majority of the House of Lords against the principle, looking at the constitution of that majority, is far from satisfactory; but if it were much greater, the evil of permanent disunion on such a question between the two branches of the Legislature would be extreme."

The day after Peel had written this letter—namely, on the 12th of August—the great Prostestant or Orange anniversary of the relief of Derry was celebrated in that city by a public dinner given by the Orange gentry of Derry. Mr. George Dawson, one of the members for the county, a brother-in-law of Sir Robert Peel, and Secretary to the Treasury, was present, and made a speech which was the first sign of a new policy on the part of the Government, and which created tremendous excitement.

"The state of Ireland," said he, "is an anomaly in the history of civilised nations. It is true that we have a Government to which an outward obedience is shown, which is responsible to Parliament, and answerable to God, for the manner of administering its functions; but it is equally true that an immense majority of the people look up, not to the legitimate Government, but to an irresponsible and to a self-constituted association for the administration of the affairs of the country. The peace of Ireland depends not upon the Government of the King, but upon the dictation of the Catholic Association. It has defied the Government, and trampled upon the law of the land; and it is beyond contradiction that the same power, which banished a Cabinet Minister from the representation of his county (Clare), because he was a Minister of the King, can maintain or disturb the peace of the country just as it suits the caprice or ambition of those who exert it. The same danger impends over every other institution established by law. The Church enjoys its dignity, and the clergy enjoy their revenues, by the laws of the land; and we know not how soon it may please the Catholic Association to issue its anathemas against the payment of tithes. . . . It depends upon the Catholic Association, no man can deny it, whether the clergy are to receive their incomes or not.

. . . It depends upon a single breath, a single resolution of the Catholic Association, whether the landlords are to be robbed of their rents or not. So perfect a system of organisation was never yet achieved by any body not possessing the legitimate powers of Government. . . .

"Now, gentlemen, with such a state of things staring us in the face, there comes the last question—What is to be done? Can we go back to the Penal Laws? God forbid that such an experiment should be made; it is revolting to common sense; it is revolting to the dignity of man. Can we persevere in our present system? The statement which I have made, and the firm impression made upon my mind by an anxious attention to passing events, is, that we cannot remain in our present situation. Something must be done. There is but one alternative—either to crush the Catholic Association, or to look at the question with an intention to settle it. Let us exercise all our ingenuity; let us argue with all our subtlety—there is no other alternative; and with such a conviction upon my mind, I feel myself called upon to exhort my countrymen—men whom I have the honour of representing—to abstain from irritating harangues, to pause, and to weigh well the dangers of the country—to dismiss all personal bitterness from the contemplation of a whole nation's welfare, and to devise some means, with satisfaction to all parties, for restoring the predominance of established authorities, and giving security to the recognised, the legal, the constitutional institutions of society. I speak here as a member of Parliament, as a member of the Government, and as a citizen of the world."

The sensation caused by this speech was tremendous, not merely among the audience who heard one of their most trusted, fire-eating champions throw down his sword, but in the country, as the echoes of the speech reached the most distant parts. It was the more unexpected as it was the first occasion on which the Platform was used by a prominent member of the Government for the announcement of a change of policy of the most momentous consequence.

Much discussion followed whether the speech was made with or without the sanction of Sir Robert Peel, or whether it expressed his views. Sir Robert Peel's letter of the 11th

August, above referred to, if not justifying the conclusion that Mr. Dawson was expressing the views of his brother-in-law, makes it at any rate clear that Sir R. Peel's views at the time were on the highway to the conclusion expressed by Mr. Dawson, which had so startled the kingdom. Moreover, it is fair to infer that as Mr. Dawson was not at once called on to resign for compromising the Government, the views he expressed were practically those of the Government.[1]

In the meantime, while the Government was considering whether to concede or to hold out, the Association was continuing its work. "It became obvious to the multitude," writes Lord Cloncurry in his *Personal Recollections*,[2] "that the exhibition of physical force was doing its work. The Ministers were seen to falter, and both the people and their leaders perceived that it was time to press upon a wavering foe."

The provincial meetings assumed a different form from that which they had hitherto done. Thus, at Clonmel, "The whole town presented the aspect of a continued triumph. There were 50,000 peasants present, collected from the neighbouring counties. They presented all the externals, not of a loose and riotous rabble, but of a well-ordered, well-disciplined levy *en masse* from the mountains around. During the meeting, which continued for three days, they were observed till late in the evening in full military array, with their respective bands of music, and headed by officers, parading about through the town."

In the course of the autumn serious apprehensions were felt by the Government as to the consequences which might

[1] In 1826 (January or February) Peel wrote to Dawson, with reference to a speech the latter had just previously delivered: "I have never sought to control the opinions of others, but I have felt very anxious, on account of the official relation in which you stand to me, that when you express your opinion on Irish affairs, you should make it clearly understood that you are speaking exclusively in your individual capacity. When I read your speeches at Derry, I could have no doubt that the general impression must be that those speeches were made after previous communication, and in conceit with me."—*Sir Robert Peel, from his Private Correspondence*, edited by G. S. Parker, p. 392.

In this speech of 1828 Mr. Dawson, so far from making it "clearly understood" that he was speaking exclusively in his own capacity, spoke "as a member of the Government."

[2] *Personal Recollections of the Life and Times of Lord Cloncurry*, p. 333.

ensue from great meetings such as these. A communication on the subject was conveyed from the Viceroy to Mr. Sheil, who was informed that any outbreak would inevitably delay the settlement of the question of emancipation. "Sheil undertook that, as far as depended on his exertions, a stop should be put to the processions in question."[1] He urged this strongly at the meeting of the Catholic Association on the 25th September. He said: "I am at a loss to see any benefit to be derived from these meetings and marchings to which so much anxious attention has lately been directed, beyond the bare evidence which they afford of the colossal power of the people, which bestrides the land. I had rather show the Government the giant in repose than exhibit this mighty stirring of his limbs. It is excellent to have a giant's strength, but it is rash to use it after this gigantic fashion. The people are reconciled. The Government must see pretty clearly what they could do at a signal (God forbid that it ever should be given!); enough has been done, and I own that I see many objections to these assemblies. . . . Let us, by gentle remonstrance, disperse these assemblies, and prove with what facility Irishmen can be controlled."

On the 30th September the Irish Government went a step farther and issued a Proclamation, pointing out that the great meetings which were being held were illegal, being "a manifest offence, and an open breach of the law," and warning the people to discontinue holding or attending them. The leaders of the Association endeavoured to quiet the excitement, and to discourage the people from holding these meetings; and on the same day as the Government Proclamation was issued, O'Connell issued an Address to the men of Tipperary, enjoining "The strict observance of order and tranquillity, and the discontinuance of demonstrations calculated to cause exasperation and alarm." Resolutions were also passed by the Association dissuading the people from holding these disciplined assemblages.

Though Mr. Dawson had publicly declared the necessity of concession, Peel himself made no sign. He spoke at a public dinner given to him at Manchester on the 6th October, but said no word on the Catholic question, nor made any remark

[1] See M'Cullagh's *Sheil*, p. 24.

of any political interest, though every effort was made to draw him into doing so.

In England the Platform gave no help towards Catholic emancipation—rather the reverse, in fact, for in the latter part of 1828 some meetings took place against emancipation.

The most memorable of them was that of "the landed proprietors, clergy, and freeholders of the county of Kent," which was held at Penenden Heath on the 28th October. The proceedings at it were lively. Upwards of 20,000 persons attended. An eye-witness has given the following account of it:—"The whole mass upon the left, deep and dense, presented at once the evidence of the strength of the Protestant party. On the right hand the opposers of the object of the meeting were assembled in an immense body. In the waggon next to the Sheriff on the right, which was that of the Earl of Radnor, stood his Lordship with a number of friends. . . . A succession of other waggons closed the right wing. . . . Between the two wings was a large cavalcade of farmers drawn up like troops of horse. Behind them was an immense quantity of vehicles, consisting of private and public carriages, with clusters of freeholders hanging about them. Within the circle which was formed by the waggons stood upon the ground a dense body of the peasantry, who arranged themselves on the left or the right wing according to their respective political predilections. The whole scene presented a most extraordinary and impressive exhibition."[1]

A Mr. Gipps proposed a Petition to the Legislature, stating the alarm of the Protestant freeholders of Kent at the proceedings of the Catholic Association, and praying the Legislature to adopt such measures as would best preserve entire the Protestant religion as established at the Revolution. "A great uproar" arose from some remarks he made, and he had to change the topic. Lord Camden spoke in favour of the Catholics and was hissed. During Lord Darnley's speech the interruptions were very frequent; he was assailed with cries of "Old prosy!" "Stuff—nonsense!" "Don't twaddle all day." A Mr. Shee spoke amid great interruption and cries of "Off! off!" and but little of his speech could be heard. Lord Teyn-

[1] *Sheil's Speeches*, by Macnevin, p. xxx. See also *The Examiner*, November 1828.

ham "hoped that the freeholders of Kent would not disgrace themselves by uproar and confusion"—the expression of which hope led to "shouting." "A great question like this," he said, "should be calmly considered." After a few more remarks, he was told he was "An old fool"; and he wound up his speech amid "vociferations."

Sheil, having heard of the intention to hold this meeting, determined on attending it. He did so, and spoke, or rather essayed to speak, but he was so much interrupted as scarcely to be heard. Cobbett tried to address the meeting, but the clamour against him was "incessant and almost deafening." Hunt also attempted to address the meeting, but was refused a hearing, and a tremendous outcry was kept up. Ultimately, the proposed Petition was carried by a large majority.

Though a county meeting, it afforded little encouragement as to the way in which a question involving religious convictions or passions would be discussed on the Platform.

Somewhat later a county meeting of Devonshire was held against concession to the Catholics, some 16,000 to 17,000 persons being present. Here also several speakers addressed the meeting in favour of the Catholics, but there was considerable interruption.

Time went on, and still the Government made no sign. On the 9th November the Prime Minister dined at the Mansion House, London, and spoke, but said nothing political.

By this time, Peel, at any rate, must have been convinced that concession was preferable to civil war in Ireland. But his real difficulty was with the King. "In all the communications which I had with his Majesty on this subject," wrote Peel in his *Memoirs*, "his determination to maintain these laws was most strongly expressed.[1]

"In a letter which I received from his Majesty in 1824, he thus expresses himself: 'The sentiments of the King upon Catholic emancipation are those of his revered and excellent father; from these sentiments the King never can, and never will deviate.'

"All subsequent declarations of opinion on the part of the King," continues Peel, "were to the same effect; and the events which were passing in Ireland . . . irritated his

[1] Peel's *Memoirs*, vol. i. p. 276.

Majesty, and indisposed him the more to recede from his declared resolution to maintain inviolate the existing law."

December passed, and "at the commencement of the month of January 1829 his Majesty had not yet signified his consent that the whole subject of Ireland, including the Catholic question, should be taken into consideration by his confidential servants. . . .[1]

"I now feared," wrote Peel (2d–3d January), "that the difficulties were almost insuperable. There was the declared opinion of the King, the declared opinion of the House of Lords, the declared opinion of the Church, unfavourable to the measures we were disposed to recommend."[2]

At last, just three weeks before the meeting of Parliament, the King gave his consent for the Cabinet, as a whole, to consider the state of Ireland; but that even was not final, for "The consent hitherto given (by the King) had been strictly limited to the submitting of advice to the King by his Cabinet on all questions relating to Ireland, without any pledge as to the adoption of that advice by his Majesty."[3]

On the 5th February Parliament met, and the King's speech was delivered. "Though worded," writes Peel, "after the manner of royal speeches, with all due reserve and cautious qualifications, no one could doubt the import of the terms. They were justly construed to imply an intention on the part of the Government to make a decisive effort to adjust the Catholic question."[4]

The gist of the King's speech was that, as the Catholic Association still existed, Parliament should give him such powers as would enable him to maintain his authority; and when this essential object had been accomplished, Parliament should take into its deliberate consideration the whole condition of Ireland, and should review the laws which imposed civil disabilities on his Majesty's Roman Catholic subjects. Accordingly, on the 10th of February a Bill was introduced giving the Lord Lieutenant of Ireland power to suppress any Association or meeting which he might think dangerous to the public peace, or inconsistent with the due administration of the law, and also the power of interdicting certain meetings.

[1] Peel's *Memoirs*, vol. i. p. 274.
[2] *Ibid.* p. 278.
[3] *Ibid.* p. 299.
[4] *Ibid.* p. 310.

Peel, in introducing the Bill, on the 10th February said: "It was the intention of the Government to suppress the Roman Catholic Association; and he would ask, Could it be doubted that the existence of such a body was inconsistent with the spirit of the Constitution? Could it be suffered that a society of this kind, whose objects were indefinite, and might be changed at pleasure, could be allowed to exercise its power? Could it be denied that it was inconsistent with the public tranquillity and dangerous to the public safety?"[1]

The struggle between the Government and the Association, however, as regards the dissolution of the latter, never came to a head. Before the Bill passed it was well known that the disqualifications under which Roman Catholics suffered would be removed. To have courted an unnecessary struggle would, in all probability, have been fatal to the realisation of the objects of the Association, and the Association accordingly dissolved itself. At a meeting of the Association on the 12th February Sheil moved that the Association be dissolved. "The object of this body was," he said, "and is, Catholic emancipation—that object is, in my judgment, already obtained. Nothing except our own imprudence can now defeat it. The end being achieved, wherefore should we continue to exist? What are we to do? In a few days an Act of Parliament will put us down. How is the interval to be employed? In making of harangues, forsooth, in the delivery of fine fragments of rhetoric, and in proclamations of our own dignity and importance? If the Minister acts a false part in our regard, we can readily rally again; but if a fair and equitable adjustment of the question be made, he is an enemy of his country who would perpetuate its divisions. The course which I recommend is this: let us determine to dissolve; let us pass a series of resolutions declaratory of our motives for so doing; let us protest against any unnecessary abandonment of the rights of citizens; let us discontinue the collection of the rent, but preserve the Finance Committee, in order to pay our debts, and wind up our pecuniary concerns; let its meetings be private, in order that there may be no pretence for alleging that we maintain a shadow of the Association; and let its measures be subject to the revision of an aggregate meeting.

[1] *Parliamentary Debates*, vol. xx. p. 179.

"After considerable debate the motion was carried, and this memorable confederacy, which, under various forms, had existed for a period of nearly six years, separated, to meet no more."[1]

So ended the first part of the Government scheme of action. Early in March, Peel made his statement as regarded the second part of it, and introduced a Bill for the removal of Roman Catholic disabilities. He took the opportunity of asserting the supremacy of Parliament, and its right alone to deal with the question. "The Parliament, and the Parliament alone, will I ever acknowledge to be the fit judge of this important question. The people at large may express their feelings and opinions, and they should always be received with deference; but, sir, we are not bound to conform to those opinions, or to refer to their decision questions affecting the general interests of the country, on which it is the peculiar province of Parliament to decide."[2]

The principle of the Bill was the abolition of civil distinctions and the equality of political rights. Catholics were to be admitted to Parliament, and, with two or three exceptions, to every office under the Crown or in corporations.

But as a set-off against this concession, and with a view to getting rid of the electorate, suddenly become dependent on the Roman Catholic priesthood, the 40s. freeholders in Ireland were disfranchised,[3] and the qualification of an elector in the counties was raised to £10 freehold. The Government proposals were adopted by both Houses of Parliament, and assented to by a reluctant Sovereign, and thus this long-debated, long-discussed question, this question which had wrecked more administrations than one, was at last solved and settled. That this consummation was reached, however, at the time it was, was solely and entirely due to the action and power of the Platform backed by organisation. It was the Platform which brought the question to the point at which it had to be dealt with: it was organisation which gave the Platform strength to do so. Greville, writing contemporarily,

[1] M'Cullagh's *Sheil*, vol. ii. p. 59.

[2] *Parliamentary Debates*, vol. xx. p. 738.

[3] It was estimated that more than two-thirds of the constituency of Ireland was disfranchised by this measure.

clearly acknowledges this fact. He said, "To O'Connell and the Association, and those who have fought the battle on both sides of the water the success of the measure is due. Indeed, Peel said as much, for it was the Clare election which convinced both him and the Duke that it must be done, and from that time the only question was whether he should be a party to it or not. If the Irish Catholics had not brought matters to this pass by agitation and association, things might have remained as they were for ever, and all these Tories would have voted on till the day of their death against them."[1]

Of the wonderful character of the organisation a few words more may be said. Wyse, in his Introduction to his *History of the Association*, which was written in 1829, while the impressions of the events he had just witnessed were still quite vivid, said,[2] "There is not, I believe, in the history of this or of the neighbouring countries an instance of more extensive and perfect organisation than the late Catholic Association.

"Its ramifications were as minute, as general, as connected as the most complicated portion of the muscular system. . . . The Association was supposed to be a mere tumultuary body, starting up from a chaos of confused and ungovernable elements, the creature of excitation, and with views as inconsistent with general constitutional liberty, and especially with the order and security of the British Constitution, as any of those sudden assemblages of Catholics and Covenanters, which were flung together at the outset of the Civil Wars in either country by the first fury of our religious dissensions.

"But this was judging rashly. The Catholic Association was a coalition of a very different order; it had a method in its madness, and an object in its tumult, which a close observer and a constant attention only could discern. It was not possible to combine in the same mass greater powers of popular excitation, more undisputed sway over the popular heart, and more minute attention to the nice machinery by which the details of public business require to be conducted. Neither was it a mere ebullition from the rank passions and the turbulent ambition of modern times; it was of long, and slow, and patient growth. Its strength was not known until

[1] Greville, vol. i. p. 168, 6th February 1829.
[2] Wyse (Introduction, p. 3, written in 1829).

it had been brought into direct collision with the Government; it was not even fully appreciated by the very hands which wielded it, until its temper had been brought out by hostile attack. It was then suddenly perceived that a body had been growing up unnoticed, *without* the Constitution, which might, in its due season, disturb from its foundations the Constitution itself, coextensive with the immense majority of the population, and reflecting, in its utmost energy, the entire form and pressure of the popular mind."

Sheil's testimony as that of one who knew the whole machinery of the Association may also be quoted.

Speaking at the Catholic Association on the 12th July 1828, he said: "In no page of history will there be discovered such an example of consolidated passion, and concentrated energy, and of systematised action, as is at this moment presented to the contemplation of every political observer by the actual state of Ireland. . . . The Irish people are not only organised, but that organisation in all its details is minutely perfect."

And, speaking a little later, he said: "The Catholics had attained the perfection of national organisation and popular discipline. They had almost reached the excellence of military array. But an immense population thus united, thus affiliated, thus controlled, in such a state of complete subordination, afforded matters of the most solemn meditation."

Sir Henry Parnell, in a speech which he made in the House of Commons in 1825, has given a description of the material on which the great Irish orators had to work, and which explains the facility with which some of these results were accomplished. He said: "The population of Ireland, we know, from the census of 1821 was five years ago nearly 7,000,000. These millions do not live in villages as the people of England do, perfectly obedient to the laws, under little other control than that of the parish constable; but they live hutted over the whole face of the country, free from almost all control and superintendence. These millions for the last thirty years have been training from time to time, and from county to county, in all the practical courses of secret conspiracies and open insurrections. The sympathy of grievance and of religion that is universal among them forms a basis for carrying on, with effect, the most extensive schemes of popular organisation. If any fixed determination to make a great popular effort should seize possession of their minds, in vain would the Catholic nobility, the Catholic lawyers, and even the Catholic clergy, exert their utmost endeavours to check them, and universal ruin and destruction must be the inevitable consequence of any such popular effort."[1]

Such material as this for agitation did not exist in England; the power which the Catholic clergy exercised in Ireland had no counterpart in England; but, nevertheless, certain very pregnant lessons were taught the English people by the Irish example.

Wyse thus summed up the movement in Ireland:[2] "Catholic emancipation, it will be seen, has not been achieved by a *coup de main;* liberty has not come to the Catholic by accident; nor is it, as has been falsely surmised, the gift of a few leaders; but its seeds have, year after year, been plentifully sown in the mind of a whole people, until the appointed moment for the sure and abundant harvest had fully arrived.

"The moral force of patient and unceasing effort in a just cause, confiding fully in the God of justice and its own might, has been adequately proved; the certainty of final triumph, when truth and reason are the combatants, is placed beyond a doubt; and if this great lesson, and no other, had been taught by the late struggle, it would have been well worth all the sacrifice and delay."

The moral which he thus conveyed appealed directly and forcibly to the vast body of the people of England, for they too had their emancipation to strive for—not a religious, but a political emancipation—emancipation from Parliamentary disabilities, long demanded, long striven for—whose seeds had been plentifully sown and re-sown in the mind of a whole people—a just cause—with truth and reason and equity on its side. The difficulty of the English people hitherto had been, how to achieve their object. The means were now revealed to them. They had been shown what the Platform, backed by organisation, could do—against what tremendous odds it could strive, and yet emerge victorious. That was a great lesson to have learned. That it was heeded at the time, at least by

[1] Hansard, vol. xii. p. 231. [2] Introduction, p. 7.

some, may be inferred from a leading article in the *Examiner* of the 31st August 1828, which said: "The state of public feeling is, indeed, at this instant, favourable to the consideration of Parliamentary reform, and it is desirable that agitation and organisation which have been working such wonders for Ireland should be made assistant to this great object for the Empire."

That it was heeded a little later by all, the events of the next few years were to prove, when the principles deduced from the Irish illustration were put into triumphant operation.

CHAPTER XV

THE FIRST REFORM ACT AGITATION

From the history of the Platform, so far as it has already been given, one important political principle may be deduced—namely, that an outbreak of Platform agitation inevitably follows on the occurrence of distress and pressure at home, or on revolution or any great popular movement abroad. In the one case hunger and misery force men to cry aloud, and the Platform enables them to lay their complaints before their fellow-countrymen, and to seek a remedy for their distress. In the other case, the contagion of popular excitement seizes on the minds of considerable numbers of men, and stirs them to action, which also seeks an outlet by the Platform.

Where a train of circumstances had long pointed to some great reform long desired, or where the foreign popular movement possessed anything in common with the popular cause in England, Platform agitation was sure to be on a larger scale, and of a more resolute and determined character than it would otherwise have been. The truth of this principle was now about to recieve further confirmation. First distress, then foreign revolutions, were to awaken the Platform to vigorous life and action.

The quiescence of the Platform, which has been mentioned as so noticeable in 1825, continued for some years. No event of startling importance awakened it. The question of Catholic emancipation, exciting as it was in Ireland, scarcely ruffled the calm of the Platform in England. Even the great question of Parliamentary reform had so far ceased to be agitated in the country, that during the space of six years, from 1824 to 1829, there was not a single Petition on the subject presented to Parliament.[1] Lord John Russell, its most ardent

[1] See *Croker Papers*, vol. ii. p. 94.

Parliamentary advocate, speaking on 3d May 1827 in the House of Commons, acknowledged that there was "a great lukewarmness" about it. But the lukewarmness was soon to be raised to boiling-point; the silence or quiescence, which was purely superficial, was soon to be broken by the roar of a united people, or, to use the description adopted by Croker, "Reform was in a very slumbering state, but of so combustible a nature that when the match was once applied, it blazed up and exploded with a fury that surprised and astonished and alarmed those who had introduced it, as some leading men of the Whig Cabinet have honestly confessed to me."[1]

And here, on the eve of the great agitation for reform, it is desirable to recall as shortly and succintly as possible what it was the Platform had been teaching for so many years, what had been the instruction now about to produce an irresistible national demand for the reform of Parliament, and which had brought about that state of feeling so soon now to produce tremendous results. With the teaching of the Platform up to 1793 we are sufficiently familiar. As persistently since then, as circumstances and Governments admitted, the necessity of reform had been inculcated, as the first step towards the amelioration of the condition of the people. The people were reminded that in 1793 it had been proved that 154 men, peers, and great commoners, together with the Treasury—or, in other words, the Ministers—or, in other words, the Crown—by their simple will or direction, returned a decided majority in the House of Commons, and that statement practically still held true.[2]

The Platform had taught, and taught persistently, that the evils which oppressed the country arose from extravagant expenditure; that there was a great deal of corruption in

[1] Croker to Guizot, 14th July 1857, *Croker Papers*, vol. iii. p. 374.

[2] In 1827 Croker sent Canning a memorandum of the number of members returned to the House of Commons by the influence of some of the peers.

Tories.—Lord Lonsdale, 9; Lord Hertford, 8; Duke of Rutland, 6; Duke of Newcastle, 5; Lord Yarbro, 5, etc. etc., or a total of about 27 Tory peers returned 96 members.

Whigs.—Lord Fitzwilliam, 8; Lord Darlington, 7; Duke of Devon, 7; Duke of Norfolk, 6; Lord Grosvenor, 6, etc. etc., or a total of about 19 Whig peers returned 54 members.—See *The Croker Papers*, vol. i. p. 368.

Parliament; that Parliament bestowed iniquitous pensions, and retained costly sinecures for the purposes of corruption; that an overwhelming debt had been incurred; that unnecessary establishments were maintained, and a profuse expenditure indulged in; and that all these evils had arisen and grown to their portentous extent, from a want of that control which alone was to be secured by a real representation of the people.

And what was more, Parliament paid no heed to the wishes or views of the people. The members of Parliament who, by the Tory fiction, were supposed to be their representatives, ignored, where they did not actually oppose, them; their Petitions were spurned, or if received, were relegated to oblivion,—all this to such an extent that the people, out of pure despair, ever now and again gave up the practice of petitioning as absolutely useless.

It is impossible to give any approximate estimate of the meetings which had been held where these views were inculcated or expressed from the Platform, and embodied in Resolutions or Petitions. In the popular constituencies they had been preached, with ever-increasing vehemence, at the successive elections. They had been contested, in a very small degree, from the Platform by those interested in maintaining these abuses, but discussion on the Platform only served to emphasise the truth and justice of the popular cause, for the weight of argument was all on the popular side.

But another, and even greater, lesson than this had been taught by the Platform, dwelt on incessantly by it—a lesson which commended itself to the people by its very simplicity as a living principle, by its absolute incontrovertibility—namely, that no Government could be satisfactory to the people, or could be expected to deal fairly with their interests, which they, the people, did not themselves choose.

Though the Platform had for some years been silent on the question of Parliamentary reform, the subject itself was moving to a crisis. The iniquitous bribery practised at the General Election of 1826 had been so bad that Parliament had been forced to take cognisance of it in two or three of the most flagrant cases. The boroughs of Penryn and East Retford were selected as chief among sinners, of whom there were not a few. In the latter place the price of a single vote was twenty guineas, and of a double vote forty guineas. A deep-laid plan for enforcing this payment had been uniformly acted on by the electors from 1796 to 1818, and winked at by an unreformed Parliament. In 1827 two Bills were introduced which resulted in the declaration that these corrupt boroughs were to be disfranchised. But one of the Bills was dropped in the Lords, who evidently approved of these practices, as they would not punish them, and the other never got out of the Commons; and so the sore was kept open for another year. Then, in 1828, Bills were again introduced, proposing to give the Penryn seat to Manchester, and the East Retford seat to Birmingham. Again they met a similar fate, and again did electoral corruption receive the practical sanction and approbation of Parliament. The next year the more general question was brought forward by Lord Blandford,[1] who moved two resolutions, which went to declare that there existed a number of boroughs, the representation of which could be purchased, and others in which the number of electors was so small as to render them liable to the influence of bribery, and that such a system was "disgraceful to the character of the House of Commons, destructive of the confidence of the people, and prejudicial to the best interests of the country."

His motives in making this motion were different from those which had previously animated Parliamentary reformers. The fact, however, that it was made, and not his motives, is what concerns us. It met with the usual fate, and was rejected.

Reformers in Parliament might have gone on struggling fruitlessly till doomsday with futile Resolutions, and Bills and Amendments, if the decision on the question of the reform of the representation was to remain in the hands of Parliament; but the people had become too powerful and intelligent to be restrained much longer by the barrier of a corrupt Parliament with its fictitious popular representation. The decision was about to be taken out of the hands of Parliament; the nation, with whom ever the ultimate arbitrament of all questions lies, was to take into its own hands the settlement of its Constitution, and the first sharp, but most impressive lesson was to be administered to Parliament that it

[1] *Parliamentary Debates*, 1829, vol. xxi. p. 1672.

was the servant, not the master, of the people—that Parliament was for the people, not the people for Parliament.

Place, in language not one whit too strong, has thus described the state of affairs at this time, and the evil consequences: "This scandalously corrupt state of the House in 1793 was somewhat increased in 1831, and against this infamous power, and the infamous manner in which it was used, the people had to contend. The necessary misgovernment of an irresponsible King, and irresponsible House of Peers, and a luxurious, rich, overbearing, benumbing clergy, with a House of Commons thus chosen, or rather appointed, the long war and its multiplied horrors, the waste of human life, the amount of human suffering, the unparalleled waste of the public money, the enormous amount of taxation consequent thereon, the long war from the time of the Petition to the year 1814, when taken in the aggregate, were not the greatest evil to the nation which its vicious and vitiating Government produced. The bribery, the perjury, the corruption, the immorality, and the consequent, enormous, and widespread criminality and debasing notions it produced, encouraged, and maintained all over the country; the consequent debasement of the notions of the people, was much more lamentable than all the other evils, enormous as they were, and will be scarcely believed to be possible by posterity."[1]

Distress was to awake the Platform from its lethargy. By the end of 1829 distress was settling down on the country. The business of the country had largely increased; the imports were larger; the exports greater than ever before; the volume of trade was far greater, and the wealth of the country had greatly increased. But large classes of the people had not participated in the progress. A continued fall in prices had been going on throughout the year—a continued reduction in wages, and ever diminishing employment. "The peasantry," wrote *The Times*[2] on the 20th January 1830, "with their wretched wives and children, are really an oppressed and ruined people; their bodily powers are impaired; their moral qualities are degraded; innocence and cheerfulness have fled with the last vestiges of self-dependence and comfort from their humble dwellings."

[1] Place, MSS., 27,789, p. 387.

[2] Leading article.

The civic industrial classes were also in sore need. In Preston one-third of the entire population was receiving relief. In other places great distress prevailed. Here and there meetings were held by distressed weavers and other artisans, disclosing their sufferings and their sad condition.

Greville, in his *Memoirs,* from his town view of things, wrote under date 17th January 1830: "The country gentlemen are beginning to arrive, and they all tell the same story as to the universally prevailing distress, and the certainty of things becoming much worse; of the failure of rents all over England, and the necessity of some decisive measures, or the prospect of general ruin."[1] The country gentlemen party, anxious enough at other times to cry out against and legislate against the Platform, when others had recourse to it, where having recourse to it themselves, and by petition pouring their woes into the ear of Government. Early in January 1830 "The owners and occupiers of land in Ely" held a meeting and petitioned the House of Commons "To take into consideration the present state of the agricultural labourers, and to adopt such measures for their relief as to your Honourable House shall seem meet."[2]

County meetings were held in seversal places. *The Times* of the 20th January remarked: "The agricultural interest, or to speak more properly, the country gentleman interest, goes on complaining with much diligence and noise."[3] And on the next day it wrote: "Meetings are becoming frequent throughout the country, and they all seem to turn on the uneasiness occasioned by some severe distress affecting one or more orders of the community; but there is none in which we do not find the peculiar and unexampled sufferings of the labouring classes dwelt upon as a matter most deeply to be deplored, and received by the hearers as a fact not open to denial;"[4] and on 22d January it wrote: "The meetings, and resolutions, and petitions of the landed gentlemen are going on."

Added to the distress there was another source of discontent—coming from the Tory party. The action of the Ministry

[1] Greville's *Memoirs,* vol. i. p. 266.
[2] *The Times,* 4th January 1830.
[3] *Ibid.* 20th January 1830.
[4] *Ibid.* 21st January 1830 (leading article).

as regards the concession of Catholic emancipation had produced almost a total disorganisation of their followers and supporters, many of whom felt that Ministers had betrayed their trust.

The Examiner, in an article written in January 1830 on "The Progress of Opinion," stated that many who were formerly Tories had changed their opinions. "The meetings in the country indicate the current of the public mind, and the declining influence of the Executive. Men who were formerly most abject in servility now talk loudly and boldly of the people's rights and wrongs, and stand forward in the character of agitators. Country gentlemen, magistrates, and even clergymen, appear in the parts of demagogues." The Tory party had practically been broken up by the action of its leaders on the questions of Catholic emancipation.[1]

Place, in narrating the events of this time, says: "In the autumn and winter of 1829 there had been much rioting in country places—many threshing machines had been broken, and stacks had been fired. In the early months of 1830 these enormities had increased, and were spreading from one county to another with fearful rapidity, and as the incendiaries could not be detected, great alarm prevailed. . . .[2]

"A general persuasion existed as to the existence of severe distress. The debates in Parliament confirmed the impression and increased the alarm.

"Here was enough, and more than enough, coupled as it was with declamations out of doors, to make those who take opinions on trust to believe, that the country was on the 'verge, nay, in the very gulf of bankruptcy.'[3] Here was enough to alarm the timid; here was enough to excite the working people to whom no change, as they thought, could do any harm, and the consequence was a persuasion, to a greater extent than had perhaps ever before prevailed, that a break-up was at hand, though many who held this faith did not know what they themselves meant.

"The debates in the Houses of Parliament were well calculated to keep up the excitement out of doors, which acted

[1] *The Examiner*, 24th January 1830. See also *Croker Papers*, vol. iii. p. 374.
[2] Place, MSS., vol. i. 27,789, p. 168.
[3] *Ibid.* p. 141.

again on the Houses, and kept up the excitement within doors."[1]

Meetings were held at a vast number of places. "To such an extent had the common people been acted upon," says Place, "that they were in a state bordering on mischief, if they could have seen how, by being mischievous, they could have destroyed the National debt, and freed the country from the taxes levied to pay the dividends; and they were countenanced in this to a considerable extent by the speeches made at country and other large public meetings, as well as by some speeches made in Parliament, by many cheap publications, and by some of the newspapers, and by pamphlets."

Birmingham, the unrepresented, set the Platform agitation for Parliamentary reform once more actively going, this time on such a scale that it would no longer be stayed.

The movement had a modest beginning. On the 14th December 1829 Mr. Thomas Attwood and fifteen other gentlemen met at "the Royal Hotel," "called together by a circular" "signed by six tradesmen." "This little meeting then founded the Political Union for the Protection of Public Rights," the forerunner and example of many similar institutions.[2] In the document in which they set forth the objects of the Union they said: "The experience of the last fifteen years must certainly have convinced the most incredulous that the rights and interests of the middle and lower classes of the people are not efficiently represented in the Commons House of Parliament. . . .

"On whatsoever side we turn our eyes, we find subjects of the highest public importance everywhere demanding the public attention, and everywhere requiring the legal interference of the industrious classes. The vindication of the National Justice, the equalisation and reduction of the National Taxes, the protection of Public Rights, the redress of Public Wrongs, the necessity of Reform in Parliament, and the relief of the National distress, all require that the National Mind should slumber no more. Under these views and impressions,

[1] Place, MSS., vol. i. 27,789, p. 144.

[2] See *Life of Thomas Attwood*, p. 129, by C. M. Wakefield (Harrison and Sons), 1885, London. Printed for private circulation only. The book is, however, in the British Museum, and therefore, I presume, quotable from.

it is therefore that we propose to form in Birmingham a General Political Union of the industrious classes for the protection of Public Rights."

The following were the principal objects of the Union: "To obtain by every just and legal means such a reform in the Commons House of Parliament as may ensure a real and effectual representation of the lower and middle classes of the people in that House. . . . To promote peace, union, and concord, among all classes of his Majesty's subjects, and to guide and direct the public mind into uniform, peaceful, and legitimate operations, instead of leaving it to waste its strength in loose, desultory, and unconnected exertions, or to carve a way to its own objects, unguided, unassisted, and uncontrolled. To collect and organise the peaceful expression of the public opinion so as to bring it to act upon the legislative functions in a just, legal, and effectual way. To influence by every legal means the election of members of Parliament, so as to promote the return of upright and capable representatives of the people."

Rules and regulations were also made as to the duties of the members of the Political Union. Amongst them the following: "To bear in mind that the strength of our Society consists in the peace, order, unity, and legality of our proceedings; and to consider all persons as enemies who shall in any way invite or promote violence, discord, or division, or any illegal or doubtful measures. Never to forget that by the exercise of the above qualities we shall produce the peaceful display of an immense organised moral power which cannot be despised or disregarded."

"Thus was established what was probably the most successful, the most powerful, and the most peaceful and orderly organisation ever known in England." [1]

In order to place this scheme before the public, a public meeting was held on the 25th of January. It was "the largest meeting ever assembled within the walls of a building,"—some 12,000 to 15,000 persons were present—and it lasted from ten in the morning till nearly five in the afternoon.[2] Numerous speeches were made.

A resolution was moved by Mr. Attwood "That in the

[1] *Life of Attwood*, p. 137.

[2] *The Times*, 27th January 1830.

opinion of this meeting the general distress which now afflicts the country, and which has been so severely felt at different periods during the last fifteen years, is entirely to be ascribed to the gross mismanagement of public affairs; and that such mismanagement can only be effectually and permanently remedied by an effectual reform in the Commons House of Parliament; and this meeting is also of opinion that for the legal accomplishment of this great object, and for the further redress of public wrongs and grievances, it is expedient to form a general Political Union between the lower and the middle classes of the people in this town." Other resolutions were also passed; a Political Council was formed to carry out the aims of the Union; subscriptions were invited, and the meeting pledged itself to use strenuous efforts to carry out these objects. In a later speech, with the view of removing any misapprehension as to the nature of the Union, he said they did not propose a political club—in those he had not much faith—but the union of the people of England.

"Such an exhibition of public feeling," said the report in *The Times*, "or one which has excited so intense an interest throughout the whole neighbourhood, is not in the recollection of man." In a leading article on the subject, however, that same paper said: "The whole thing is nonsense, and may probably die away quietly." But subsequent events proved how incorrect was such a prognostication.

On the 23d February 1830 a meeting was held in London at the Mansion House of Merchants and others asking for an inquiry on the subject of the distress, and at which a resolution was carried that it was vain and childish and delusive to expect that the distresses would ever be relieved till there was a real effective and radical reform of the House of Commons. A meeting was held at Aylesbury at the end of February,[1] and a Petition adopted, "That your petitioners have long observed with the deepest sorrow the apathy and indifference with which their petitions are received, and which they can only attribute to the notoriously corrupt and imperfect state of the representation of the Commons in your honourable House; and in thus taking the only constitutional method they possess of making known their own insupportable grievances, they

[1] See *The Times*, 1st March 1830.

regret to say, that they entertain but little hope of redress until a thorough, effectual reform shall have been accomplished in the said representation of the people." In March 1830 meetings for Parliamentary reform were held at Leeds, and in Worcestershire and Kent.

The Platform was evidently rapidly awaking to the question again. "Other (besides Birmingham Union) meetings for reform were held in many places, at which resolutions and petitions were voted, which went much farther than those of the Birmingham Union, and there was a display of oratory and knowledge all over the country to an extent far beyond what was supposed to have existed."[1]

The Birmingham Political Union held a large and successful meeting on the 17th May. A considerable number of members had, in the meanwhile, joined the Union. The views adopted by the Union were by no means extreme. At this meeting the Council stated that after mature consideration they had decided not to claim universal suffrage, vote by ballot, or annual Parliaments, but to confine themselves to the ancient and well-tried lines of the Constitution.

During the session of 1830, with a steadily rising popular feeling in the country, the state of representation was brought before the House of Commons in various forms. Birmingham had been mocked by the refusal of the House of Commons to transfer to it the representation of the borough of East Retford. Manchester had been mocked by the refusal of the House of Commons to transfer to it the representation of the rotten and corrupt borough of Penryn; and now, when the proposal was once more made to give these two great cities, and Leeds, with their enormous wealth, their huge numbers of intelligent and patriotic citizens, the right of sending representatives to Parliament, the House of Commons negatived it by 188 votes to 140. Nor did Parliament rush blindfold on its fate in this refusal, for, as Huskisson pointed out to the House, "the consequences of continued refusal to amend even moderately what might be amended were becoming most visible."

The more indefensible a position is, the more obstinately sometimes it is held, and this was the case in the struggle

[1] Place, MSS., 27,789, p. 147.

now approaching a crisis. For what system was more hopelessly indefensible in reason or argument than the system of Parliamentary representation then existing? With what vestige of reason, for instance, could it be contended that the Mayor and thirty aldermen of Bath were so much wiser, more immaculate, and altogether more capable than every other man in the city, that they should select the representatives for Parliament and the others not? Or with what vestige of reason could it be contended that the thirty-three self-elected magistrates of Edinburgh should elect a member of Parliament who was presumed to be the representative of the 130,000 inhabitants of that city, though the inhabitants had nothing to say to the election? And Edinburgh and Bath were very far from being single specimens of this absurdity. Or how could people be brought to believe in arguments as to the justice of the arrangement by which great cities like Manchester and Birmingham, with thousands of men as intelligent and highly educated and capable as any in the kingdom, were excluded from any voice and any influence even in making the laws affecting their lives, their businesses, their property, whilst representation was given to peddling little boroughs, which meekly followed the behests of a boroughmonger, whose exalted ideas of government extended no further than to support the corruption which filled his pockets, and the system which gave him social and political eminence? Happily the fictions, the absurdities by which these evils had been defended were at last about to be ruthlessly brushed aside. But while Parliament was still engaged in opposing itself to the wishes of the people on this subject, the King died (on the 26th of June 1830), and William IV. reigned in his stead.

Place makes an interesting comment on one indication of the change that had passed over the people. He says: "Addresses to William IV. on his accession poured in, yet neither in number nor in style as in former times; numbers of them spoke of reforms, and hoped and believed in changes, which would have been called indecent at the accession of any preceding king of the House of Hanover."[1]

The few pending matters of necessary business in the

[1] Place, MSS., 27,789, p. 153.

Houses were hurried to completion, Parliament was prorogued by the King on the 23d July, and dissolved immediately afterwards.

It was a momentous event, this dissolution; for here ended the old order of government, here practically began the new. Into the next few years, and following each other with bewildering rapidity, were to be crowded events and experiences such as the people had never gone through before.

Three general elections were to take place in the next two and a half years, general elections very different from any previous ones. An agitation was to rage at fever-heat, in comparison with which all previous agitations had been local, trivial, or ephemeral. Issues of the most tremendous import, pregnant not alone with the interests of large masses of the people hitherto practically unrecognised by the State, but of the nation itself, were to be raised and settled. And all these things were to be done and to be decided, for the first time in the history of our country, not by Parliament, which, so to speak, was the culprit, who was to be tried, but by the people. Startling though the event might be—something quite without precedent—it was nevertheless the fact—a very tremendous fact making its mark on the destinies of our country and of our race to the end of all time.

And as the issue now lay with the people, so had they to find the means of expressing themselves, both for purposes of discussion and for decision. Parliament was of no use, for the real discussion was outside Parliament, and the Press, valuable though the help it could give, was quite inadequate, for the discussion had reached an acuter form than writing.

The Platform alone remained. It had been tried previously with varying, but on the whole with encouraging success. To it now the people sprang, and found in it the fulfilment of their requirements; and in the great struggle now being entered on, it reached a position hitherto undreamt of.

During all July—in fact, since the illness and approaching death of George IV. had brought in view the certainty of a general election—candidates had been actively canvassing the constituencies. It is worthy of note that when the dissolution actually took place no ministerial manifesto was issued to the electors setting forth the issues on which the election was to be fought, no speech was made by a Cabinet Minister to give the cue to the followers and supporters of the Government.[1] The Government counted on an addition to their majority, and, in the days of rotten boroughs, could afford to scorn recourse to any such superfluous action. On the side of the Opposition the nearest approach to a manifesto was a speech from Brougham in Yorkshire on 26th July. As a candidate for the greatest constituency in England, and as a conspicuous member of his party, his speeches claimed general attention. He said, "We have emancipated the Catholics and given peace to Ireland. I say now, let us emancipate all the middle, the industrious, and all the humble class of our fellow-subjects, and let us see England tranquil, and in peace, and contentment. My principles on the subject of monopoly are plain and short. I will have no monopoly, positively no monopoly." He spoke against the Corn Laws. He declared in favour of Parliamentary reform (though against the ballot), of extending the right of voting to the great towns of England, and to inhabitant householders, and he was for shortening the duration of Parliaments. "I have no manner of doubt that this election will do much towards Parliamentary reform. I believe there are three questions which your example and your exertions on this occasion will carry in England as effectually as the election in the county of Clare carried the Catholic question, Parliamentary reform, a revision of the Corn Laws, and the extinction of Colonial Slavery.

Brougham's position at the time, prominent though it was, was scarcely sufficiently high to impose his ideas without question on the whole popular party, nor was that party sufficiently united to admit of any one person dictating to them; but, nevertheless, many followed the lead given them, and in many elections the question of Parliamentary reform figured in the front of the battle. But whilst all eyes were turned on the elections, an event suddenly occurred which imported new excitement into the contests.

The Government of France was overthrown, and the French King was driven into exile, not by mere Parliamentary vot-

[1] Peel spoke at Tamworth on the 30th July, but his speech was mostly of a personal character, in no sense a party manifesto. For a report of it see *The Lichfield Mercury* of 13th August.

ing, but by force of arms. The struggle long raging there between tyranny and liberty came to a crisis.

On the 28th of July 1830 *The Times* published copies of the Ordinances of the French King, Charles X., dated 25th July.

The first abolished the freedom of the Press. "All the benefits to be derived from free discussion are thus at once destroyed. No political rights can be defended, no political wrongs can be denounced, without the permission of those whose conduct is implicated."

The second demolished almost equally effectually the popular branch of the French Legislature. The number of members was reduced from 430 to 258, the franchise of three-fourths of the electors destroyed, and restrictions imposed which practically placed the constitution of the Chamber absolutely and completely in the hands of the Sovereign.

The Ordinances were promptly resisted. Paris rose in arms, and after a bloody but short struggle the populace triumphed. The King and the Ministers fled. The members of the Chamber of Deputies met and assumed the government.

On the 2d of August, in so short a time did it all happen, *The Times* published the Proclamation of the Deputies: "Frenchmen, France is free. Absolute power raised its standard; the heroic population of Paris has overthrown it. Paris attacked has made the sacred cause triumph by arms, which had triumphed in vain in the elections."

By decree of the Deputies, Charles X. and his descendants were excluded from the throne, and the Chamber of Peers was reduced by a third, and the Duke of Orleans was made head of the State.

This great and startling event made itself at once felt in England.

"Excited as the people generally were," says Place, "the elections tended to increase and continue the excitement; and in the midst of their exertions to influence the electors to return Liberal candidates, a circumstance occurred which carried their enthusiasm to the greatest height. This was the Three Days' Revolution in Paris, the news of which, when it arrived, caused an almost unparalleled ecstasy." [1]

[1] Place, MSS., 27,789, p. 158.

This startling revolution was hailed as an omen of success by the reformers. The elections had begun on 30th July, and some of them were over before the news of the impressive events could influence opinion. But it was quickly turned to account as regards those still to come, and public sympathy in England sided at once with the popular party in France.

"The news," says Place, "greatly disconcerted the Ministry and the privileged aristocracy generally. . . . The people generally were glorified at the result, and their exultation was remarkable for its fervour and its continuance. . . . The impression the events in Paris made on even the least intelligent of the people was such as will never either be effaced, or to any extent be forgotten by them." [1]

By the 2d of August the events in France were utilised in election speeches. Sir Robert Wilson, speaking at Southwark, said: "We saw in France a generous nation contending for its rights—for its freedom, and for the maintenance of the law against one of the most wicked, desperate, and felon ministerial acts of treason that had ever been perpetrated."

And at the Surrey election Denison said: "France had held out a proud example to the world. The people of that country had not been so submissive to their Ministers as our House of Commons had been."

It is very strange, when so much depended on this election, and such vast issues were at stake, that the anticipations of the result were not intensely keener than they appear to have been.

It had for some time been very generally recognised that the political education of the population had been advancing by leaps and bounds, that the perception of misrule had become acuter and more general, that Liberal principles had been sinking ever deeper into the public mind and permeating new classes, that the temper of the people had grown less patient under misgovernment, more self-assertive, that the people themselves had become more self-confident as to their capacity for taking their due share in the government of the country. But that these important changes should much affect the elections appears scarcely to have been given a thought, and the result of the elections seemed to come as a surprise.

[1] Place, MSS., 27,789, p. 163.

From sources very different in their views may be taken a few extracts from contemporary writers. "The elections here," wrote Greville in his *Memoir* on the 31st of July (1830), "are going against Government, and no candidate will avow that he stands on Government interest, or with the intention of supporting the Duke's Ministry, which looks as if it had lost all its popularity."[1] And a fortnight later he wrote: "Our elections are still going against Government, and the signs of the times are all for reform and retrenchment, and against slavery."[2]

"Wherever," wrote the *Annual Register*, "the elections approached to the character of being popular, no candidate found himself a gainer by announcing that he had been, or intended to be, an adherent of the existing Government."[3]

"In Norfolk," wrote Cobbett, "the old Tory Woodhouse has been shoved aside by a man who has pledged himself to reform. In Cambridgeshire the Duke of Rutland's brother, or cousin, or something, has been put out by a private gentleman, who made a solemn declaration he would vote for radical reform. In other counties no very great change as to the principles of the men, but everywhere reform has been sounded in their ears, and nowhere has there been found a man bold enough to say that he was not for some degree of reform in Parliament."

The Examiner wrote:[4] "Liberality has had extraordinary victories; bad men of great influence have been thrown out from the strongholds of their power, and the election of popular candidates has been carried in defiance of a hostile aristocracy."

But volume-speaking was the fact "unprecedented in the Parliamentary history of England that not one Cabinet Minister sits in Parliament by the voice of any portion of his Majesty's subjects, except Sir G. Murray, and he for a Scotch county, which is, like the rest of the Scotch counties, more rotten than most English rotten boroughs.[5] . . . At no one place where the public voice could be raised did any member

[1] Greville, *Memoirs*, vol. ii. p. 20. [2] *Ibid.* p. 29.
[3] *Annual Register*, 1830, p. 146. [4] *The Examiner*, 22d August 1830.
[5] See *The Result of the General Election, or, What has the Duke of Wellington Gained by a Dissolution?* London, 1830.

of the Government attempt to show himself. All took refuge in rotten boroughs."

The result of the election, viewed superficially, was the diminution by between twenty or thirty of the number of votes on which Ministers could rely, but there was a far deeper lesson to be read from them than this. In the words of a contemporary observer: "When mariners observe the sea to heave and roll in swelling waves while scarcely an air is stirring, they lay their account with a coming gale, take in their lofty canvas, reduce their top-hamper, and make all snug for what may happen. . . . There is a force in the country beginning to act, which is not seen on the surface. There is a power in operation which is not suspected in its individual component parts, but which speaks broadly in the aggregate type. The swell of opinion is rolling in before the tempest; of drops, separately of insignificance it is composed, but how mighty is the united mass!"[1]

And another writer observed: "The people of England have begun to exert the power with which extended knowledge arms countless numbers, and they will, beyond all doubt, obtain an influence in the management of their own affairs commensurate with their just title to it. They have, therefore, thoroughly discovered their own strength. Yorkshire, Devonshire, Cambridgeshire, Surrey, even Leicestershire, certainly Suffolk, bear witness to it."[2]

Before Parliamennt met another fillip had been given to popular feeling in England by a revolution in the Netherlands. By the treaty of Vienna Belgium had been united with Holland. "The inhabitants of Brussels rose in insurrection against the local taxes. Having succeeded, they extended their views to the destruction of the Government, and the separation of the Netherlands from Holland. They repulsed the King's troops in an attack upon Brussels; they established a provisional Government; they convoked a national congress; they declared the Netherlands an independent State; they excluded the House of Orange from the throne, and set about the election of a new King."[3]

[1] *The Examiner*, 22d August 1830.

[2] *The Result of the General Election* (*of* 1830), *or*, *What has the Duke of Wellington Gained by a Dissolution?*

[3] *Annual Register*, 1830, p. 144.

This event afforded another instructive example to the British people how easily a united people could overthrow an unpopular Government.

Nor did the effect of the revolution in France cease with the elections. Numerous meetings were held specially for the purpose of expressing sympathy with the French people. "This great event," said a speaker at one of them, "reads a lesson at once to Governments and to the people. To the former it says, Never trust your own strength in opposition to the will of the nation; while to the people it says, Never allow your rights to be violated, but when the blow is struck, defend your liberties with your lives."

Brougham, the chosen of Yorkshire, in apologising for not accepting an invitation to a public dinner in celebration of the event, wrote: "The authors of the glorious events you have met to celebrate have done far more in three days to make despotism impossible, either in France or England, than its vile abettors can now accomplish in as many ages."

In Edinburgh a meeting was held for congratulating the French on their Revolution of "the Three Days"; and "similar assemblages took place all over Scotland, assemblages, in Scotland, where a revolution, which had just dethroned a monarch, was applauded openly, and with no opposition or disapprobation! Who could fail to see the indication of our own state which this fact implied?"[1]

In Birmingham the Political Union had a dinner, at which some 3700 persons were present, "to commemorate the recent glorious Revolution in France"; and the toast of "Honour, gratitude, and prosperity to the noble people of France" was drunk amidst cheers.[2]

Attwood, speaking at it, said: "We will go on in our peaceful and legal career, and by God's grace we will recover the liberties of our country—not by violence, anarchy, or brute force, but by the peaceful, organised, and magnificent display of the will of the people. When the barons of Runnymede recovered the liberties of England from the tyrant John, they took up the bow, and the spear, and the battle-axe, and the sword, and they were justified in so doing. Thank God, we have no occasion now to take up murderous and destructive

[1] Cockburn's *Memorials*, p. 467. [2] On 11th October, 1830.

weapons like these; the progress of education and knowledge has changed this state of things; our weapons are union, truth, justice, and reason; our sword is 'the sword of the spirit,' which is the will of the people, and let no one doubt that this great moral sword is not efficient for every just and useful purpose."

These meetings, and the language used at them, are worthy of notice for another reason than that of showing how the Revolution abroad affected the agitation for Reform—namely, they afford the means of making a most interesting comparison between the tone and manners of the Platform and public meetings at this time, and at the time of the previous French Revolution in 1792. The occasion was identical—the overthrow of a despotic Government by the people. Then, there had been ludicrous bombast and tawdry claptrap sentiments in imitation of the wild utterances of the revolutionists, and sympathy was so exaggerated that patriotism even disappeared in the effusive praise of the French revolutionists. Now, however, the language, though sympathetic, was not unpatriotic, nor were the incitements to imitation of the violent character they had been in the end of the last century. No one can fail to be struck with the great improvement, and the fact was encouraging, marking very clearly the progress which the British people had made in political education, intelligence, and moderation.

Independent of the political example set by Europe towards popular principles, the other great incentive to agitation—namely, distress—was continuing actively at work. Poverty and want were extending ever wider. Large numbers of the people, feeling the pinch and stress of hunger, and groping blindly and helplessly in the dark for some remedy, betook themselves, not to the Platform, but to the most questionable of all remedies—violence. The Platform had already been giving warning of coming trouble.

"Many of the numerous county Petitions presented to Parliament previous to the Dissolution, representing the distressed condition of those of the lower orders who depended on agriculture, had predicted that, unless their situation could be bettered, it would be impossible to restrain them from outrages, and violations of the public peace." [1]

[1] See *Annual Register*, p. 149, 1830.

"The harvest was scarcely over when these anticipations were realised." The disturbances began in the county of Kent, and spread first into the neighbouring counties, then over nearly half of England. "Night after night conflagrations were lighted up by bands of incendiaries; corn-stacks, barns, farm-buildings, and live-stock were consumed; and threshing-machines were destroyed; bolder bands attacked mills, and demolished the machinery, and levied money." A few meetings of the half-starved and starving labourers were held; but ignorant and helpless as they were, it was to violence they had recourse. Thus, from one cause or another, the public mind in all classes of society was deeply agitated.

The new Parliament met on the 26th of October; it was formally opened by the King on the 2d of November; and the very same day the Duke of Wellington, the Prime Minister, made an emphatic pronouncement against reform.

He said: "I shall not hesitate to declare unequivocally what are my sentiments upon it. I am fully convinced that the country possesses at the present moment a Legislature which answers all the good purposes of legislation, and this to a greater degree than any Legislature ever has answered in any country whatever. I will go further, and say that the Legislature and the system of representation possess the full and entire confidence of the country—deservedly possess that confidence—and the discussions in the Legislature have a very great influence over the opinions of the country. . . . The representation of the people at present contains a large body of the property of the country, and in which the landed interests have a preponderating influence. Under these circumstances I am not prepared to bring forward any measure of the description alluded to by the noble lord (a reform measure). I am not only not prepared to bring forward any measure of this nature, but I will at once declare that, as far as I am concerned, as long as I hold any station in the government of the country, I shall always feel it my duty to resist such measures when proposed by others."[1]

The Times commenting, a short time after, on this speech wrote: "The declaration (of the Duke of Wellington) against all reform, formidable enough as it was in itself, was rendered

[1] *Parliamentary Debates*, 1830, vol. i. p. 52.

yet more ominous by the apprehension that it was meant to cover also all other abuses and extravagances, and to protect the yet smoking remains of that system by which the nation has so severely suffered in its social comforts and enjoyments."[1]

Despair would have settled down on the country had it not been at once perceived that this vehement declaration of the Prime Minister had sealed the fate of the Government. On the 15th of November the Government was defeated on a question concerning the "Civil List," and immediately resigned. Lord Grey, the veteran reformer, was sent for by the King, and on the 23d received the Seals as Prime Minister.

"The new Government will find plenty to occupy their most serious thoughts, and employ their best talents," wrote Greville on the 21st November; "the state of the country is dreadful; every post brings fresh accounts of conflagrations, destruction of machinery, association of labourers, and compulsory rise of wages. Cobbett and Carlile write and harangue to inflame the minds of the people, who are already set in motion and excited by all the events which have happened abroad;" and on the 28th he wrote: "There has been nothing new within these three days, but the alarm is still very great, and the general agitation which pervades men's minds unlike what I have ever seen. Reform, economy, echoed backwards and forwards, the doubts, the hopes, the fears of those who have anything to lose, the uncertainty of everybody's future condition, the immense interests at stake, the magnitude and imminence of the danger, all contribute to produce a nervous excitement which extends to all classes, to almost every individual."[2]

On assuming office Lord Grey at once stated that the question of Parliamentary reform would be taken up by the new Government.

"No sooner," says Place, "was the declaration of Lord Grey made than it was considered as the declaration of Ministers, and there was a simultaneous movement, not only of the Political Associations, but of the reformers all over the kingdom, as if there had been mutual communication among them, and mutual agreement to proceed in the same manner for the same purpose, although there was no such communication, no agree-

1 *The Times*, 16th November 1830. 2 Greville's *Memoirs*, vol. ii. p. 68.

ment to do anything. There was a persuasion that Ministers ought to be kept up to their promises, vague as they were, and pushed on as far beyond them as possible, and made as much as possible dependent on the people." [1]

The Times, in a leading article of 27th November, pointed out what meetings and associations, or, in other words, what the Platform, under the changed circumstances of the time, might do to bring about the realisation of reform: "Beyond all doubt the necessity for a reform of Parliament is the main and prime necessity under which this country labours. It is a long while since this truth was discovered and displayed energetically in speech and writing by intelligent men throughout the Empire, but it is not very long since the people began to entertain hopes of acting successfully on that knowledge, because facility of communication through the Press, and that of co-operation by means of meetings and societies, had not yet been so far matured as to teach the people that they need but unite to be irresistible. The present Parliament was elected by a nation bent resolutely on reform of Parliament."

The country was not, however, going to be content with action at election time, but determined to persevere in making its voice heard, and to keep up pressure on the representatives.

"The systematic way," says Place, "in which the people proceeded, their steady perseverance, their activity and skill astounded the enemies of reform. Meetings of almost every description of persons were held in cities, towns, and parishes; by journeymen tradesmen in their clubs, and by common workmen who had no trade clubs or associations of any kind. Meetings of these people were held in all the great towns, and speeches were made at them; the manner of the speakers, and the matter of their speeches were very generally superior to those which could have been made even a few years ago by their employers. So numerous were the meetings which passed resolutions urging Lord Grey on, and pledging themselves in every way to support him, that the morning newspapers were compelled over and over again to declare their utter inability, not only to give accounts of the proceedings, but even in any way to take any notice whatever of an immense number of them." [2]

[1] Place, MSS., 27,789, p. 204.

[2] *Ibid.* pp. 252, 253.

All through the winter, while unfortunate half-starved peasants, driven to desperation by poverty and want, were having recourse to violence and crime, instead of appealing through the Platform for help, and whilst the law was dooming these wretched victims to the scaffold and the convict ship, the more intelligent classes were giving expression through the Platform to their views as to the real source of all the evils that afflicted the country. Scotland too was making herself heard on behalf of Parliamentary reform. Meetings were held at Edinburgh, Forfar, Kirkcaldy, and numerous other places, and resolutions passed demanding an extension of the franchise. Conscious, as it were, that the Platform was the only power that could carry the measure, *The Times* did its best to incite the people to have recourse to it.[1]

"We trust there is not a county, town, or village in the United Kingdom which will not meet and petition for a reform in Parliament." Soon, "the nation was meeting everywhere." Meetings were held in Cambridgeshire, Berkshire, Middlesex, Lincolnshire, Kent, Northumberland, Manchester, Bristol, Norwich, Reading, and a host of other places. The more formidable kind of meetings—those organised ones of the Political Unions—were increasing in frequency also. A meeting was held in Birmingham on the 13th of December 1830—a town's meeting in support of the Ministry. Attwood was at it and spoke. He said: "It gives me great satisfaction to perceive that Political Unions are spreading everywhere—from Devonshire to Caithness they are studded throughout the country. In the extremities of Fifeshire and Forfar, for instance, in Glasgow and Paisley, in Leeds, Manchester, and Liverpool, in Sheffield, Norwich, Coventry, and many other places, they have taken deep root, and I trust they will flourish for the benefit of the people." Resolutions were passed thanking the King for dismissing the Wellington Administration, and calling upon the people to support their patriot King and the new Ministers.

"This was a stimulating meeting," remarks Place; "and the Birmingham Union being now acknowledged as the leading voluntary political association, it produced the intended effect, and its proceedings were adopted at an immense number of public meetings."[2]

[1] See *The Times*, 1st December 1830.

[2] Place, MSS., 27,789, p. 211.

On the 20th December Parliament was adjourned to the 3d February 1831, and during all that time the country kept the agitation vigorously going.

On the 3d February 1831 *The Times* wrote: "The reform meetings throughout England begin to be almost too numerous for us to notice. Two features are common to most of them —first, an expression that the meetings will be accepted by Ministers as a support and encouragement; second, there runs throughout their proceedings an evident persuasion that a full and uncompromising reform of Parliament offers the sole security which can be devised against some dreadful convulsion."

One county, Cornwall, met a slight rebuff from its High Sheriff, who was requisitioned to convene a meeting. His reply is illustrative of the ideas prevailing even then among some as to the Platform. He wrote: "That he doubted the prudence of the assembly of large masses of people at a time of public excitement like the present; the House of Commons was the only proper place for the discussion of reform, as it contained all the discretion and temper of the country." The meeting was, nevertheless, held and reform petitioned for.

Place, referring to the agitation in January and February 1831, says: "The business, for such the people really made it, was immense, and was carried on as systematically as it could have been, had there been an arrangement made for the whole of it; yet there was not even the smallest communication between places in the same neighbourhood; each portion of the people appeared to understand what ought to be done, and each did its part as if it were an arranged part of one great whole." [1]

The short recess gave Lord Grey and his colleagues time to frame their scheme of reform. Brougham, in his Memoirs, says: [2] "The state of the reform question was now so entirely different from what it had been in former times, that the principles were wholly different from those which guided the rational and considerate reformers thirty or even twenty years before. In those days there had been a complete schism in the reform party." Now, however, as he proceeded to point

[1] Place, MSS., 27,789, p. 251.

[2] *The Life and Times of Lord Brougham*, by himself, vol. iii. p. 49.

out, in the urgency of the general necessity for some reform, differences were being sunk, and the Cabinet were happily able to frame a measure on which all were agreed.[1]

Thanks to the generosity which permitted the publication of the correspondence which passed between the King and his Prime Minister, during the acute struggle now being entered on, we have the means of tracing, in the innermost councils of the State, the effect of every move made by the Platform; and the comments of the King, and of the Prime Minister, on the passing events, throw a flood of light upon some of the most important and difficult problems and occurrences of the time.

Only one letter of Lord Grey's, previous to the introduction of the Reform Bill into the House of Commons, need be referred to. On the 15th January 1831 he wrote to Sir Herbert Taylor, the King's Private Secretary: "I am myself convinced that public opinion is so strongly directed to this question, and so general, that it cannot be resisted without the greatest danger of leaving the Government in a situation in which it would be deprived of all authority and strength. . . . An attempt to postpone it would be fatal to the character of the Government, and would lead to its dissolution under circumstances still more disastrous than those which would follow such a result if his Majesty withheld his assent from the measure which may be submitted to him by his Ministers."[2]

Early in February there is a letter from the King, giving his views on the proposal of his Ministers as regards reform: "Great stress," he says, "is laid upon the general opinion of the people, as being in favour of an extensive reform; but his Majesty very much doubts whether there be sufficient ground

[1] There is a curious agreement of opinion between Francis Place and *The Quarterly Review* as to the reason of the Whig leaders so suddenly taking up the reform question.

Place says: "Fear works wonders. It was fear, sheer fear, which at length induced the Whigs to make the sacrifices they did, and to take, to the extent they did, part with the people."—Place, MSS., 27,789, p. 391.

And *The Quarterly Review* wrote (1831, vol. xliv. p. 561): "What can be the motive of all these sudden conversions to the cause of Parliamentary reform? The answer is short enough, and must be on the lips of every one who is not afraid to look at the truth. It is the dread of *physical force*. The events of the three days of July at Paris have given for a time, to popular insurrection, a predominance of character such as it probably never possessed before at any period of the history of mankind."

[2] *Correspondence between William IV. and Lord Grey*, vol. i. p. 65.

for this conclusion. He cannot consider public meetings as a just criterion of the sentiments of the people. The objects of those meetings have, in general, been the promotion of discontent and the disturbance of the public peace."[1] Upon mature consideration, however, he gave his full assent to the ministerial proposals.

The public meetings which the King could not consider a just criterion of the sentiments of the people were expressing themselves pretty plainly. Turn to some of the Petitions decided on by a popular meeting at this time, and we get there a very clear idea of what the Platform was saying, for its teaching was but an enlargement of, a dissertation on, a commendation of, the prayers of these Petitions. Look at the Petition from a meeting at Norwich.

"Where distress is of a public nature, and can be traced to legislative causes, men begin to lose their respect for the laws, and are ready to encounter dangers the most appalling in opposition to them. . . . That the distress has been caused by an overwhelming weight of taxation, partly for the payment of an enormous public debt, partly for the maintenance of innumerable pensions, and sinecure offices, and inordinately overpaid or unnecessary establishments—military, civil, and ecclesiastical. That measures reforming these and other evils can only be safely carried into effect by a Parliament enjoying the full confidence of the people and elected by them."

Look at another Petition from Worcestershire in January 1831.

"That your honourable House, instead of representing the opinions, feelings, and interests of the great body of the people," etc., "has, by a series of acts, commenced, forwarded, and upheld a monstrous expenditure of public money, which has mainly tended to enrich and increase the influence of a corrupt boroughmongering aristocracy.

"Your petitioners are of opinion that this hitherto wanton and profligate expenditure of public money, this overwhelming system of taxation, are not only rapidly impoverishing, degrading, and sinking the middle classes and working classes of his Majesty's subjects into one general mass of misery and ruin,

[1] *Correspondence between William IV. and Lord Grey*, vol. i. p. 98, 4th February.

but producing also the greatest discontents throughout the whole community," and the petitioners very naturally prayed for a radical Reform Bill.

The *Annual Register* of this year gave a summary of the statements in the Petitions adopted at this period, but at the same time used the occasion for a criticism on, or almost condemnation of, the Platform. That criticism has been so often since repeated that it is as well to refer to it here as in any other place.[1] "Meetings," said the writer, "were held in all parts of the country—in counties, in towns, and in parishes—for the purposes of getting up Petitions, which were at once to be the result and the support of the declared intentions of the Government. Such expressions of opinion are at all times easily obtained; and, in reference to such a topic, they bear on the solution of the question only in so far as they prove the fact of the existence of an unsatisfied desire in masses of the population, in regard to their political condition. . . .

"The degrees, by which the power of the popular body might be increased, were infinite; and the question how far its increase was fitting and safe, or how far necessary to secure the objects of good government, was a question to be decided by sound reason—not by the mere fact that certain bodies of men desired political power. The Petitions, however, which were now industriously manufactured in every part of the country, were almost uniformly found wanting in this, the only intelligible question that could arise. Thus one set of petitioners prayed for 'the equalisation and extension of the right of suffrage'; but whether they meant such an extension and equalisation as would convert the government into a democracy, or some more modified degree of change, they either did not know, or were afraid to declare. Others announced that 'for the sake of everything that is truly valuable in society, a real, substantial, and effectual reform in the representation of the people is become absolutely necessary'; but what would amount, in the opinion of the petitioners, to a real, substantial, and effectual reform, and whether a reform, meriting, in their eyes, the honour of these epithets, would not be inconsistent with the permanent and useful existence of the other branches of the Constitution, was left

[1] *Annual Register*, p. 2, 1831.

to conjecture. When the petitioners departed from these unmeaning generalities, the demands which they put forward were—the annihilation of all influence on the part of the aristocracy in returning members to the House of Commons, the shortening the duration of Parliaments, the extension and equalisation of the elective franchise; but how it was to be extended was left untold, except in those Petitions which demanded that the right of suffrage should be universal. A large proportion of these Petitions further set forth that no measure of reform, however radical might be the changes which it would introduce, would prove an effectual remedy, unless it provided that all votes in future should be given by ballot."

Such criticism displays the antipathy existing then to the Platform. It was ridiculous to expect the Platform to draft a Reform Bill, yet this is what the writer seemed to expect.[1] The Platform, at that stage of its existence, discharged its functions in confining itself to a simple demand for reform; and it discharged it very efficiently. Through it the millions of voices calling for reform made themselves heard within the portals of the Legislature, and, up to the very eve of the introduction of the Reform Bill, meetings were being held, and Petitions adopted, for reform.

At last Lord Grey's Government gave to the country the result of their deliberations. On the 1st of March 1831 the keenly expected measure was introduced into the House of Commons. The Bill was far more sweeping in its character than even the most sanguine reformers had anticipated. At one stroke most of the rotten boroughs were to be obliterated. It proposed the total disfranchisement of all boroughs which had less than 2000 inhabitants at the date of the last census. Of such boroughs there were 60, returning 119 members. It proposed the semi-disfranchisement—that is to say, the taking away of one of the two representatives of boroughs with less than 4000 inhabitants; of these there were 46; and the semi-disfranchisement of Weymouth, which returned four members

[1] From the 5th of November 1830, when Parliament met, up to the 4th of March 1831—the period at which the reform proposal was fairly before the country—645 petitions were presented to the House of Commons for reform, 280 for the ballot, 182 for short Parliaments.

—168 seats were thus placed at the disposal of the Government; but as the Bill proposed that the House of Commons should be reduced in number, from 658 to 596 members, only 106 seats were actually left for distribution among new constituencies, or for additions to existing ones.

It was proposed to give five additional seats to Scotland, and three to Ireland, and one to Wales; that each of seven large towns should send two members, and twenty other towns one member each. London was to have eight members more, and it was proposed to add fifty-five members to English counties. So much for the seats. As regarded the franchise, it was to be extended to £50 leaseholders, and £10 copyholders in counties, and to £10 householders in boroughs. The poll was to be taken in two days; and instead of one polling place in each county there were to be several.

The Bill was received with universal joy by all classes of reformers; the general enthusiasm was "utterly indescribable" —bells ringing, flags flying, illuminations, every symptom of rejoicing.

The Platform came at once to the aid of the Government, and there was an almost unanimous expression of approval throughout the country. "The whole nation is in movement for the sake of petitioning Parliament to pass the Bill. Every parish throughout the metropolis, every district throughout the kingdom, is in motion."

The Birmingham Political Union at once took measures for supporting the Ministers, and on 7th March a meeting of 15,000 persons was held, at the Repository, for the purpose. Attwood was in the chair. He said that the Government proposal was not all that he could wish, but that it would be better to support it in its entirety than to run the risk of alienating many of the middle class by bringing forward a more radical measure. He declared his conviction, that it was admirably calculated to restore the liberty and the happiness of the people.[1]

It is interesting finding the Press again urging the people to Platform action. On the 10th March *The Times* wrote: "Let every meeting throughout the kingdom adopt resolutions, the strongest that language can convey, in favour of the

[1] *Life of Thomas Attwood*, p. 157.

Bill in all its parts. Let this be done instantly; let it be done unanimously."[1]

Other portions of the Press took up the same line. "While the contest is pending," wrote one provincial paper, "the people ought to come forward in numbers outnumbering all former public assemblages, in zeal outdoing all former enthusiasm, in perseverance exceeding all former determination."

The people needed little incitement. Deep determination had taken possession of them, and in counties, cities, towns, and parishes they were giving expression from the Platform to their desires. Even Cornwall, from which twenty seats were to be taken, joined in the chorus for the Bill. "The people have almost exceeded our hopes," wrote *The Times*. "They have far outstripped our utmost efforts to keep pace with their still increasing ardour in the cause of reform, so far as those efforts might have aimed at presenting to our readers even a faint outline of what is taking place every hour of each succeeding day at meetings held throughout every county in England, and attended by numbers, wealth, intelligence, high reputation, and consequent moral power, such as never before were seen, or imagined, in connection with any political question at the most animated period of English history."[2]

Place has given a short but pointed explanation of the support which was given to the Bill by the people who derived no immediate benefit from it. He said: "The people have to a great extent been taught, as well by circumstances and examples as by precepts, that the nearer the institutions of the nations approach towards self-government, the better they must be for the people. On this occasion they saw that the Bill to reform the House of Commons was a step towards improving the government of the country, and they took it with firmness and alacrity. Their proceedings were those which alone could induce the corrupt House of Commons to carry the Bill, and were therefore, under all the circumstances of the case, the best they could adopt."[3]

"The excitement is beyond anything I ever saw," wrote Greville on the 5th March. On the 7th he wrote: "Nothing talked of, thought of, dreamt of, but reform."

[1] See *The Times*, 10th March 1831. [2] *Ibid.* 15th March 1831.
[3] Place, MSS., p. 282.

On the 11th March there is another interesting entry in his *Memoirs:*[1] "It is curious to see the change of opinion as to the passing of the Bill. The other day nobody would hear of the possibility of it, now everybody is beginning to think it will be carried. The tactics of the Opposition have been very bad, for they ought to have come to a division immediately, when, I think, Government would have been beaten; but it was pretty certain that if they gave time to the country to declare itself, the meetings and addresses would fix the wavering and decide the doubtful. There certainly never was anything like the unanimity which pervades the country on the subject; and though I do not think they will break out into rebellion if it is lost, it is impossible not to see that the feeling for it (kept alive as it will be by every sort of excitement) must prevail." And on the 20th of March he wrote: "Reform the people will have, and no human power, moral or physical, can now arrest its (the Bill's) career."

The debate on the second reading soon came on, and on the morning of the 23d of March, at three o'clock, the House divided, and the second reading was carried by a majority of one "in the fullest House that ever was known,"—303 having voted for it and 302 against it; and this though, according to Lord Grey, "the activity, the intrigue, the falsehood that was used to influence votes (against the Government) is not to be described."[2]

How tremendous must have been the pressure of outside opinion on members of Parliament when such a result could be obtained in the unreformed Parliament.

Already, while the Bill was under discussion, it had become apparent to the Government, at least, that there would have to be a new election before the opposition to it was overcome.

The day before the division on the second reading Lord Grey wrote to Sir H. Taylor (22d March 1831): "We did not cause the excitement about reform. We found it in full vigour when we came into office. . . . The excitement which now exists is directed to what is, I think, a safe and legitimate object. In the event of a dissolution, it would act in support of the King and Government. If a contrary direction is given

[1] Greville, vol. ii. p. 126.

[2] *Correspondence of William IV. and Earl Grey*, vol. i. p. 201.

to it, you probably will see associations all over the country; and when once they have felt their power, the history of the Catholic question will show the consequences that may be expected."[1]

And the same day Sir H. Taylor wrote to Lord Grey: "His Majesty has considered the period of general election to have been, at all times and under all circumstances, a period of disorder, of general relaxation, and more or less of outrage; and he has been strongly impressed with the fear that, from the spirit of the times, the disturbances and lawless acts which prevailed some months ago, the illegal combinations which are still in existence, though not at present in active operation, those disorders which attend a general election would be carried to extremes, without reference even to any extraordinary excitement produced by the agitation of the question of reform and its failure. His Majesty has not concealed his apprehension of associations for the purpose of forcing forward the measure, although there should not be a dissolution; but he has not considered that they would endanger the tranquillity and the security of the country in the same degree as large assemblages of the lower orders, in every part of the country, at one and the same moment, which would be held under sanction of the law."[2]

The following day again some interesting correspondence took place.

Lord Grey wrote to the King's private secretary: "The extent of the public feeling as to the measure that has been proposed will be differently estimated by different persons. But I believe there never was a sentiment so general, or rather so nearly universal, as that which now prevails. Let any impartial person look at the meetings in all parts of the country, the number and description of the persons attending them, and the unanimity of their decisions, to which scarcely, in any instance, an opposition has been attempted; and I think there can be little doubt of the opinion he must form."[3]

Sir H. Taylor replied to Lord Grey, 24th March: "With regard to the meetings that take place, it may be questioned whether those who attend them express the opinions of the

[1] *Correspondence of William IV. and Earl Grey*, vol. i. p. 186.
[2] *Ibid.* p. 189.
[3] *Ibid.* p. 199.

most respectable or most influential portion of the community. They are almost invariably the advocates and supporters of the object for which they are called together; and, upon a popular occasion, the great majority are of the very lowest class. The opponents, those who know that they will not be suffered to raise their voices, seldom attend, and unanimity is thus placed beyond the power of dispute."[1]

The small majority by which the second reading of the Bill had been carried made it at once apparent that there was no prospect of carrying the Bill through Committee, to say nothing as yet of the House of Lords; but this narrow division, so far from causing the Platform to slacken in its work, only gave it additional energy. "County meetings go on, parochial meetings go on, the zeal increases everywhere."[2]

On the 14th April Greville[3] wrote: "Though the opinion of the country is universally in its (the Bill's) favour, people are beginning to think that it may be rejected without any apprehension of such dreadful consequences ensuing as have been predicted." Less than a week later the Tories determined to run the risk, and on the 19th April they succeeded in carrying a separate resolution hostile to the principles of the Bill, the Ministers were defeated, and the Bill was lost. The Government took instantaneous action, the King himself helping.

"Parliament was prorogued," says Jeffrey, "on the 22d April, after a scene of bellowing and roaring and gnashing of teeth on the part of the adversary in both Houses, which it was almost frightful to look at;" and the next day it was dissolved. The day after that the King, evidently overwhelmed with anxiety and work, wrote: "The times are awful."[4]

Never, in the history of the country, had so momentous a crisis arisen, never were great exertions by the people so imperatively required. The goal long striven for was at last in view, there before them, only one great effort more, and it would be reached; and they gathered their strength for a final rush. A Reform Bill had been actually proposed, triumphed

1 *Correspondence of William IV. and Earl Grey*, vol. i. p. 204.
2 *The Times*, 26th March 1831.
3 Greville, *Memoirs*, vol. ii. p. 134.
4 *Correspondence of William IV. and Earl Grey*, vol. i. p. 245.

even for a moment, and had then been defeated—so far had they got, farther than ever before, and now Parliament was dissolved, and it rested with themselves whether the Bill should ultimately be carried to a triumph.

The King's speech had put the issue clearly enough to the country, but indeed all men could understand it. It is, however, to be recorded that the Minister who was practically the leader of the party in the House of Commons made a public speech outside the House of Commons which was to act as an election cry. It is the first instance I have been able to find of what has since become a recognised practice—namely, of a leading Minister making a speech on the eve of a general election which gives the cue to his party in the country.

On the 25th April a meeting was held of Mr. Brougham's friends (brother of Lord Brougham), who was standing for Southwark. Lord J. Russell spoke at it in favour of Brougham. In the course of his speech he said: "On this occasion the electors had more than a common duty to perform, for they were called on not merely to select men, the best fitted to defend their rights and interests, but to answer by their conduct this question put to the electors of the Empire by his Majesty in dissolving Parliament, 'Do you approve, ay or no, of the principle of a reform in the representation?'"

And now that Parliament was actually dissolved, and the issue put shortly and clearly before the country, from one end of the kingdom to the other burst forth the articulate voice of the people. Their voices, and the voices of their leaders, rang from the platform, now suddenly raised into a mighty political engine. From thousands of platforms rang the question, 'Reform, ay or no,' with all the additional embellishments with which the varied talents or tastes of the speakers could adorn it. Not only on one day either was it reiterated, but day after day, as the contests prolonged themselves into weeks. And from thousands of meetings speaking by the Platform came back the reply, 'The Bill, the whole Bill, and nothing but the Bill.'

Nor were the electors now, as heretofore, the only persons interested in the proceedings. Outside them, standing on the threshold of the Constitution, were great numbers of the people waiting to be enrolled as citizens of the Empire,[1]—the inhabitants of the wealthy cities of the North and other places, where lay so much of the wealth and intelligence of England, and who at last were to be enfranchised, and to become part participators in their own government; and outside them again the still larger masses, who even yet were to be excluded from citizenship, but who felt that in helping their comrades, they were helping themselves forward too.

The brunt of the battle fell upon the electors, and fired with enthusiasm, their votes were recorded for reform candidates, in defiance of intimidation, in scorn of bribery, and at the risk of persecution and loss; but "great emergencies lift men's minds above ordinary considerations, and carry them on to exalted acts of heroism," and with many electors it was little short of heroism to vote for reform.

Dover had the honour of leading the van, by setting the first example to England of a constituency returning two reformers; London city sent four reformers; and Middlesex, ever true to the Liberal cause, sent two—all she could.

In Somersetshire, on the day of the election, about five o'clock of the morning, a numerous body of electors and others assembled. By the time they reached Wells, the county town, their numbers amounted to some 15,000 or 20,000. Candidates were proposed—reformers and anti-reformers; the immense body of people held up their hands for the two reform candidates, and the demonstration was such that the Tory or anti-reform candidates there and then resigned. In some places, however, the anti-reformers did not succumb without a contest, though with indifferent success. Northumberland, Kent, Lancashire, Essex, and Sussex, all returned two reformers each. In Cumberland the Lowther interest, long predominant, tottered and fell. In Gloucestershire the Beaufort interest collapsed. Interests long paramount were as chaff before the breath of the people.

"The county members, as Sefton says, are tumbling about like ninepins." [2]

[1] Lord J. Russell estimated that the Bill would add 60,000 to the electorate of London, and 260,000 to that of England, and 60,000 to Scotland. See Hansard, vol. xi., 1831.

[2] Greville, *Memoirs*, 26th April 1831, vol. ii. p. 139.

In Worcestershire so popular was reform that no temptation of a bribe would make people forfeit the good opinion of their fellow-townsmen and countrymen, and the Tory candidate was defeated, though helped "by fourscore hired attorneys." In Dorsetshire the anti-reform candidate thought to appeal to the selfish feelings of his hearers by saying that the Bill would rob the inhabitants of Dorset of one-half of their representatives, and was silenced by the cry, "They are not ours"; "We disown them"; and they promptly disowned him too.

"Nothing could go worse than the elections," wrote Greville on the 7th of May: "Reformers returned everywhere, so much so that the contest is over, and we have only to wait the event, and see what the House of Lords will do;"[1] and on the 11th he wrote: "The elections are going on universally in favour of reform; the great interests in the counties are everywhere broken, and old connections dissevered. . . . Everywhere the tide is irresistible—all considerations are sacrificed to the success of the measure." The enthusiasm reached even a close borough, for at Banbury the patron withdrew his nominee after two votes had been recorded for him, "there being six independent electors of the borough who voted against him."[2]

Old Sarum, however, no storm could touch, no popular enthusiasm affect, no Platform oratory move. At nine o'clock one morning, that month of May, under an elm tree, might have been seen a table and two chairs, and, accurately counted, some thirteen persons—two of whom were members of the dissolved Parliament,—the rest, we may presume, the Sheriff and his assistants, possibly some of them spectators. A few minutes, some few forms gone through, and the two late members are again members, elected, if it could be so called, for the last time; and soon after, as if to emphasise its being really the last time, some 200 reformers—non-electors need it be said—come with banner flying, cut down the tree, and divide it into small portions—mementoes of the last election in the rottenest of rotten boroughs.

Great as had been the anxiety of the people of England on the subject of the elections, and enthusiastic as they had been, they had been, if possible, surpassed by the Scotch. But Scotland could do little more than be enthusiastic, for in

[1] Greville, *Memoirs*, vol. ii. p. 141. [2] *Ibid.* p. 142.

Scotland, as has been already told, there was not a vestige of popular or real representation; there were no popular constituencies; all were close boroughs or close counties, of the very closest description. From 2500 to 3000 voters, according to different returns, constituted the electoral body for the whole of Scotland. "The hustings were things that Scotland never saw. Even county meetings were not accessible to the populace, for only certain qualified ratepayers had a voice in them, and in Moray a county meeting was held at which eight persons were present, and as five of those voted against reform, Morayshire was claimed as an anti-reform county. Still worse was it in Bute.[1] At one election for that county, within the memory of man, when the day of election came, only one person qualified to vote attended, and that person was the Sheriff. He took the chair; he constituted the meeting; he called over the names on the roll of freeholders; then he answered his own name; then he took the vote for a præses and elected himself; then, last of all, he moved and seconded his own nomination; he put the representation to the vote, and was unanimously returned."

Scotland, however, was not going to be dumb.

The enlargement of the electorate from 3000 to 63,000 was too exciting a possibility to be treated with quietude. Great towns with their populations of 25,000, 50,000, and 100,000, under these circumstances were not going to be silent, whatever anti-reformers might wish, and large and enthusiastic meetings were held in them, and the Platform gave voice, and Petitions were adopted in favour of reform. A Petition at Edinburgh, originated at a public meeting, had 21,000 signatures, "signed by nearly the whole of that portion of the inhabitants who were considered as leading persons in society there." Indeed, in some two or three places, where the formalities of election brought into prominence the exclusion of the people from the privilege of the franchise, the people were unable to restrain their feelings, and violent riots took place. These however were exceptional, and *The Times*, reviewing the whole election, was able to write:[2] "There never, we believe, occurred

[1] See Speech of the Lord Advocate for Scotland on second reading of the Scotch Reform Bill.—*Parliamentary Debates*, vol. vii. p. 529.

[2] *The Times*, 24th May 1831.

an election in either part of the United Kingdom wherein so little of actual violence was had recourse to."

The Government watched the elections throughout the country with deep anxiety. That even they had underrated the state of the public feeling on the subject is evident from the letter of Lord Grey to Sir H. Taylor, written on the 3d May: "All the elections, except those of Schedules A and B (the condemned boroughs), prosper beyond our most sanguine expectations;" and on the 6th May he wrote: "The enclosed list will show you that the elections are going on better and better. The freeholders of Northampton have insisted upon putting up Lord Milton in conjunction with Lord Althorp, and declare that they will bring them in free of expense."[1]

The King's mind was, however, disquieted within him. On the 17th of May he wrote to Lord Grey:[2] "The fact is, that the King had noticed with extreme pain and alarm the early effects produced in this country by the contagious example of the French revolution. They followed close upon his accession to the throne, and preceded, by somewhat more than the same interval, the change of Government, and the introduction of the Reform Bill. They have been very striking; and although the introduction of a popular measure by the Government, with the declared sanction of the King, has secured to both the support of the great mass of the people, and expressions of favour and attachment, it is impossible not to trace, in much that has taken place and manifested itself in the course of the elections, and the popular demonstrations, the seeds of revolution—a disposition generally hostile to the aristocracy of the country,—a strong inclination to introduce a form of government purely democratical, and other symptoms, which are calculated to raise the apprehension that those who may now appear and express themselves satisfied with the measure of reform introduced, have ulterior objects in view, towards which they trust this may prove a stepping-stone."

It is difficult to realise the tremendous part which the Platform took in this election—the last of an unreformed Parliament. The newspapers of the day convey necessarily but a most inadequate idea of its work, for a line was all there was

[1] *Correspondence of William IV. and Earl Grey*, vol. i. p. 253.
[2] *Ibid.* p. 266.

to record what often was a most effective speech, a sentence or two all to describe even an important meeting. Still, they enable us to clearly see that at no previous general election had the Platform been so extensively used, that never yet had its power been so strikingly manifested.

The people of the country were almost at white-heat of excitement, easily to be moulded and influenced by the power of public speech; they had learned, in process of years, that no expression of their views and of their feelings carried such weight as when spoken from the Platform, and they availed themselves fully of what to many of them was a new-found engine of political power.

The new Parliament met on 14th June 1831, and the Government immediately reintroduced their Reform Bill. The true results of the elections were seen on the second reading which took place on the 8th of July, when there was a majority of 136 votes in its favour—367 members voting for the Bill, and 231 against it. Lagging somewhat in its progress through Committee, it was finally passed by the House of Commons on the 21st of September, with some alterations which it is unnecessary here to refer to, by 345 votes to 236, and sent to the House of Lords.

The country, which had been fairly quiescent while the Bill was progressing through the House of Commons, at once gave evidence of watchfulness. Rumours got abroad that the Bill would be rejected by the Lords, as the temporary quiescence of the people had been interpreted by some as a sign of reaction or growing indifference to the fate of the measure. It was necessary to disprove this malicious calumny; it was necessary for the people to remind the Lords that they were in earnest, and not to be trifled with, and meetings innumerable were forthwith everywhere held.

Greville, in his *Memoirs*,[1] depreciatingly remarks: "A thousand mushroom orators and politicians have sprung up all over the country, each big with his own ephemeral importance, and every one of whom fancies himself fit to govern the nation."

Place gives a very different and a truer version: "The meetings in counties, cities, and boroughs, showed, by the

[1] Greville, *Memoirs*, vol. ii. p. 208.

speeches of those who took leading parts in them, that they were very generally well qualified to judge of the state of the country and the merits of the Reform Bill, and were remarkable proofs of the great improvement which had been going on, and was still going on, all over the kingdom—proofs too that great changes in Government must be made, as certainly as that a really intelligent people cannot be governed like barbarians; to this plain fact none seemed blind, a number of the peers alone excepted, on whom experience cannot operate."[1]

"The people were now again," as Place terms it, "in a state of ebullition. The meetings in counties, cities, boroughs, towns, wards, and parishes became again so numerous that the London newspapers were obliged to apologise for not being able to give account of by far the largest portion of them, and it was again demonstrated that the people were fully resolved to have the Reform Bill passed."[2]

The Platform resounded with warnings and advice to the peers. One or two examples will suffice to convey an idea of the views propounded.

At a meeting of the Livery of London, at which the Lord Mayor presided, one speaker said: "The people of England alone should dictate to their rulers. Should this Bill by any unforeseen possibility be defeated, how did the noble conservators of rotten boroughs propose to retain their countrymen in allegiance to a defective political system? If it were to be negatived, would its foes answer for the existence of trade, and the prosperity of the realm? Did they flatter themselves into the belief that they could induce the people to pay taxes at the bidding of the reptiles in Schedule A (the boroughs which were to be entirely disfranchised), and the fiat of the half-palsied Schedule B (the boroughs that were to be half disfranchised), of which one part was dead, while the other still maintained its vitality? The peers could not be insane, and he therefore presumed that it was their intention to pass it rather than imperil their own existence by supporting a power as invidious as it was unjust, as dangerous to them as it was hateful to the people."

Another speaker said: "If the peers should be so rash as to

[1] Place, MSS., 27,789, p. 421. [2] *Ibid.* pp. 417, 419.

reject the Bill—if they should be so absolutely insane as to provoke the danger of being swept away, still would the nation be where it was."

Another said: "If the Lords rejected the Bill, they would not be taken by surprise when they came to discover the unavoidable results. The people, he would forewarn their Lordships, would not thenceforward pay taxes, nor would they be justified in so doing, when the country had decided that the Constitution was not what it ought to be."

Another said: "Let the Lords refuse this Bill if they dare, and if they do, dearly will they rue their obstinacy hereafter. . . . Should the present Bill be defeated, we shall bring their Lordships another Bill demanding a little more, and then should they still dare to resist the might, and insult the majesty of the people of England, which heaven forfend, united as one man will we come forward with a Bill of Reform, in which their Lordships will find themselves inserted in Schedule A."

Another important meeting was held in London—namely, of the merchants, bankers, and traders of the city of London, convened by the Lord Mayor, who presided. A Petition to the House of Lords was adopted. Their Lordships were reminded that the demonstrations in favour of the Bill had been unanimous throughout the kingdom, that the rejection of the Bill would spread dismay, that commerce would be paralysed, the labouring classes deprived of employment, and public credit fatally endangered.

A great meeting was held at Liverpool, another at Manchester, another at Chester, and a host of other places, all of them to petition the Lords to pass the Bill. Nearly every part of Scotland joined in the demonstration of public feeling. Middlesex, Kent, Surrey, Yorkshire, Berkshire, Hertfordshire, and several other counties held meetings, and at each and all of these meetings for hours a stream of Platform oratory was poured forth, spurring the people on to fresh exertions, raising ever greater hopes of the results of reform, instilling a deeper determination to gain them. Of one of these meetings—namely, the one at Derby—Lord Brougham, in the course of the debate on the second reading in the House of Lords, read an account which he had received from a friend.

"Some very good speeches were delivered at Derby, and you will perhaps be surprised when I tell you that much the best was by a common mechanic. He exposed with great force of reasoning the benefits which the lower classes would derive from the Reform Bill, and the interest they had in being well governed. He showed as much good taste and feeling as he would have done had he been a member of St. Stephen's. He is, of course, a man of talent, but there are many others also to be found, not far behind him."

The most important meeting of all, however, was that which was held at Birmingham on 3d October.

The Birmingham Political Union, evidently with misgivings of the treatment which the Bill would receive in the House of Lords, held a meeting on the day on which the debate on the second reading of the Bill was to begin, and resolved on a Petition to their Lordships to pass the Bill. Previous meetings had been held indoors. This one was held out of doors. At half-past eleven the people began to arrive. Then came the leaders of the Union, and then the members of the Staffordshire Union, until at last there were some 100,000 to 150,000 persons present, with bands and banners. It was a notable meeting, as showing what the Platform had come to—a greater meeting by far than the celebrated Manchester meeting of the 16th August 1819. Attwood took the chair. He congratulated them on having assembled in such numbers at the call of the Birmingham Political Union—of that formidable and patriotic body whose influence was felt not only throughout all the towns of that district, but throughout every part of England. They had acquired that position by courage, patriotism, and public spirit, tempered by prudence, caution, and discretion, submission to the law, mingled with determination to correct the law—these were the qualities by which they gathered up their giant strength, and by means of which they would use that strength for the recovery of the rights, liberties, and happiness of the people. . . .

"The most illustrious man in Europe, La Fayette, had told them forty years ago that 'for a nation to be free it was sufficient that she wills it.'

"Look around at this immense and magnificent assemblage in the very heart of England; see this prodigious mass of brave and upright men assembled together to support their good and patriotic King, and who, with such a spectacle before them, could possibly doubt that the British nation willed that the Bill of Reform should pass, and therefore that it must pass."

One of the speakers, referring to the eventuality of the Lords refusing to pass the Bill, said: "Failing all other constitutional means of obtaining the success of the reform measure, he solemnly declared that he would be the first man to refuse the payment of taxes, except by a levy on his goods" (tremendous cheering). "I now call upon all who hear me, and are prepared to join me in this step, to hold up their hands." (An immense forest of hands was immediately elevated, accompanied by vehement cheering.)

"Extraordinary was the excitement which this great meeting created throughout the country. Nothing of the sort had been witnessed in England before. Friends and foes were alike astonished at the peaceful, orderly, and unanimous conduct of its proceedings."[1]

The Times, referring to this meeting, wrote:[2] "There were neither military, nor policemen, nor magistrates present, nor any coercive power, save a deep sense of the obligations of rectitude and duty supported by a profound conviction that the purpose for which that meeting met together was altogether incompatible with licentiousness, violence, or disrespect for the peace of society. No symptom accordingly of disorder, or even of ill-humour, appeared in any quarter of that tremendous meeting, for well might it be called tremendous."

The influence of this meeting must have been strong on Lord Brougham when he made his splendid speech in the House of Lords in favour of the second reading of the Bill: "It is said the present representative system works well!" he exclaimed. "Then why does the table groan with Petitions against it? . . . It works well! Whence then the phenomenon of Political Unions—of the people everywhere forming themselves into associations to put down a system which you say well serves their interests? . . . Those portentous appearances, the growth of later times, those figures that stalk

[1] *Life of Thomas Attwood*, p. 178. [2] *The Times*, 5th October 1831.

abroad of unknown stature, and strange form—unions, and leagues, and musterings of men in myriads, and conspiracies against the Exchequer—whence do they spring, and how came they to haunt our shores? What power engendered those uncouth shapes, what multiplied the monstrous births, till they people the land? Trust me, the same power which called into frightful existence, and armed with resistless force, the Irish Volunteers of 1782—the same power which rent in twain your Empire, and conjured up thirteen republics—the same power which created the Catholic Association and gave it Ireland for a portion. What power is that? Justice denied—rights withheld—wrongs perpetrated—the force which common injuries lend to millions—the wickedness of using the sacred trust of Government as a means of indulging private caprice—the idiocy of treating Englishmen like the children of the South Sea Islands—the frenzy of believing, or making believe, that the adults of the nineteenth century can be led like children, or driven like barbarians? This it is that has conjured up the strange sights at which we now stand aghast." [1]

The Lords, however, disregarded the Petitions, which were so numerous that one day a waggon-load of them was presented; [2] they defied the Platform—defied the manifest feeling of the country. The large majority in the House of Commons should have been sufficient warning to them; but unable or unwilling to recognise that they had now to deal with the nation, and not merely with a House of Commons, and unwilling without a struggle to accept a measure which most of them regarded as leading inevitably to a revolution, and which on the face of it relegated them to a far lower position in the Constitution than that to which they considered they were entitled, they rejected the Bill on the morning of the 8th of October by 199 votes against 158.

On the rejection of the Bill by the Lords the House of Commons passed a resolution by 329 votes to 198, the object of which was to prevent Ministers resigning by pledging the House of Commons to support them, and much plain, and some minatory speaking was indulged in by some of the mem-

[1] *Parliamentary Debates*, vol. viii. pp. 263, 269.
[2] Place, MSS., 27,789, p. 437.

bers. But, as has before been pointed out, the nation had taken the settlement of this question into its own hand, and the House of Commons occupied in reality only a secondary, though an instrumental part in it. This fact cannot be too unreservedly recognised, for even in the more popularly written histories of this great struggle the impression conveyed is, that all turned on the persevering action of the House of Commons. That was not the case. The whole motive power—the whole driving force came from the people. The news of the rejection of the Bill was received throughout the country with the most intense indignation and excitement. In spite of all their petitionings, in spite of all their meetings, and all their declarations, in spite of the manifest unanimity and determination of the nation, in spite of the fact that the House of Commons, by passing the Reform Bill, had declared its own incapacity, and that its constitution could no longer be maintained, in spite of all these things, the Lords, aided by the almost full strength of the episcopal vote, had defied the nation. The people sprang instantaneously to the Platform to give expression of their feelings.

On the 10th October *The Times* wrote: "Our paper of to-day is dedicated to the description of that just indignation which is felt by the British people on the rejection of their Reform Bill. Everywhere they are in movement. We can hardly sum up the various constituent bodies that are appointing meetings, and the rapidity of the proceeding is no less remarkable."

"As fast as the news of the rejection spread," writes Place,[1] "meetings were held in counties, cities, boroughs, towns, parishes, and wards, in Unions, and Clubs, and of promiscuous bodies of people. Some of these meetings consisted of larger numbers than had ever before been brought together at the places where they were held. The tone in all of them was the same. To support the King and his Ministers in every way, and at any cost—of money, time, or life—everywhere the people were in concert, and would not have shrunk from any demonstration which could have been required of them, or which they thought would be agreeable to Ministers, and calculated to promote the passing of the Reform Bill."

Again did the "Bankers, merchants, and traders of the city

[1] Place, MSS., 27,790, p. 51.

of London" assemble; again did the counties meet; again did the inhabitants of the great new cities and towns assemble in their thousands and tens of thousands. On the 10th October some 30,000 persons met in Marylebone, but there not being enough room for them there to hold a meeting, they moved on to Hyde Park, and thence to Regent's Park, by which time there were some 80,000 persons collected together.

Joseph Hume, M.P., presided, speeches were delivered by him and several others, and strong resolutions were passed "That this meeting have learned with deep regret and indignation that a majority of the House of Peers have presumed to reject the Bill proposed by a Liberal Ministry—sanctioned by our patriotic King—and received by the people with gratitude and satisfaction. That this meeting cannot any longer tamely submit to this arrogant usurpation of the people's rights by any 200 individuals, particularly so when many of them are personally interested in upholding the present defective and corrupt system of representation and government."

The reintroduction of the Reform Bill was urged on Ministers, a resolution of thanks was accorded to the King for his paternal regard for the welfare of his people, and finally, a resolution was passed threatening the non-payment of tithes and taxes if an anti-reform Government should supplant Lord Grey's Government.

As Mr. Savage—"one of the most outrageous of the leaders of those of the working classes who would not consent to any reform, unless it included themselves, by means of universal suffrage and vote by ballot,"[1]—said, "He advised the people to use every constitutional means in their power before they resorted to physical force to obtain their rights. . . . He would tell the recreant peers that the minds of men, and not stocks and stones, should be represented."

Patience and constitutional courses were strongly recommended by all the speakers. "And," says Place, "these proceedings tended greatly to calm the people, and to lead the working people into the right path." On the same day there was an immense meeting of the Liverymen of the city of London in the Guildhall. In the metropolis, parish after parish

[1] Place, MSS., 27,790, p. 12.

held meetings—parishes which formed the suburbs of London, and contained nearly a million of inhabitants. On the 12th October a tremendous demonstration took place—a procession of some 100,000 to 300,000, mostly respectable shop-keepers and superior artisans and working men, with loyal addresses from the different parishes in London which were presented to the King. "It was necessary to convince our enemies," wrote one of the principal promoters of the demonstration, "that the people were in earnest, and that, if they have been hitherto quiet, it has only been a quiet resulting from confidence in the Government. We have shown them that we *can* do, and *mean* to do something if circumstances should require it."[1]

From one end of the country to the other, from north to south, from east to west, the flames of excitement blazed high. From Edinburgh came the report, "The dejection and dismay produced by the first reception of the news was soon succeeded by a determination to resort once more to the constitutional means of making our wrongs known, and obtaining our rights. The whole country is again on the move. Meetings have been held or are about to be held in Glasgow, Dundee, Perth, and a host of other places."

In some places the language used from the Platform was strong. Thus one speaker said: "They must have the Bill —the Bill or the barricades."

In some places, unfortunately, the Platform did not suffice as a vent for excited feelings. Riots of a more or less serious character took place at Nottingham, where the mob attacked and burnt down the castle of the Duke of Newcastle, at Derby, and at a few other places, but these were solitary exceptions. The people behaved with marvellous self-possession and self-restraint, and contented themselves with making plain to all men their determination to get reform, feeling confident that ultimately their cause must triumph, without their tarnishing it with violence or bloodshed. Strenuous efforts were made by the leading reformers on all the leading Platforms to repress all violence as disastrous to the cause of reform; and the Council of the Birmingham Political Union, the leading union in the country, issued an Address to their fellow-countrymen, exhorting them to stand firmly by the King and Lord Grey.

[1] Place, MSS., 27,790, p. 35.

It concluded as follows: "Without blood, without anarchy, without violation of the law, we will accomplish the most glorious reform recorded in the history of the world."

Fortunately, the situation was not embarrassed by any difficulties as regards the action of Ministers. Their course was quite plain. A general election having been recently held on this particular question, another was unnecessary, the general sense of the country being sufficiently clear. For Ministers to resign would have been a scandalous desertion of their posts. Their resignation would have been useless too, as the Tory party could not possibly have carried on a government with so large a majority in the House of Commons against them. Ministers, therefore, determined on the only remaining course to be adopted—namely, to wind up the necessary business of the session as quickly as possible, to prorogue Parliament for a short recess, to summon it again, and again send up the Reform Bill to the Lords.

The announcement of this course gave general satisfaction, but great alarm manifested itself at the rumour that Parliament was not to meet again till January. It was impossible for the people to be stretched out so long on the rack of expectation and excitement. A meeting of the committees and delegates of the various parishes in London was convened for the 12th October, and was held at the Crown and Anchor Tavern in the evening, "to consult on the best means of giving effectual support to the King and the Government, and on the measures necessary to secure the peace and safety of the metropolis." [1]

After many speeches a Memorial to Lord Grey was adopted, which set forth the firm conviction of the meeting, "that unless Parliament be prorogued for the shortest possible period of time (not exceeding seven days), and that the Reform Bill be then again introduced, and the necessary means be adopted to secure its becoming the law of the land, this country will inevitably be plunged into all the horrors of a violent revolution, the result of which no one can predict."

Forthwith a deputation, consisting of one representative of each parish, started off to present the Memorial to Lord Grey, or, as it was afterwards described "to beard the Minister at midnight."

[1] See Place, MSS., 27,790, p. 54.

When Lord Grey, who had been dining out, reached Downing Street, he found the deputation waiting for him, and there and then, at this midnight reception, received their Memorial, and listened to the speeches made. He gave some replies, and the deputation withdrew.

"The whole matter," says Place, who was one of the deputation, "was very simple, and the impression made on every one was—(1) That Parliament would be prorogued till after Christmas; (2) that a Bill more palatable to the Lords would be proposed; (3) that no new peers would be made; (4) that if the people became tumultuous, the armed force would subdue them."[1]

The proceeding from its novelty produced a very considerable sensation both within the Houses of Parliament and among the people.

At the enormous number of meetings which followed in the next few days "the speakers were energetic and eloquent, their resolutions and petitions were clear and determined—they deprecated a long prorogation, prayed for a short one, and for the reintroduction of Lord John Russell's Bill."[2]

On the 20th October Parliament was prorogued, and the date fixed for its reassembly was the 22d November.

On the same day a great meeting of the Northern Political Union took place, and was attended, it was said, by some 50,000 persons. There was also a meeting at Birmingham, and one of some 20,000 persons at Edinburgh.

At this latter a resolution was passed "That in the present excited state of the public mind, in the fearful crisis in which the country has arrived, the people, with most fervent loyalty and devotion to his Majesty, feel that any undue delay on the part of his Majesty's Ministers in bringing forward a Bill equally as efficient as that which has been lost, will diminish the confidence which the country has hitherto reposed in their exertions. The people, therefore, look to the throne for the accomplishment of their wishes, and the salvation of the Empire from impending calamities."

And here reference must be made to the very serious riots which broke out at Bristol on the 29th of October, lest the accusation might be made that, to omit them, would be omit-

[1] Place, MSS., 27,790, p. 65. [2] *Ibid.* p. 96.

ting the proof of one of the gravest charges against the Platform, that of exciting the passions of the people to violence and plunder. The Recorder of Bristol was Sir Charles Wetherell. He was a member of Parliament, and had been most outspoken in his hostility to, and denunciation of the Reform Bill. Place says of him: "His abuse of the people was remarkably gross. He was vindictive from passion, and savage in his manner and words. He manifested a singularly evil disposition, uncontrolled by judgment, or exhibited himself with violence which implied that at times he was hardly sane."[1] The Criminal Sessions were to be held, and he came to attend them. His entry into the town was made the occasion for a demonstration of hostility to him. The demonstration developed into rioting, then into attacks on people and houses, then to destruction of property, the firing of houses, attacks on the military, and for some days Bristol was the scene of fearful violence and disorder. Owing to the imbecility of the magistrates, the mob was allowed its own way for a long time, and it was not until the military took energetic action, and many lives were lost that order was restored. I do not think that this occurrence, deplorable in itself, and most strongly to be condemned could, in any way, be reasonably charged against the Platform.

There had been no immediate excitement caused at Bristol by the Platform. No meeting for the purposes of discussing Sir Charles Wetherell's conduct had been announced or held, no speeches had been delivered inciting to any outbreak, the popular gathering was altogether dissociated from the Platform, and was meant to be, not the verbal expression of popular disapprobation, but a physical demonstration of it.

By the Tories and anti-reformers it was at once used as an argument against reform. Even Greville, in commenting on this transaction, wrote: "The spirit which produced these atrocities was generated by reform, but no pretext was afforded for their actual commission; it was a premature outbreaking of the thirst for plunder, and longing after havoc and destruction, which is the essence of reform in the mind of the mob."[2]

But even this is not a fair statement of the case. In every society, and particularly in a large city, there is a substratum

[1] Place, MSS., 27,790, p. 125.

[2] Greville, vol. ii. p. 209.

of criminal, or needy men, ever ready to avail themselves of any opportunity for plunder and disturbance. The opportunity came with the helpless incapacity of the authorities, for no effectual means had been taken either to prevent or put down a riot, and the criminal and reckless classes availed themselves of the neglect. No other explanation is needed, but the event produced a great sensation all over the kingdom.

It was not rioting, however, which chiefly engaged the anxious consideration of the Ministers, and of the King; there was another phase of the agitation which seemed more dangerous and portentous, and with greater capacities for mischief —this was the organised form of it displayed by the "Political Unions."

The first of these, and the prototype of many others, had been, as we have seen, "the Birmingham Political Union." Several other similar Unions had been formed in other parts of the country—some of them with large numbers of members. Letters of Lord Melbourne [1] to Sir H. Taylor describe the progress of the Political Unions: "The Political Unions, as far as I can learn, are undoubtedly extending themselves, increasing their numbers, and completing their arrangements. [2] . . .

"In Birmingham the Political Union is numerous, but it is not looked upon with favour by the more respectable of its inhabitants. . . . In Manchester and the manufacturing parts of Yorkshire and Lancashire these Political Unions have not prevailed to the same degree, nor have they the same consistency and popularity as in Birmingham. In London it exists, but is not as yet formidable. They are established also in many parts of Scotland, but I am not aware in what numbers, or how composed. . . . I feel quite certain that any attempt to put them down by law would only end in giving them consequence and importance, and would perhaps constitute them the acknowledged organs of public feeling, of which at present they are only the symptoms. It is the public feeling which is dangerous, not the Political Unions."

The rejection of the Bill by the Lords gave a great impetus to the extension of these Unions.

[1] *Lord Melbourne's Papers*, edited by Lloyd C. Sanders, p. 129, dated 24th and 26th September 1831.

[2] See *ibid.*, edited by Lloyd C. Sanders, p. 133.

Place, writing of this precise period, throws some light on the way in which the Unions were really acting. He says: "The continual alarms, the silence of Ministers, the suspicion this created respecting them, and the fear always entertained of the King (changing his opinions) were causes of great moment, and fearfully agitated the people. The Unions were most appropriately adapted to the circumstances of the times. They kept the people, who flocked to them in vast numbers, steady, caused them to rely upon one another, prevented partial ebullitions, and produced a conviction of the utmost importance, namely, the certainty, of a simultaneous movement all over the country, should a movement become inevitable."[1]

The Times strongly urged their formation. Writing on the 27th October it said: "At the risk of being charged with repetition, we must inculcate upon the people of this country the urgent and even solemn duty of forming themselves into political societies throughout the whole realm, and watching over the progress of the reform question. . . . The Political Union of the metropolis is just established, and Sir F. Burdett, as becomes a distinguished patriot, has consented to take the chair. This will do good. It is obvious that the best organisation for a 'Union' protective of political rights is one which, under a change of circumstances, might be turned, not to hostile or aggressive purposes, but to the pure and simple defence of those rights, as well as of individual persons and property, by arms. We say again, form 'Unions' everywhere."[2]

And a couple of days later it defined more fully the nature of its recommendation: "These Unions were to be for the promotion of the cause of reform, for the protection of life and property against the detailed but irregular outrages of the mob, as well as for the maintenance of *other* great interests against the systematic violences of an oligarchy made desperate by opposition."

A very important meeting of "the inhabitants and householders of the metropolis" was held at Lincolns Inn Fields on the 31st October, to form themselves into a Political Union.[3] Sir F. Burdett took the chair. "The object of the

[1] Place, MSS., 27,790, p. 238. [2] *The Times*, 27th October 1831.
[3] *Ibid.* 1st November 1831.

present meeting," he said, "was the adoption of the best means for the securing the success of the Reform Bill. Among these means none appeared so feasible and efficient as a great National Union, having for its sole object the obtaining of good government, and preserving social order."

This meeting was notable for one strange coincidence. At it, and speaking at it, were types or representatives of three generations of Platform agitators—the past, the then present, and the future—meeting thus once on the same Platform, in their strange and chequered careers, and then parting for ever.

The past was there in the person of Thelwall, who approved of the proposal of the Union, and urged them all to unite. "He thought he might take this liberty," he said, "having through a long life, through good report and bad report, been the uncompromising advocate of the rights of the people, having had the honour of being tried for high treason in 1794, in the good old time of Pitt, and Eldon, and Toryism." He urged them to avoid such needless splittings into parties as could only serve to advance the designs of the enemies of good government.

The present was typified in the chairman, Sir Francis Burdett, who, from the awakening of the Platform after Pitt's repression, and for a quarter of a century after, had, most usefully and advantageously for the people, filled the role so conspicuously and brilliantly performed by Fox.

The future, in Lovett, the framer of the far-famed "People's Charter," who came forward as a working man to propose an amendment; "he would first inquire what the middle classes wanted, except to make them, the working men, the tools of their purposes. There was no use in preaching up patience to the starving people of this country. If the middle classes were really sincere, they would see that the working class were better clothed and fed. He moved a resolution in favour of manhood suffrage.

It was the first voice of "Chartism"—Chartism which, later, came forward to move, and ultimately to carry, many amendments, not to the Reform Bill, but to the Reform Act; but the nation then was intent on the Reform Bill and nothing else, straining every nerve to get that, and Lovett, with his

Chartist ideas, was listened to with impatience, and finally howled down.

The declaration of the Union which was formed at this meeting set forth that "This is not a Union of the working classes, nor of the middle classes, but of all reformers, of the masses—of the millions. The National Political Union is essentially a union of the people, and is the first instance on record of the nation breaking through the trammels of class to associate for the common interest in a common cause."

Its objects were thus defined: "To obtain a full, free, and effectual representation of the middle and working classes in the Commons House of Parliament; to support the King and his Ministers against a corrupt faction, in accomplishing their great measure of Parliamentary reform; to join every well-wisher of his country, from the richest to the poorest, in the pursuit of such an important object; to preserve peace and order in the country, and to guard against any convulsion which the enemies of the people may endeavour to bring about; to watch over and promote the interests, and to better the condition of the industrious and working classes; to give opportunities, by frequent discussion, for eliciting the best means by which the above object may be carried into execution."

Place draws attention to the beneficial effects following the formation of this Union. He said: "We were on the very verge of a fearful convulsion, that for a time the people did not quite know what to do; but the formation of the National Political Union gave a turn to their hesitation, and was of all but inappreciable importance."[1]

Some of the extremer members of the working classes were not content with this programme of the National Union, and they formed another Union for themselves, entitled the "National Union of the Working Classes," whose programme went much farther, and included universal suffrage, annual Parliaments, vote by ballot, and the levelling of hereditary distinctions. They determined to hold a meeting, and a deputation on the subject waited on Lord Melbourne, the Home Secretary. He told them that the proposed meeting would be seditious, and might possibly come within the provisions of the law against high treason.

[1] Place, MSS., 27,791.

Lovett, who was one of the deputation, told Lord Melbourne that "He held it a great injustice that the middle classes should be allowed to have their Unions and their open-air meetings, and that the working classes, who were really ground down to the dust, should be prevented having theirs. The working classes were in a dreadful state of destitution, and such meetings were like so many safety valves for passing off irritated feelings!"

But Lord Melbourne's advice prevailed, and the idea of holding the meeting was abandoned. The Government, however, made preparations to prevent any disorder should the idea of a meeting be persevered in—military were held in readiness, and special constables sworn in.

It was in reference to this proposed meeting that Sir H. Taylor wrote on 4th of November to Lord Grey:[1] "His Majesty is by no means displeased that the measures contemplated by the meeting in question are so violent, and in other respects so objectionable, as he trusts that the manifestation of such intentions and such purposes may afford the opportunity and the facility of checking the progress of the Political Unions in general, the introduction and establishment of which, the King orders me to say, he cannot too often describe as being, in his opinion, far more mischievous and dangerous than any proceedings of a more avowed and violent character, palpably illegal and treasonable."

The subject of the Political Unions anxiously engaged a great deal of the King's and Lord Grey's attention, and many letters passed between them about it. As the Unions were the organisation which gave so much strength to the Platform, the views set forth in the correspondence must be briefly referred to.

On the 6th November (1831) Lord Grey wrote to Sir Herbert Taylor:[2] "The alacrity and zeal shown by the middle classes in enrolling themselves as special constables for the preservation of the public peace has been most satisfactory; and I feel great hope that the late events (evidently the Bristol riots are referred to), distressing as they have been, will eventually be productive of good. Everything, however, depends upon the successful adjustment of the question of

[1] *Correspondence of King William IV. and Earl Grey*, vol. i. p. 401.
[2] *Lord Grey to Sir H. Taylor*, 1831, vol. i. p. 403.

Reform, and it will be a fatal mistake if those by whom it has hitherto been resisted should be encouraged in the belief that the public feeling in this measure can be repressed.

"It is by the fear of this opposition that the Political Unions, which had been formed at Birmingham and other places before the change of Government in November last, have been extended. In every sentiment expressed by his Majesty as to the nature and tendency of these Unions I entirely agree. It is impossible to shut one's eyes to the danger of their becoming permanently established. To discourage them as much as possible is equally the duty and the interest of his Majesty's Ministers. But as long as they keep within the limits of the law it does not seem possible to take any measures for their suppression. . . . For this evil the best and surest remedy will be the passing of the Reform Bill, and for this object all the influence of the Government must now be decidedly and vigorously exerted."

The next day Sir H. Taylor wrote to Lord Grey "That the King hopes that the successful and satisfactory adjustment of the reform question may have the effect of quieting the country, but he does not see in what degree such violent and illegal proceedings can be connected with either the support of, or the opposition to, the Reform Bill, nor that the Unions were directed exclusively to this object." After referring to the proceedings at Bristol, and the proposed meeting which had been abandoned, Sir H. Taylor mentioned certain reasons "which caused his Majesty to look with so much jealousy and uneasiness to the proceedings and designs of these political and other Unions, abstractedly from the question of Parliamentary reform, which he considered to be advanced by them as a plea for projects decidedly revolutionary, entertained before any expectation had been indulged in of the introduction of the Reform Bill, and not likely to be abandoned when that Bill shall have been carried."[1]

In reply to this letter Lord Grey wrote, saying that the Government partook in the King's sentiments on the character and effect of the Political Unions; but he went on to say: "Neither do I dissent from the opinion that the Political Unions have been originally instituted with views directed to

[1] *Lord Grey to Sir H. Taylor*, 1831, vol. i. p. 407.

other objects besides a reform of Parliament, and that many of their leaders—making this, from the advantage of the moment, their pretext—would be desirous of keeping up these Societies after that object was attained, for the sake of maintaining their own influence and power. But it is not the less true that these Unions have received a great impulse and extension from the rejection of the Reform Bill; and that many persons, not otherwise disposed to do so, have been induced to join them for the purpose of promoting that measure. It is also undeniable that the middle classes, who have now shown so praiseworthy an alacrity in supporting the authority of the Government, are actuated by an intense and almost unanimous feeling in favour of the measure of reform. . . . If the question of reform can be settled, all the sound part of the community would not only be separated from, but placed in direct opposition to, associations whose permanent existence every reasonable man must feel to be incompatible with the safety of the country. Under such circumstances these Unions could not long continue to exist, and all the real influence and power of society would be united with that of the Government in putting them down."[1]

As the month of November went on, and the Government did not show by their action their intention of expediting the meeting of Parliament for the purpose of again sending the Reform Bill to the Lords, the country got more impatient, and Political Unions and Associations were formed everywhere. One county meeting after another was held, and in many of them the greatest people in the county took part, throwing their influence into the scale in favour of the Bill. The activity of the people is described in *The Morning Chronicle* of the 19th November: "Political Unions are now the order of the day. Throughout England, Scotland, and Ireland, but more especially Scotland, they are to be found everywhere;" and *The Glasgow Evening Post*, referring to Scotland, said "Political Unions are springing up rapidly in every town and village in the country, and if they hold on at the same rate for a few weeks, there will not be a place found where the people will not have associated together for the purpose of first obtaining their rights, and then renovating the corrupt and antiquated institutions of the country."

[1] *Correspondence of William IV. and Earl Grey*, vol. i. p. 410.

And *The Chronicle* further wrote: "The object of the Political Unions is to secure reform, happen what may. If reform be carried without delay, well and good, but if any unforeseen difficulty occurs the Unions will bring the force of an united people instantly to bear on the depositories of power."

The extreme tension of feeling that existed, the doubts as to the House of Lords reversing their treatment of the Bill when it reached them, and the consequent probability that the people would be called on to make even greater exertions than they hitherto had done, led the Birmingham Political Union to improve on its organisation.

On the 15th of November the chiefs of that Union promulgated a scheme, whereby it was proposed to class the members in local sections under officers of various grades and denominations, and subject to a system of rule and discipline by which their whole collective physical force might easily and almost instantaneously have been made available, whenever it should be judged desirable to bring it into action; and this plan, it was intended, should be the model for the general organisation of the Political Unions throughout the country.

This scheme, which was so much in advance of anything that had hitherto been attempted, instantly attracted the attention of the Government.

On the 16th of November Lord Grey wrote to Lord Melbourne (the Home Secretary): "The sort of organisation which is now proposed is not calculated for the discussion of public questions, or for petitions upon them. It is of a military character, for active purposes, now alleged to be for the preservation of the public peace, but easily convertible to any other objects. Unarmed as a body, they possess arms as individuals, and being previously formed into companies, and regiments, and divisions under the name of tithings, etc., they may at any moment appear as an armed and disciplined force. The danger of this I need not point out to you. The question is how to deal with it."[1]

"The plan," wrote Lord Grey to Sir H. Taylor on the 18th of November, "for the constitution and organisation of the Birmingham Union is now before us. Of its dangerous and unconstitutional character there can be but one opinion."[2]

[1] *Lord Melbourne's Papers*, p. 136. [2] *Correspondence*, etc., vol. i. p. 424.

The opinion of the law officers of the Crown was taken, and was quite decisive on the illegality of the proposed organisation.

Fortified by this opinion a Proclamation was issued by the King on the 22d November, which described Unions or Associations with such an organisation as being incompatible with the performance of the duty of subjects, at variance with the acknowledged principles of the Constitution, and subversive of his Majesty's authority as supreme head of the State; and such Associations were declared to be unconstitutional and illegal, and all the lieges were commanded to abstain from joining them.

In obedience to the Proclamation, the Political Union of Birmingham abandoned the proposed new form of organisation. The Proclamation was accepted, said Mr. Attwood, not in a hostile spirit, but as a "wise, friendly, and beneficial measure on the part of Ministers towards the people."

The mere proposal of the scheme, however, was an impressive incident, and must have been suggestive of much to those who were still holding out against reform. Though thus checked, the Union, in its old form, did not cease from agitation, nor was it by Birmingham alone that agitation was continued. Growing signs of impatience were shown by the country, until the announcement was made that Parliament would be called together before Christmas to pass the Reform Bill.

Parliament met on the 6th of December. The Reform Bill was at once reintroduced, with some alterations;[1] the second reading was carried on the 16th December by an increased majority—324 votes to 162—a majority of exactly two to one, and the House adjourned to the 17th January 1832.

As there was a general persuasion during this month of January that the Reform Bill would pass the Commons, there was little political matter to cause excitement in the country. Soon after the middle of February, however, symptoms of activity among the people began to be visible; and on the 18th, when the Ministers dined at the Mansion House, the Prime Minister availed himself of this extra-Parliamentary

[1] The most important was, the abandonment of the proposal to reduce the number of members.

occasion to allay the rising excitement or fears of the people. He said: [1] "That Ministers had difficulties to contend with, all would admit, but none except those who had shared these difficulties could justly appreciate their amount. He hoped, however, in time they would all be overcome. . . . He was aware of the anxiety felt by the public on this subject, and he would not allow himself to doubt that their wishes would be realised, for the great measure was advancing steadily to a certain and successful issue. They might rest assured that no effort on the part of himself or his colleagues would be spared to aid in perfecting that great work. If it had experienced some delays, they might be assured the fault was not with them. They had used their best endeavours to accelerate its progress, and he hoped the time was not far distant when they would be able to congratulate each other on its completion."

Place,[2] writing of this period, said: "The great body of the people were self-assured that either the Reform Bills would be passed by the Parliament, or that they should, by their own physical force, obtain much more than they contained, if they were rejected; and it will be seen presently they were resolved to use that force. It was, however, on every account desirable that matters should not be pushed to extremities, and excepting a comparative few, none had any wish to resort to force."

Once more—namely, on the 23d of March—the Reform Bill emerged from the House of Commons. Once again did the Bill reach the Lords, followed thither by the keenest popular anxiety. The second reading was moved on the 9th of April. For days its fate trembled in the balance, whilst everything that could be urged by the speakers on either side was given utterance to. At last the end came, and the closing scene of that ever memorable struggle was strikingly fine and appropriate. The debate had been carried on all through the night, speaker had followed speaker. Lord Grey, the Prime Minister, the veteran statesman and reformer, who had given his life to the advocacy of reform, rose to sum up and conclude the debate. It was late when he began his speech, and he spoke "from the kindling dawn into full sunlight,"

[1] *The Times*, 20th February 1832.

[2] Place, MSS., 27,790, p. 291.

typifying as it were the entry of this great nation into the full sunlight of its manhood and strength. At seven o'clock on the morning of the 14th the House divided, and the momentous decision was come to—184 peers were in favour of the Bill being read a second time, 175 were against its being so read, and thus, by the narrow majority of nine, the House of Lords decided that the Reform Bill should be read a second time.

It is impossible to describe the keenness of the anxiety that prevailed while the decision hung in the balance. In this great crisis of the fate of the measure the whole nation stood by, jealously watching. The decision had been in their favour, but by so narrow a margin that the safety of the measure was by no means assured, and so, that in the last moment there should be no falling away on the part of the Ministers or the assenting peers, again did the people make their voice heard.

A large number of meetings were held with the view of putting pressure on the Lords to carry the Bill unmutilated. Thus, at Edinburgh, a meeting of 50,000 persons was held on the 24th, and a Petition despatched to the Lords, praying them to pass the Bill. Numerous other meetings were also held; some asking with somewhat ominous sarcasm for greater reforms even than those embodied in the Bill—"the Bill—or more." The Easter recess found the Bill unadvanced—a reason for more popular demonstrations to hurry its progress. As the enemies of reform alleged that a change in public opinion had set in, and that the people were becoming indifferent to the fate of the Bill, the Political Union of Birmingham decided on giving a crushing answer to such a calumny; and on Monday, the 7th of May, there was assembled in Birmingham "A meeting of reformers, the most magnificent for its strength and numbers, the most formidable from its union and enthusiasm—the most impressive from its order, discipline, and resolution that ever was seen in England or in the world."[1]

"The meeting was for the purpose of refuting the false and unfounded representations of the indifference of the public mind to the great cause of Reform," and to petition the House

[1] See *The Times*, 9th May 1832.

of Lords to pass the Bill. At a very early hour of the morning the people began to collect in front of the hustings. About ten o'clock the Political Unions began to arrive.

"The Grand Northern Division" was, at the very lowest, estimated at 100,000 persons—the procession extended over four miles, and there were upwards of 150 banners and eleven bands of music. The procession of the Grand Western Division extended over two miles, and there were seventy banners and nine bands. That of the Grand Eastern Division had eight bands and thirty banners, and consisted of about 5000 people. The Grand Southern Division consisted of 20,000 people, was accompanied by six bands, and had twelve banners. These estimates were exclusive of the population of Birmingham, some 140,000. "Upwards of 200 bands were in attendance, and from 700 to 1000 banners waved over the assembled throng."

Attwood was chosen chairman. "The enemies of the people," he said, "have told their Lordships that the country is indifferent in this great cause. If we hold no meetings, they say that we are indifferent; if we hold small meetings, they say we are insignificant; and if we hold large meetings, they say that we are rebellious and wish to intimidate them." . . . He said that he would rather die than see the great Bill of Reform rejected or mutilated in any of its great parts or provisions; and his statement was received with "immense cheering, which lasted a considerable while." "I say," he exclaimed—and the phrase was a true one—"that the people of England stand at this moment 'like greyhounds on the slip,' and that, if our beloved King should give the word, or if this Council should give the word in his name and under his authority, the grandest scene would be instantly exhibited that was ever witnessed on this earth before. . . .

"Give us a House of Commons who are identified with the Commons, and with the feelings and interests of the Commons, and everything will be right in England.

"Now I must beg leave to explain to you the absolute necessity of the peace, the order, and the strict legality which you have always exhibited. But for these great qualities our cause would have been lost. Within the law the people are as strong as a giant, beyond the law they are weak as an infant. See the prodigious strength which this meeting has peacefully and legally accumulated. . . .

"Hitherto our exertions have been confined in direct operation to this town and neighbourhood. Suppose now we should erect the standard of the Birmingham Union in London, nine-tenths of the whole population of that great city would answer to the call whenever it should be unfurled under the sanction of the King and of the law. . . .

"Your destinies, and the destiny of your country, are at this moment in the hands of the House of Lords. We have met this day for the purpose of discharging our duty to them. If that august assembly should neglect to discharge their duty towards us and our country, upon their heads alone will rest the awful responsibility of the tremendous consequences which may ensue."

Other speeches followed, and then the people repeated in a loud voice the pledge: "With unbroken faith, through every peril, and privation we here devote ourselves and our children to our country's cause"—a proceeding which was followed by loud cheering and waving of hats for several minutes, and then the meeting quietly dispersed.

It was on this same day, the 7th of May, that the motion was to be made that the House should go into Committee on the Bill. The division was expected to be a very close one. Place has left us a thrilling picture of the state of the public mind: "On that day," he says, "the excitement was raised up to the highest pitch it had hitherto attained. It was to a very considerable extent a holiday. Solicitude was not only visible in the countenances of men, but in their words and actions also. Anxiety made them neglectful of business concerns to an extent never before observed. They seemed to say, 'Let us wait until to-morrow; let this day pass as it may, we can attend to nothing directly until we know the fate of the Reform Bill.'"[1]

The die was soon cast. The more reckless or privilege-loving section of the peers were blind to demonstrations, deaf to the popular voice. A motion was made, which the Government declared would, if passed, be fatal to the Bill. Nevertheless it was carried, in the teeth of this declaration,

[1] Place, MSS., 27,792, pp. 203, 204.

by a majority against the Government of 35. Ministers, adopting the last available course, advised the King to create a sufficient number of peers to overcome the opposition. He hesitated at this last jump and refused, and Lord Grey and his Cabinet resigned.

As a sharp shock of earthquake sends all the inhabitants of a town tumbling pellmell into the streets, so the news that the Reform Bill was in peril sent nearly the whole population flying to the Platform and to public meetings. Once more they assembled in their tens and hundreds of thousands, scarce a town or a place not joining in the national outcry. Once more their spokesmen ascend the Platform to give utterance in terms of firm decision to the course now to be pursued, and clearer and more decided than ever ring back the assenting cheers. No child's play now, but downright grim earnest. Such excitement had never before been witnessed in the country. The House of Commons was besought or instructed to withhold supplies to the Executive. The determination to refuse to pay taxes was very generally expressed. "No Bill, no taxes" became the portentous password of agitation, and plain, unmistakable references to the people arming were received with ominous murmurs of approval.

Place says, "That the people would at a moment's warning rise in insurrection, no doubt could any longer be entertained."[1]

Fortunately, the demonstrations of the Platform were sufficient.[2] The Duke of Wellington—the leader of the Tories—who had been asked by the King to form a Government, declared himself unable to do so, and the Ministers who had resigned were recalled. On taking office again, they stated that "They conceived that they had secured the means sufficient to enable them to pass the Reform Bill, and therefore that they should continue in office."

The discussions on the Bill were then resumed in the House

[1] Place, MSS., 27,793, p. 142.

[2] From the 9th to the 19th May two hundred and one meetings were chronicled in *The Times* and *Morning Chronicle;* but that the list was far from complete is clear from the statement made by these papers of their inability to report them or even to notice them in a vast number of cases. 290 Petitions were presented to the House of Commons between the 8th and the 23d May 1832 to withhold supplies.—Place, MSS., 27,794, p. 347.

of Lords; many of the Tory peers absented themselves both from the debates and the divisions; and after a short time it passed the Lords, and having received the Royal Assent on the 7th of June, became law. The victory was won, the people had triumphed.

One closing scene of this great agitation may be described. On the intelligence reaching Birmingham that the Bill was safe, an impromptu meeting of rejoicing was got up the very same day, and some 40,000 or 50,000 persons were present at it. Attwood, as usual, was in the chair. Advancing to the front of the platform, amidst the most enthusiastic cheering, he said: "My dear friends, I feel so much gratitude to Almighty God for the escape which the nation has had from a most tremendous revolution, that I cannot help wishing that our reverend friend near me would publicly return thanks to our wise and beneficent Creator for the success of our righteous cause."

No sooner was this intimation made than all hats were doffed, and "the most deathlike silence pervaded the immense assembly."

The Reverend H. Hutton then, in a most impressive manner, offered up the following thanksgiving: "O Lord God Almighty, who orderest the affairs of all men, behold Thy people before Thee with grateful and rejoicing hearts, looking up to Thee as the Author of every blessing. We thank Thee for the great deliverance Thou hast wrought out for us, and the great and bloodless victory which Thou hast conferred. . . . Grant that we may so use and improve the great privileges Thou hast conferred upon us, that we may secure them to us and to our children, for Thy glory, and for the universal benefit of the family of man."

CHAPTER XVI

THE PLATFORM AFTER THE REFORM ACT

It is impossible in any brief compass to summarise the effects of the great struggle for reform, and the changes introduced by the Reform Act of 1832.

The Times, in an article written ere the dust and din of the battle had well subsided, wrote: "The Session accomplished, without social confusion, or civil bloodshed, a mighty political revolution. It has wrested usurped power from the hands of an arrogant and domineering oligarchy, to lodge it with the great body of the people. It has conferred upon the property, knowledge, and intelligence of the country that control over the national resources, and that privilege of adapting the laws to their interests, which has hitherto been engrossed by the prejudices, selfishness, and corruption of a boroughmongering faction. It has reinstated men in their rights; it has attached them to the Constitution, by making them sharers in its benefits; it has rendered civil convulsions almost impossible, by providing the means of a legislative adjustment of differences between antagonist parties; and it has opened a path to all the social improvements of which an active and enterprising people are susceptible."[1]

Many years were to elapse, however, before the mighty change could be appreciated in all its bearings; if, indeed, we are even yet in a position to gauge its full effects. It has been well said that this great Act "was to politics what the Reformation was to religion; it made reason the recognised standard instead of authority."[2] Certain it is, that with its enactment a completely new departure was taken by the nation; and with the light of experience since gained, it can-

[1] *The Times*, 17th August 1832.

[2] *Edinburgh Review*, April 1845, vol. lxxxi. p. 502.

not be doubted that the nation, in the choice she made, chose wisely and chose well.

It is, I think, no exaggeration to say that this great measure effected a revolution—one more genuine in its character, and more lasting in its consequences than any of the Revolutions which had taken place on the Continent—not a revolution of devastation, such as that of which France had been the theatre, but the greatest, the most desirable of all revolutions, a revolution of progress.

The powers of government long held and wielded by the Crown and a very limited class passed into the hands of the great middle class of the country, and the first step was taken towards making the people—as they should be—the ruling power in the country. It is impossible to overestimate the share which the Platform had in effecting this great revolution.

From the days of Chatham the cause of reform had been upheld and carried on by the Platform despite its being, time after time, scouted from even the popular chamber of the Legislature; it had been kept alive through adversity and evil repute for whole generations by the Platform, and in spite of prohibitive laws against meetings and speeches, and suspensions of the Habeas Corpus Act, and every discouragement which the wit of a dictatorial government or oligarchy could devise.

In former agitations the Platform had been used first by one section then by another, never before by all united. Upon this occasion it was adopted by the whole people, and its power was irresistible.

By itself, the House of Commons, once it was converted to reform, could never have carried reform against the opposition of the Tory party and the House of Lords. It was the Platform which compelled Ministers to endeavour to satisfy the popular demands; and when Ministers had made the effort, it was the Platform, with its impressive meetings and determined language, which compelled the House of Commons to accept the ministerial proposal; and when the House of Commons had accepted them, compelled a still more reluctant House—the House of Lords—to do so too.

Perhaps the most striking fact in connection with this great revolution was, that it was effected peaceably and without bloodshed, for the instances in which loss of life occurred scarcely call for notice. Though in a few places there was rioting, yet it was never on a formidable scale,—there was no massing of an armed people, no struggle with the military, no barricades, such as neighbouring countries had given examples of.

The explanation of this extraordinary immunity from violence and bloodshed, of this marvellous calmness and restraint, is to be found partly in the eminently law-abiding and order-loving character of the people. But still more was the result due to the Platform, where for years and years public discussion of this question had been carried on, where reason had been pitted against reason, and argument against argument, until men had got accustomed to argue instead of coming to blows, and to rely on truth, and justice, and right, triumphing in the end.

Place, who was well qualified to express an opinion on the subject, bears testimony to the admirable character of the people. He says: "He who will make himself master of all the circumstances of the case, of the multiplied oppression in Church, in State, in corporations, the widely spread circumstances calculated to demoralise the people, the vast number who are more or less dependent on the Church, the State, the corporations, and other institutions who must necessarily be inimical to every sort of reform, will be compelled to confess that, upon the whole, for a people roused to action as they were, opposed as they were, likely to be injured as vast numbers of them were by their attention to public affairs, their conduct was more rational and more effective than was that of any people at any former time similarly circumstanced, and as conscious of their power as were the people of Great Britain during the proceedings on the Reform Bills."[1]

For long the struggle had been one between right and might. At last, thanks mainly to the Platform, right and might got on the same side, and then the struggle was over—reform was won, and with it the door was opened for the progress of the people.

The first great result of the agitation for the Reform Act was to install the Platform formally among the great political

[1] Place, MSS., 27,789, p. 391.

institutions of the country—to raise it at once into one of the governing authorities of the kingdom. It had been tried, and had proved itself to be a mighty instrument of power in the hands of the people; it had demonstrated to their complete satisfaction its boundless utility; it had shown its perfect adaptability to all their needs; it had placed in their hands a ready weapon of attack as well as of defence; it was in harmony with the most marked features of the national character; it breathed the very essence of freedom; it had become, during the last few years of fierce agitation, a part and parcel of the public life; it had overcome the hitherto invincible might of the Tory party; and, henceforward, it was to be a great power in the State.

Looking back at that eventful period, and with the light of subsequent history, we can clearly enough discern that the problem which the English people were beginning to work out was how, within the existing lines of the Constitution, to secure a system of government wherein the wishes and views of the people should prevail—a system by which the largest amount of self-government could be obtained, or, to use other words, a system which would bring the people to be, to the utmost extent possible, "legislators themselves," and also their own executive. Mr. Bryce, in his great work on *The American Commonwealth*, has pointed out that this is the fundamental idea of the American Constitution.[1]

"The phrase 'Government by public opinion,'" he says, "is most specifically applicable to a system wherein the will of the people acts directly and constantly upon its executive and legislative agents. A government may be both free and good without being subject to this continuous and immediate control. Still, this is the goal toward which the extension of the suffrage, the more rapid diffusion of news, and the practice of self-government itself, necessarily lead free nations; and it may even be said that one of their chief problems is to devise means whereby the national will shall be most fully expressed, most quickly known, most unresistingly and cheerfully obeyed. Delays and jerks are avoided, friction and consequent waste of force are prevented, when the nation itself watches all the play of the machinery, and guides its workmen by a glance.

[1] *The American Commonwealth*, by James Bryce, vol. iii. p. 24.

Towards this goal the Americans have marched with steady steps, unconsciously as well as consciously. No other people now stands so near it."

This too was the goal to which the English people were also "unconsciously as well as consciously" striving, and the true appreciation of this cardinal fact is the key to the rise and progress and extraordinary power and popularity of the Platform. The people's desire was, and is, not merely to make the laws for themselves, but to have the executive of the country under their direct control also. They felt it was their right, and they were determined to obtain it. But the English people had to strive for this goal on different lines from those on which the Americans worked. The Americans had a blank sheet of parchment on which they could inscribe whatever system they thought best calculated to give effect to their ideas. The English had no such blank sheet. They had to contend against laws and institutions which had been handed down from the remote past, and against authorities who not alone obstructed them, but were actively and relentlessly inimical to their objects, and they had, perforce, to keep their endeavours within the lines of the constitution of King, Lords, and Commons. Any other procedure would have subjected them to the penalties of high treason. It is a remarkable fact that, in all the agitations which had taken place up to this time, there had been no intention of altering the form of the Constitution. Universal Suffrage and Annual Parliaments were the avowed objects of the most extreme men; and, by their opponents, these objects were denounced and stigmatised as revolution; but theoretically, at least, both of them were possible without subverting the form of the Constitution, though they would very certainly have altered the balance of these great authorities. The alteration of that balance was, however, absolutely necessary if the people's objects were to be obtained. The theory of the Crown, the House of Peers, and the House of Commons having equal and co-ordinate authority looked very pretty, and worked very satisfactorily for the Crown and the Peers, but it did not work satisfactorily for the people or Commons. Revolution by force, however, had not only at no time been desired by any considerable number of men, but was nearly impossible;

and reformers, with true instinct, recognised that the real, and indeed the only possible road towards the wished-for goal of self-government lay through the House of Commons. Once they could secure an absolute majority in the House of Commons they were masters of the situation, and could then proceed to work out their ultimate aims and objects. When we consider then the true meaning of and effect of the great principle striven for by the reform agitation, we can better understand the heat of the battle.

The Quarterly Review of 1831 affords an amusing illustration of the horror with which the new vista of popular government was regarded by those who had hitherto enjoyed the monopoly of government.

"How," asks the appalled and terrified writer—"how, on the principles laid down by Ministers, and promulgated in the name of the monarch, is *any* will or wish of the people—that is to say, of the electors—to be resisted or even discussed? If the people, even in the present state of representation, have *an omnipotent* voice on the subject of reform, if its mandates are to be obeyed as the final decision of the last resort on a *theoretical* question,—how can it be resisted upon any *practical* question—on the Corn Laws—on tithes—on a church establishment—on every branch of taxation—on cash payments—on the equitable adjustment—on public credit—on slavery—on the policy of maintaining our eastern and western colonies—on an army—on a navy—on primogeniture—on the division of property—on the expediency of maintaining the *Unions*—on the ballot—on universal suffrage—on the utility of an hereditary peerage—and finally, on the necessity for an hereditary monarch? Every one of these questions has been set afloat on the public mind in the *wake* of REFORM."[1]

The answer to the question which, as years went on, became the actual answer was, "No will or wish of the people is to be resisted." The voice of the people was to be, in all these questions, theoretical or practical, "the final decision of the last resort."

The nation had come to the parting of the ways described by Canning[2] as "a limited monarchy," and "a crowned repub-

[1] *The Quarterly Review*, vol. xlv. p. 539, 1831.
[2] Speech at Manchester, 31st October 1812, see Kaye's *Canning*, pp. 78, 79.

lic"; and the nation had chosen the latter. That above everything was the meaning, the significance of the reform agitation.

The simplest and most manifest way for the people to secure the object they had in view was, by influence over the House of Commons; and as this could only be secured by influencing in detail its component parts, their main efforts were directed towards gaining control over those who nominally were their representatives.

In considering this subject one has to bear in mind what are the actual principles and facts of "representative government." They are a little startling when put nakedly.

Lord Brougham, in his work on *The British Constitution*,[1] gives a very clear definition thereof. He says: "The essence of representation is, that the power of the people should be parted with, and given over, for a limited period, to the deputy chosen by the people, and that he should perform that part in the government which, but for this transfer, would have been performed by the people themselves. All these several things must concur to constitute representation." And he goes on to enlarge on the separate parts of this definition, or, so to speak, to dissect them.

(1) "The power must be parted with, and given over. It is not a representation if the constituents so far retain a control as to act for themselves. They may communicate with their delegate; they may inform him of their wishes, their opinions, their circumstances; they may pronounce their judgment upon his public conduct; they may even call upon him to follow their instructions, and warn him that, if he disobeys, they will no longer trust him, or re-elect him, to represent them. But he is to act—not they; he is to act for them—not they for themselves. If they interfere directly, and take the power out of his hands, not only is the main object of representation defeated, but a conflict and a confusion is introduced that makes the representation rather prejudicial than advantageous.

(2) "The people's power must be given over for a limited time. This is essential to the system. . . . If the delegation be for ever, the body of representatives becomes an oligarchy,

[1] Chapter iii.

elective indeed, but still an oligarchy, and not a representative body.

(3) "The power must be given over for a limited period to deputies chosen by the people. This is of all others the most essential requisite. If any authority but the people appoint the deputies, there is an end of representation—the people's power is usurped, and taken from them.

(4) "Finally, the representatives are to perform that part in the government which would otherwise have been performed by the people."

A little further on he makes one addition to this definition. He states again of representation: "It is the people parting with and giving over their power, for a limited period, to deputies chosen by themselves;" but, he adds, "Those deputies fully and freely exercising that power instead of the people."

Now, if this be a true definition of representative government, and I think it must, in its main features, be taken as such, it is evident that it falls very far short of complying with the requirements of a democracy.

The dangers of it were very well described, so far back as 1812, in an admirable article in *The Edinburgh Review*[1] on "The Rights and Duties of the People," and I cannot do better than quote it.

The writer said: "The delegation of the greatest of all trusts—that of government—necessarily implies a surrender of the function itself, and with the function much of the power, and leaves the people, in some degree, at the mercy of those whom they choose for their trustees during the whole term of the appointment. Hence the danger of those trustees abusing their delegated authority in such a manner as to weaken the control of the people over them—and by rendering themselves more powerful and less accountable, to make the resumption of the trust more difficult. It is quite manifest, therefore, that there is nothing of which the Constitution, in a State like England, ought to be more jealous than any step towards independence on the part of the representatives—any attempt of theirs to acquire a substantive and separate authority—either an existence not created, or attributes not bestowed by the people."

[1] *The Edinburgh Review*, vol. xx. p. 405, November 1812.

The problem which lay before the people of England was a wholly new one in the science of government—namely, how far, consistent with the maintenance of a system of representative government, of the Crown, and of an Upper Chamber, could a democracy secure absolute self-government, and supreme control in the government of the nation both as regarded its internal affairs and its external relations.

The problem, which seemed almost insoluble, has been in great measure worked out by the adoption of the Platform as a great controlling power over the representatives, controlling them in two ways—first by publicly exacting pledges from them previous to their election, and next by putting pressure on them whilst Parliament is sitting, should the occasion arise.

I have already mentioned the views held at different times on this subject of pledges, and of responsibility to constituents, and have shown how the tendency all along was towards the greater dependence of a representative on his constituents. That the principle of responsibility to constituents had reached a more advanced form in 1829 than at any previous period was proved by Sir Robert Peel, who, when he determined to propose to Parliament the great measure of Roman Catholic emancipation, felt it his duty to resign his seat for the University of Oxford. He has himself placed on record the reasons for this step.

"I cannot deny that in vacating my seat I was acting upon the impulse of private feelings rather than upon a dispassionate consideration of the constitutional relation between a representative and his constituents. I will not seek to defend the resolution to which I came by arguments drawn from the peculiar character of the Academic body, or from the special nature of the trust confided to its members. Still less will I contend that my example ought to be followed by others to whom may be offered the same painful alternative of disregarding the dictates of their own consciences, or of acting in opposition to the opinions, and disappointing the expectations of their constituents. I will say no more than that my position was a very peculiar one, that I had many painful sacrifices to make, and that it would have been a great aggravation of them if it could have been said with truth that I was exercising an authority derived from the confidence of the University to promote measures injurious, in her deliberate judgment, either to her own interests or those of the Church."[1]

In his letter to the Vice-Chancellor of Oxford (4th February 1829) resigning his seat, and stating his intention of recommending an adjustment of the Catholic question, he said: "I cannot doubt that the resistance which I have hitherto offered to the claims of the Roman Catholics has been one of the main grounds upon which I have been entitled to the confidence and support of a very large body of my constituents; and although I discontinue that resistance solely from the firm belief that perseverance in it would be not only unavailing, but would be injurious to those interests which it is my especial duty to uphold, yet I consider myself bound to surrender to the Ministry without delay the trust which they have confided to me."

"Peel," wrote Croker, on the 31st of January 1829, with evident disgust, "has written to place his seat at Oxford at the disposal of his constituents. In my mind, and so I told him, a democratical and unconstitutional proceeding, and a precedent dangerous to the independence of the House of Commons."[2]

And yet "dangerous" as he pronounced it, a greater than he, Canning, had declared that, should differences arise between him and his constituents, he would resign. But far worse, from Croker's point of view, than this individual instance were the proceedings at the General Election of 1831, which, it is to be remembered, was a direct appeal to the electorate on a particular subject, as a tremendous impetus was then given in the direction of tightening the control of the electors over their representatives, or, in other words, of reducing representatives more to the position of delegates. *The Quarterly Review*, in an article published in July 1831, refers to this: "The late 'appeal to the people,' which the King has been advised to make, differs essentially, vitally, in the spirit, the manner, and the time in which it was made, from what the Constitution understands by that phrase. *Virtual representation* has been made a term of obloquy, and *direct representation* is, as every man sees, *mere delegation*. The King appealed to his people for their sentiments on the Reform Bill; the people

[1] See *Memoirs of Sir Robert Peel*, vol. i. p. 311.
[2] Croker's *Memoirs*, vol. ii. p. 7.

at the hustings catechised the several candidates, and bound them, as they thought the King's wishes required, to support the Reform Bill, which course they are in duty and honour pledged to follow, whatever change their private opinions may have undergone, or may undergo. Such votes his Majesty is advised to consider the voice of his people, and in such votes the Ministers profess that the ultimate power and sovereign will of the State is actually vested."[1]

Another contemporary work, the *Annual Register*, may also be quoted in reference to this matter at this election: "Nor was it sufficient to save a candidate from the storm which had been raised that he should be willing to lend his mind to the reform of the representation. It was demanded of him that he should pledge himself in everything to this particular measure. The candidate was not to be sent to Parliament to exercise his understanding, as a reformer, on the principles of reform which ought to be applied, and the manner of their application. He was taken, specially bound to give up the power of thinking, to renounce all exercise of the understanding, if he should be burdened with such an encumbrance, and to retain merely the power of saying Yes to every proposition which Ministers might make in order to carry through the particular plan which had been already proposed. The new House of Commons was not to be a deliberative body, chosen to decide on great measures of public policy; it was to be nothing more than an assembly of delegates, nominated as a mere organ by which the popular sanction might be given to a ministerial proposal. . . .

"The question raised at the election was not whether the power of the democracy ought to be increased, but whether it ought to be increased in the manner proposed by Ministers. The electors were requested not to choose legislators, but to be legislators themselves; not to elect men to whose understandings they could trust, but to select speaking-trumpets, on whose voices they could rely."[2]

This question evidently exercised considerably the minds of political thinkers at the time, and very properly so, for therein was really concerned the vital essence of the popular move-

[1] *The Quarterly Review*, July 1831, vol. xlv. p. 539.
[2] *Annual Register*, 1831, p. 151.

ment which had begun some seventy or eighty years previously, which has continued down to the present day, and which has as yet by no means spent its force.

I venture on one more quotation from *The Quarterty Review* of this time, as it sums up the Tory views of the period on this important subject: "One word here, by the way, on this very constitutional doctrine, which maintains that representatives are sent to Parliament, not to exercise an independent judgment, but to speak the will, and obey the instructions, of their constituents, and which, if pushed to the utmost, would obviously deprive Parliament altogether of the character of a deliberative assembly,—a doctrine which has long enough been in favour on the hustings, but hitherto rarely hazarded within the walls of the House itself, and universally repudiated, we believe, by every writer worth naming. The point, indeed, is properly one of authority and principle, and cannot now be affected by the views which any individual may entertain of what would be expedient or desirable. It has been held so far back as the reign of Elizabeth, that each member of the House of Commons is deputed to serve, not only for his constituents, but for the whole kingdom; and consequently, that so far from being the mere organ of his constituents' will, he is not at liberty even to consult their interests, except in so far as those are compatible with the interests of the rest of the community. In noticing the first assertion of this great principle, Mr. Hallam observes that it is 'a principle which marks the distinction between a modern English Parliament and such deputations of the estates as were assembled in several continental kingdoms—a principle to which the House of Commons is indebted for its weight and dignity, as well as its beneficial efficiency, and which none but the servile worshippers of the populace are ever found to gainsay.' [1]

"We need not swell our article with quotations, which are in the mouth of every one, from the writings and speeches of Mr. Burke, Mr. Fox, Mr. Grattan, and other great men of modern times, all unanimous in the affirmation of the same principle, as a fundamental rule of the Constitution. It is a principle, too, as clearly founded in right reason as any part of our ancient institutions. For, to assert that the *will* of the

[1] *The Quarterly Review*, April 1831, vol. xlv. p. 262.

constituent *ought to be* the *rule* of the representative, is to assert (what is clearly an untenable proposition) that the constituent may fairly be presumed as competent to legislate for himself and the nation at large as the representative whom he deputes; or, failing that presumption, that the wishes and caprices of the constituent ought to be gratified at the expense, not of his own interests only, but those of the country. No man, we suppose, will be found to maintain gravely such palpable absurdities. Nor should we have thought the point altogether worth the space we have bestowed on it, but for its bearing on a practice which has of late been gaining ground very rapidly, of shackling the free judgment of members of Parliament in regard to particular measures, by pledges demanded and given, either during an election or with a view to secure their return in case of a dissolution; a practice which we hold to be not only at utter variance with this constitutional principle, but one, in every point of view, of most pernicious influence and example. There are few members of Parliament, we believe, who are not in some degree sensible that, in conceding such pledges, they are deviating from the strict line of their public duty.

"But it may not have occurred to all of them, that every approximation to the universal adoption and application of such practice is, in real truth, a revolutionary approximation to the very worst sort of republican Government—to a republic, namely, in which the affairs of the State are conducted, not by deputies as in America, but by the people themselves in aggregate masses."

The keenness and determination of the people in this matter, in the great crisis of their fate, may be illustrated by an event which Greville, writing on the 20th July 1831, stigmatises as "one of the most disgraceful scenes (produced by the Reform Bill) ever witnessed."

"On the question of the disfranchisement of Appleby, a certain Alderman Thompson, member for the city, who stood deeply pledged to reform, voted for hearing counsel in defence of the borough, on which there was a meeting of his ward, or of certain of his constituents to consider his conduct. He was obliged to appear before them, and after receiving a severe lecture, to confess that he had been guilty of inadvertence, to make many submissive apologies, and promise to vote no more but in obedience to the Minister."[1]

The triumphant passing of the Reform Act, which was the first demonstration of the effectiveness of the course adopted of electing men whose functions partook more of the character of delegates than of representatives, was not likely to lessen the tendency in this direction. Already, once the passing of the Reform Act was secured, and before the elections consequent thereon, the subject of pledges from candidates occupied considerable attention.

Place says: "It was evident that in places where the people would, for the first time, be called upon to exercise the right of voting for representatives (they) would be benefited by a clear exposition of the nature of Pledges, and the pointing out such as might reasonably be required of any candidate who professed himself a reformer. The Bill was considered a means to an end, and not at all, as Lord Grey and some of his colleagues represented it, a final measure.

"It therefore became necessary that some recommendation on the subject of Pledges, which would apply to all persons, and might be used in all places, should originate somewhere, and in no place could it originate so well as in the Council of the National Political Union, and by no body could such a paper, when composed, be so fully and so usefully distributed. . . .

"The subject of Pledges had occupied the attention of all the more active reformers, meetings had been held, resolutions had been passed; . . . but they all differed, many very widely."[2]

Place proceeded to summarise the views held by different people: "The propriety of exacting any pledge was questioned by some well-disposed persons—others made no question of the matter but insisted that no pledge whatever should be demanded or even expected. Others, and those by far the most numerous body, wished to exact pledges for even the most minute particular, or very many indeed respecting which the widest difference of opinion existed.

"By those who were the most rational and best qualified to judge, it was thought advisable that the opinions of candi-

[1] Greville, *Memoirs*, vol. ii. p. 166.

[2] Place, MSS., 27,796, p. 45.

dates on all the great leading questions should be accurately obtained, and pledges on those alone demanded."[1]

Public meetings were held on the subject.[2] The first which reported its proceedings was a meeting of the Liverymen of London on the 19th June (1832). The meeting appointed a Committee which made a report. The report stated that "members chosen to be representatives in Parliament ought to do such things as their constituents wish and direct them to do." That, in order for the electors to have the best possible ground for reliance on the candidate, he should give the following pledge: "That I will omit nothing within my power to cause, in the very first session, a total abolition of tithes, a repeal of the assessed taxes, and the taxes on malt and soap. These having been repealed, I pledge myself to the immediate consideration of the revision of the Corn Laws. To do everything in my power to cause the abolition of all sinecures and all unmerited pensions—a repeal of the Act of daring usurpation called the Septennial Act.

"I will at all times and in all things act conformably to the wishes of a majority of my constituents deliberately expressed, or I will resign to them the trust with which they have honoured me."

The National Political Union issued a leaflet on the subject of Pledges, 11th July 1832 (written by F. Place): "Every elector should recollect that his representative is elected for the unreasonably long period of seven years, and that he may therefore set his constituents at defiance for that period.

"It is then indispensably necessary that the conduct, as well private as public, of every candidate should be scrutinised, and the result made known, and that pledges should be given by him to the electors in the most solemn manner. . . .

"The pledges to be given by candidates should be as general as possible; the understanding as to their execution as particular as possible. No man should be expected to attempt anything at such an unseasonable time as would subject him to the imputation of folly; no one should bind himself in such a way as would compel him to perform such acts to save his

[1] Place, MSS., 27,796, p. 46.

[2] See on this subject articles in *The Examiner* of 1st and 15th July 1832, said to be by Mr. John Mill.

pledges as would make him a hypocrite; much must be left to the judgment of the representative. . . .

"The pledges that candidates should be required to give seem to be—

I. Parliamentary Reform—Shortening the duration of Parliaments—and Vote by Ballot.
II. Law Reform.
III. Financial Reform.
IV. Trade Reform—the abolition of all monopolies, more especially that of the Corn Law—Free Trade in every respect.
V. Church Reform—under which head was classed the equalisation of the Church Establishment, ceasing to compel any one to pay for the maintenance of any particular doctrine he does not approve—and Abolition of Tithes.
VI. Abolition of Slavery.
VII. Taxes on Knowledge."[1]

The Home Secretary, writing to Sir F. Lamb, said: "I do not myself much like the complexion of the public meetings of constituents, of which I read in newspapers. They seem to me to be very violent, to be disposed to go a great way, and to be demanding pledges in a very positive manner, which are given rather too readily, and to too great an extent."[2]

The Duke of Wellington's opinion is also interesting. He wrote to Croker, 6th March 1833: "The mischief of the reform is, that whereas democracy prevailed heretofore only in some places, it now prevails everywhere. There is no place exempt from it. In the great majority it is preponderant. To this, add the practice of requiring candidates to pledge themselves to certain measures, which is too common even among the best class of electors, and the readiness of candidates to give these pledges, and you will see reason to be astonished that we should even now exist as a nation."[3]

It was, of course, objectionable to some when pledges were given for reform. No objection, however, was raised to persons pledging themselves to support and defend the existing Constitution in State and Church.

[1] Place, MSS., 27,796, p. 144. [2] See *Lord Melbourne's Papers*, p. 146.
[3] Croker's *Papers*, vol. ii. p. 206.

The tightening of the rein on the representatives was shown in the first year after the passing of the Reform Act, in the case of Sir J. Hobhouse, one of the members for Westminster, and Chief Secretary for Ireland. He was so bound by declarations on the Platform at election time to oppose the taxes which the Government were imposing that he resigned his office, and also his seat, but came forward again for re-election. The electors, however, refused to re-elect him, and he was beaten.

Another straw showing which way the wind was blowing was a speech in the autumn of 1833 by Mr. Hill, M.P.,[1] who met large bodies of his constituents at Hull, for the purpose of explaining to them his Parliamentary conduct, and offered to resign to them the power confided to him, if that conduct were not satisfactory to them. He declared that he should adopt that course annually, for the purpose of giving them, so far as he was concerned, an efficient control over the representation.

The Reform Act of 1832 had in effect terminated the fiction of government by virtual representation, which the Tories so fondly believed in, and substituted actual representation in a considerable degree.

Greville, in his Diary, shows us the effects in the new House of Commons of this increased supervision of constituents over their representatives. Writing in July 1833, he says: "The truth is, that the House of Commons is in such a state that it is next to impossible to say what Ministers can or ought to do, or what the House will do. There is no such thing as a great party knit together by community of opinion. . . . Every man is thinking of what he shall say to his constituents, and how his vote will be taken."[2]

The other process by which the Platform supplemented the deficiencies of representative government was by instructing, or, if necessary, putting pressure on the representatives while Parliament was sitting.

It must be remembered that the Reform Act did not alter the duration of Parliament, and, therefore, that it left the constituencies without any control over their representatives during the long interval between the elections. The subject

[1] See *The Examiner*, 3d November 1833, p. 697.

[2] Greville, *Memoirs*, vol. iii. p. 17.

had already engaged a certain amount of attention and consideration.

The writer in the *Edinburgh Review* in 1812, already quoted, refers to it, and defends the practice of holding public meetings on this very ground. He says:[1] " . . . It is essential to the freedom and stability of our happy Constitution, as well as to the right administration of our affairs, that the people should have the practice of frequent public meetings, at which the discussion of their great interests may be undertaken, their voice raised boldly, yet peacefully to the Parliament and the Prince; and their sentiments made known without reserve. This practice, so far from being inimical to the representative system, or in the least degree inconsistent with it, flows naturally from it, and gives it life and vigour. For surely it cannot be pretended that the people of England are, only once in seven years, to exercise the right of interfering with the management of their affairs; and that this interference is to be confined rigorously to one function—the choice of their delegates. Were this the case, only see with what powers those delegates are invested, and consider, both how impossible it would be to find persons worthy of so dreadful a trust, and how ridiculous to elect them for more than a few months. . . . The elective franchise—the whole system of representation—may safely be pronounced at an end from the moment that the people confine themselves to the exercise of this one political function. . . .

"Even if the duration of Parliaments were reduced to three years, still, in the changeful scene of political affairs, unforeseen events arise, upon which the representative could not possibly have had a previous understanding with his constituents, and must be left wholly in the dark as to their feelings and opinions, and oftentimes as to their interests, if he has no opportunity of learning those by their own free and united deliberations. Some unexpected rupture with foreign powers —some novel measure affecting trade—some new invention in the art of taxing—some extraordinary stretch of prerogative, —all these incidents may demand a communication between the Parliament and the people which popular meetings alone can fully and safely maintain."

[1] *Edinburgh Review*, vol. xx., 1812, p. 411.

One constituency, the city of London, was constantly in the habit of holding meetings and "instructing" their representatives as to how to vote on particular measures which had suddenly and unexpectedly come to the front. Occasionally, but very rarely, a few other places followed this example.

In Westminster there was a practice in obedience to which the representatives were obliged annually to appear before the represented to render an account of their proceedings, and to receive such instructions with respect to their future conduct as the circumstances of the times rendered expedient; and in several of the large constituencies a similar practice was followed. This afforded a certain amount of control over the representative, and the liability to dismissal at the end of the Parliament if he misconducted himself added to that control. But this was far from being very generally practised, and in many constituencies, even after the Reform Act, there were ways innumerable in which members made peace with their constituents. But what the Reform Act certainly did was to increase the desire of the electors to exercise control over their representative, and there was no means so impressive as informing him by the Platform and by resolutions come to at a public meeting. The Reform Act gave therefore a great incentive to public meetings having this object in view.

We shall see how, in later years, this desire became ever stronger, and the progress which has been made towards rendering the representatives more dependent on the views of their constituents.

Another very important practical effect of the Reform Act on the Platform was to instal it formally and lastingly in a large number of places where hitherto its use had been only occasional—that is to say, in the constituencies created by the Act. It is true that fifty-six boroughs had been totally disfranchised, but they were mostly boroughs where the voice of the Platform was never heard, or if heard at all was the merest form. The new constituencies were large towns and cities, not one of which had a population of less than 10,000 persons. Forty-one such constituencies were now created by the Reform Act, and henceforward, in every Parliamentary election that took place in them, the Platform would fill an important part in the proceedings. This alone would have been an important result, but when coupled with the fact that an enormously increased number of people were taking part in the political life and action of the nation, it gave a tremendous impetus to the use of the Platform.

That the interest of the people in politics had increased was proved by the greatly increased number of contests which took place at the first general election after the Reform Act. The old Parliament was dissolved on the 3d of December 1832, and the country was plunged into the excitement caused by the exercise of its newly acquired rights.

There were 50 contests in English and Welsh counties, 144 in English and Welsh boroughs; there were 17 contests in Scotch counties, and 16 in Scotch boroughs; or a total for Great Britain of 227—a number considerably more than double the number of contests some fifteen years before (95) at the General Election of 1818; just four times as many as at the election of 1790 (57); more than ten times as many as at the General Election of 1761—with such rapid strides had interest in politics and Government progressed.

The diminution in the number of days during which the poll was to be kept open scarcely affected the use of the Platform at this election, for the length of time between the passing of the Act and the election admitted of a prolonged course of canvassing and electioneering.

Of the first Edinburgh election (1832) Lord Cockburn wrote: "This was the first time that the people had ever exercised the elective franchise. . . . People stared at the very sight of the hustings—all from curiosity, many with delight, some with unaffected horror. One party saw in these few rare planks the fulfilment of a vision long cherished; another the end of a system which they had hoped to perpetuate." [1]

That other influences besides the Platform affected some constituencies, even after the passing of the Reform Act, must be acknowledged.

Greville, in his *Memoirs*, gives an account which, coming from the representative of one concerned, may be accepted as true. He wrote: [2] "Yesterday I dined with Robarts, and after

[1] Lord Cockburn's *Life of Lord Jeffrey*, vol. i. p. 339.

[2] Greville, *Memoirs*, vol. iii. p. 184, 1st January 1835.

dinner he gave me an account of the state of his borough (Maidstone), and as it is a tolerably fair sample probably of the real condition of the generality of boroughs, and of the principles and disposition of their constituencies, I will put it down. There are 1200 voters; the dissenters are very numerous, and of every imaginable sect and persuasion. He has been member seventeen years; the place very corrupt. Formerly (before the Reform Bill), when the constituency was less numerous, the matter was easily and simply conducted; the price of votes was as regularly fixed as the price of bread —so much for a single vote, and so much for a plumper, and this he had to pay. After the Reform Bill he resolved to pay no more money, as corruption was to cease. The consequence was that during his canvass none of the people who had formerly voted for him would promise him their votes. They all sulked and hesitated; and, in short, waited to see what would be offered them. I asked him what were the new constituencies. 'If possible worse than the old.' The people are generally alive to public affairs—look into the votes and speeches of members, give their opinions—but are universally corrupt. . . . The one prevailing object among the whole community is to make money of their votes; and though, he says, there are some exceptions, they are very few indeed."

It would, however, have been unreasonable to expect that practices so long encouraged and indulged in would at once cease on the passing of the Act. A disease that had worked its way into the blood could not be cured but by a prolonged course of treatment. The first great step towards cure had been taken, and in spite of all malpractices, such as described by Greville, the electors appeared to look upon speeches from candidates and others as part and parcel of an election. Thus the Platform became more recognised, more indispensable at every election, and the gradual improvement in the tone of the Platform gradually worked an improvement in the principles and dispositions of the electors.

Another way in which the reform agitation acted on the Platform and added enormously to its power and consequence was in the important matter of organisation. It must be apparent from what has already been said that, except in the cases of the Political Unions, the agitation was, as a whole

—even to the very end—entirely unorganised; each constituency and each great unfranchised town acted by itself. Indeed, with such rapidity did the various scenes of the great drama pass, and so suddenly did the great crisis arise, that, through want of time, no consultation with nor communication between different parts of the country was possible. The opinions of the people coincided in all material points—they knew what they wanted, and that was a sufficient bond of unity.

But even such local organisation as was had recourse to increased the power of the Platform. Frequently to hold public meetings, frequently to discuss all the changing political events of the day, frequently to give expression to the conclusions arrived at, and to convey them to the Government, with the sense that a good deal of weight attached to their representations,—these were occurrences which could not pass over any place or section of the people without leaving considerable and lasting impressions behind; they taught the people the habit of resorting to the Platform, and taught them to regard it with the respect befitting the expression of the public opinion.

In the parts of the country, however, where the larger Political Unions had been established, there was a very powerful organisation backing the Platform, and it may be affirmed that the reform agitation was the first in England which had any real organisation at its back. In the previous agitations such organisations as these had been, were, in comparison with these Political Unions, utterly insignificant; and no fact testifies more to the enormous strides which the Platform had made in power since those times than the existence of these great Political Unions.

There was not, as yet, one general organisation with a directing centre; to such perfection the Platform, as an engine of political power, had not progressed; there were only different centres of organisation in different parts of the country, but they were very powerful within their respective spheres, and were practically new phenomena. Ireland had just given an example of political organisation combined with the Platform such as the world had not yet seen, and the experiment had been crowned with complete success. In England, in the one matter on which the people had most set their heart, they were long thwarted. Petitions to Parliament proved unavailing; it was natural, therefore, that ideas of organisation and of a show of strength should find favour with many, as the means of wringing from the Crown and upper classes that which they would not concede to justice and right. Thus the Political Unions came into prominence and power, giving the full aid of their strength to the Platform. The scope and effect of the Birmingham Political Union has been described by a son of Attwood, the founder of the first of them. He said: "The services rendered by the Political Union consisted (1) in creating public opinion in favour of reform; (2) in producing the strongest possible proof and manifestation of such public opinion without any infraction of the law; and (3) in keeping up public spirit, maintaining enthusiasm at boiling-point, and preventing any reaction, or appearance of reaction, such as in most cases follows after great efforts and sacrifices."

This, however, is but an imperfect summary of the work of the Political Unions. They did more than this. They "taught the people to combine for a great public purpose without breaking any of the salutary restraints of law, and without violating any of their obligations as private citizens. They divested the physical force of the country of its terror and lawlessness, and made it conducive to the ends of the highest public benefit."[1]

A more vivid and thrilling description of the work done by the Platform and the "Political Union" of Birmingham in the reform agitation[2] has been given by an American writer, Elihu Burritt, who spent some years of his life in the manufacturing districts of England.

"Birmingham," he says, "is distinguished above any other town in Christendom for organising a political force, which had hitherto acted like the lightning, the tornado, or earthquake, in sudden wasting or wasteful explosions. Under the leadership or inspiration of Thomas Attwood public opinion won the greatest victory it had ever achieved without blood. Under him it was raised from an impulsive brute force to a moral power which the mightiest wrong could not resist. It

[1] See a speech in commendation of Attwood by Grote.—*Life of Attwood.*

[2] *Walks in the Black Country*, by Elihu Burritt, p. 16.

was a perilous crisis for England. In almost every town or village there was the sharp crack of fiery sparks showing how the very air the people breathed was charged with the electricity of their passionate sentiment. The approaching tempest gathered blackness, and its thunderclouds revealed the bolts that were heating and hissing for their work of wrath and ruin. Very few thoughtful men can now doubt that the storm would have burst upon the country with all the desolation of civil war, if Thomas Attwood and the men of Birmingham had not drawn the lightning out of the impending tempest by the rod of moral force, which was grasped and wielded by his steady hand. From the central hill of the town he lifted up his revolutionary standard with this new device—'Peace, Law, and Order.' This white flag, and not the bloody banner of brute force and brute passion, which had been raised in other times at home and abroad, to right political wrongs, was the *drapeau* of the Political Union which he formed and headed in the metropolis of the black country. . . .

"On the grand march to political right and power, the masses stood shoulder to shoulder with their leaders. It was a great copartnership and fraternisation of the classes. They showed to European Christendom a spectacle it never saw or conceived before—what had never been seen or imagined in England before. That was a mighty mass meeting of the people which could be counted by ten thousands, and nine in ten belonging to the working classes—a waving sea of faces, with 100,000 eager listening eyes turned towards the speaker, gazing at principles and resolutions which no human voice could utter in the heaving of the vast multitude, but which were raised in great letters on standard boards one to each half acre of men. That was about the grandest sight ever witnessed. It is computed that full 100,000 men were numbered in some of these outdoor meetings, who were swayed with indignant emotion, and listened with wrathful eyes, and clenched fists to the story of their political wrongs, till they looked like an army massed for battle. . . .

"It is said that at some of these monster gatherings of strong-willed and strong-handed men, with fierce faces, begrimed with the grease and coal-dust of their factories, forges, and mines, Attwood's face would pale at the thought of the deluge that would follow the outburst of all that brute power, should it break the holding of his hand and trample on the banner of his device—'Peace, Law, and Order'; but it held them fast to the end."

The existence of these Political Unions had long continued to be a source of anxiety to the King. The possibility of their becoming all-powerful, and endeavouring—once they had tasted power—to supplant the Government itself excited his fears, and he was very anxious that they should be suppressed. Fortunately, he had a wise Prime Minister, who thus wrote to him: "Upon the whole, Earl Grey feels it to be his duty humbly, but explicitly, to repeat his unchanged and conscientious opinion, that nothing could be more injurious to your Majesty's service, nothing more dangerous to the public peace and security of the Empire, under the present circumstances of the country, than any attempt, by new and coercive enactments, to suppress institutions which are not prohibited by any existing law, and which, if they should transgress the bounds of duty prescribed to all loyal subjects, he confidently trusts the authority and the power of the Government will be found sufficient to restrain."[1]

The counsel was wise, and was timely given, and events soon proved that it was correct. Once the Reform Act was passed, once the great measure was obtained which the Unions had been formed to secure, their rationale ceased, their work was accomplished, and the bond of cohesion between their members was broken. So soon, indeed, after the passing of the Act, as October 1832, a great split took place in the Birmingham Union, the workpeople at Birmingham breaking off from it—a public break off, at a large public meeting—and the formation of another, and of course weaker Union by those who broke off—"The Midland Union of the Working Classes." The reasons for its formation were stated by a Mr. Massey, who said: "The Whigs had miserably deceived them in the Bill, and in all their measures, and the Union which at present existed was pledged not to agitate the public mind for any further reform for some time to come. In these momentous times, however, the working classes were fully resolved not

[1] See *Correspondence between Grey and William IV.*, vol. ii. p. 473, 19th June 1832.

to stand still, but to press onwards until they had obtained the whole of their rights."[1]

By 1833 the National Political Union in London was virtually extinct. Many of the others throughout the country had ceased to meet, many more were quietly dying out, and none could be maintained in a state of vigour. Even the Birmingham Political Union, once so powerful, shared the common fate, lost its power and influence, and at last expired.

Place makes an admirable and most just comment on the decline of these Unions. He says: "Such associations can never flourish, but in times when the people are greatly and justly excited, by some particular movement of the Government, or when some great difficulty occurs, and the Government, either from incapacity or wilfulness, becomes apathetic. In either case the people will sometimes, not always, determine that a change of some sort shall be made." But he adds: "Circumstances such as these have hitherto been of rare occurrence in the country; they will be less and less rare in future. Public opinion is only of recent growth, but it will continue to grow with increasing rapidity, and will become more and more potent. It is only of late years that the masses of the people have ever shown a deliberate disposition to act together for any purpose."[2]

Here the people had determined, the change had been made, the excitement had passed, and therefore the Political Unions ceased to flourish. Viewed as a whole there can, indeed, be little doubt that the Political Unions really saved the country from a great convulsion, for when the real crisis of popular indignation and determination came, they exercised a powerful restraining influence on the people. Nevertheless, it was by their means that the Platform was ultimately successful in its long struggle for Parliamentary reform, and the moral was left for future generations, that in any great popular struggle the Platform, to be successful, requires a powerful organisation at its back.

"The National Union of the Working Classes," to which reference has been already made, and which altogether was of a lower and more extreme grade than any of the other Political Unions, did not expire quite so quickly. It was, in reality,

[1] Place, MSS., 27,796, p. 330. [2] *Ibid.* pp. 205, 206.

utterly insignificant, but its existence is interesting in connection with the political associations of the time, the more especially as endeavours were made to fix the stigma of its extravagances on all political associations, popular meetings, or platformings of the time. It had sprung out of another society, which was a branch of Robert Owen's plan for establishing "a new order of society." It held weekly public meetings at the Rotunda in the Surrey Road, which were sometimes well attended.

Place tells us that "Several of the leaders and principal speech-makers were ill-informed men entertaining very narrow notions; some among them were utterly dishonest men, whose purpose was confusion, that they might plunder; and these notions, scarcely disguised at all even in public, and carefully inculcated privately, were inimical to the better sort of working people, and by the alarm they occasioned, prevented vast numbers joining the Union."[1]

Its views on reform may be judged from a speech made at its meeting on the 16th April 1832: "With regard to the Reform Bill, it was grounded on property and not on rights, and therefore iniquitous and unjust, for it allowed the greatest villains to have the rights to which the honest and industrious man was entitled, but could not obtain them because he did not possess those things of which the congregated tyrants of the world had deprived him."[2]

Place, who was seldom blind to the failings of agitators, and who is perpetually letting us behind the scenes of agitation, says: "The leaders, like other fanatics, imagined they had great power, and also, like other fanatics, although they never had the most remote chance of carrying any one of their resolutions into effect, they proceeded as if they were continually effecting some of their purposes, and progressing in all of them. This was the character of the Union during the remainder of its existence."

The fanatical idea of a National Convention was mooted in the Society, and a public meeting was announced to be held at Cold Bath Fields on 13th May 1833, "To adopt preparatory measures for holding a National Convention, the only means of obtaining and securing the rights of the people."

[1] Place, MSS., 27,791, p. 281. [2] *Ibid.* 27,796, p. 303.

The resolutions to be proposed contained a "Declaration of rights." "All men are born equally free, and have certain natural and unalienable rights, any infringement on which is a gross violation of the laws of nature, and ought to be resisted."

The Government issued a Proclamation declaring the proposed meeting illegal and dangerous to the public peace. The meeting, nevertheless, was attempted, but the police promptly interfered, and it was dispersed in two or three minutes, not however before many persons were hurt, and one policeman stabbed and killed. The action of the police appears to have been hasty and unnecessarily violent, and the coroners' jury returned a verdict of "Justifiable homicide" on the grounds that the Riot Act was not read, nor any proclamation made, ordering the people to disperse, that the Government did not take the proper precautions to prevent the meeting from assembling, and that the conduct of the police was ferocious, brutal, and unprovoked by the people.

The proceedings did not, however, in any way help the Union.

Place tells us that "The year (1833) ended, leaving the Union in a state of much depression. The nonsensical doctrines preached by Robert Owen and others respecting communities and goods in common, abundance of everything man ought to desire, and all for four hours' labour out of twenty-four; the right of every man to his share of the earth in common, and his right to whatever his hands had been employed upon; the power of masters under the present system to give just what wages *they* pleased; the right of the labourer to such wages as would maintain him and his in comfort for eight or ten hours' labour; the right of every man who was unemployed to employment, and to such an amount of wages as have been indicated, and other matters of a similar kind, which were continually inculcated by the working men's Political Unions in small pamphlets . . . had pushed politics aside, to a great extent, among the working people. . . .

"A very large proportion of the working people in England and Scotland became persuaded that they had only to combine, as it was concluded they might easily do, to compel not only a considerable advance of wages all round, but employment for every one—man and woman—who needed it, at short hours.

"This notion induced them to form themselves into Trades Unions in a manner and to an extent never before known. . . . It was impossible, under these circumstances, that the National Union of the working classes, or any other such Political Unions, could flourish or even exist at all."[1]

This Union accordingly soon expired, and thus ended the last of the Political Unions of the reform agitation period. Nor, for a time, was there any revival of them; indeed, when the next organisation in support of the Platform was attempted, it was on somewhat different lines.

In another way besides those already enumerated, the reform agitation had proved the cause of a most important and remarkable advance in the status of the Platform. This was its adoption by Cabinet Ministers. To such importance had the Platform risen that Ministers, for the first time in our history, thought it worth their while, indeed, found it necessary, to address personally, out of Parliament, not merely their constituents, but other gatherings of the general public. Moreover, so increasing were the demands of political life that speeches during Parliament were quite inadequate to meet the public expectation or desire for information, and the country was no longer content to be, during the long Parliamentary recess, without some sign of life on the part of those who were governing them.

Previous to the final agitation for the Reform Act this had not been the case. Canning's occasional speeches had been quite an exception. Lord Liverpool, during the whole of his long premiership, never, so far as I have been able to ascertain, made a political speech outside Parliament. The Duke of Wellington occasionally but very rarely spoke in public, and then not much on politics. As Prime Minister he spoke once during the recess of 1828–29, when the country was eager to know the policy of Government as regards Catholic emancipation, but he avoided politics. Peel did exactly the same. During the winter of 1829, and the whole of 1830, no political speech was delivered by any Cabinet Minister outside Parliament. There was no ministerial manifesto, by speech, outside Parliament before the General Election of July 1830; no speech of any consequence was made by a Cabinet Minister at

[1] Place, MSS., 27,797, pp. 290, 291.

the general election; and in *The Times* of that period I have found no reported speech even of an ordinary member of Parliament to his constituents, except at the actual time of the general election.

But with the agitation for reform, matters in this respect soon changed. Thus, on the 24th September 1831, a great Parliamentary dinner was given to Lord Althorp, Chancellor of the Exchequer, and Lord John Russell, by about 300 members of the House of Commons who were in favour of reform, and it was utilised both as a demonstration in favour of reform, and as an occasion for the leaders of the party to speak a few words to the country. *The Times* called it "A novel and imposing gathering which will interest the present generation, and make the event remarkable in times to come." Again, on the 16th November 1831, a dinner was given by the reformers of Wiltshire to Lord Lansdowne, then a Minister, at which he made a long speech, strongly dwelling on the necessity of preserving peace and order. "Those who abetted the approach to violence were enemies of reform."

On the 11th July 1832, after the battle was over, Lord Grey, the Prime Minister, and Lord Althorp, were presented with the freedom of the city of London. Both made speeches of thanks. Lord Grey said: "My share of merit in this transaction (the Reform Act) is comparatively small. It has been owing to the zealous and powerful co-operation of the people by whom I have been assisted that we have been successful. It is to the exertions of the people, under the sanction of a beneficent King, that the successful accomplishment of this work is to be ascribed;" and speaking later at the dinner given in his honour, he said: "The first cause of the success of reform was the firm determination, the calm moderation, and the well-tempered zeal by which the people of England supported it," and he enlarged upon the advantages of the change which had been effected.

That the practice rapidly grew is shown by an article in *The Examiner* of 29th December 1833, entitled "The Harangues of the Ministers." "The customary ministerial dinner circuit has just concluded," says the writer, "and we ask whether there is anything in panegyric to match the speeches of the different members of the Government in commendation of themselves and their Administration."

Lord Brougham, the Lord Chancellor, and a Cabinet Minister, spoke at York. Lord John Russell, a Cabinet Minister, made a political speech at a dinner at Plymouth; Mr. Stanley, Secretary of State for the Colonies, made one at Manchester; whilst less important members of the Government, such as Mr. Thomson, Vice-President of the Board of Trade, and Mr. Macaulay, Secretary of the Board of Control, also figured on the Platform.

A sentence in Macaulay's speech shows that the practice extended even further. He said: "I know that some members of Parliament on meeting their constituents after the late eventful session have thought it necessary to come before them with the tone of humility, and the language of self-defence."[1] Lord Durham, also, who had been a Cabinet Minister, though not in office at the time, made a regular political speech at a dinner at Gateshead relative to reform, and another a few days later at Sunderland. Altogether these speeches went far towards making a diminutive autumn campaign, now so familiar to us, and so indispensable a part of public life and requirements.

These then were the principal effects which the reform agitation had upon the Platform: to instal it formally among the great political institutions of the country; to introduce it permanently into numerous places where hitherto its use had been only occasional; to associate it with skilful and powerful organisation; and finally, to inveigle even the Ministers of State into adopting it as a means of communication with the people.

After a quiescence of years—a period of rest, as it were, for the work that lay before it—the Platform had suddenly been called into action. For two years almost the whole population of Great Britain used it as an engine of political power, and when the great struggle was over and won, the honour and glory of victory rested with it. Just as some warrior of old attributed his victory to the excellence of his sword, so the people could attribute their victory to the excellence of their new weapon of political warfare. Its temper had been well proved. Backed by a powerful organisation it had overcome all obstacles, the people acclaimed it as their own; Ministers

[1] *The Examiner*, 17th November 1833.

and statesmen and politicians of all ranks and parties, recognising its strength, had freely and unreservedly adopted it; henceforth its position was assured as a great power in the State; henceforth all men might know that there was a tremendous reserved popular force which, in any really great popular crisis, could be brought into decisive action.

The interest of the history of the Platform for some few years immediately ensuing the passing of the Reform Act, centres in the growth of the practice of Ministers and ex-Ministers, and prominent politicians resorting to it for the advocacy or the explanation of their policy and views—for to this period is to be assigned the origin of what has become so remarkable a feature in the political life of this kingdom.

The autumn campaign of 1833 was notable, but the autumn of 1834 presented an even more remarkable instance of the change that had come over great public men in this respect—this was no less than a Platform tour, by no less a personage than Lord Brougham, the Lord Chancellor of England, and a Cabinet Minister.

The tour was through Scotland. He visited many places, and in almost every town of consequence that he passed through he resorted to the Platform, quite in the peripatetic style of Orator Hunt and previous Platform celebrities, and delivered speeches.[1]

"At one place," says the *Annual Register*,[2] "he would not hesitate to go the utmost lengths of ultra-radicalism; in another he would speak in such a way as would have induced the Conservatives to hail him as their own; to-day the House of Peers would be the subject of his eulogy; to-morrow it would be held up to scorn and ridicule. Sometimes the violations of decency became ludicrous. At Inverness he assured his audience that he would write to the King by that night's post to inform his Majesty of the loyal sentiments they entertained."

There was a general outcry against his conduct. *The Times*,[3] writing some little time after, said: "There could

[1] For an account of this tour, see *Lives of the Lord Chancellors*, by Lord Campbell, vol. viii.; also the newspapers of the time.

[2] 1834, p. 335.

[3] See *The Times*, 17th November 1834.

not, indeed, be a more revolting spectacle than for the highest law-officer of the Empire to be travelling about like a quack doctor through the provinces puffing himself and his little nostrums, and committing and degrading the Government of which he had the honour to be a member."

Greville, too, describes him making more mountebank exhibitions than he did in the House of Lords, and exciting the unquenchable laughter of his enemies, and the continual terror of his friends.[1]

The tour was to bring forth unexpected fruit.

Independent of it, another remarkable event occurred this same autumn in connection with the Platform. In the course of the session of 1834 Lord Grey resigned the office of Prime Minister, and was succeeded by Lord Melbourne.

Scotland felt herself under peculiar obligations to Lord Grey, having been enfranchised by him, and so Scotland determined to do him honour. An invitation was accordingly sent him, and he was given a great public reception, finishing up with a grand banquet at Edinburgh, at which he, the ex-Prime Minister, made a regular Platform speech. His reception began at the border.

In the centre of the bridge over the Tweed a triumphal arch was erected. Here he was met by large numbers of people, and, a procession being formed, continued his journey to Coldstream, where he was presented with an Address of gratitude and made a speech in reply.

"It has been truly said in the Address just read that this great measure was necessary to ulterior reform. Much has been done, more indeed than could have been expected, considering all the circumstances and difficulties of the time, to promote the great work of reform. Much yet remains to be done, but I am satisfied that the means of effecting all that is necessary for the purposes of good government, and for preserving the peace and order of the State are now in our possession. . . . It is necessary that in resolving to effect what is necessary, we should equally desire to avoid being led away by the hurry of popular excitement, and not fall into the opposite extreme, which would be prejudicial to the best interests of the country."

[1] Greville, *Memoirs*, vol. iii. p. 133.

At Kelso a magnificent reception was given him, and several Addresses were presented him. Here he made a long speech in reply.

Again he urged moderation. "The purpose for which this great measure has been granted is not that of undermining and disturbing, but of upholding and securing the fundamental principles and essential forms of the Constitution. It was a work of protection and of peace, and not, as stated, of revolution."

At Dalkeith he was presented with an Address, and replied to it, but the crowning reception was at Edinburgh. Here a huge procession escorted him through the streets—which were filled with immense throngs—and he was presented with the freedom of the city; also with the freedom of Glasgow and other cities, and with a large number of addresses.

In the evening the great banquet took place, and he delivered a speech—a regular political speech.

Again he preached moderation. "I trust we shall persevere to make such further improvements as the increased intelligence of the people and the necessity of the times may render expedient. In doing this I am sure I need not say to such a meeting as this, that we should carefully abstain from pressing any extreme or violent changes."[1]

An ex-Prime Minister thus touring the country and delivering one Platform speech after another was a new feature in English public life.

Lord Brougham, who was just finishing up his tour, and was present at the banquet, replied to the toast of his Majesty's Ministers: "I am one of those Ministers, and my noble friend is another, who have never feared the people. I rejoice, delight, and glory in office, and out of office, in every opportunity of meeting the people to render an account to them of my stewardship, and face to face with them to tell them what I think, even when I happen to differ with them."

Lord Durham, ex-Cabinet Minister, also spoke: "I am one of those who see with regret every hour which passes over the existence of acknowledged but unreformed abuses. (Rapturous applause.) I do not object to the deliberation with which reforms are conducted, but I object to the compromise

[1] See "The Grey Festival," etc., Edinburgh, 1834.

of those principles. I object to the clipping and the paring and the mutilating which must inevitably follow any attempt to conciliate enemies who are not to be gained."

Great was the wrath of the King over this sudden elevation of the Platform into favour in such high quarters. On the 5th November 1834 his private secretary wrote to Lord Melbourne: "His Majesty has not ceased to deprecate the practice, which has more especially obtained lately, of giving great dinners, which are a sort of political assembly at which topics are introduced, which necessarily lead to crimination and recrimination when parties are split as at present; and he also objects to 'itinerant' speechifying, particularly by individuals holding high offices."[1]

The opportunity soon came when he was able to show his anger in another way than mere words. Lord Spencer died. On 12th November Lord Melbourne wrote to the King that, consequent on the death of Lord Spencer, and the promotion of Lord Althorp to the House of Peers, the King might wish to make other arrangements, and he went down to Brighton to present the letter.

The King replied on the 14th November: "His Majesty conceives that the general weight and consideration of the present Government is so much diminished in the House of Commons, and in the country at large, as to render it impossible that they should continue to conduct the public affairs in the Commons."[2]

"Nothing," wrote Greville, "could be more peremptory and decisive; and not a loophole was left for explanation or arrangements, or endeavour to patch the thing up;"[3] and a little later he added: "Their (the Whigs) case is one of rare occurrence. Unceremoniously kicked out, not resignation following ineffectual negotiations, or baffled attempts at arrangement, but in the plentitude of their fancied strength, and utterly unconscious of danger, they were discarded in the most positive, summary, and peremptory manner."

The change of Government was owing (Sir Robert Peel has told us) "to the direct intervention of the King."[4] Well

[1] Sir H. Taylor to Lord Melbourne, see *Lord Melbourne's Papers*, p. 217.
[2] See *Lord Melbourne's Papers*, p. 222.
[3] Greville, *Memoirs*, vol. iii. p. 144. [4] Peel's *Memoirs*, vol. ii. p. 32.

might "the town" have been "electrified," as Greville tells us it was, by the intelligence that Lord Melbourne's government was at an end. That within less than three years after the passing of the great Reform Act a Liberal Government should be summarily dismissed, and be succeeded by a Tory Government, was beyond all apparent possibilities.

Lord Brougham's Platform tour had produced startling fruit. Lord Melbourne, in enumerating the motives which led the King to dismiss him and his colleagues, mentioned, "The recent conduct of the Chancellor, and the absolute disgust and alienation which it had created in the King's mind;" and in a letter to Lord Brougham he himself (14th February 1835) wrote: "I must, however, state plainly that your conduct was one of the principal causes of the dismissal of the late Ministry; and that it forms the most popular justification of that step."

The outgoing Prime Minister made two speeches outside Parliament on the subject of his dismissal. Shortly after his arrival at his own place in the country, on the 1st December 1834, an Address was presented to him by the town of Derby, and he availed himself of the occasion to do the hitherto unprecedented thing of using the Platform for the purpose of explaining the reasons of his dismissal by the King—explaining them too at considerable length.

Having stated the incidents that had occurred to the Ministers in consequence of Lord Spencer's death, he said: "Upon this event taking place, it became my duty to take his Majesty's pleasure as to whether he would command me to make arrangements for filling up the vacancies which had been thus occasioned; and his Majesty was pleased to come to the determination that he would not impose upon me that duty, but would resort to other advisers. This is the short and simple statement of the facts which have actually taken place.

"It has been affirmed that the late Cabinet was dissolved, not by the determination of his Majesty, but its own internal differences and divisions; that there existed in it such dissentient and contradictory opinions as must necessarily have led to its early, if not its immediate, dissolution. I seize this opportunity of giving to this assertion a clear, distinct, emphatic denial. There were in the Cabinet shades of opinion, as there always must be amongst men who think and act freely and conscientiously, but there was no such difference of opinion upon great impending public measures as was likely to interfere with the harmonious and united action of that administration."[1] He used the occasion also to give advice as regarded the future conduct of the different sections of the Liberal party.

Greville calls the speech "extremely temperate and reserved;"[2] but he makes no comment on the fact of its being absolutely the first occasion in which the ministerial explanation of a change of Government was made outside Parliament and from the Platform.

Remarkable as this occurrence was, and memorable in the history of the Platform, the action of the incoming Prime Minister was, if possible, more so. His own account which he has left us in his Memoirs best describes it.

"Immediately after the completion of the Cabinet I proposed to my colleagues that I should take advantage of the opportunity which the approaching election would afford; and in an Address to the constituent body of Tamworth, declare the general principles upon which the Government proposed to act. My colleagues entirely approved of this course."[3]

In that Address he said: "In seeking the renewal of my political connection with you, I feel it incumbent upon me to enter into a declaration of my views of public policy, as full and unreserved as I can make it, consistently with my duty as a Minister of the Crown.

"You are entitled to this, from the nature of the trust which I again solicit, from the long habits of friendly intercourse in which we have lived, and from your tried adherence to me in times of difficulty, when the demonstration of unabated confidence was of peculiar value. I gladly avail myself also of this, a legitimate opportunity, of making a more public appeal—of addressing, through you, to that great and intelligent class of society of which you are a portion, and a fair and unexceptionable representative—to that class which

[1] See *The Derby and Chesterfield Reporter*, 4th December 1834.

[2] Greville, vol. iii. p. 166.

[3] Peel's *Memoirs*, vol. ii. p. 58.

is much less interested in the contentions of party than in the maintenance of order and the cause of good government, that frank exposition of general principles and views which appear to be anxiously expected, and which it ought not to be the inclination, and cannot be the interest of a Minister of this country to withhold."

The real purport of this Address is well explained in an article in *The Quarterly Review.* "Sir Robert Peel's Address is—in *itself* and independently of its topics—a proof that he accepts, and will, unfettered by old customs and traditions of government, endeavour to meet the exigencies of the times. When before did a Prime Minister think it expedient to announce to the *people,* not only his acceptance of office, but the principles, and even the details of the measures which he intended to produce, and to solicit—not from Parliament, but from the people—'that they would so far maintain the prerogative of the King as to give the Ministers of his choice not, indeed, an implicit confidence, but a fair trial?' In former times such a proceeding would have been thought derogatory, and impugned as unconstitutional, and would have been both; but the new circumstances in which the Reform Bill has placed the Crown, by making its choice of Ministers immediately and absolutely dependent on the choice of the several constituencies, and, in the first instance, quite independent of the concurrence of the assembled Parliament have rendered such a course, not merely expedient, but inevitable."[1]

It is, of course, evident that this Address does not strictly fall within the province of a history of the Platform, for it was not a speech but a written address, but it is interesting as showing the altered ideas of a Conservative Prime Minister as to his relationship to the constituent body.

He supplemented this Address shortly afterwards by a speech at the Mansion House, where he dined on the 23d December: "I may undertake to say, on the part of his Majesty's Ministers, that it will be our object to attain, and if necessary to confirm, the confidence of the people, not by rash and precipitate pledges for the removal of everything that may appear at the first superficial and imperfect view to be an evil—not by undertaking to make every concession hastily demanded by

[1] *The Quarterly Review*, vol. liii. p. 265.

popular feeling—not by rashly promising relief with respect to everything that may be complained of as burdensome—not, I say, by giving rash and hasty pledges; . . . but by candidly admitting it to be our duty narrowly to examine every allegation of grievance, every suspected abuse, and when the existence of grievances is proved, and when abuses cannot be denied, to attempt a remedy, but only after mature consideration, and looking at every question in all its complicated bearings upon the interests of the country. That course is necessary, in order to afford relief, and apply remedies, with effect." The Address and this speech sounded the keynote to the Tory party for their conduct in the contest to be fought out in the general election.

That the party political leaders were waking up to a sense of the importance of extra-Parliamentary utterances is further shown at this time by the action of Lord John Russell, soon to be installed as the leader of the Opposition. Before the dissolution of Parliament was announced, he went down to Devonshire, and on the 2d December addressed a great meeting of his constituents at Totness,[1] and endeavoured to show that the position which the Conservatives were assuming as reformers could not be reconciled with their past conduct. "His speech was generally accepted as an excellent exposition of the views of the Whigs at the time, and was reprinted from the local papers, and placarded throughout the county."[2] A fortnight or so later he spoke at a county meeting in Devonshire, and then again addressed his constituents.

Other speeches at this period also display a marked difference of tone, and the appreciation of a great difference in the relative position of representatives and their constituents, and of what was due to the latter. Thus Lord Stanley, on his nomination for Lancashire, entered into an elaborate explanation of his refusal to accept the invitation made to him by Sir Robert Peel to join the new Government.

"It appeared to myself and my friends that our public duties would be best discharged by declining the proposal. If we had agreed to join the new Government for the purpose of strengthening it in those liberal measures, which I believe it must and will carry into effect, to what calumny and miscon-

[1] See *The Times*, 8th December 1834. [2] Walpole's *Russell*, p. 212.

struction would our motives have been exposed? Would not the people have regarded us as having formerly resigned merely that we might rise upon the ruins of the Government which we had quitted?"

Parliament was dissolved on the 30th December 1834, and the elections took place in January 1835. The contested elections were by no means so numerous as they had been in 1832, —145 boroughs in Great Britain were contested, as against 160 in 1832, but the great falling off was in the counties, 47 contests only taking place in Great Britain as against 67 in 1832, or a total of 192 contests as against 227 in 1832. Writing on 7th January 1835, Greville said: "The elections, as far as they have gone, are rather against the Government, but not showing any material difference in numbers—sufficient, however, to prove in point of fact, Peel's declarations have produced little or no effect, and that the various considerations that have been urged on the country, and the appeals to its reason, have been all alike thrown away." [1]

Before the elections were over—namely, on the 16th January 1835—Peel made a speech [2] at a banquet which he gave to his constituents at Tamworth, and afforded the first instance in our history of the Prime Minister of the day using the election Platform for the purpose of making a full declaration of his policy. To such high position had the Platform attained.

He expressed his regret that he had not been able to speak to them before the election: "These are not the times when public men can affect ministerial reserve, and fancy themselves exempted from the duty of frank communication with those whom they represent. It is because I am a Minister of the Crown that I court rather than shrink from the opportunity of such communication. It is by the result of public discussion that, as a Minister, I hope to succeed—by dispelling unjust suspicions—by removing unfounded prejudices—by refuting the misstatements which ignorance or malignity may put forth. It is by these instruments that truth will ultimately prevail, and that justice will ultimately be done; and of these instruments I shall never hesitate fully and freely to avail myself."

[1] Greville, *Memoirs*, vol. iii. p. 188.
[2] *The Times*, 26th January 1835, abridged from *The Staffordshire Advertiser*.

He sketched out his intentions. "The people of England," he said, "are anxious, I believe, to preserve in their full integrity the prerogatives of their ancient monarchy. They are anxious also to preserve the free and independent action of every branch of the Legislature; they are anxious to maintain the Church and its connection with the State. . . . This object I am determined to maintain. But it is quite consistent with that object to relieve any real grievance, and to remove any civil disadvantage, under which those who do not concur in the doctrines of the Established Church may labour. My opinon is that, with that course, coupled with a sincere desire to promote rational and well-matured improvement, the people of England will be content—nay, more, that of that course they will cordially approve."

The first division, which took place in the new House of Commons, showed sufficiently plainly the result of the general election. It resulted in the defeat of the Government by 10 votes, 306 having voted for them and 316 against them. It was a great pull up for the Conservative party to have made so soon after the Reform Act, but it was not quite sufficient. Defeat quickly followed defeat in Parliament, and Sir Robert Peel was soon urging on the King, who was much averse to it, the necessity of a change of Government.

On the 25th March he wrote in a Cabinet memorandum: "Nothing can, in my opinion, justify an administration in persevering against a majority but a rational and well-grounded hope of acquiring additional support, and converting a minority into a majority."[1]

And on 29th March he wrote to the King, deprecating the continuance of the Cabinet in office: "Your Majesty must bear in mind that this vote will follow a succession of votes adverse to the views of your Majesty's Ministers; that there is great public evil in permitting the House of Commons to exhibit itself to the country free from any control on the part of the Executive Government, and usurping, in consequence of the absence of that control, many of the functions of Government."[2]

The King at last yielded. Sir Robert Peel's Government

[1] Peel's *Memoirs*, vol. ii. p. 89.
[2] *Ibid.* p. 91.

resigned on the 8th of April, and Lord Melbourne was appointed to succeed him.[1]

From the time of Lord Melbourne's reaccession to power down to the close of the reign of the King, we find the practice of Ministers and other politicians having recourse to the Platform becoming ever more and more general.

Sir Robert Peel, so far from feeling himself debarred from the Platform by the fact of his having been Prime Minister, frequently resorted to it—in fact, seemed to rely on the Platform as the best means of gaining the widest publicity, and securing the greatest attention. Thus he made a great speech at a dinner at the Merchant's Tailor's Hall on the 11th May 1835, and he used the occasion for an appeal to the public for support for Conservative principles. He expressed the intention of his party to correct real abuses and to promote real economy. He said: "The Government of the country, and the mode in which it is conducted, allow me to tell you, must mainly depend upon the constitution of the House of Commons"; and he urgently pressed the necessity of gaining an effectual influence on the popular branch of the Legislature.

"We do not disguise that it is our firm resolution to maintain to the utmost of our power the limited monarchy of this country—to respect the rights of every branch of the Legislature—to maintain inviolate the United Church of England and Ireland—to maintain it as a predominant establishment in the possession of its property and of all its just privileges. Such it is our firm resolution to preserve it. We will submit to no compromise, and we will exercise every privilege which the Constitution has entrusted to us for the legitimate maintenance and support of the Constitution in Church and State. This is the appeal we make to the middle classes of the com-

[1] One interesting fact culled from the pages of Greville's *Memoirs* may here be stated. Writing on the 15th February 1835, he said: "I went yesterday to see the two Houses of Parliament. The old House of Lords (now House of Commons) is very spacious and convenient. For the first time there is a gallery in the House of Commons reserved for reporters, which is quite inconsistent with their standing orders, and the prohibition which still in form exists against publishing the debates. It is a sort of public and avowed homage to opinion, and a recognition of the right of the people to know through the medium of the Press all that passes within those walls."—Peel's *Memoirs*, vol. iii. p. 205.

munity—to those who are the depositaries of the elective franchise.

"We will not allow, if we can prevent it, by any the most plausible pretext, such an infusion of democracy into the institutions of this country as shall essentially change their theory, and by slow degrees deprive us of the advantages we have so long enjoyed under our limited monarchy and ancient institutions. Now, that is what I apprehend by the Conservative principle, and such is the ground on which we make an appeal to the country at large for the maintenance of our principles. . . .

"Proclaim to the country from this, the centre of the metropolis, that, entertaining principles of moderation, you still will stand by the ancient walls, the ancient landmarks of the Constitution, that you will rally round the monarchy and protect it in its just prerogatives, protect the independent exercise of the authority of the House of Lords, and maintain, firm and inviolable, the rights of the Established Church. You will stand by, in the emphatic language of Acts of Parliament, the Protestant Government and Protestant religion of this country."

Another ex-Prime Minister, the Duke of Wellington, was also present at the banquet, and made a short speech.

The Platform was not, however, to be confined to ex-Prime Ministers. In the autumn of 1835 O'Connell, imitating the example of Lord Brougham in the previous year, made a political tour through the north of England and Scotland, and addressed numerous large meetings, advocating the reform of the House of Lords.

The violence of his language rather damaged the Government, with whom he declared himself to be in union, as, "instead of being fitted to convince and convert the rational and soberminded, it only excited disgust and some degree of alarm."

The Whigs felt the consequences in some elections which took place shortly after the close of the session. At Devizes a Conservative replaced a Whig, and in Northamptonshire Lord Fitzwilliam's eldest son was defeated. Lord Melbourne, in despair, remarked: "It seems to me easy to get through the sitting of Parliament. The vacation is the trying time."[1]

[1] See Walpole's *Russell*, vol. i. p. 248.

An opinion which, coming from the Prime Minister, is the very strongest testimony to the great change which had taken place as regards the practice of political speeches during the Parliamentary recess and the recourse to the Platform by party leaders or prominent politicians.

The Whigs found it necessary to disclaim all participation in schemes and opinions which had become so obnoxious; and Lord J. Russell, the Home Secretary, took the opportunity, at Plymouth, where an Address was presented to him, to express the views of the Government.

Referring to the obstructive conduct of the House of Lords, he said: "The same party which prompted and led this resistance have been opposed to every Liberal measure which has been proposed for the last seven years; and upon all the most important of these measures their resistance has ended in a confession that the struggle was hopeless." But he added: "Fortified by past victories, relying firmly on future progress, I earnestly recommend you to look for the triumph of further measures of reform rather to the effect of public opinion, enlightened and matured by knowledge and discussion, than to organic changes which cannot be proposed without causing division, nor carried without risk of convulsion, and which, even if carried, would be of very dubious benefit, indeed, to the popular cause, but of unquestionable danger to the monarchy. . . . To the great landmarks of our liberties I must steadily adhere; of the principles which pervade our primitive institutions I am an ardent admirer; to the Constitution of the country, in all its branches, I stand pledged by feeling, by opinion, and by duty."

There was another circumstance which was bringing the Platform into wider use by members of Parliament at this particular period—namely, the close equality in the Parliamentary strength of the two great parties. This equality rendered each of them the more energetic in their efforts to gain a majority in the country, and the Platform was pressed into service by both of them.

The *Annual Register* of 1837 has described their proceedings: "The assembly of Parliament had been assigned to the last day of January (1837), but the business of political discussion did not await that time to commence its operations.

Meetings took place in all parts of the country under the auspices of the several parties which divided public opinion, for the purpose of arraying their strength, and declaring their views, preparatory to the more important struggle that was about to take place in Parliament.

"These meetings have their importance as indications of opinion; and public men, moreover, have often, on the occasions of them, the opportunities of a more clear and decided expression of their sentiments and views than the objects and limits of a Parliamentary debate will allow them."[1]

On the 5th January 1837 the reformers of Bath gave a public dinner to their representatives, which was attended by most of the leading radicals of the country, who took the opportunity of renewing a public profession of their political faith.

Sir William Molesworth set forth the views of the Radical party. He said: "The sincere reformers must begin to act independently. They were advised to dismiss minor differences. Was the ballot a minor difference? Was the repeal of the ratepaying clauses—was an extension of the suffrage—was an abolition of the Church rates—was an abolition of the Corn Laws—was an abolition of the Irish Church—was a reform in the army—was a reform in the universities—were all these questions of minor import?" He then went on "with many forcible arguments" to show the necessity of the popular party acting firmly and independently. "At any rate there was but one course for the popular party; they ought, on every possible occasion, to make known their principles, to labour by reiterated argument and incessant discussion to diffuse their opinions among the masses. By such a manifestation they would be able to excite the people afresh to enthusiasm."

"A meeting, much more imposing in its numbers and accompanying circumstances," was that which attended the banquet which was given by the Middlesex reformers on the 23d January, in honour of their representatives, Mr. Byng and Mr. Hume. Drury Lane was chosen as the scene of this political festivity. Tables for 1100 were laid out on the pit and stage, and the boxes were filled with well-dressed spectators. There was a great deal of speaking, and among the toasts drunk was one, "The sovereignty of the people."

[1] *Annual Register*, 1837, p. 11.

As regarded the Conservatives the writer in the *Annual Register* tells us they were not idle; "on the contrary, it was the extraordinary activity which they had exercised in every method of application to public opinion from the very close of the preceding session that had principally roused the ministerial and popular parties to something of correspondent exertion." They trusted that "a little more popularity was all that was wanting to restore them even to present power. With this view they have addressed themselves to the use of every act of popularity; meetings, chiefly festive ones, of Conservatives were held in every part of the country, and local associations organised for the defence and diffusion of their principles."

The *Annual Register* further observed: "We do not discover that any of the Ministers personally came forward on these occasions either with a declaration or a defence of their own policy. The only exception was that of the Irish Secretary, Lord Morpeth. At a dinner given in honour of himself and his colleague at Leeds, he took occasion to enter at some length into the present state of political questions, and of the conduct which his party had hitherto held in their discussion or settlement."[1]

By far the most important meeting at this time was one which took place on the 13th of January, at Glasgow, in honour of Sir Robert Peel, a banquet of over 3400 guests—and here Sir Robert Peel made a great party speech:[2] "Let us," he said, "come to the main point, for I do not wish to conciliate your confidence or support by hoisting false colours. I mean to support the national establishments which connect Protestantism with the State in the three countries. Then, again, I avow to you, that I mean to support in its full integrity the House of Lords. I support it as an essential and indispensable condition to the maintenance of the Constitution under which we live, as tantamount to the maintenance of the British Constitution. Do you also concur in that expression of opinion? And if you do, it is a timely declaration of it. The hour has arrived when, if these are our feelings, we must be prepared to act upon them."

[1] *Annual Register*, 1837, p. 31.

[2] The report of the speech occupied five columns in *The Times*.

He then entered into an elaborate defence of the House of Lords.

"If you will abolish prescriptive authority—if you will make one predominant democratic assembly—then prepare yourselves, not for the institutions of the United States, but for that terrible and fiery ordeal through which France has passed."

After a glowing eulogy of the British Constitution, he concluded with the expression of the hope that "From those walls should go forth a spirit inviting the people to rally in support of their Constitution."

With the opening of Parliament the Platform campaign ceased. Before the session was over the King died (20th June 1837). Here, then, at the end of the reign of the Sovereign, but for whose wise discretion England might have been the scene of a bloody civil war, we may for the present leave this aspect of the Platform and turn to another and more important one already looming large over the political horizon.

It is, I think, evident from what has been stated that one of the immediate results of the reform agitation, and of the Reform Act, has been the adoption of the Platform by Ministers and party leaders, and other politicians, as an instrument of party and political warfare—that was a great and momentous event in the history of the Platform.

The increasing use of the Platform was indeed only natural. Once the reform agitation had accustomed large masses of the people to take, not alone an active interest in political matters, but an actual part in the realisation of political measures, and once the Reform Act had opened the door of the Constitution to larger masses of the people, it was inevitable that some greater means for the expression of political views and feeling, and for the discussion of political schemes, should be devised than those afforded by Parliament.

Moreover, as the country advanced in wealth and population, vast interests grew up which rendered the work of Government of far greater complexity, and of far more unintermittent a character than previously. The country could not stand still while Parliament was in recess, and so the need had arisen for extra-Parliamentary speech; for information from the Government when questions could not be asked in the House; for counsel from the leaders when Parliament was not sitting; and the Platform was had recourse to as affording the best medium for communication. Once resorted to by one great party in the State, the other in self-defence had to take to it too; and thus, slowly at first, but gathering momentum as time went on, a great portion of party strife was transferred from the arena of Parliament to the Platform, and an autumn session of the Platform gradually became almost as regular a function as the winter and spring session of Parliament.

Yet one additional Platform speech must be quoted, though delivered some little time after William IV. had died, as it was destined to attain fame, and one particular phrase in it was to pass into a political axiom. Speaking at a dinner on the 7th August 1837, after the Tamworth election, Sir Robert Peel, after referring to the growth of Conservatism, said:[1] "They should remember that they had a duty to perform. It might be disagreeable and indeed inconvenient to them to attend the registration of voters which annually takes place throughout the country. All this may be revolting, but you may depend upon it that it is better you should take that trouble than that you should allow the Constitution to become the victim of false friends, or that you should be trampled under the hoof of a ruthless democracy. The advice which has been given to some persons was, 'Agitate, agitate, agitate'; the advice which I give you is this, 'Register, register, register.'"

His advice was taken, and the result was to show that, under the then existing state of the franchise, "registration" was more effective than "agitation."

[1] See *The Morning Chronicle*, 9th August 1837.

PART IV

CHAPTER XVII

THE FIRST CRISIS OF CHARTISM

THE Reform Act had not been law for more than a very few years before fresh signs of popular agitation began to display themselves, and the Platform was again called on to take a conspicuous part in public affairs. Within that comparatively short period the lower classes of the people had learned that they had not gained much by that great measure. They had helped the middle classes to force reform from a reluctant House of Commons, and a hostile House of Lords; their numbers had added to the moral and argumentative force of that movement—a physical force which could not be ignored; their voices and their cheers had swelled the volume of sound that awed Parliament into compliance with the demand for reform; but the result had only been to place the predominating power of the State in the hands of the middle class. They themselves had apparently profited little, for though, on the one hand, the constitution of Parliament had been made far more popular, and more susceptible to popular influences, yet, on the other hand, the numbers of those prepared to withstand any further great or subversive innovation had been considerably increased.

Every successive agitation in this country, in its transition from feudalism to democracy, lets us deeper and deeper into the depths of human needs, and brings us closer and closer to some of the most tremendous problems of human existence; and the agitation for further reforms now beginning, and which was soon to become known as "Chartism," brought the Government and thinking men of the nation face to face with problems hitherto resolutely ignored, or kept at as great a distance as possible.

The increase of population which has already on more than

one occasion been referred to was going on, as rapidly as ever, at the rate of a thousand a day, some said; and the increase had been mainly among the civic industrial population, being six times greater in the towns than in the country. Villages had become towns; towns had become large cities; tracts of country, previously almost uninhabited, had become thronged with people, and large masses of men were densely gathered together in new places. Trade, commerce, manufactures had also been rapidly increasing; new resources had been developed; new industries had been created; new manufactures had been started; and new methods of manufacture multiplying a thousandfold the produce of labour. But with the increasing wealth of the country little additional advantage had accrued to the toiling millions. Their existence was scarcely as yet recognised by the State; their moral and religious welfare was ignored and neglected by the State Church; their scanty food was taxed to the extremest limit, for the purpose of adding to the means of the wealthiest and most limited class of the community.

"A great mass of our unskilled and but little skilled labourers," writes Place about this period, "are in poverty, if not in actual misery. A large portion of them have been in a state of poverty and great privation all their lives. They are neither ignorant of their condition nor reconciled to it; they live amongst others who are better off than themselves, with whom they compare themselves; . . . and they come to the conclusion that the difference is solely caused by oppression—oppression of bad laws, and avaricious employers. To escape from this state is with them of paramount importance; among a vast multitude of these people not a day, scarcely an hour, can be said to pass without some circumstance, some matter exciting reflection, occurring to remind them of their condition, which, notwithstanding they have been poor and distressed from their infancy, and however much they may *at times* be cheerful, they scarcely ever cease, and never for a long period cease, to feel and to acknowledge to themselves, with deep sensations of anguish, their deplorable condition."[1]

And now once more these growing masses, actuated by feelings of misery and discontent, were beginning to stir. The

[1] Place, MSS., 27,819, 1836, p. 9.

elder among them could remember the agitation which ensued on the cessation of the war with France—could vividly enough remember Peterloo, and the repression that followed. With all, the agitation for reform was still fresh in memory, and ideas some way or other had reached even the lowest and poorest of them, in the midst of their squalor, ignorance, starvation, and hardships of every kind, that they had "rights."

No wonder then that, with masses sunk in poverty and ignorance, there should be groanings and upheavings, and searchings for mitigations of evils heavy and scarce to be endured; no wonder that in their dumb pain and anger they should often turn on and seek to destroy what seemed to them the immediate cause of their suffering and of their degradation, or that they should think of destroying the State and substituting themselves as governors.

Large movements took place among these people during the years 1833–35. Disappointed with agitation for political objects they directed their efforts to matters more directly affecting their social life, their wages, and hours of working, and numerous Trades Unions were formed. So far had they got, and so numerous were their Unions that, according to Place, who was a close observer of their proceedings, and personally acquainted with many of the principal men, "the leaders of all these Unions, with but few exceptions, had succeeded in persuading themselves that the time was coming when the whole of the working men would be ready to rise *en masse*, and take the management of their own affairs—that is to say, the management of the affairs of the nation into their own hands."[1]

Pending this consummation, the movement, by a natural transition, drifted towards political action, for the changes wanted would, they now conceived, be easiest attained by political changes on a large scale. But with such extreme and violent views as were publicly avowed, the working people were little likely to get such aid from the newly enfranchised middle classes as they required for their success. Nor, indeed, were they themselves at the time very favourably disposed to the middle class, for some of the legislation of the reformed Parliament affected them sorely.

[1] Place, MSS., 27,791, p. 333.

"They felt," Place tells us, "great disappointment at being abandoned by those whom they said they had supported to the utmost of their power, and for whom *they* had carried the Bills. The consequence of this was the total abandonment of all reliance upon the middle class to an extent which never before was entertained by them. This laid them open to the wild speculations of visionary men who meant well, and to projectors of all kinds—good, bad, and indifferent."[1]

Previous agitations, and more especially the Reform agitation, had familiarised all ranks and classes with the Platform, and had given proof of its power and effect. To it these great masses of the labouring classes therefore once looked for aid; to it once more had recourse, to express the sorrows which lay on their hearts, to tell the grievances which oppressed them.

And now the occasion had come, the need had arisen for a great popular leader—one who should have truly depicted the miserable condition of the people, and formulated their real wants; one whose voice like that of a great prophet of Israel should have thundered in the ears of the rulers of the country, carried conviction to their hearts, and wrung from them the remedies that were wanted. None, however, arose; and the people, left to themselves, without guidance, fell a prey to a set of misleaders—men who darkened counsel by words without knowledge, and whose pernicious and foolish advice tended but too often to aggravate and intensify the evils they suffered under instead of mitigating or removing them. These leaders had, unfortunately, a very clear field for their operations.

"The amount of knowledge among the many," wrote Place at this time, "is lamentably defective, though its increase is certainly great. Some among the working people, a large number among themselves, but a very small number in comparison with their class, are much better informed, more rational, and in all respects superior men, to any who could formerly have been found in their class. But even these men, with few exceptions, have not yet arrived at that state when men rely upon themselves; they are still in but too many cases liable to be drawn aside from the true course, and led into errors. Many again, who are neither so well informed as these men, and generally not so honest, are ready on every

[1] Place, MSS., 27,819, p. 24.

occasion, when a display can be made, to become leaders of large bodies, and to influence still larger bodies, to make what they call demonstrations, most of them absurd, and demonstrating nothing but their folly. . . .

"The great body of the working people who take part in political proceedings are still open to the delusions of ill-informed, and to dishonest agitators, the field of operation for whom has of late years been greatly enlarged. These ever active men are enthusiasts as much misled as those who follow them. The doctrines by which the people are misled are founded on what are called inherent indefeasible rights, which are made to include whatever particular object may be aimed at: by notions of equality in respect to property, and by the doctrines promulgated by Robert Owen, now known under the name of Socialism.

"The most mischievous nonsense propagated is that which pretends to assure the deluded people that poverty will, by the adoption of the proposed measure, be wholly removed, and that the time is all but at hand when these predictions will be accomplished. These to them mischievous notions led them to the conclusion that they could associate nearly the whole of the working classes in one great confederation, which, in a short time, would gain possession of all the power and property in the nation, and compel the submission of all to their rule, never for an instant doubting that their rule would be the most wise and beneficent that could be imagined—be, in fact, a millennium in which peace, plenty, and happiness would abound."[1]

And now, for the first time in the history of the country, the Platform must be looked to exclusively as the exponent of the feelings, and ideas, and aims of a very large portion of the population. Other exposition of their opinion there was practically none, for, with the exception of one or two newspapers, the few which represented their views were ephemeral in character and limited in circulation, whilst none of them reached those classes who would have to be influenced if reforms were to be obtained.

Unfortunately, on this occasion, the Platform appears in its least attractive aspect, time after time affording evident proof of most of the evils its most inveterate enemy could charge it

[1] Place, MSS., 27,819, p. 6.

with. Reasons there are that it was so, excuses and palliations also in abundance, but the fact itself cannot be denied. Still, on the whole, it was fortunate that the Platform was there, even with all its attendant evils, for it was a vent for the feelings of the masses of the population, which, otherwise, might have found a far more dangerous and disastrous form of expression, and it afforded a means of diagnosing the evils of which it was the most informing symptom.

Gammage, who has written a rambling, ill-arranged, and illiterate, but still most useful *History of the Chartist Movement*, and who was himself a Chartist lecturer and agitator, has pointed out that "It must be borne in mind that, down to about this period, with the single exception of the time of the Consolidated Trades' Union, even the more enlightened of the working classes had been but little accustomed to public speaking. The Platform [1] had been almost exclusively occupied by the upper and middle classes, and it could hardly be expected that the working men, deprived in a great measure of educational advantages, would become Ciceros in a day. But the dawn of the Chartist movement was quite an era in working class oratory. It gave to the humblest the opportunity of raising his voice in public meeting, and that opportunity was not disregarded, but, on the other hand, was embraced with avidity." [2]

The grievance first fastened on by the people was the Poor Law of 1834, which, by a strange fate, had been almost the first-fruits of the reformed Parliament. The abolition of outdoor relief, the separation of the family in the workhouse, and many other of its provisions were regarded with the utmost aversion, and with widespread horror. "The operative looked upon the repeal of the 43d of Elizabeth," wrote Gammage, "and its substitution by the new enactment, as a cancelling of the bond which had hitherto bound them to the richer classes, as the breaking of the last link in the chain of sympathy. Huge prison-like workhouses had risen up in various parts, serving to remind the poor of their coming doom.

[1] This is one of the first instances of the use of the word "Platform" in its generic sense.

[2] *The History of the Chartist Movement*, p. 24, by R. G. Gammage. London, 1854.

With scanty wages, in many instances insufficient to support life in a tolerable state of comfort, there was nothing before them but misery in the present, and the Bastile in the future, in which they were to be immured when the rich oppressor no longer required their services."[1]

But there were other grievances as well. "At that time, too," continues Gammage, "the factory system was on so wretched a footing as to be monstrously oppressive to its victims. . . . Wages were so low as to compel thousands of parents to send their children to the mills, where they were worked beyond the powers of endurance. It was with tottering limbs that the poor young creatures staggered from the factory to their cheerless home." And worse if possible than work in the factories, and the state of the factory population, was work in the mines, and the state of the mining population. In fact, what with new Poor Laws, the want of factory laws, dear food, poverty, starvation, misery, there were grievances enough, evils enough, to account for discontent among the people, and to furnish endless subjects of the most impassioned speech from themselves or from those who felt with them, or from those who wished to gain notoriety by using the sufferings of the people for their own selfish or ambitious ends.

The Platform was soon utilised to make the country ring with complaints on this subject. Emerging into prominence in the early stages of the agitation against the Poor Law, which later culminated in, or merged into Chartism, came Richard Oastler. He had been "a steward to a gentleman of property, a man of great animal powers, active, persevering, a ready writer and fluent speaker, of undoubted courage, and entertaining the very best intentions to serve the mill and factory-workers, and most especially the unfortunate and helpless children employed in the mills."[2] Yorkshire was the principal scene of his labours, and there he carried on a most determined Platform campaign against the Poor Law, attending meeting after meeting to denounce it, addressing his hearers "in an eloquent and fiery strain,"—"Arm, Arm, Arm,"

[1] *The History of the Chartist Movement*, p. 62, by Gammage.

[2] He was styled the "King of the Factory Children," from the long and earnest advocacy of their cause.—Place, MSS., 27,820, p. 150.

being the oft-repeated exhortation with which he finished his speeches. And emerging also into prominence about this same time was another man, who was also to become a notoriety of the Platform, the Reverend J. R. Stephens, a dismissed Wesleyan minister. Francis Place, whose qualification to judge is acknowledged by Stephens's biographer, described him as "a fanatic, possessing great command of language and great power of declamation."[1] His labours lay mostly in Lancashire. His biographer,[2] in a eulogistic and by no means complete account of his life, says: "To his just and generous mind the grievances of the poor were intolerable, and he was for redressing them; and if not redressed by the humanity of those in authority, then he was for redressing them by combination, by public agitation, and by whatever agencies he believed to be justifiable in the sight of God."

Numerous were the meetings held in the manufacturing parts of the country against the new Poor Law, by these and other less known men, and numerous also were the meetings for shorter hours of labour. Gradually the meetings increased in number; and in the winter of 1837–38 they were very frequent. These anti-Poor Law and other meetings in the north of England were not, however, the only evidence of agitation; they were not the only meetings at which the Platform was telling the dolorous tale of the condition of the people. In the summer of 1836 the seeds of a greater movement were beginning to crop up,—the movement known by the name of Chartism—so called from the fact of the people who participated in it adopting a proposed Charter as the basis or embodiment of their demands, just as the barons of old formulated their demands in the Magna Charta which they presented to King John.

"Chartism," wrote Carlyle in 1839—when some years' experience of the agitation had given material for forming an opinion on it—"means the bitter discontent grown fierce and mad, the wrong condition therefore, or the wrong disposition, of the working classes of England. . . . Food, shelter, due guidance, in return for his labour—candidly interpreted, Chartism—and all such *isms* mean that."

[1] Place, MSS., p. 150 (27,820).

[2] See *Life of J. R. Stephens, Preacher and Political Orator*, by G. J. Holyoake, p. 78.

"Chartism," according to another contemporary writer, who expressed himself somewhat strangely, was "no more than the cry of millions suffering under a diseased condition of society"[1]—as if that were not enough, not far too much.

But however Chartism may have been defined, no more momentous movement has occurred in England in modern times. It may have been rendered, at times, ridiculous and foolish by the conduct and characters of some of the men who came to the surface, and who were reputed its leaders; indeed, it would be easy by selecting the worst passages in the speeches made at the meetings of the people, and by holding up to ridicule the characters of most of the leaders, to present Chartism as something altogether to be condemned and repressed, in the interests of peace, of order, of society, of the country itself. Folly enough was uttered from the Platform by some of the blatant fools who sought more to gratify their own vanity than to ameliorate the condition of the people—schemes so wild as to stamp their authors with fatuous imbecility were paraded for the regeneration of society—passions base and brutal betrayed themselves at times among some of the people; but these almost necessary concomitants of popular agitation should not make us lose sight of the real nature of the movement, or of its portentous gravity. Stripped of these accessories it was practically and actually what Carlyle said the French Revolution was—"A revolt of the oppressed lower classes against the oppressing or neglecting upper classes."

It raised not only political questions of the greatest magnitude, going down to the root of all politics, but it brought also into prominence questions of the deepest social consequence.

"These Chartisms, Radicalisms, Reform Bill, Tithe Bill, and infinite other discrepancy and acrid argument and jargon that there is yet to be," said Carlyle, "are *our* French revolution; God grant that we, with our better methods, may be able to transact it by argument alone."

The best hope of this prayer being granted lay with the unrestricted use of free speech and free discussion; and it was here that the Platform, despite all its faults and dangers, once more was to render the most incalculable inestimable service to the nation.

[1] See *The Monthly Chronicle* on "Chartism," 1840.

The actual beginning of the movement was a modest one. At a meeting of a few persons assembled at 14 Tavistock Street, Covent Garden, in the month of June 1836, William Lovett brought forward a rough sketch of a prospectus for a Working-men's Association. The prospectus set forth amongst other things that, "Among the causes that most contribute to the perpetuation of abuses and corruptions in every department of the State, and the indifference manifested towards the interests of the millions, none have been more pregnant with evil than the divisions and disputes among the working classes themselves.[1]

"The great variety and clashing of opinions on all important subjects, political and social, the contradictory and deficient evidence relating to the true condition of the labourer, the conflicting means suggested to remedy what each conceives to be the paramount evil, together with the bickerings and triflings of the most honest and influential among them, have long been subjects of regret and causes of vexatious disappointment."

Lovett himself, in his autobiography,[2] describes his and his friends' efforts to form associations, and he says, "We found that we had collected together a goodly number of active and influential working men, and the question arose among us, whether we could form and maintain a union formed exclusively of this class, and of such men. We were the more induced to try the experiment, as the working classes had not hitherto evinced that discrimination and independent spirit in the management of their political affairs which we were desirous to see. A lord, a M.P., or an esquire was a leading requisite to secure a full attendance, and attention from them on all public occasions, as well as among those who called themselves their betters. They were always looking up to leadership of one description or another, were being swayed to and fro in opinion and action by the idol of their choice, and were rent and divided when some popular breath had blown that idol from its pedestal. In fact, the masses, in their political organisations were taught to look up to great men (or to men professing greatness) rather than to great principles. We

[1] Place, MSS., 27,819, p. 35.

[2] See *The Life and Struggles of William Lovett in his Pursuit of Bread, Knowledge, and Freedom*, by himself (1876), p. 91.

wished, therefore, to establish a political school of self-instruction among them, in which they should accustom themselves to examine great social and political principles, and by their publicity and free discussion help to form a sound and healthful public opinion throughout the country." Lovett and his friends accordingly, on the 16th of June 1836, started "The London Working-men's Association." Its principal objects were "To draw into one bond of unity the intelligent and influential portion of the working classes in town and country; to seek by every legal means to place all classes of society in possession of their equal, political, and social rights; to use every exertion to remove those cruel laws that prevent the free circulation of thought through the medium of a cheap and honest Press; and to promote by all available means the education of the rising generation and the extirpation of those systems which tend to future slavery."

An association, however, was of little use without the Platform to bring it into notice, and to explain its objects. Accordingly, after the lapse of some time, a meeting was convened by the Association, and one February day in the following year a crowded gathering took place at the Crown and Anchor Tavern in the Strand. "There were eleven speakers at it—all working men, and besides them two who were not of the working class—namely, Feargus O'Connor and J. Bell—both of whom were considered intruders." [1]

"A Petition of Grievances" was adopted which previously had been drawn up by Lovett. It set forth the injustice and anomalies of the existing representative system, and advocated remedies which afterwards were known as "the six points" of the Charter—namely, Universal Suffrage, Annual Parliaments, Equal Electoral Districts, the Abolition of Property Qualification, Vote by Ballot, and Payment of Members.

"The prayer of that Petition," says Lovett,[2] "formed the nucleus of the far-famed *People's Charter*, which may be said to have had its origin at this meeting. The public meeting was the most crowded, and at the same time the most orderly one I ever attended. All our resolutions were unanimously agreed to, and our Petition signed by about 3000 persons." It was determined to embody the Petition in a Bill which was to

[1] See Place, MSS., 27,819, p. 48. [2] Lovett's *Life*, p. 102.

be introduced into Parliament, and which was to be called "The People's Charter"; but before the Association had made progress with this work the King died (20th June 1837), and further action had to be postponed until the assembly of the new Parliament.

In the meantime the Association issued an Address to reformers, in the hope of influencing electors. Its terms help to explain the cause of the Chartist movement: "It is now nearly six years since the Reform Act became a part of the laws of our country. To carry that measure, despite the daring advocates of corruption, the co-operation of the millions was sought for, and cheerfully and honestly given. They threw their hearts into the contest, and would have risked their lives to obtain that which they were led to believe would give to all the blessing of liberty. Alas! their hopes were excited by promises which have not been kept, and their expectations of freedom have been bitterly disappointed. . . . In the course of a few weeks this Bill will be prepared and printed for circulation under the title of 'The People's Charter,' and will form a rallying point for radical reformers—a standard by which to test all those who call themselves friends of the people. . . . Let those great principles, therefore, form the pledge of every candidate who presents himself on the hustings. . . . You formed yourselves into societies—you met and petitioned by thousands to force a measure in which you were not included; show, therefore, by similar demonstrations that you are not unmindful of your own interests. . . . True it is that your Petitions are but little regarded in the Houses of Parliament, but still we know that it is the most efficient means of creating, guiding, and ascertaining public opinion." [1]

The general election which ensued on the King's death, judging by the number of contested elections, showed rather an increase of political interest throughout the country, as there were contests in 219 constituencies in Great Britain as against 192 in 1835; but it left Lord Melbourne and his Whig Ministry in much about the same position in the new Parliament as they were before—that is to say, without a sufficient majority to carry any real liberal measure against the Tory opposition in the House of Commons, and the still more powerful opposition in the House of Lords.

[1] Lovett's *Life*, p. 115.

The election effected no change in the feelings or desires of the lower classes; those lay far too deep to be touched by the superficial and remote effect of the transfer of a few votes one way or the other in the House of Commons. But there was one moral they drew from it.

Place says: "The late elections had demonstrated to them (the people) that the whole process of electing members to the House of Commons was one of gross bribery, undue influence, and intimidation, the remedy for which could alone be found in a great extension of the suffrage, reducing the various denominations of voters to one, and securing their independence by the ballot." [1]

In addition to their Address to the Electors, the Working-men's Association adopted an Address to the Queen.[2] On expressing their intention to present it, they were informed that official usage prescribed that an Address could not be presented personally to the Sovereign except at a levee, when the Petitioners must be in Court dress. They replied that, "with every respect for the forms which make personal cleanliness and respectful behaviour necessary qualifications to approach her Majesty, we have neither the means nor the inclination to indulge in such absurdities as dress-coats, swords, and wigs," and they accordingly sent the Address to the Home Secretary to present. "We find," said these men, "the bulk of the nation toiling slaves from birth till death—thousands wanting food, or subsisting on the scantiest pittance, having neither time nor means to obtain instruction, much less of cultivating the higher faculties and brightest affections, but forced by their situation to engender enmity, jealousy, and contention, and too often to become the victims of intemperance and crime."

Even a more graphic description of the condition of the people was given by Lovett and John Collins in a book called *Chartism*, which they wrote in prison in 1840.[3]

"What worse can those experience on earth who, from earliest morn to latest night, are toiling in misery, yet starving while they toil; who, possessing all the anxieties of fond parents, cannot satisfy their children with bread; who, susceptible of every domestic affection, perceive their hearths desolate, and

[1] Place, MSS., 27,819, p. 116. [2] September 1837.
[3] *Chartism*, by William Lovett and J. Collins.

their little ones neglected, while the wives of their bosoms are exhausting every toiling faculty in the field or workshop, to add to the scanty portion which merely serves to protect their lives of careworn wretchedness? Men thus steeped in misery and standing on the very verge of existence cannot philosophise on prudence; they are disposed to risk their lives on any chance which offers the prospect of immediate relief as the only means of rendering life supportable, or helping them to escape death in its most agonising forms."

With much truth has it been said by Gammage:[1] "It may be doubted whether there ever was a great political movement of the people without a social origin. The chief material object of mankind is to possess the means of social enjoyment. Secure them in possession of these, and small is the care they have for political abstractions. It is the existence of great social wrongs which principally teaches the masses the value of political rights."

Unfortunately the lower classes of England at this time were steeped in social wrongs. And now the Platform was once more in full activity—meetings for Reform of Parliament, meetings for the Ballot, meetings against the new Poor Law, meetings against the Factories, meetings for Universal Suffrage. Scarcely even in the reform struggle was the Platform so appealed to; but never yet had it sunk to such depths as it now reached, for the people, left to themselves by the middle and upper classes, ignorant and uneducated, not knowing whither to turn for some alleviation of their condition, submitted themselves willingly to the lead of false guides, who, using the Platform for the purpose of influencing and controlling them, led them deeper and deeper into trouble and disaster.

The Chartist movement was not, however, to be got under way by any one man or any one association. Just as a large river is made up by the contributions of numerous streams, so the Chartist agitation resulted from the actions of several men and several associations, each working on independent lines.

The plan of proceeding started by Lovett not being deemed satisfactory by all, Feargus O'Connor and a few of his friends made an effort to set up another association which would be more conformable with their own notions.

[1] Gammage, p. 14.

Feargus O'Connor, who soon was to rise into notoriety as the leader of the Chartists, and to fill a conspicuous position in the agitation, was the nephew of Arthur O'Connor, who had been an exile in the United States of America ever since the Irish Rebellion of 1798. He had been elected Member of Parliament for an Irish constituency on the passing of the Reform Act, and had belonged to the party of O'Connell, but having quarrelled with him, transferred his scene of operations to England, and joined those who were agitating against the Poor Laws, for factory legislation, or for any other reform they wished to obtain—"Taking," as Place says, "whatever means he could to lead and mislead the working people." He started in 1837 a newspaper called *The Northern Star*, which quickly became recognised as the organ of the Chartists. Deficient in all the qualities which go to make greatness, yet possessed of many which soon make a man notorious, he quickly came to the front, despite the fact of his not being one of the working people. He was a powerful and a popular speaker. "Out of doors," says Gammage, "the thunder of his voice would reach the ears of the most careless and put to silence the most noisy of his audience;"[1] but his speeches were made up of the wildest declamation, of the veriest rant, and all are vitiated by vanity or selfishness, and are completely devoid of the ring of earnestness or sincerity which is observable in the speeches of so many of even the most violent and bombastic of the Chartist orators.

He and his friends, in their endeavour to start a movement independent of the Association, called a public meeting (9th June 1837) at the Crown and Anchor Tavern in the Strand for the purpose of forming a Central National Association, "in order to obtain universal suffrage, protection for the native industry, and the total abolition of the infamous Poor Law Bill."

One of the speakers, Bernard by name, said his plan was to get a law passed by which ten shillings should pay for a sovereign, and sixpence for a shilling.

James Bronterre O'Brien said that the people of Yorkshire were sick of speech-making, and wished that something should be done. He said in plain English he would not give a damn

[1] Gammage, p. 52.

for moral force unless he knew that there was another in the background prepared to come and relieve the moral force, if moral force was insufficient to carry the point. He recommended that at the next general election they should proceed to the hustings in every borough and endeavour to procure a majority on a show of hands, and unless the returning officer consented to take the poll universally, the people should consider the men as their representatives and no others. If proper arrangements were made, he did not despair of getting 400 democrats returned. He should recommend these men to proceed to St. Stephens to take their seats, not by force, but they should assume they would be allowed to sit there. By way of doing honour to these men, it might be as well that 200,000 of the able-bodied subjects of the King should accompany them, not to fight—nothing of that sort—but to show the great sympathy which existed for the new representatives. . . . He was not for employing force, not now at any rate, not until they could not do without it, and they could do with it.

Another association or body which was also beginning to take part in the agitation about this time was the Political Union of Birmingham. It had been revived after the financial panic of 1836 mainly by Attwood, who, Place says, was "the besotted advocate of an alteration of the currency"; but it was a very different sort of body from that which had figured so prominently in the Reform agitation. It held its first public meeting on the 19th June 1837, and other meetings in the course of the autumn.

The Working-men's Association was in no way deterred by the rival proceedings of O'Connor. With the view of helping localities to form associations similar to itself, and also of rousing the slumbering energies of the masses, it selected certain persons as "missionaries" or emissaries for these purposes. Most prominent among these was Henry Vincent—"the young Demosthenes of English democracy," as Gammage calls him. "For fluency of speech he rivalled all his competitors. . . . He had every capacity for exciting the multitude, but to give stability to their wakened minds was a very different thing. With a man of his stamp it was no difficult matter to rouse every passion into active life, but to form and mature the judgment did not lie within his province. . . . Wherever he appeared, he drew forth the most enthusiastic responses. Among the Welsh too his fervid declamation awakened every sympathy of the heart. Excitable as that people are, his thrilling tones, as he depicted the burning wrongs of the toiling classes, fanned their passions into a flame which no after prudence could allay."[1]

Place says "that these emissaries were themselves deluded, and they deluded others with the expectation that the time was come, and therefore they had only to associate and demand what they wanted to obtain it. This was mischievous doctrine though sincerely promulgated."[2] It resulted, however, in the formation of many local associations. The agitation continued throughout the autumn of 1837. By the end of the year the Working-men's Association had "attained a station which had never before been attained by any body of working men. . . . They were, however, mistaken in one principal particular. They persuaded themselves that the *six* points of reform which they had adopted would be speedily obtained; they mistook those who countenanced their proceedings for the nation, and expected they would so overawe the Parliament as to induce the members of both Houses to concede all they demanded, and so fixed was this persuasion that it was impossible to convince any *one* of them that he was in error in this particular. They were sure, therefore, to mislead themselves and all who relied upon them."[3]

The new Parliament, the first of our present Sovereign's reign, met in November. Its opening was looked to with some anxiety. Great was the disappointment when all reference to such changes as the ballot or an extension of the franchise was omitted in the Queen's speech, and dismay was produced when Lord John Russell, as the mouthpiece of Ministers, and leader of the House of Commons, made an occasion to declare that Government would not countenance any changes, much less assist in the great changes proposed out of doors, and likely to be moved within the House. "The excitement caused by this conduct was very great, and the conduct of Ministers was freely canvassed. It was reprobated by the Political Associations."[4]

[1] Gammage, p. 17. [2] Place, MSS., 27,819, p. 59. [3] *Ibid.* p. 63. [4] *Ibid.* p. 160.

The Birmingham Political Union, seeing the progress the radical reformers in London were making, began to think of putting itself forward as leader in the movement.

Attwood, "becoming more violent as the prospects of realising his absurd currency schemes became ever more remote," said: "The middle classes could not be moved; they were choked with pride, jealousy, and servility. The masses of the people constituted the only hope of the country. Into their hands the destiny of the country must be committed. Without them universal anarchy was certain. . . . The Union must bring 2,000,000 of men together to stand by them, and move legally at the word of command. They must raise the masses in the large towns, and bring them to act centrically, legally, and simultaneously upon the Parliament."[1]

The Union decided on sending deputies throughout the kingdom to establish Political Unions, and, at a meeting held at Coventry on the 3d January 1838, with this object Mr. P. H. Muntz, one of the Birmingham leaders, said: "He had great hopes when the Queen came to the throne that a better system would be adopted. He was wofully disappointed, and nothing now remained but agitation, and such a display of popular opinion and popular strength as would procure for the people a voice in the Legislature, without which they could not expect any amelioration of their condition."

There were thus two organisations that had sent out Platform missionaries or organisers to awake the people, and besides the men thus sent, Stephens and Oastler were addressing meetings on their particular subjects, and Feargus O'Connor and his friends were also actively engaged in holding meetings and making speeches. The Platform was, in fact, hard at work throughout the country instilling into the minds of the people such lessons as the leading popular orators chose to present to them.

It is quite to be believed that, as Place tells us, "There was great excitement at the commencement of the year 1838. It had spread into the southern and eastern counties, and into South Wales. Birmingham was the centre of the midland counties, as Manchester and Newcastle were of the northern counties, and Edinburgh and Glasgow were of Scotland. It

[1] Place, MSS., 27,819, p. 164.

was rapidly spreading in every direction. The so-called Liberal members of the House of Commons, who had assisted to procure the Reform Act in 1832, and had led the multitude to expect many important changes favourable to their class, abandoned them, and confederated together to prevent any further political changes; . . . the middle classes had subsided into a state of quiescence and abject submission in which the Parliament did its utmost to keep them, and the working classes were left wholly to themselves, and to some extent under the guidance of leaders, some of whom have been shown to be equally ignorant and dishonest."[1]

Some extracts from some of the speeches being made at this period by some of the leaders will show to what purposes the Platform had now been turned, and what extreme language was sometimes being used.

At a meeting at Newcastle on 1st January 1838 the Rev. J. R. Stephens said: "The people were not going to stand this, and he would say that sooner than wife and husband, and father and son, should be sundered, and dungeoned, and fed on 'skillee'—sooner than wife or daughter should wear the prison dress—sooner than that—Newcastle ought to be, and should be, one blaze of fire, with only one way to put it out, and that with the blood of all who supported this abominable measure. He was a revolutionist by fire—he was a revolutionist by blood, to the knife, to the death. . . . It would be law for every man to have his firelock, his cutlass, his sword, his pair of pistols or his pike, and for every woman to have her pair of scissors, and for every child to have its paper of pins, and its box of needles (here the orator's voice was drowned in the cheers of the meeting), and let the men, with a torch in one hand and a dagger in the other, put to death any and all who attempted to sever man and wife."[2]

At a meeting at Glasgow in the same month he said: "If they will not reform this, ay, uproot it all, they shall have the revolution they so much dread. We shall destroy these abodes of guilt, which they have reared to violate all law and God's Book. If they will not learn to act as law prescribes, and God ordains, so that every man shall, by his labour, find comfortable food and clothing, not for himself only, but for

[1] Place, MSS., 27,820, p. 4. [2] Gammage, p. 65.

his wife and babes, then we swear by the love of our brothers, by our God who made us all for happiness, by the earth He gave for our support, by the heaven He designs for those who love each other here, and by the hell which is the portion of those who, violating His Book, have consigned their fellow-men, the image of their God, to hunger, nakedness, and death; we have sworn by our God, by heaven, earth, and hell, that from the east, the west, the north, and the south, we shall wrap in one awful sheet of devouring flame, which no arm can resist, the manufactories of the cotton tyrants, and the places of those who raised them by rapine and murder, and founded them upon the wretchedness of the millions whom God, our God, Scotland's God, created to be happy."

"Of such as the above," remarks Gammage, "were the speeches of Mr. Stephens generally composed." Pointing once to a monster mill he exclaimed, "You see yonder factory, with its towering chimney; every brick in that chimney is cemented with the blood of women and little children." On another occasion he said: "If the rights of the poor were trampled underfoot, then down with the throne, down with the aristocracy, down with the bishops, down with the clergy, burn the church, down with all rank, all title, and all dignity."[1]

Other speakers also were almost if not quite as violent. Thus, on the 8th of January 1838, a meeting of the Working-men's Association was held at Leeds, with the object of petitioning for universal suffrage. Some 1500 to 2000 persons were present. A speech was made by Beaumont, who has already been mentioned, who referred to the rebellion in Canada, and said:[2] "Gosford and Colborne should be hanged, and justice would not be done them, unless Russell and Melbourne and Peel were hanged with them. Now, my friends, you are here the representatives of British justice; you know the defence set up by the Ministers through their hired advocate, the Press; you have heard my charges against them, and have weighed the evidence. How say you? Are John Russell and Lord Melbourne guilty of treason, robbery, arson, and murder? or are they not guilty? (Cries of 'Guilty.') Such of you as give your verdict of guilty hold up your hands (here

[1] Gammage, p. 66.

[2] Place, MSS., 27,820, p. 18.

the whole meeting held up their hands). Hearken to your verdict. You say the monsters are guilty of murder, treason, robbery, and arson, and so you say all. (Cries of 'Yes, yes, we do.') Oh, how I wish I could give effect to your most righteous verdict by pronouncing judgment of death and execution according to law on these detestable violators of the laws of God and man. (Loud cheers.)"

A dinner was given in the evening after the meeting. Speaking at it Dr. Taylor said: "The time for physical force had arrived; . . . it was high time to lay down the spade and take up the sword."[1]

Beaumont also spoke and said: "I am a man for physical force. . . . It is not by talking but by taking the sledge-hammer and knocking out the tax-gatherers' brains that any good can be done;" and he went on to make some further remarks, but this time "he was met with such a volley of hisses and groans that he could scarcely make himself heard at all, and quite in a paroxysm of rage, and grinning and clenching his fists, as if becoming completely ferocious, he exclaimed"—but what he further said need not be given. His conduct confirmed the statement that he was insane—a fearful infliction, but affording a sad comment on the Platform that such men should be listened to at all.

On the 15th January 1838 the Political Union of Birmingham held a great meeting in the Town Hall, and made a declaration of their principles by passing a resolution in favour of Universal Suffrage, Triennial Parliaments, and Vote by Ballot.[2]

Attwood, at this meeting, strongly urged obedience to the law. "By peace, law, order, loyalty, and union, the people are powerful for good; by tumult and disorder they become weak as infants. A mob never yet possessed power, but an outraged indignant people are omnipotent. . . . We know you, and we know our country well, but in the midst of the mighty masses of men that we must bring into political activity in every town in England, Scotland, and Ireland, not excepting London itself, we cannot but be sensible that the follies of some, and the guilt of others, may possibly lead great masses astray. In one short hour of error or crime

[1] Place, MSS., 27,820, pp. 23, 24. [2] *Ibid.* pp. 44. 45.

immense mischief may be done to our cause and to our country. If ever the people suffer their cause to be stained by crime, they will be attacked and crushed by the law."[1] Such counsel was, unfortunately, rare.

On 5th February 1838 a meeting of delegates of various branch societies of the South Lancashire Anti-Poor Law Association was held at Manchester.

Stephens, who spoke at it, said: "If the Act were established, it should be eye for eye, tooth for tooth, wife for wife, child for child, man for man, blood for blood. (Cheers.) So help him God and his country." Oastler followed. He "seriously warned the Ministers against pushing the people too hard. (Loud cheers.) . . . He knew the assassin's knife would be used if they were to be tricked out of their rights. . . . It was time he should speak out. Ministers had already pursued their crawling, dirty, bludgeon, shabby career too far. (Loud cheers.) And if they thought the inhabitants of those hills and valleys would tamely submit to be cheated against law out of their rights, they might expect, for he knew they would meet with, sudden death on the part of their own friends. (Cheers.) He was sorry to speak in this style. He had been considered an incendiary, a bloodthirsty man. He was one of those rather who had spoken right out in order to prevent those consequences which must follow if Ministers persevered in their course."

At Rochdale, on the occasion of a similar meeting, Stephens said: "If it were right to confiscate the property of the people by abrogating the 43d Elizabeth, it is right for the poor to take a dagger in one hand, and a torch in the other, and do the best for themselves."[2]

At the same meeting Oastler again flamed forth his anathemas: "I tell you churchmen, I tell you dissenters, before I would submit to such an Act, I would set the whole kingdom in a blaze. I am no incendiary, but I have affection in my heart, and will breathe out."

And so the agitation went on. These and similar attempts to influence the people against the new Poor Law not long after had the effect to be expected from them. And "blood was

[1] See *The Times*, January 1838.

[2] *The Examiner*, 10th February 1838, p. 88.

spilt—the blood of the innocent, and the blood of the misguided." The case is an illustration of the danger of the Platform.

"A madman, whose real name was said to be Thom, appeared at Canterbury about the year 1833 under the assumed name of William Courteney. His manners were pleasing, and his elocution fluent and impressive. He successively stood as candidate for the city of Canterbury, and East Kent, but failed. He was subsequently convicted of perjury, and on proof of his insanity he was sent to an asylum, from which, after a period, he was discharged. Once at liberty he resumed his old connection with some of the idle and ill-disposed peasantry, inflamed of late by harangues against the new Poor Law Act, and formed a band of about a hundred. A farmer, whose servant had been seduced from his service to join the band, sent a civil officer to bring him back to his work. Thom shot the constable dead. A military party, accompanied by several magistrates, forthwith endeavoured to arrest him. He shot the officer dead, and was then shot dead himself. His followers attacked the soldiers, who in self-defence had to fire, and altogether some fifteen lives were lost. The band then dispersed." [1]

Among the numerous meetings held in the course of the spring of 1838 there is one which deserves special mention, as presenting a new phase of the Platform. This was a meeting of the women of Birmingham. The idea originated apparently with Mr. T. C. Salt, a member of the Birmingham Political Union, who has also left an account of it in a letter he wrote [2] to Mr. Ebenezer Elliot: "I sent you, last week, a Birmingham journal, with a very much curtailed account of the meeting of women. I *alone* of Birmingham reformers dared either to convene it or to attend it. There could not have been less than 12,000 women there. A more beautiful and moving sight was never seen; a meeting more enthusiastic or more orderly never was assembled. It was evident that the iron had entered into their soul, and that they felt deeply, and resolved religiously, that their children's children should not be trampled on as they had been.

"I mention this meeting to you because it forms part of my general plan. I believe (I might say I know) that hitherto

[1] *The Examiner*, 3d June 1838, p. 346. [2] April 1838.

the women have thought so little upon politics, and being so utterly ignorant of the connection of our system with their poverty and degradation, that they have either not interfered, or persuaded their husbands from meddling with politics as a thing of no profit. We cannot afford their neutrality or hostility. They must be our enthusiastic friends."[1]

The meeting was held on the 2d April in the Town Hall. Salt spoke: "He looked upon the sight before him," he said, "as one which no mortal eyes had ever seen—a meeting of women surpassing in numbers that of any body of men ever assembled in that vast hall. . . . He held as an article of his faith that nothing was really well done unless it were done by women. The men in 1832 made a sad bungling job of the Reform Bills. . . . The men of England took the lead then, now the women of Birmingham would obtain the immortal honour of setting an example to the women of England, which would be of the utmost consequence to all."[2]

In the course of his speech he, for the first time, propounded the idea of a National Petition. He said: "While similar meetings were being held elsewhere, they might obtain the signature of 3,000,000 of men to a National Petition demanding a restoration of their rights. He proposed that the day on which the Petition was presented should be the day to be kept as a solemn observance throughout Great Britain, and thenceforth the people should resolve to abstain from every excisable article."[3]

Resolutions were passed, one of them inveighing against Parliament for persisting in maintaining Corn Laws for making food dear, and trade laws to make labour cheap—for having given monopoly to the wealthy, and competition to the poor, and who, while they have maintained the interests of the pension list of State paupers, have enacted Poor Laws calculated to deprive the victims of their iniquity of their last refuge. And another, that the time has arrived when the general inquiry has produced conviction in every sound and inquisitive mind that the interest of all can only be protected by all being represented in the Legislature, and they pledged themselves to support universal suffrage, annual Parliaments, and other measures of reform.

[1] Place, MSS., 27,820, p. 26. [2] *Ibid.* p. 69. [3] *Ibid.* p. 70.

A more important meeting was that which was held on the 3d May[1] at Hunslet Moor, near Leeds, for the purpose of forming a great Northern Union. There Feargus O'Connor was present, and spoke, and there was much vague declamation. It was agreed that the Union should be formed. Collins, one of the Birmingham deputies, addressed the meeting, and carried with him the enthusiasm of those present to the highest. The meeting declared that they and the men of the North would follow Feargus O'Connor to the death, and pledged themselves to make atonement for their former apathy by making up for it by increased energy.

"From this time," says Place, "Feargus O'Connor became the Apostle of the North, the constant travelling dominant leader, and at length, as will be seen, in his own conceit, the master of the Radicals."[2]

Lovett, who has given a description of the state of the political reformers at this period, tells us that they were "Not merely split into numerous parties, but each was pursuing its own political purpose to the prejudice of all practical measures. One party was loud in condemnation of the Poor Laws; another was contending for an increase of Paper Currency as the only specific for the national grievances; another was depicting and deprecating the horrors of the Factory System; another praying for a Short Time Bill; another for a 'Tax on Machinery'; another for Household Suffrage; another for the Ballot."

Lovett[3] and the Working-men's Association got at last as far as actually to publish "The People's Charter."[4] It made its appearance on the 8th May 1838, together with an Address to the Radical Reformers of Great Britain and Ireland.

It was in the unattractive form of a Bill—a Bill to provide for the just representation of the people of Great Britain and

[1] 1838. [2] Place, MSS., 27,820, p. 135. [3] Lovett's *Life*, p. 172.

[4] The words "People's Charter" were not quite new.

A pamphlet, entitled *The People's Charter*, had been written by a physician, and sold by Brooks, the stationer in Oxford Street, in 1832. In it was the following: "The people must remember that the battle of freedom is but begun, and that its next, its grand, its sacred objects are a free Press, universal suffrage, vote by ballot, and annual Parliaments. They must remember that the best means of obtaining these is to enrol themselves in Political Unions, to call incessant public meetings, and widely diffuse such works as the present."—Place, MSS., 27,796, p. 26.

Ireland in the Commons House of Parliament. It proposed to enact (1) that every male inhabitant of twenty-one years and upwards, with the exception of foreigners, lunatics, or criminals, should be entitled to vote for the election of a member of Parliament, or, in other words, universal suffrage; (2) that the United Kingdom be divided into 300 equal electoral districts; (3) that the voting should be by ballot; (4) that Parliament should only last a year; (5) that no qualification for membership should be required other than the choice of electors; and (6) lastly, that members of Parliament should be paid.

"The object of this Bill, according to the Address, was to cause the radicals of the kingdom to form a concentration of their principles in a practical form, upon which they could be brought to unite, and to which they might point *as a charter they are determined to obtain.*"[1]

Lovett adds that "The People's Charter" "excited among the industrious classes a more extended and united public opinion in its favour than perhaps any other political document that has issued from the Press." And that, after its publication, the majority of all of the conflicting parties for different reforms gave up their separate hobbies, and decided on contending for it as the first effectual step towards all political and social improvement.

The Birmingham Political Union also made a move forward at this time. After many meetings of the Council of the Union a public meeting was held in the Town Hall on the 14th May 1838, when, after many speeches, certain important resolutions were adopted. The first decided on the appointment of seven delegates to proceed to Glasgow, where a great demonstration was being organised.

It was further resolved to present to Parliament a National Petition, which was read to the meeting. *Five* points were set forth in it—not "*six* points," as in the Charter—"equal electoral districts" not being in it.

The Petition had been drafted by the Council some short time before the Charter was published. The two documents came from independent sources, and the difference among historical writers as to the "*five* points" and the "*six* points"

[1] See "Address from Working-men's Association."—Lovett's *Life*, p. 169.

of the Charter is thus explained; some speaking of Chartism as defined by the National Petition, others as defined by "The People's Charter."

The Petition humbly showed "That we, your petitioners, dwell in a land whose merchants are noted for their enterprise, whose manufacturers are very skilful, and whose workmen are proverbial for their industry. The land itself is goodly, the soil rich, and the temperature wholesome. It is abundantly furnished with the materials of commerce and trade; it has numerous and convenient harbours; in facility of internal communication it exceeds all others. For three and twenty years we have enjoyed a profound peace. Yet, with all these elements of national prosperity, and with every disposition and capacity to take advantage of them, we find ourselves overwhelmed with public and private suffering. We are bowed down under a load of taxes; our traders are trembling on the verge of bankruptcy; our workmen are starving; capital brings no profit, and labour no remuneration; the home of the artificer is desolate, and the warehouse of the pawnbroker is full; the workhouse is crowded, and the manufactory is deserted. We have looked on every side, we have searched diligently, in order to find out the causes of a distress so sore and so long continued. We can discover none in nature or in Providence. Heaven has dealt graciously by the people; but the foolishness of our rulers has made the goodness of God of none effect. . . . The few have governed for the interest of the few, while the interests of the many have been sottishly neglected, or insolently and tyrannously trampled upon.

"It was the fond expectation of the people that a remedy for the greater part, if not for the whole, of their grievances, would be found in the Reform Act of 1832. They were taught to regard that Act as a wise means to a worthy end; as the machinery of an improved legislation, where the will of the masses would be at length potential. They have been bitterly and basely deceived. The fruit which looked so fair to the eye has turned to dust and ashes when gathered. The Reform Act has effected a transfer of power from one domineering faction to another, and left the people as helpless as before. . . .

"We come before your honourable House to tell you, with

all humility, that this state of things must not be permitted to continue; that it cannot long continue without seriously endangering the stability of the throne, and the peace of the kingdom; and that if, by God's help, and all lawful and constitutional appliances, an end can be put to it, we are fully resolved that it shall speedily come to an end. . . .

"We perform the duties of freemen; we must have the privileges of freemen. We demand Universal Suffrage. . . . We demand the Ballot. . . . We demand Annual Parliaments. . . . Universal suffrage will, and it alone can, bring true and lasting peace to the nation. We firmly believe that it will also bring prosperity.

"May it therefore please your honourable House to take this our Petition into your most serious consideration, and to use your utmost endeavours, by all constitutional means, to have a law passed, granting to every male of lawful age, sane mind, and unconvicted of crime, the right of voting for members of Parliament; and directing all future elections of members of Parliament to be in the way of secret ballot, and ordaining that the duration of Parliament so chosen shall in no case exceed one year, and abolishing all property qualifications in the members, and providing for their due remuneration while in attendance on their Parliamentary duties."[1]

Another idea which originated with the Birmingham Political Union was that of a National or General Convention. It was proposed that forty-nine of the largest towns should elect or appoint by public meeting, delegates who should meet in London, and take charge of the National Petition and arrange for its presentation to Parliament; and it was evidently expected that the body thus formed should become a people's Parliament, which should make its influence powerfully felt in the Legislature.

On the morning of the 21st of May (1838) the deputation which had been appointed in Birmingham to proceed to Glasgow reached the neighbourhood of that town. At the Toll Cross an arch had been erected, decked with evergreens, and with a motto on it—"Moral force will emancipate the world." A little farther they were met by a procession of reformers, and were escorted to the place of the meeting, "accompanied

[1] Place, MSS., 27,820, p. 374.

on both sides by thousands of spectators with deafening cheers."

"It was computed," says Gammage, "that not less than 200,000 of the stalwart sons of labour displayed their toil-worn faces in the gigantic gathering."[1] "The upturned faces when seen from the hustings was a most surprising and beautiful sight, causing the most solemn feelings."[2]

"The meeting was wholly composed of working men. Not a solitary member of what are called the respectables of the high middle class, with the exception of the chairman, took part in the proceedings." After a few sentences from the chairman, a Mr. Gillespie spoke. He said: "This is a great, a grand, a glorious day. That heart must be cold, indeed, which would not be raised into enthusiasm at the sight before me. No tyrant king spreads his banners before them to lead them to the field of slaughter. No political priest stains his sacerdotal robes by going forth with the Bible in one hand, and the sword in the other, leading on the infatuated people to the commission of murder. Justice and Mercy are emblazoned on our shields, law, order, and loyalty, and unanimity, on our banners. They had assembled to demand those rights which they believed Heaven had granted them, but man withheld from them."

Several resolutions were passed. One "That the Reform Bills having failed to realise the reasonable expectations of the people, it has become necessary for the masses again to exert their power in procuring those political rights, and that voice in the election of representatives which is the inalienable inheritance of Britons, and which can alone secure a fair remuneration for labour and the peaceable possession of property."[3] Resolutions were also passed in favour of the ballot, payment of members, for the repeal of the Corn Laws, and of commercial restrictions, and for the adoption of the National Petition; and it was also decided that a delegate be appointed to proceed to London to act in concert with those deputies from other parts of the country who might be appointed for similar purposes.

Attwood made a long speech: "Men of Glasgow," he said,

[1] Gammage, p. 27. [2] See the report of the *Birmingham Journal*.
[3] Place, MSS., 27,820, p. 111.

"unconquered men of Scotland, I come amongst you from the heart of England. I bring with me the blessings of your English countrymen, their expression of deep sympathy for your sufferings and wrongs, and the expression of their firm determination to unite with you in obtaining relief from those sufferings and redress for those wrongs, and in restoring the prosperity and vindicating the liberty of our common country. . . .

"I am reproached with being an agitator. I have never agitated but for the good of my countrymen. It was the cries, the misery of my countrymen, that made me an agitator. . . .

"Follow up the proceedings so well commenced to-day by sending a delegate to London. I know that there are forty-eight other towns which will do the same; and when those delegates are assembled in London, and backed by the Petition of 2,000,000 of men, I should like to see the House of Commons which would set them at defiance. (Thunders of applause.) But if they should be mad enough to despise your Petition, then I would have you to proclaim a solemn, sacred, universal strike, not of masters against men, not of men against masters, but of all together against the common enemy. Your cause is just and righteous and holy. You have only to cling fast to it in order to achieve victory." [1]

Several other speakers followed. Edmonds from Birmingham said: "You are now, for the first time, invited to co-operate with Englishmen for the common benefit of both countries, and more especially for yourselves—the working classes." He approved of the motto "Moral Force," but at the same time he would assure them "that unless the Physical Force was not called into action with the moral demonstration of public opinion, the moral would have no weight without the physical power. The truth was the Moral was the Shadow, the Physical was the Substance."

Dr. Wade, a deputy from the Working-men's Association of London, and "a minister of the Church of England," presented the Charter to the meeting, and recommended its "six points," and union with perseverance as the means of obtaining them.

[1] Place comments on this proposal: "Mr. Attwood is a sad example of this want of power to reason, of dull, besotted muddleheadedness, yet he was not alone among his associates."

The deputation did not confine their operations to Glasgow, but proceeded to other towns in Scotland. The next day a great meeting for the county of Renfrew was held at Elderslie—the native place of Sir William Wallace—and a delegate was elected to attend the proposed Convention. Part of the deputation then proceeded to Kilmarnock, where a large meeting was held on the 30th May, then to Stirling, Perth, and Dundee; part went to meetings at Cupar, Fife, and Dunfermline. Banquets and soirées were also given in their honour. At all of these meetings, resolutions, similar to those at Glasgow, were adopted, and the Petition was put in course of signature. When the deputation got back to Birmingham, a public reception was given them, and speeches were made, describing their successful tour in Scotland.

On the 27th of June the men of the Tyne and Wear held a meeting on Town Moor of Newcastle—"One of the most magnificent arrays of moral and physical power ever exhibited by the masses of this country." The chair was taken about midday by Mr. Doubleday—"a veteran champion of democracy"; "the Moor presented what the foes of progress would denominate a truly awful appearance,"—some 80,000 persons, it was estimated, being present. Amongst the speakers was a working man named Ayr. As Gammage regarded his speech as "one of the best specimens of the working class oratory of that period," an extract from it may be given. Ayr said: "He was proud of the thousands which they had banded together this day, to worship at the altar of freedom. The sword of oppression hung over them, but if need should be, they would draw the sword of justice, and never return it to the scabbard till justice should be done to the wronged and outraged people of England. . . .

"He would advert to a portion of the resolution which he held in his hands; it declared that they would use every means, not every legal means, mark, but every means for the attainment of universal suffrage. He could not help again alluding to the monarchy; hitherto they had reigned for themselves, but he declared before that vast assembly, and in its name, that if it did not reign for the good of the millions it should not reign at all. The famishing and the helpless, the widow and the orphan, future generations were looking up to them for support, and should they look in vain? The interests of working men were everywhere the same, and the oppressors would find that working men were about to be everywhere united. Knowledge was power, and union was strength, and in the diffusion of knowledge that was now spreading around, and in the union that had now sprung up among the people, he foresaw, and that too at no distant period, the downfall of aristocracy all over the world."[1]

At Sunderland a large meeting took place. One speaker, referring to their co-operation with the middle classes for Parliamentary reform, said: "They had been deceived, basely deserted, but they now stood forward again in their own might and majesty, and again they would triumph." O'Connor spoke at it, and said: "I would rather die a freeman than live a slave. When the Constitution of my country tells me I have a right to carry arms, my own wisdom tells me when I ought to use them—these are not my maxims but those of the greatest statesmen. Should I fall there will be others to supply my place."

At Nottingham there was a great demonstration on the 31st July; and at Northampton a series of meetings were held early in August; and then, on the 6th August, a great meeting was held at Birmingham for the purpose of selecting eight delegates to the proposed Convention. Some 200,000 persons, according to Chartist accounts, were present. Attwood, in the course of a very long speech,[2] suggested a national strike for a week. "Suppose the delegates in Convention should command a sacred week, when no plough or shuttle should move, no anvil sound throughout Great Britain—a sacred week during which every man should cease from labour. In that great week we will do no work until we have first done the work of the nation. Let there be a proper union and agreement amongst the people, and then, if there should be occasion for it, the forty-nine delegates would have but to stamp with their feet upon the ground, and 2,000,000 of men will answer the call, and if that will not do, 5,000,000 of men will repeat it. But there will

[1] Gammage, p. 32.

[2] "His speech, as reported in the *Birmingham Journal*, occupies by measurement a column of close printing 2¾ inches wide and 21 feet long."—Place, MSS., 27,820, p. 172.

be no occasion for it. We shall have all we want without having recourse to it. If we are forced to it, then I say let the enemies of the people take the consequences." [1] He praised the people, and promised them the reward of their perseverance, and said: "That if the Government dared to arrest him in the execution of his peaceful purpose, 100,000 men would march to demand his release."

Feargus O'Connor also spoke, and made a violent speech: "When he saw the wealth, the strength, the power, and the virtue of the people before him, he recognised the meeting as the signing, sealing, and delivering of the great moral covenant this day entered into by the people."

"He went on," says Place, "with his usual volubility, looseness, and inconsiderateness. He deprecated all agitation for the 'Corn Laws,' as he did 'every other crotchet.' He appeared before them as the representative of 3,000,000 of determined minds and stalwart arms. There was not a man amongst them who was not satisfied to trust the moral power of the nation, even to down-bending, even to submission, even to a fawning pliability for expediency. They were ready to do this rather than to rush into any maddening conflict. They might be sure that the man who was for marshalling physical force would be the first to desert it whenever it was in reality resorted to, still he would not be understood to imply that he was contented to live a slave.

> "No! come he slow or come he fast,
> It is but death that comes at last.

But when the moral strength was expended, and the mind drawn out at last, then, as Mr. Attwood had said, if wrong should come from any party, cursed be that man who refused to repel force by force. He had travelled over 2000 miles in the last six months. He had seen the soldiers intrude upon the meetings of the people, whom, every one of them, as if prepared for better days, stood unawed. He had told the soldiers that if they were going to begin the work of carnage, to give him time to muster his battalions, and if 2,000,000 were not sufficient, 5,000,000 would stand up to do them justice."

[1] Place, MSS., 27,820, p. 173.

The comments on this speech are interesting; they show the rift which was afterwards to widen into a split that was fatal to the Chartist agitation. "It may," wrote William Lovett, "be said to be the first *Chartist meeting* at which O'Connor introduced his physical force notions, or rather his Irish braggadocio about arming and fighting, for to fight himself formed no part of his patriotism."

"Such indiscretion," wrote Gammage,[1] "was laying the foundation of a schism which could only be productive of the most fatal consequences to the success of the movement;" but, as if in extenuation of the fault, he adds: "The strongest language was at that time the most popular."

Place, commenting generally on the meeting, says: "From the speeches made, it may be safely concluded that all of the speakers were fully persuaded that the six points of the Charter would be extorted from the Government early in the session."

On the 17th September the first public meeting of the Chartists in London was held at the Palace Yard, Westminster. It was presided over by the High Bailiff, and it was estimated that some 10,000 to 15,000 people were present. Resolutions were proposed and passed in favour of the Charter and of the National Petition, and the people of the United Kingdom were recommended to hold meetings and appoint deputations to their representatives to support and vote for the People's Charter and the National Petition.

Eight persons were appointed "to unite with the delegates that may be selected by other meetings to watch over the Charter and Petition when they are presented to Parliament." Lovett opened the proceedings. He said: "In order that there may be no mistake as regards the object of this meeting, I have been requested, on the part of the Working-men's Association, to say that whatever speculative opinions we may entertain, they form no part of our present agitation. We mean what we say when we declare that the People's Charter contains a full measure of political justice, which would give to the people the means of redressing all wrongs, and that, with God's help, we mean to obtain it. The National Petition embraces all the objects and the same principles of just

[1] Gammage, p. 51.

representation as 'the Charter,' and having already been hallowed by the approbation of hundreds of thousands of signatures will, I trust, be respected by this assembly."

Ebenezer Elliot, afterwards known to fame as the Corn Law rhymer, also spoke. He said: "Your enemies tell you that meetings like this mean nothing. But I tell them that when people cheerfully pay out of their poverty for such meetings as this, they mean a great deal; for they mean that the people are in earnest; and when nations are in earnest they get their rights. You are told too, by many of your friends, that you should not now agitate for the franchise. Why not? Because for want of it you have been robbed of everything. A strange argument. But that you may agitate for it and obtain it, I wish to convince you of two things—that you can obtain it if you will, and that if you do not speedily obtain it, taxation will drive your trade to other countries, and you will find yourselves in the streets, without wages, without food, and without the possibility of obtaining either, unless you devour first your oppressors, and then perhaps each other. . . . Let no other object divert your attention from the franchise which contains all good objects, as the acorn carries within itself the oak and his fortunes."

The most interesting speech was that of Mr. J. T. Leader, one of the members for Westminster. "The sight before him was glorious. It was a vast assemblage of working men, met to consider what were their rights, and to determine, by every legal means, to gain the moral influence in the country which would enable them to assert and to maintain them.

"In former times, when many thousands of people were called together, the meetings were convened by a few leading men, not of the working classes, who spoke to the masses for the purpose of inducing them to aid any purpose of their own, and what was the consequence? This, the passions of the people were appealed to, and the leaders having thus gained the notoriety they sought, they deserted the people they had deluded. The people must trust to themselves. Every man amongst them had cause to reason and judge for himself, and ought not to let his judgment be blinded by others. This meeting was called by working men; it had been addressed by working men; they did not speak to the passions of their hearers; they gave reasons, and used arguments, quite as well as was done in the House over the way; yet we are told the people ought not to have the franchise; they are by far too ignorant and don't know how to use it. For my part, I never heard better arguments, nor the English language better spoken than to-day. Such being the case, I recommend the working people to look to themselves, and to themselves alone. I look upon this meeting and the agitation out of which it grew as a great step in a grand moral struggle. They must go on in this way; it was agreed that this was a grand moral struggle in which they would succeed." He proceeded to give some wholesome and helpful counsel.

"They were engaged in no child's play. They had not undertaken an easy task. Let them all, in their efforts, bear in mind that it was by reason, by argument, by obtaining that moral influence which the masses must obtain, that they could eventually succeed in all things. By at all times opposing violent counsels, by setting their faces against violent language, and refusing to participate in violent deeds, they would find safety and the best means of success."

"The speech," said Gammage, "fell but coldly" upon the great body of the meeting, but the people were soon restored to their element by a speech from O'Connor, and a stronger incitement to physical force from one Richardson, of Manchester, who stated that "if the National Petition should fail, he could not attempt to say what would be the consequence. Rifles would be loaded; that would be the next step, no doubt, and he defied the power of any Government or any armed Bourbon police to put them down."

Place, commenting on this meeting, wrote that it was a very remarkable one.[1] "Very remarkable, as showing the ardent state of feeling of the working people to an extent never before witnessed in Westminster. Few, indeed, of the middle class took part in these meetings anywhere, Birmingham alone excepted."

He comments on the cost many of the working men must have been subject to, coming from far parts of the country to attend it, and as regards the speeches he remarks that: "It

[1] Place, MSS., 27,820, p. 210.

may be as truly said that the speeches would bear comparison with those made at public meetings by their betters."

The meeting at Westminster was speedily followed by other large meetings at Bath, Sheffield, and Liverpool, "where O'Connor gave a loose to his tongue."

On the 24th September 1838 a great meeting of the radicals of Manchester and its environs was held on Kersal Moor. It was said that some 200,000 or 300,000 persons were at it, with 20 bands and 200 banners, one banner with a picture of the Peterloo Massacre, and the words "Murder demands justice."

Gammage, in his description of this meeting, says: "stern were the countenances of the men in that vast assemblage. Their haggard emaciated features bore evidence of suffering, and were more than sufficient to excuse their wrath at the conduct of their oppressors."

Mr. John Fielden, M.P., presided. Stephens and O'Connor were the principal speakers. This was the exordium of Stephens's speech: "I ask to-day, with such a sight before me as the world never before beheld—I ask what is it that makes this mighty movement of the masses of the people of England? What was it that has shaken England herself to her very centre, and brought her laborious, industrious, peaceable, loyal, united, determined sons to this great, this glorious gathering? I ask what means this mighty movement. There must be something greatly wrong which these hundreds of thousands have come here to right, or to have righted for them."

It was a most pertinent question; it was a true answer. There was something greatly wrong, many things greatly wrong, but he and the orators of his sort were scarcely the men to set things right.

In this same speech he gave an explanation—which is most instructive—of what he meant by the term Universal Suffrage: "If any man asked him what he meant by universal suffrage he would tell him. He meant to say that every working man in the land had a right to a good coat on his back, a good hat upon his head, a good roof for the shelter of his household, a good dinner upon his table, no more work than would keep him in health whilst at it, and as much wages as would keep him in plenty, and in all the enjoyment of all the pleasures of life which a reasonable man could desire."

He concluded thus: "I will only say, before I withdraw from your notice, that in beholding this mighty mass of living, moving, ethereal spirit, in beholding this sea of heads, this ocean of intellectual patriotism, of religious determination, in beholding this great gathering—the mighty mustering of the manhood and womanhood and childhood of Lancashire—I have in my hand, or rather your chairman has in his hand, a fulcrum on which he shall place the lever to move every mountain of oppression and opposition which has hitherto stood between you and your object. I will continue to support the resolution (adopting the Charter) in the manner in which you have heard me support it—mind and soul, heart and arms—as far as I can, and as you can with me. We will carry the People's Charter." [1]

Gammage bears testimony to the deep enthusiasm of those present. He says: "Notwithstanding that, during the latter period of the meeting, the rain poured in torrents, it seemed to produce no impression on that enthusiastic and excited throng. The dense mass seemed welded together, and were so intent on their object, that nothing could turn them aside from the path they had chosen. The meeting was peaceable in the extreme, and at its conclusion no religious assembly could have dispersed in a more orderly manner."

These are specimens, examples, or illustrations of the Platform at this period. They leave a pitiable picture in one's memory—these meetings of hard-working, or would-be hard-working men—the bone and sinew of the land—sunk in poverty and ignorance, seeking relief, groping, as it were, for counsel, crying, as Carlyle so well expresses it, "Guide me, govern me, I am mad and miserable, and cannot guide myself"; and in reply, getting only such evil counsel as that given in the speech above quoted—only such, for in the upper sphere of society, or in Parliament, scarce one was found who would stoop so far as to endeavour to counteract such teaching except by force.

It would be impossible to enumerate the meetings which took place about this time; the Chartist newspapers of the time are full of reports of them. In nearly every part of the country, where there were working men of the industrial

[1] Place, MSS., 27,820, p. 226.

classes they were held, and Wales and Scotland joined in the agitation.

A meeting of some exceptional interest was held on the 25th September at Sheffield. Ebenezer Elliot, the Corn Law rhymer, was chairman. He wound up his speech with the following question and answer: "Will your enemies help you? From the time of the first murderer they have been what they are; they poisoned Socrates; they crucified Jesus; and do you think they will help you? No, no; you must help yourselves."

One of the speakers, a Mr. Ironside, made a very interesting speech, too long to quote more than its peroration. "In conclusion," he said, "allow me to give you a little advice. Be clean, be temperate; by these you will add much to your comfort, much to your happiness. You will become more thoughtful and inquiring, and consequently better acquainted with your social and political condition. You will soon become more powerful than mere numbers can ever make you. Brute force may be overpowered, but mind cannot.

"Fixed on the eternal and immutable pillars of truth, high and majestic it raises its head, like the Himalaya Mountains; it bids defiance to the contending storms that assail it on every side, fruitlessly exhausting their fury upon it. For a time the clouds of ignorance may hide it from view; anon its outline will be shadowed forth through the mists that envelop it; suddenly it breaks into full light, looking lovelier than before, rejoicing in its strength, its pristine splendour, its surpassing beauty, its stupendous majesty, and with a single glance withering the paltry arguments of the self-styled 'rational and practical reformers.'"

Place gives a long account of this meeting "for the purpose of showing what might in time be expected from the working people, if uninfluenced by the travelling demagogues, who were crazy as Beaumont and O'Brien, or had sinister interests to promote, as they and O'Connor had, or the Birmingham men (meaning Attwood and his friends). . . . The men of Sheffield were left to themselves. . . . The speakers, one and all, showed that they were unacquainted with the leading principles of political economy, or even so much of the science as related to profit and wages; and they, therefore, believed it was in the power of the Government to cause constant employment at good wages to every working man and woman in the country at all times and for ever. . . . The conduct of the people was good, as it always is when they are left to work in their own way for any proper purpose. Scarcely have they ever deviated from the right course unless when led astray by their betters, or interrupted by power.

"The speakers were all fluent men; their speeches were quite as much to the purpose as those of their betters usually are, and better than they sometimes are even amongst men who are supposed to be 'educated.' . . .

"The whole of what passed at the meeting, the manner in which the business was conducted, the speeches—all may be taken as proofs of the advance the working people have made in knowledge, and as indications of the much greater progress they will make. These are all new things, and when the men of the present day are compared with the men of half a century, or even a quarter of a century ago, are all but wonderful. Their improvement has been mainly the work of themselves, and is, therefore, the more creditable to them; it might by judicious means be rapidly increased and widely extended, but this would require assistance not likely to be given.

"The aristocracy fear the spread of information amongst the masses. This has been shown in their public acts. It has been expressed to me over and over again many times without the least disguise and in many ways. . . . Assistance to promote schools (for the children of tradesmen and persons of small income) was refused on the grounds that 'the lower orders' ought not to receive the education of gentlemen. The contemptuous manner in which not only the working class, but the tradesmen class, are usually spoken of by the upper class, and those who ape them, and the words *lower classes*, as applied to them, have lessened the respect paid to the aristocracy more, perhaps, than any other single thing whatever."[1]

On previous occasions, under the tithe of such provocation as these meetings afforded, or of such alarm as they created, the Government had almost instantaneously applied to Parliament for extra powers involving the suppression of public meetings, and even the suspension of the Habeas Corpus Act.

[1] Place, MSS., 27,820, p. 247.

Times, however, had changed. The Reform Act had been passed, and now the Government acted on very different lines; but it was a very different Government and a very different House of Commons from those of 1817–19. Curiously enough too the first declaration of the new policy of the Government was made from the Platform. Lord John Russell, the Home Secretary, dined, on the 3d of October, with the Mayor of Liverpool. It was only a semi-public dinner, but the speech he made at it found its way into the papers. He is reported to have said: "He would not, before such a party, wander into the field of politics; but there was one topic, connected with his own department, upon which he might be allowed to dwell for a few moments.

"He alluded to the public meetings which were now in the course of being held in various parts of the country. There were some, perhaps, who would put down such meetings. But such was not his opinion, nor that of the Government with which he acted. He thought the people had a right to free discussion. It was free discussion which elicited truth. They had a right to meet. If they had grievances, they had a right to declare them, that they might be known and redressed. If they had no grievances, common sense would speedily come to the rescue, and put an end to those meetings.

"It was not from free discussion, it was not from the unchecked declaration of public opinion that governments had anything to fear; there was fear when men were driven by force to secret combinations; there was the fear, there was the danger, and not in free discussion."[1]

How great a difference from the system of government in 1817–19, and the still remoter period of 1792–1801.

This being the policy of the Government, the meetings went on unchecked; but signs of division among the Chartists themselves began to be disclosed. Lovett points this out. He says: "The Charter was rapidly enlisting converts, and earnest supporters, when a few mad advisers, by furious appeals to the passions of the multitude, stirred up the demons of hate, prejudice, and discord, to obstruct its onward progress." And Gammage says: "The bone of contention was the nature of the means to be employed for the attainment of

[1] *The Liverpool Albion*, 8th October 1838.

their common object, for upon the object itself there were no visible signs of disunion. The cause of the Charter was espoused by advocates of two different schools. The first consisted of those who contended that the people's rights must be secured by moral means alone. The other was composed of the more determined, who could not conceive that the ruling classes would bow to anything short of physical force, and who generally made use of threats in the course of their various speeches. . . . Anything more unfortunate than this division could scarcely have occurred." [1]

During this month of October a large number of meetings were held, and the tide of Platform oratory flowed rapidly. On the 18th "there was a prodigious meeting on Hartshead Moor, near Bradford." There was a very large attendance, estimates varied from 30,000 to 300,000. The speeches were violent in their tone. "What was it that gained the independence of America? It was common sense and American rifles," said one speaker. "If ever the people of England mean to obtain their independence, if ever they calculate upon uprooting the tyranny which now depresses their industry, they too will have to provide themselves with rifles."

And now, as the autumn evenings grew longer, and the people could ill spare a day's wages for the sake of attending a meeting, they took to holding their meetings at night by torchlight. The first of these meetings was held on the 29th October at Bolton. "Rings were formed in the marketplace of torch-bearers, which, at a distance, had the appearance of immense circular fires, producing a novel, picturesque, sublime, and beautiful appearance."

Gammage gives a graphic description of these torchlight meetings. He says: "In the autumn of 1838 the meetings began to assume a formidable character." "For a short period the factory districts presented a series of imposing popular demonstrations. . . . It is almost impossible to imagine the excitement caused by these manifestations. To form an adequate idea of the public feeling, it was necessary to be an eyewitness of the proceedings. The people did not go isolated to the place of meeting, but met in a body at a starting-point, from whence, at a given time, they issued in huge numbers,

[1] Gammage, p. 93.

formed into procession, traversing the principal streets, making the heavens echo with the thunder of their cheers on recognising the idols of their worship, and sending forth volleys of the most hideous groans on passing the office of some hostile newspaper, or the house of some obnoxious magistrate or employer. The banners containing the more formidable devices, viewed by the red light of the glaring torches, presented a scene of awful grandeur. The death's-heads represented on some of them grinned like ghostly spectres. The uncouth appearance of thousands of artisans, who had not time from leaving the factory to go home and attend to the ordinary rules of cleanliness, and whose faces were therefore begrimed with sweat and dirt, added to the strange aspect of the scene. The processions were frequently of immense length, sometimes containing as many as 50,000 people; and along the whole line there blazed a stream of light illuminating the lofty sky, like the reflection from a large city in a general conflagration. The meetings themselves were of a still more terrific character. The very appearance of such a vast number of blazing torches only seemed more effectually to inflame the minds alike of speakers and hearers. O'Connor, Stephens, and M'Douall were frequent attendants at these meetings, and their language was almost unrestrained by any motive of prudence. Incitements to the use of arms formed the staple of the speeches of the two latter. . . . Stephens did not hesitate to declare that the ruling classes were nothing better than a gang of murderers whose blood was required to satisfy the demands of public justice."

Encouraged by impunity, the language of some of the Chartists became more violent. On the 5th of November a meeting was held at Norwich—"The people," it was remarked, "came forward for the first time on their own account in joyful thousands to lift up their voices in concert with their brethren of the North, in demanding their just rights." Stephens was present, and made a violent speech: "These poor men have children who are dear to them, and they say to themselves there is no chance that things will be better; let us strike the blow even though we lose our lives. . . . I tell the men of Norwich, the great towns of the north are not worth twelve months purchase—twelve months purchase did I say, not more than twenty-four hours purchase. England stands on a mine; a volcano is beneath her; you may dance on it; you may pluck the flowers from its surface, but it only sleeps. The train is laid, the match is lighted, and unless the distress and misery of the poor be met by good feeling and speedy remedy, no man can tell what a day, what an hour may bring forth. . . . Hitherto the people have been held in leash; they can be held back no longer; they must be slipped."

He proceeded to recommend an appeal to arms in a most atrocious way: "No Government can, and no Government shall exist in this country that will not repeal the new Poor Law Amendment Act. We will give ourselves no further trouble about it; we will never ask it again, but we will have it; for husband and wife God has joined together, and neither men, nor devils, shall put them asunder. Men of Norwich, fight with your swords, fight with pistols, fight with daggers, fight with your torches. Women, fight with your nails and your teeth; nothing else will do; every English husband will fight to the death for the wife of his bosom, and every English father will fight till he dies for his children. Mothers will not be behind. Husbands and wives, brothers and sisters, will war to the knife; so help me God."

On the 5th of November a meeting was held at Preston. At this meeting one of the delegates to the approaching National Convention spoke and said, referring to the Government of the Whigs: "I hope we shall soon get rid of them all. I hope the time will come when we shall string their heads up on the scaffold."

At a dinner at Manchester on 6th November, in celebration of the birthday of Henry Hunt, who had died in 1835, O'Connor delivered a fulsome eulogy on him,—"A man on whom no particle of praise could be honestly bestowed," says Place. His speech is notable as an effort to fix a time for the accomplishment of the Chartist objects: "Now was the time for universal suffrage—the nation demanded it, justice required it, and God would grant it. Let them fix a period to the existence of suffering. Let them say they would receive all moral instruction to prepare and fit them for it—to prepare themselves for the exercise of the right till the 29th September next; and let them tell the moral philosophers that unless it was given them on the 29th, they would give them Michaelmas goose on the 30th."

On the 8th of December a mill was burnt down at Ashton-under-Lyne, the result of incendiarism, and direct incitement by Stephens. On the same night a torchlight meeting was held at Bury, in defiance of a notice from the magistrates pointing out its illegality, several thousand persons being at it—Stephens, Feargus O'Connor, and others making violent and inflammatory speeches.

At a meeting at Rochdale, F. O'Connor is reported to have said: "He had preached peace all his life, but at the same time he was always prepared for war. One of those torches (pointing to one near him) was worth a thousand speeches. It spoke a language so intelligible that no man could misunderstand." And he told his hearers "That they would be justified in taking those torches and burning down the inhuman Bastiles."

Meetings of the character of these torchlight gatherings were plainly passing beyond the purposes of discussion and petitioning, and were becoming mere demonstrations of physical force. The Government, while determined not to interfere with the former, could not with safety permit the latter, and on the 12th of December they issued a proclamation against meetings by torchlight.

"Whereas great numbers of evil-disposed and disorderly persons," said the Proclamation, "have lately in some parts of Great Britain assembled themselves together after sunset, by torchlight, in large bodies, and in a tumultuous manner, with banners, flags, and other ensigns, and have continued so assembled until a late hour of the night, and by loud shouts and noises, and by the discharge of firearms, and the display of weapons of offence, greatly alarmed the inhabitants of the neighbourhood of such assemblies, and endangered the public peace, etc. We do hereby warn and command all persons to desist from such assemblies at their peril, and do further command all justices, constables, etc., to use their utmost endeavour to prevent all such illegal assemblies, and to bring the offenders to justice."

"To say that the appearance of the proclamation was the cause of great excitement," wrote Gammage,[1] "were to convey

[1] Gammage, p. 108.

a very inadequate idea of the state of popular feeling. That feeling had been worked up to such a feverish state that a sort of delirium now seized upon the people, and thousands expressed their determination to trample the proclamation under foot and set the Government at defiance." They did not, however, do so, and the torchlight meetings were virtually abandoned.

On the 27th December the Government took a farther step, and Stephens was arrested. The charge against him was that he told the people "that to destroy a Poor Law guardian was doing God service," and that his language applied to several gentlemen named. He was committed to Liverpool Jail to take his trial on a charge of misdemeanour, but was allowed out on bail. A witness described the meeting where he had thus spoken. It was at Leigh. Between 2000 and 3000 persons were at it. They commenced assembling at about nine o'clock in the morning. Stephens arrived at twelve. There was a cart for hustings, and Mr. Stephens spoke from it for two hours and thirty-five minutes—for how much longer is not known, as the witness to this fact then went away."

Another sentence in his speech ran as follows: "What I mean to say is this: God has perhaps raised up you to fire down those buildings (alluding to the houses round about), and perhaps even that venerable church which our forefathers have erected."

"The agitation caused by the apprehension of Mr. Stephens was very remarkable. The whole body of radicals felt it, and in Manchester and its environs great apprehensions were entertained of fearful riotings and extensive mischief. All the Associations called meetings, and vast numbers of people came to Manchester ready for mischief."[1] But nothing actually occurred. The blow struck by the Government had, however, considerable effect. It was a first warning to the Chartist orators that there were limits to the abuse of free speech.

In reviewing the speeches made at the Chartist meetings so far, and in endeavouring to obtain a clear view of the action of the Platform throughout this period, it appears that the speeches made fall, roughly, into three classes or categories. The first—speeches of unknown, ill-educated, ignorant men,

[1] Place, MSS., 27,820, p. 360.

describing with much difficulty of utterance the heart-moving, heart-breaking condition of themselves and thousands upon thousands of their fellow-workmen. The second—speeches from the more moderate and intelligent and better class of working men—men who, though advocates of even extreme reforms, such as universal suffrage, honestly urged the people to a pacific line of conduct. "Meet and petition—meet and petition, until Parliament grants your requests." The third—speeches from professional peripatetic agitators, such as Feargus O'Connor, Stephens, and others who have been named; who, dazed with the facility with which revolutions had been made abroad, applied the same standard to Great Britain, and, totally devoid of any idea of the vast centralised disciplined power of the executive, or the measureless, though passive, reserves of force at its back, lashed themselves into ever greater fury, and encouraged in ever more decided and outspoken terms an appeal to physical force.

There were no speeches from men who might have led the people into right paths—no speeches controverting the thousand ridiculous assertions made by the most feather-headed of the Chartist orators—so far everything spoken was on one side.

"It is melancholy," says a contemporary writer,[1] "to contrast the present demonstrations with the conduct of the working classes in 1830; then what different leaders, what different opinions, what practical sense, what tempered firmness. Who could suppose that in 1838 the schoolmasters had given place to the Cades? who could suppose that the multitude, who profess to be so sharpsighted, could be blind to what every one else sees—the sordid and mendicant ambition of the Massaniellos they have chosen? . . .

"We are not among those who would limit political power to the boundary of the middle class. We are not among those who think that the Government of the multitude is dangerous in itself. The condition of the working classes, their prospects, their hopes, their welfare, must ever be vitally connected with the objects of an enlarged philosophy or generous statesmanship, and we do most deeply lament to see them at this time of day throwing themselves into the hands of men who are so evidently making the awful passions of the mass

[1] See *The Monthly Chronicle*, September 1838.

subservient to a mendicant ambition or a feverish vanity. What a different spectacle these meetings might have exhibited if a different spirit had pervaded them! How formidable would they have been, how vast a moral influence would have belonged to them, *if* their demands had been rational, and if their audience had imparted a loftier temper to the orators, if they had conciliated the fears they have now provoked, if they had indignantly scouted appeals to force and promises of plunder, if they had refused to be divided from other sections of their countrymen, and taken their stand as a people, not as a class. But now, while disowning and reviling all other superiority, they demand to be an aristocracy themselves—they and they alone must rule."

It is interesting to have another criticism on the Chartist meetings generally from another source, one which at first sight one might have anticipated would have been friendly.[1] The Chartists had sent an address to the Precursor Society in Ireland, which had been started by O'Connell, and they got an elaborate reply signed by him, in which the following passages occur:—"We are compelled by a sense of justice and a love of truth to reprobate in the strongest terms the mode in which many of your public meetings are conducted. We entirely disapprove of the language of intimidation and violence, the incitements to arms, the aspirations for revolution, the total contempt for the legal and constitutional bounds within which political agitation should be restrained, the sanguinary ferocity of your Oastlers, O'Connors, Stephenses, shouted for and responded to by the dupes of a useless and insane declamation. We not only abhor the illegal and criminal nature of such proceedings, but we are disgusted with their folly and fatuity. We ask you earnestly why you do not disclaim the men who thus wickedly and foolishly injure the cause of reform? They justly alarm all men of property, and throw against you the sagacious multitude of persons who have learned from history and experience the enormous mischiefs which result from tumultuous or sanguinary changes in the political state."

It was most deplorably unfortunate that the people had fallen into such hands as those of Feargus O'Connor, and

[1] See *The Examiner*, 9th December 1838.

some of the other men who have been named—unfortunate, indeed, that such men should have been allowed to seize on the Platform and hold possession of it to mislead the people. Men such as Harney,[1] who attended a meeting at Smithfield early in this same year, and appeared on the Platform, wearing a red cap of liberty, in imitation of the French revolutionists; he who wished to be considered the "Marat of the English Revolution," and who scrupled not to flourish his dagger at public meetings, in order to give point to his perorations.[2] Or even such men as Frost, who got, at least, as far as leading the thousands of the Welsh miners to the muzzles of the soldiers' guns at Newport, but disappeared after the first few shots had been fired, and as soon as he had learned that the matter was grim earnest, different somewhat from blatant braggadocio on the Platform.

Place, who was acquainted with all, or nearly all these men, has left us a whole gallery of portraits of them. "Vincent and Hartwell" he describes "as being desirous of a convulsion of any sort, in the hope that it might lead to a revolution. Vincent had a family taint of insanity which at times made him uncontrollably desirous of mischief. At other times he was mild and considerate and good-natured, and was generally liked by those who knew him. Hartwell was a cunning, ill-disposed man, an intriguing, undermining, reckless fellow, who at length became disliked and shunned by his fellows. . . . Hetherington was an honest man, with too little brains to guide him; one who always intended to do good, but seldom understood the way to accomplish his own wishes." Bronterre O'Brien he describes as "a three-parts insane and savage man." Stephens as a "malignant, crazy man, who never seemed exhausted with bawling atrocious matter."[3]

"This Mr. Stephens had been used to address the people, and to dogmatise as he pleased—had learned how to lead them at will. He spoke to their ignorance, he spoke to their prejudices, which he understood. He had won their hearts

[1] "Harney," says Place, "was a very young man; he had some time previously contrived to live by hawking unstamped newspapers about the streets, for which he had been committed to prison more than once. He was afterwards employed as shop-boy by Hetherington."—Place, MSS., 27,821, p. 5.

[2] Lovett, p. 203.

[3] Place, MSS., 27,821, p. 226.

wherever he had been. Before he took the active part in political meetings O'Connor was the general, the great mob orator; but Stephens soon became the superior in certain places containing a large number of people. He was now their idol to whom they bowed down, and had he desired to become the great leader of the working people of the North, and used but ordinary discretion, O'Connor would soon have been cast into the shade. A Government prosecution took him out of the field, and left O'Connor the unopposed and sole master of it."[1]

O'Connor, Place describes as "the most restless of them all, who, by his volubility, his recklessness of truth, his newspaper, his unparalleled impudence, and by means of the talkative mischievous (men), whom he either paid or combined with to enable to pay themselves, triumphed over every other agitator. His vanity could only be gratified, and his purse filled by the course he had taken, and as he was the best qualified, best constituted man amongst the leaders for his purpose, so he, in a short time, pushed aside all his competitors, and reigned lord paramount. . . . He seems never to have had any of the feeling denominated principle, and is utterly ignorant of every principle of political economy. He seems to be, and always to have been, governed by a most rancorous disposition towards every person, and body of persons, whose conduct does not at every moment conform to his notions; in other words, who does not at all times acknowledge him as his or their leader, and thus minister to his mischievous and absurd vanity.[2] He knew that he could only hold the people to himself by increasing the enmity between the working and all other classes of the people. This, therefore, he sedulously laboured at. He never seems to hesitate at denying anything he has said when it may suit his convenience to do so, saying it again, and denying it again, yet he has still (September 1841) the confidence of an immense number of people.[3]

"O'Connor's oratory," Place says, "was desultory, vague, shallow, wandering, misleading. Yet both the manner and the words of O'Connor are well adapted to the heterogeneous assemblages he addresses. His statements are put forward with all the confidence of a man who thoroughly understands

[1] Place, MSS., 27,820, p. 267. [2] *Ibid.* p. 3. [3] *Ibid.* 27,821, p. 20.

what he talks about. The air of mastership he puts on, the matter being in detached portions, and consequently compressed in short essays, his general earnestness and good-humour, tell well upon the unread and loose-thinking people, and constitute him the ablest mob orator of the day.[1]

"Multitudes of men, relying upon what he and others had told them at public meetings of the absolute power of themselves, whom they called the people, were satisfied that the whole body, or nearly the whole body, of the working people were fully prepared for action. They also believed that when O'Connor said, 'Universal Suffrage would be the law of the land on a certain day,' that it would be as he said; and with equal credulity and absurdity they now believed that Universal Suffrage would be the law of the land within three months from the meeting of the Convention. Ill-informed men as these were, and withal so credulous, were easily collected, kept together, and led in the very loose manner in which they were associated by the exhortations of their orators, and the matter with which they crammed them. . . .[2]

"So completely blinded were all the misleaders of the people by their own egotism, that they were fully persuaded the full measure of the reforms they demanded would, in a short time, be granted."

Though the principal leaders of the Chartists were actual or but thinly veiled advocates of physical force, now and then some of the speakers at the meetings would repudiate the idea of violence or force. In Birmingham Mr. Douglas and Mr. Muntz frequently reprobated it. At a great meeting, held at Colchester on the 17th November, one of the speakers said: "They say we contemplate plundering and bloodshedding, but we cast back the calumny with the utmost contempt on our slanderers. We tell them we are lovers of our fellowmen, and of the just rules of good society; that we abhor even the contemplation of plundering, and are incapable of contemplating murder. We want good government, peace, our rights, not bloodshed."

A more important announcement was made at a torchlight meeting held at Edinburgh to consider certain resolutions which had been agreed to by the delegates from the Radical

[1] Place, MSS., 27,820, p. 163. [2] *Ibid.* 27,821, p. 20.

Associations of Scotland. "These resolutions," said the chairman, "condemn in the strongest terms all appeals to physical force, and pledge us to renounce all connection and co-operation with those who make or approve of such appeals." They were readily adopted.

Lovett too protested against "the great injustice" of branding all the radicals of England as the abettors and followers of O'Connor, Stephens, and such men; but these protests were scarcely heard, or heeded amidst the louder and more vehement declarations of the leaders of the physical force party.

Before proceeding to an account of the doings of the Convention which by this time had been elected, reference must be made to a matter ignored as much and as long as possible by the Chartists, but destined, nevertheless, to affect most materially the future of Chartism.

In itself the division of the Chartists into two parties—physical force and moral force, which had already become so very apparent—would ultimately have sufficed to defeat the cause, but there was another far more subtle but more potent cause of defeat now beginning to rise into prominence—the movement for the repeal of the Corn Laws. The subject of the Corn Laws, and the agitation against them, will be treated of in a subsequent chapter, and it is undesirable to refer to them here more than is absolutely necessary; but this much it is necessary to point out here that the intrusion of the question of the Corn Laws into the politics of the day was the real turning-point in the Chartist agitation.

Up to this the people, left to their own devices, had fallen the prey to a set of noisy, more or less ignorant, violent, impracticable men, and, driven almost to despair by hardship and sufferings, had echoed and re-echoed the foolishness of the men who had imposed themselves on them as leaders. From this time on some of the wisest and most eloquent men in the nation were to take in hand the redress of that grievance which gave to the Chartist agitation much of the strength it possessed, and were gradually to wean large portions of the people from the more violent agitation.

It is difficult to fix any precise date for the entrance of the Anti-Corn-Law agitation into competition with Chartism. This much is certain, and is practically all that is wanted to be known here, that towards the latter part of the year 1838 the subject is noticed by some of the Chartists. Thus Lovett, writing of the Chartist meeting at Westminster in September 1838, said: "Another circumstance tending to create bad feeligs, disunion, distrust between the middle and working classes, was the proposed agitation against the Corn Laws;" some of the working classes believing "that the object aimed at was not so much the repeal of those unjust laws as it was to frustrate their agitation in favour of political reform."

At first the Chartists would not hear of any agitation for the repeal of the Corn Laws, though in the National Petition they had declared "That the laws which make food dear, and the laws which make money scarce, must be abolished." Their view was that, with a Parliament in which landlord interest predominated, to obtain a repeal of the Corn Laws was as difficult an undertaking as to obtain the "six points" of the Charter, and that the latter was far preferable, as securing them not only very promptly a repeal of the Corn Laws, but a repeal as well of all those other laws which pressed upon them, and made their existence so unendurable. They were, moreover, suspicious of the quarter from which the proposal came.

Gammage gives expression to this suspicion. He wrote: "As soon as the middle class manufacturers perceived that the people were in earnest in their movement for the suffrage, they strained every nerve to draw them aside from the pursuit of their object. They knew that the Charter meant an end to the reign of social monopoly, and they turned anti-monopolists themselves, but the only monopoly which engaged their attention was that of the landlords. They described the Corn Laws as the one great source of social misery of the working classes, and the repeal of those laws as the panacea for all their ills." [1]

"The bait did not, however, take so easily." The reasons given by various men amongst the Chartist body for not going with the League widely differed. With a very large number it was a detestation of the social tyranny exercised by the manufacturers which led them to believe that anything coming from such a quarter was not likely to be very favourable to their interests. Some, doubtless, were instigated by the fear that their own position in the popular favour might be endangered.

[1] Gammage, p. 112.

At Birmingham an agitation for the repeal of the Corn Laws was negatived by an overwhelming majority of Chartists, but at Sheffield the Chartists were defeated. Here, however, Ebenezer Elliot, himself a Chartist, sided with the Anti-Corn-Law people, remarking, "I am for your Charter, but I am not for your being starved to death first."

During December 1838 and January 1839 numerous Anti-Corn-Law meetings were broken up or disturbed by Chartists. Feargus O'Connor declared against them, as may be gathered from the following headings in his paper, *The Northern Star:* "Defeat of the Corn Law Repealers at Rochdale"; "Glorious Defeat of the Corn Law Repealers at Bradford"; "Anti-Corn-Law Agitation; Triumphant Defeat at Huddersfield of the Whigs."

When the Chartist Convention met, it passed a resolution, deprecating and opposing all agitation for the repeal of the Corn Laws until the fate of the National Petition and of the Charter had been determined by Parliament.

At the Anti-Corn-Law meetings many of the most respectable, wealthy, and intelligent men of the mercantile and manufacturing classes attended. And as it appeared to be by this time held that no agitation could be carried on without a central body or convention, delegates from the great manufacturing and commercial towns were sent to London, who were to form a body to watch over and direct the opposition to the Corn Laws.

Thus practically there were two Conventions sitting simultaneously—one of them demanding the complete abolition of the Corn Laws, the other demanding universal suffrage, annual Parliaments, and a good many other things besides; and one cannot help casting one's mind back to the period, scarce half a century previously, when the mere idea of holding a Convention sent the Government into a state of panic, which resulted in State trials for high treason, suspensions of the Habeas Corpus Act, and other severe measures. Now the Conventions were let go their own way, Parliament tolerating both with more or less calm indifference.

The National or General Convention, whose members had been "elected" or delegated by such gatherings of people as no Parliamentary election had ever caused, assembled on Monday, the 4th of February 1839, at the British Coffee House, Cockspur Street, London,—"that body, which, in the absence of an extended Parliamentary representation, was to speak the feelings, the thoughts, and the sentiments of the political helots of society."[1] The number of delegates composing it was nominally 53, many of them representing several places. It had originally been intended to limit it to 49, as it was believed that that number of deputies, but not more, were permitted by law to assemble as deputies. Lovett was appointed secretary.

Place has made some very interesting comments on the manner in which this body to which so many eyes were turned had been got together. He says: "The appointment of political delegates was a new thing, practised by persons in a hurry, and in a tumultuous meeting, the greater part, and in some cases the whole of the persons who attended the meeting, never having been told who was the candidate for their suffrages until he was proposed to them. Men thus circumstanced, to whom it was not only new, but almost, if not quite, an unintelligible business, whose generally honest enthusiasm was worked up to the highest pitch by the speakers before the candidate was named, might, as they did, vote, but it would be absurd to say they made a choice, and a good or a bad man, a wise man or a fool, an honest man or a scoundrel, was all the same to them, in their enthusiastic state; add to which that it scarcely ever happened that more persons were nominated than were to be chosen, and the imposition would be nearly perfect. To perfect it, it needed only that some one who had been elected should combine with others to promote their election, as was the case, they and no others being put forward to make the fraud perfect. It was by these various contrivances that the conspirators were solely nominated and elected.[2]

"The Convention had a very exalted idea of its own importance. It believed that it held the power of the country in its hands, and had the people at its command, and had only to proceed boldly to have the Government wholly at its command. . . . It was repeatedly shown to some of the best of them," Place says, "that they had no power whatever, but not one of them could be persuaded to believe so."

[1] Gammage, p. 116. [2] Place, MSS., 27,821, p. 87.

It was called by some "the people's Parliament," and it is recorded that at a public meeting an Address was adopted "To the really Honourable the Representatives of the Working Millions in General Convention assembled." Quite at the outset of its work, it was much discouraged by ascertaining that instead of 3,000,000 signatures to the National Petition, only 500,000 had been received, of which 100,000 were women's. Also that the great design of the national rent had only resulted in a sum of £967, and that deputies had been sent from several places, in none of which any money had been collected for their maintenance.

Shortly after their first meeting the place of meeting of the Convention was moved to Dr. Johnson's Tavern, Bolt Court, Fleet Street.

The public were admitted to the meetings, and the proceedings were reported in some of the newspapers. Its business did not progress smoothly. Very soon after its assembling the first split took place. J. P. Cobbett moved resolutions to the effect that they would not adopt any measures which might be in contempt of the law, and that their business was to superintend the presentation of the people's petitions. An amendment was carried "That the consideration of the resolution be postponed till after the People's Charter has been rejected by Parliament." Frost remarking, "Unless they could make use of weapons other than reason, no good would be effected for the people." Mr. Cobbett accordingly resigned.

For weeks the Convention met, and its members harangued; violent speeches were constantly being delivered, and by many members the adoption of what were called "ulterior proceedings" was constantly urged, and justified, if Parliament refused to grant the prayer of the National Petition. The ludicrous conceit as to their own importance is illustrated by their proceedings on the 13th February, when O'Brien moved "That this Convention request an interview with the House of Commons, on the 23d February, in the Crown and Anchor Tavern, for the purpose of disabusing the gentlemen of that House of any evil opinion they may have taken up with regard to the principles of the Chartists, and to give them every information as to the object for which this Convention have assembled."[1]

[1] Place, MSS., 27,821, p. 33.

Audacious as was this motion it was adopted with only two dissentient voices. Place remarks: "A more absurd proceeding than this could never have been carried, as this was after a discussion which lasted several hours. It showed how ill the delegates understood their own position, how extremely ignorant they were of even the most obvious particulars; yet here were several sedate, well-meaning men, of good property and good standing—men whom they who elected them looked upon as wise men—committing an absurdity which no club of working men could, if left to themselves, have committed."

On the 3d of April three of the Birmingham delegates—Hadley, Salt, and Douglas—resigned, they said, because the pledge of peace, law, and order, had been violated in spirit and in letter. "The language made use of at a meeting at the Crown and Anchor on the 11th plainly shows that the General Convention, while professing themselves the enemies of tyranny and oppression, in every form, are yet ready and anxious to peril the success of Radical Reform on an appeal to the last and worst weapon of the tyrant and oppressor." [1]

The three who had resigned were the original proposers of the National Petition and of the Convention. A public meeting was held at Birmingham, at which 40,000 were said to have been present, and a vote of censure was passed on the conduct of the delegates who had resigned. Place says their conduct was disreputable. He says: "The conduct of the Birmingham middle class men, who principally composed the Council of the Union, had caused considerable mischief—they misled the people under the pretence of bettering their condition, and they gained their confidence by repeated assurances that as long as they went on steadily they would not abandon them. By their conduct, and especially by their resignation, they have added what, to the working people, will be a truth to them, that whenever they put their trust in any of the class they will certainly be deceived and betrayed. This is a lamentable state of things, and yet there is but too much of fact in it, since scarcely any of the middle classes ever become active for the advantage of the working people, and this it is which has laid them open to the still more mischievous delusions of such men as Beaumont, O'Connor, OBrien, and others."

[1] Place, MSS., 27,821, p. 71.

The Government which had long forborne action under much provocation at length made a move. On the 17th April the first step in proceedings against the great leader Feargus O'Connor was taken. A rule was obtained by the Attorney-General to show cause why a criminal information should be filed against him for a libel on the Warminster Poor Law Guardians in Wiltshire, which was published in *The Northern Star*.

Coupled with this blow, disappointing reports reached the Convention. Dr. Fletcher, one of the delegates who had been on a tour about Birmingham, reported to that body that: "On the whole, they found amongst the people a great lack of political spirit and information. The people were all at work in consequence of the demand from the railways for iron, rails, etc., and appeared to be reaping all the fruits promised by the Reform Act. Still there was a general feeling of approbation of the Convention."

A more reassuring report was from Hetherington, who had been on a mission in Wales: "In some places the people are arming, and all were enthusiastic."

The first sign of Government action was not without effect, and some of the Convention began to show the white feather. On the 30th April O'Connor moved that the Convention after the presentation of the Petition should remove its sittings to Birmingham, "where they would sit amongst from 15,000 to 20,000 of the working classes, and in the evenings they would have meetings of thousands around them in the Bull Ring."

Lovett declared it would look like cowardice to go away, but his argument did not prevail further than that. The change was not to be made until the National Petition was presented.

The Convention had been devoting part of its energies to getting signatures to the National Petition, "Missionaries" had been sent to different districts, and meetings held, and by the beginning of May the Petition was ready. Attwood was to present it, but early in May he addressed a letter to the Convention. He stated that the language and conduct of the members "had alarmed and alienated the middle classes, without whose aid and friendly co-operation there was no hope for the working men; and they have also alarmed and alienated the less distressed, and in many instances the better disposed masses among the workmen themselves."

He said it would be most satisfactory to him before he presented the National Petition "if your Convention should think right to pass some resolutions" such as he suggested, embodying a disclaimer of all thoughts of violence and physical force in obtaining the just and legal objects of the National Petition, a denial of all wish to create discord and separation of interests between masters and men, or between the lower and middle classes of the community, and a denial of all intention to encroach upon the just rights, liberties, and interests of the people. A very long debate in the Convention ensued upon this letter, and they declined to pass any such resolutions.

On this event Place remarks: "This was one of the most extraordinary meetings of this extraordinary body. It showed more folly and less knowledge than the Convention (had) ever before shown. The request was rational, and ought to have been at once complied with. The refusal showed to the Parliament and the people that the intention, however absurd, existed to excite commotion for the purpose of destroying the Government, and this too at the instance of a small number of men who were compelled to acknowledge that the working people of the metropolis were not with them, whose 'Missionaries' showed, notwithstanding the glosses they put on their reports, that a vast majority of the working people throughout the country were not with them, who were themselves in all but a paroxysm of terror lest the Attorney-General should prosecute them, and were about to run away from London to Birmingham in the forlorn hope that the Government would be deterred from proceeding against them by the masses of the people who would support them. The truth is, the Convention never had any extensive influence in any way, and what they had was rapidly departing from them."

The Convention continued its preparations for the presentation of the National Petition which at last was deemed to be as complete as time would allow it to be made.

"The Petition is ready!" exclaimed Collins at the meeting of the Convention on the 6th May; "it is two miles one thousand five hundred and four yards, or nearly three miles in length, and it contains the enormous number of one million and a quarter signatures."

"This was a day, a sacred day," said Feargus O'Connor,—"a day on which was to be presented the groanings, the wishes, and the aspirations of the houseless, the hungry, the oppressed, and the enslaved, for redress, to the few who assumed to themselves the authority of passing bad laws, and of having them wickedly administered."

The next day the members of the Convention formed a procession, and escorted the Petition, "amidst the cheers of assembled thousands," to the house of Mr. Fielden, where Attwood was waiting to receive it.

The Chairman of the Convention, in presenting the Petition to Attwood, said: "If the prayer of the Petition were refused, the industrious classes had in their power the means of obtaining all that the Petition embraced. He knew, not only by correspondence from all parts of the country, but by direct and distinct communications, that the industrious classes would find the means of producing the beneficial results which they demanded by their Petition, should they be denied by the House of Commons."

While the Petition was being escorted in great pomp to Attwood to present, quite another scene, also of considerable importance to Chartism, was being enacted in another part of the country. Vincent was arrested for words spoken by him in Wales.

The next day O'Connor, in sudden panic at the meeting of the Convention, moved that the Convention be removed to Birmingham, "where danger could not be apprehended."

"The first act of the Tories," he said, "was to arrest one of their body, and they would arrest every member of the Convention unless the delegates placed themselves in a position where danger could not be apprehended, and that position was in Birmingham. The interference of the Tories with the principles of Chartism would justify a revolution, and the first shot fired would be a declaration of war against the people. He recommended the delegates to ensconce themselves behind a quarter of a million of men who were ready in Birmingham to defend them."

The Convention was evidently very perturbed, and indulged

in many ludicrous speeches. One member declared that "ten thousand stout hearts and strong arms would raise a glorious funeral pile over their mangled carcasses." The motion was carried by a considerable majority.

The presentation of the Petition to Parliament was delayed, owing to the defeat of the Ministry and their resignation on the 7th May.

The ministerial crisis, however, did not last long, and the Whig Ministry resumed possession of their places on the 11th May.

The Government having once made a start began to take more energetic action, and a Proclamation was issued against carrying arms. Frost, a leading Welsh Chartist, was removed from the Commission of the Peace, he having declared that "if the Ministers dared to take him off the list, the people of England would speedily put him on again." Edwards, Donaldson, and Townsend were also arrested at Newport on a charge of holding illegal and seditious meetings, and conniving together to incite persons to discontent and dissatisfaction with obedience to the laws and Government, and for attending some of the meetings prohibited by the magistrates as illegal.

The persistent incitements to violence were, in fact, beginning to have their effect. In the middle of May disturbances took place in the potteries, so serious that the soldiers had to fire.

The Convention, without waiting to witness the presentation of the National Petition to Parliament, moved to Birmingham on the 13th May, and once there, in safety, as they imagined, the violence of the language of its members increased. A great meeting was held immediately on their arrival.

O'Brien, who spoke first, said that if the Government governed them by the sword, then, by God, they would put them down by the pike. Many speakers followed him, O'Connor among the number, and very strong language was used. In the evening there was a dinner to celebrate their arrival, and more speeches were made.

The delusion of their safety was quickly dispelled, and they were shown that the Government could act even in Birmingham. On the 17th May Brown and Fussell (the latter of whom, it was subsequently stated, was a Government spy) were arrested for speeches.

The Convention, for the few days it sat in Birmingham, gave its energies to preparations for carrying out the grand idea which had been started of holding "simultaneous meetings," for the nominal purpose of petitioning the Queen to return good men to her councils, but in reality to submit certain questions to the people there assembled—namely, whether, at the request of the Convention, they would be prepared to make a run on the banks for gold; to abstain from the use of all excisable articles for a month; to deal exclusively with Chartists; to universally cease from labour for the period of a month, to be called the "sacred month"; and whether they had provided themselves with arms,—a programme which scarcely impresses one with the wisdom of its framers, for few Chartists had money to make a run on the banks for; abstinence from excisable articles would have resulted almost in starvation; few could afford to buy arms, and, as it was the want of work which afflicted them, cessation from work for a whole month was rather a curious remedy. But one must not look for much sense among these misleaders of the people.

The simultaneous meetings were to be held in Whitweek, and the arrangements having been made for thus bringing the full strength of the Platform to bear in support of their cause, the Convention adjourned on the 17th May to the 1st July. During Whitweek, from 20th to 25th May, a series of "simultaneous meetings" were held, and there was a regular orgy of Chartist oratory. "The most formidable of all the demonstrations" was that on Kersall Moor, as many as 300,000 persons being said to have been present, though this "was highly improbable." Next in importance was the meeting at Peep Green—some 200,000 persons, it was said, being at it. Here Feargus O'Connor and O'Brien spoke. The latter gave an outline of the Chartist plan. He said: "At the next general election we must have Chartists as our representatives, and when they have been elected by a show of hands, we must insist on having a formal return to that effect made by the returning officer. We shall thus have a Parliament legally chosen under the Queen's writ; and we shall then show our tyrants the difference between a Parliament nominated by 9,000,000 or 10,000,000, and one elected by 300,000 or 400,000 monopolists. The people's Parliament will meet at Birmingham, and then it may be necessary that 50,000 of their constituents should proceed thither to protect them in the discharge of their legislative duties, and when they are all thus assembled, then I will tell you what I mean to do, but not till then. I will not make a step farther until I am stronger than the law and the Constitution."

Meetings also were held at Liverpool, Newcastle-on-Tyne, Sheffield, Carlisle, Sunderland, Bath, Preston, Hull, Northampton, Glasgow, Blackwood in Monmouthshire, and a host of other places; or, as Gammage says, "in every town and village throughout Great Britain, wherever the voice of democracy could find an echo." At the Newcastle meeting the chairman, after saying that their triumph that day was perhaps owing to the Press, went on to say: "If they (the writers in the Press) had, on former occasions, told the truth as to number and behaviour, Government, no longer left in the dark, would have paid attention to our wishes and complied with our demands."

Place draws special attention to this remark, and says: "This is well expressed as the opinion of the masses. Everywhere the same notion is entertained. Even as individuals they believe that they need only to be understood to have everything acceded to that they require. They have a firm notion that whatever is pre-eminently good must be granted; they, without understanding the bearing of their subject in any direction, conclude that they understand it thoroughly; they doubt not that it is pre-eminently good, and hence the conclusion—'If the Government understood us as well as we understand ourselves and our subject, they would at once enact the Charter.' It is this persuasion, blind as it is, which keeps them together."[1]

Numerous meetings followed these. The Convention being in recess, its members were at liberty to perambulate the country and hold meetings, and the speeches they delivered were one series of covert or direct incitements to the people to arm, and of threats against the Government.

[1] Place, MSS., 27,821.

Whilst the leaders were thus perambulating and platforming, the great National Petition was at last, on 14th of June, presented by Attwood to the House of Commons, into which, as human strength could not carry it, it had to be rolled. "It was," he said, "the result of not less than 500 meetings, which had been held in support of the principles of the Petition."[1] In 214 towns and villages it had been adopted and signed, and when all the sheets of the bulky document were united, it was found to be nearly three miles long, and signed by 1,283,000 persons.[2] It was ordered to lie upon the table.

The Petition having been presented, and the "simultaneous meetings" having come off, the Convention reassembled on the 1st July at Birmingham, and took up the consideration of "ulterior measures"—that is to say, measures which would be had recourse to if Parliament turned a deaf ear to the Petition.

Several members described their proceedings during the recess. O'Connor's were the most striking of them all. He said that "At the three meetings which he had attended, above a million of people were present, fully determined to carry Universal Suffrage—morally if they could, physically if it could not be obtained without. He believed they were in the last stage of the agitation. The first stage was the creation of public opinion, the second was the organisation of public opinion, and the third was the direction of public opinion. They had created it, and its organisation was nearly completed, but he would not be for directing it until they could irresistibly direct it."[3]

In spite of all the meetings and speeches Gammage deplored the ignorance still of the people. He writes: "The means which, up to this time, had been taken for enlightening the people were comparatively trifling. Public meetings, so far as certain districts were concerned, had certainly been numerous enough, but something more than public meetings was required. The people would have been better with less of Platform oratory and more of book knowledge—a fact which seemed to be overlooked by the vast majority of their leaders, in whose estimation mere talk appeared to be the most neces-

1 *Parliamentary Debates*, vol. xlviii. p. 222.

2 See Lovett's *Life*, p. 206.

3 Place, MSS., 27,821, p. 280.

sary thing for bringing up their minds to the desired standard."[1]

Soon after the first arrival of the Convention at Birmingham riots had broken out, more or less directly due to the speeches of the Chartist leaders. The local police force being insufficient to preserve the peace, assistance from London was applied for. On the arrival of 100 police from London on the 4th of July a serious riot ensued. A meeting was being held at the Bull Ring. The police were ordered to disperse it. They were worsted in the combat, but the military who were called out put the mob to flight, and several arrests were made, a prominent Chartist, Dr. Taylor, among the number.

The next day the Convention issued a placard signed by Lovett, containing some strong resolutions passed by the Convention. On the following day Lovett and J. Collins were arrested and committed for trial on the charge of publishing and circulating a seditious libel. Harney also was arrested on a charge of a speech made on 14th or 15th May at Holloway Head.

It was evident that the Convention was not realising that immunity from arrest or prosecution which they expected to find at Birmingham. While the town was still in a state of great excitement, consequent on the rioting and the arrests, the subject of the great National Petition was brought before the House of Commons on the 12th of July by Attwood, who moved that the House resolve itself into a Committee of the whole House for the purpose of taking into consideration the National Petition. "That great Petition, unequalled in the Parliamentary history of England,[2] was produced," he said, "by the long sufferings, the injuries, the wrongs, the distresses of the working classes of the people, not only of the working classes, but of the merchants, the manufacturers, the tradesmen, the farmers, and the labouring classes of England generally. . . . He knew of no other remedy but further reform. Birmingham had waited until 1837, when many friends waited on him to take the lead in getting further reforms. . . . In his mind this Petition showed that there was great misery among the people of England which wanted redress."

[1] Gammage, p. 122.

[2] *Parliamentary Debates*, vol. xlix. p. 220.

Mr. Fielden seconded the motion. Lord John Russell, speaking on behalf of the Government, complained of the speeches of many of the Chartists whose language, he said, was not exceeded in violence or atrocity during the worst times of the French Revolution. He thought it was with very undue assumption called a National Petition, and he opposed the motion. The House was not very favourably disposed towards the Petition either, and on a division 235 voted against the motion, whilst 46 were for it, or a majority of 189 against it. And so ended the career of the first great National Petition, of which such great things had been expected, and concerning the rejection of which such dire threats had been used.

A few days after it had thus been laid to rest—namely, on the 15th July—a general expectation prevailed in Birmingham that Mr. Attwood would address his constituents. Large crowds gradually congregated; Attwood not appearing, they finally broke into riot; no police being at hand to check them, houses were attacked, shops demolished, their contents thrown into the street, carried away or burnt; several houses were fired, and two actually burnt down; the police office was wrecked. At last the police, aided by the military, appeared. On the first onset the mob dispersed, numerous arrests were made, and order was at length restored. A lamentable example this of Platform work, but one to which we cannot close our eyes; rather one whence, by the lurid light of blazing houses, a very warning and impressive lesson may be read—a lesson not against the use of the Platform, but against its abuse.

In consequence of these proceedings and the highly excited state of other parts of the country, Lord J. Russell on the 22d announced the intention of the Government to take the requisite precautions for securing the tranquillity of the country. The Government proposed to give local authorities power to create a local police force, and also proposed to increase the strength of the army; but so far as speeches and meetings were concerned, the Government intended and was content to rely on the ordinary law.

Having once begun to take active steps, the Government proceeded with vigour. Violent words had passed into violent deeds; it was time, therefore, for the authority of the law to be asserted, and the arrests of leading Chartists followed quick on each other.

On the 2d of August Lord J. Russell, in moving for a Committee of supply, after describing the state of the country and the proceedings of the Chartists, said:[1] "Lately, it appears, these societies have had a more regular organisation. The General Convention have issued a certain declaration and advice to the people, evidently intended to procure, by a general combination, an alteration of the law and the Constitution of the country. Their general object is, by means of terror and confusion, to produce a general, total, and entire change in the institutions of the country. I say that all these are symptoms of very considerable danger. . . . My own opinion is that, upon their own statements, there is no remedy which this House can give. It does seem to me that their complaints in all their placards, and in all their speeches, are complaints against the constitution of society. They complain that society is so constituted that they have not a sufficient quantity of wealth and means of support in that society, and that, by a change of the law, some new state of society will take place, by which their happiness will be increased, and their grievances redressed. I do not think that any law can pass that would at all tend to improve their condition. . . .

"While our laws, generally speaking, are well adapted to maintain freedom and preserve tranquillity, yet the means by which these two objects are to be obtained are not sufficiently well adapted to the increased population of the country. . . . He hoped that every power of free discussion would be preserved to the public with regard to the institutions of the country; and if those institutions could not brave the test of free discussion, by the result of such free discussion he thought they were bound to abide."

I have omitted one passage from this speech to give it separately, so that it may fix the deeper attention by standing singly, apart from the rest, for it is practically the justification of the whole Chartist movement; it is a terrible admission of culpability on the part of the governing classes of England up to this time, of Church, as well as of the State.

In an address from the Working-men's Association, presented

[1] *Parliamentary Debates*, vol. xlix. (1839), p. 1157.

not long before this, the men say: "Let our rulers ask themselves, when they see our prisons filled with victims, our land covered with paupers, and our streets infested with intemperance and prostitution, how much of those terrible evils are occasioned by ignorance, the consequence of their own neglect? . . . We claim education as a right derivable from society itself."

And here is Lord John Russell's answer, not directly to them, but to the state of things which evoked their complaint: "We have, particularly in the manufacturing districts, very large masses of people who have *grown up* in a state of society which it is lamentable, if not appalling, to contemplate. It is not a society growing up under the hand of early instruction, with places of worship to attend, with their opinions of property moulded by seeing it devoted to social and charitable objects, and with a fair and gradual subordination of ranks; but it is, in many instances, a society necessarily composed of the working classes, with certain persons who employ them, with whom they have little connection, regard, or subordination, and unhappily neither receiving in schools, nor in places of worship that religious and moral instruction that is necessary for knitting together the inhabitants and classes of a great country."[1]

His confession does not appear to have been received with groans, or cries of shame, either because Parliament itself was the culprit, or because the statesmen or politicians of the day had not awakened yet to a sense of their duty towards the people. But now, as we read his words, it is impossible to repress the most intense indignation at such an avowal—an avowal which covered the Ministers, the Opposition, and Parliament after Parliament with shame. What more heinous, fearful charge could have been brought by the most vehement of Chartist fanatics against the Government and the Parliament! The bitterest foe of the State Church could scarcely have formulated a more tremendous indictment against it, involved as it was too in the infamy—"grown up in a state of society lamentable, if not appalling to contemplate"—neglected all the years of their growth—that is the infamy of it—by the State Church, which stood charged with their religious and

[1] *Parliamentary Debates*, vol. xlix. (1839), p. 1159.

moral welfare—neglected, naturally enough, by an unreformed Parliament—neglected up to the date of this shameless avowal even by the reformed Parliament itself.

"Of lower classes so related to upper happy nations are not made," remarked Carlyle, writing in 1839, and he added: "To whatever other griefs the lowest classes labour under, this bitterest and sorest grief now superadds itself—the unendurable conviction that they are unfairly dealt with, that their lot in the world is not founded on right, not even on necessity and might, and is neither what it should be, nor what it shall be."

No wonder that men should think that the interests of the people could only be secured by the government of the country being in their own hands; no wonder that universal suffrage should be demanded. What was Parliament for, if it was not to look after, to guard the interests of the people? Lord J. Russell, in his explanation of Chartism, unconsciously, quite unconsciously, acknowledged its fullest justification.

Beyond the measures increasing the forces in the hands of the Executive, the Government introduced no coercive measure, but trusted to the efficacy of the existing law of the land. That was vigorously put into operation, and prosecutions were instituted under that law, and in every instance the juries returned verdicts vindicating the law where it had been violated.

The National Convention, after being sorely inconvenienced in Birmingham by the arrest of several of its members and other unpleasant circumstances, flitted back to London again. Five of the most influential of the Scotch delegates resigned, and so discouraged were the residue that a motion was discussed for the dissolution of the Convention, and the election of another. Complaints of want of money were also heard. Nevertheless, what remained of the Convention proceeded to the discussion of that supremest of their follies—"the sacred month," which had long been thought of as an unfailing weapon wherewith to compel success. Bronterre O'Brien thus explained it at a meeting at Stockport on the 15th July.

"Let not the anvil be struck within the breadth and length of the land. Let not a needle or a spade be used unless to dig some tyrant's grave. Let not a shuttle move, unless to weave the winding-sheet of some monster robber, some profit-monger, who dared to attack the people's Parliament (the National Convention). All will then soon be over." And in advocating it at the Convention, he made this foolish speech: "What he attached importance to was a holiday declared by a Parliament elected upon a general election—of a Chartist Parliament—by a show of hands, when the holiday should endure, not for a week, or a month, but for all time, till justice should be substantially done to the people."

Ultimately the Convention, having satisfied itself that the people were not prepared to carry out this proposal, abandoned it as impracticable.

In the meantime the ordinary law of the country was being energetically enforced. The people had clearly broken the law in taking part in meetings which were palpably illegal, in joining what the law stigmatised a conspiracy, and in numerous other ways; and the law, however much it might be derided in the abstract, was, once it was put in motion, stronger than those who broke it.

The month of August saw prosecutions pouring down like hail on the Chartists, and conviction following conviction. Three of the Birmingham rioters were convicted of the crime of demolishing houses, and this, being a capital felony, they were sentenced to death, but subsequently reprieved. At Barnsley 10 Chartists were arrested and committed for trial for attending unlawful meetings where seditious and inflammatory language had been used. At Sheffield 71 rioters were arrested for taking part in certain disturbances there. At Liverpool Assizes some 70 to 80 Chartists were arraigned—among them J. H. Holmes, who was convicted for seditious conspiracy and riot on 12th August. It was found that he had carried a pole with a red cap at the top and a flag bearing inscriptions, and had thus walked at the head of a concourse of people.

On the 5th August Collins was found guilty of publishing a seditious libel, and on the next day Lovett was convicted of a similar offence, and both were sentenced to a year's imprisonment. But the point of real interest in a history of the Platform is, in what manner did the Government deal with the men who had made violent Platform speeches?

Vincent, the "young Demosthenes of English Democracy,"

who had made innumerable speeches in Wales and the West of England, had delivered some speeches of a violent nature at Pontypool. He had been, as already stated, arrested in May. He was tried on the 2d August with three others. The indictment charged that the defendants, together with divers other evil-disposed persons, did conspire "seditiously to meet and assemble themselves together for the purpose of exciting discontent, etc. etc., and did then and there, by loud and seditious speeches, etc. etc., raise and excite such discontent as aforesaid."[1] Vincent was convicted and sentenced to twelve months' imprisonment, and the others to lesser terms. The Reverend J. Stephens was also tried in August on an indictment, "Unlawfully and maliciously intending to disturb the public peace, and to endanger the persons and property of, and terrify and alarm a great number of her Majesty's quiet and peaceable subjects, and to raise or excite discontent in the minds of her Majesty's subjects with the laws of this realm, and to excite them to tumult and disobedience of the laws." He was convicted and sentenced to eighteen months' imprisonment, and then to find bail to keep the peace for five years, himself in £500 and two sureties of £250 each.

At Chester Assizes four men were charged with sedition, exciting to disturb, and attending illegal meetings, and were convicted.

At Manchester five men were apprehended on warrants charging them with having uttered seditious and inflammatory language.

"The Whig reign of terror," wrote *The Northern Liberator* on 24th August, "is proceeding in all its glory." A little while after, its editor, Batchelor by name, was committed for trial for having, at a meeting at Darlington on 17th July, advised the people to arm, and for uttering sundry other inflammatory speeches. There appeared to be, in fact, little difficulty in framing an indictment under the ordinary law for violent Platform speeches.

There is a most instructive return amongst the Parliamentary papers of 1840[2] of "the numbers of persons who were confined for charges for printing and publishing seditious and

[1] *State Trials*, New Series, vol. iii. p. 1037.
[2] See *Parliamentary Papers*, 1840, No. 600—"Prisoners for Libel."

blasphemous libels, or for attending any seditious meetings, etc. etc., or for any offence of a political nature, from 1st of January 1839 to 1st of June 1840." The number was 444 persons, of whom 380 were in England, 63 in Wales, and 1 in Scotland. But the most interesting part of the return is the classification of the offences of which these people were convicted, showing, as it does, the numerous ways in which violent Platform speeches could be punished. The offences were: "Uttering seditious language at a tumultuous assembly"; "uttering seditious words"; "conspiracy to excite to arms"; "seditious and inflammatory speeches"; "seditious conspiracy, unlawful assembly, and seditious speeches"; "uttering malicious and seditious words"; "seditious libel"; "exciting the people to hatred of the Government and Constitution"; "treasonable conspiracy." A pretty large list.

Among the numbers convicted were several members of the National Convention, a circumstance which considerably thinned its ranks. Over twenty members had resigned, eight had never attended; and on 6th September 1839 the great Convention dissolved itself. Gammage comments on its career.

"Such," he says, "was the end of the first Convention, which numbered amongst its members many men of superior talents, but who were so divided upon matters of policy as to bring about results fatal to the glorious mission which they had undertaken. The great mistake of the Convention was in presuming to act before they were possessed of the requisite power to ensure success."

It has consistently been alleged against the Platform, by its opponents, that it leads to the commission of crime and violence; and late in the autumn of this year an event took place which was clearly traceable to the incitements to violence which had been steadily poured into people's ears.

Gammage, from his Chartist point of view, attributes it to the suppression of the Platform, and meetings, which had resulted from Government prosecutions.

It has already been stated that Vincent, one of the ablest of the Chartist orators, had been "awaking" the people in Wales. "This impulsive people received Vincent with open arms. He was just the man to rouse all the keener emotions of the masses whose condition was none of the best, and it was not long before a spark of fire ran from breast to breast which threatened to ignite into an inextinguishable flame."[1]

Amongst other places, Newport, a considerable town in South Wales, had been the scene of his labours. And here a tradesman and a magistrate, a Mr. John Frost, of whom mention has already been made, adopted Vincent's views. The neighbourhood of Newport, which was wild and mountainous, was densely inhabited by a mining population, the people being poor and ignorant. It would appear that they had been organised by the establishment of affiliated societies, so that on any occasion a command might be issued and circulated among the people, and obeyed.

In the week before Sunday, 3d of November, a plan was laid for a general rising of the people of that district to take place on that day. Various consultations were held at Blackwood, where there was a public-house, at which there was a large society of Chartists, and at which meetings were held. Orders were issued that the men should assemble armed on the night of the 3d of November. There were to be three principal divisions, which were to meet at a particular place some miles from Newport, on which they were to march, and to reach it about two o'clock in the morning when every one would be asleep and unarmed, and even without the "suspicion of danger." Arriving at Newport they were to attack the troops that were there, and get possession of the town. A general rising was then to take place through Lancashire, and throughout the kingdom generally, and Charter law was to be universally and instantly established.

The night was the darkest and most tempestuous known for years, with heavy rain; some of the divisions were late; nevertheless, about 5000 men advanced on Newport, armed in a sort of way, under the command of Frost.

Rumours had already reached the Mayor and magistrates, and the small company of troops, and every preparation was made to meet the emergency. The Chartists having reached Newport, an attack was made on the Inn, where the troops and constables were stationed; shots were fired in return,

[1] Gammage, p. 77.

several persons[1]—twenty, it was said—were killed, and a large number wounded, and the people then fled in a panic.

Lord Melbourne, in a letter to Lord J. Russell on this subject, wrote: "I hope now that this will go no further, but what I do not like in it is that there was a disposition to rise throughout the whole district, which was totally unknown and unsuspected until the moment before it was about to be carried into execution. If this were to be done in many places much mischief might be done. Such a mode of proceeding is a thousand times more dangerous than unions and great meetings, which are always known beforehand and provided against."[2]

The outbreak had been a serious one. The Government at once sent down a special commission to try those who had been arrested for participation in it. On the 31st of December Frost and eleven others were indicted as false traitors, who, on 4th November 1839, at Newport, together with a great multitude of false traitors, to the number of 2000 and more, arrayed, and armed in a warlike manner, with guns and pistols, etc., did wickedly and maliciously levy and make war against the Queen. They were charged with having, by force and violence, taken and seized large quantities of arms, made a forcible and violent attack on a house where the Queen's soldiers and constables were, and fired upon them, and that they maliciously and traitorously attempted, by force and arms, in a warlike manner, to subvert and destroy the Government and Constitution of this realm as by law established.

Frost and two others—Williams and Jones—were convicted. Chief-Justice Tindal, in his address to the prisoners after conviction, said: "It has been proved in your case that you combined to lead from the hills, at the dead hour of night, into the town of Newport many thousands of men, armed in many instances with weapons of a dangerous description, in order that they might take possession of the town, and supersede the lawful authority of the Queen, as a preliminary step to a more general insurrection throughout the kingdom." And they were sentenced to death; also five others who pleaded

[1] See report in *The Morning Herald*. The reporter said he had seen seventeen who were killed.

[2] *Lord Melbourne's Papers*, p. 407.

guilty. Several others were also sentenced to various terms of imprisonment. The capital sentence was subsequently commuted to transportation for life.

With the fiasco of the Newport "insurrection," and the punishment of the ringleaders, Chartism received a blow from which it took a long time to recover, if indeed it ever was quite forgotten. A great deal of restlessness was for a time visible in certain localities, and in others several small riots, scarcely to be dignified with the name of disturbances, occurred; but in most instances the offenders were indicted, convicted, and punished. The steady enforcement of the law was in fact grinding the courage out of the Chartists, and instilling discretion. A letter from Fletcher, a member of the Convention, dated September 1839, acknowledges as much. He says: "The trade of agitation is, I think, declining. The time is coming on when men must work more with their brains and less with their tongues to obtain the confidence of the people—the time when sense and knowledge will be preferred to boasting and cunning." The most that Gammage could say of this period was: "The spirit did not entirely die out." The degree of hallucination that was reached by some of the Chartists was exhibited at the York Assizes in 1840, where a Chartist was convicted, who, when sentence of seven months' imprisonment was passed on him, exclaimed, striking his hand on the front of the dock, "Well, that will produce a revolution if anything will!"

At last the leader of the Chartists, the great Feargus O'Connor, was proceeded against. On St. Patrick's Day he was put on his trial for a seditious libel. Curiously enough he was not tried for any speech that he had made, though many of them would have justified proceedings, but he was indicted for publishing certain speeches, one of which was his own, in his newspaper, *The Northern Star*.

The Attorney-General (who prosecuted him) said:[1] "There has sprung up within about two years of the present time a political sect, called Chartists, who approve of physical force. With regard to mere speculative opinion, that is free for every man, and while he seeks to spread and support his opinions by

[1] For a very full report of this case, see O'Connor's own paper, *The Northern Star*, 21st March 1840.

lawful and constitutional means, no man has a right to complain. But the sect to which I refer have formed a resolution to carry into effect their schemes by force and violence. They have formed this opinion, that property is not to be respected, and that there ought to be a new distribution of property, of which they are by force to share. Such doctrines are utterly subversive of civil society, and cannot be tolerated in any country. I charge the defendant with publishing articles in the newspaper, of which he is editor and proprietor, directly having that tendency. The system of the newspaper conducted by him has been to publish accounts, or supposed accounts, of speeches made at public meetings of those Chartists of the most inflammatory and dangerous and culpable description, and to publish those with applause and approbation, holding out the sentiments expressed in those speeches to be adopted and acted upon."

After ten minutes' consideration the jury found him guilty. Judgment was postponed until 11th May, when, after a long affidavit had been made by him that he had always advised the use of moral force, the judge remarked that, on his own showing, his moral force was little short of physical force, and sentenced him to eighteen months' imprisonment.

Here, then, may be closed the narrative of the first part of the Chartist movement in which the Platform played so conspicuous a part. The law—not "Two Acts," or "Four Acts," or "Six Acts," but the ordinary law—proved itself stronger than the Platform when the Platform was abused.

The trials of the Chartists evoked, as was only natural, a good deal of exposition of the law as regards public meetings, and the Platform; and it is to be remarked that both wider views and greater toleration for free speech are to be found in these later expositions of the law. Thus, Judge Erskine, in his charge to the Grand Jury at Newcastle Assizes in 1840, said: "By the laws of this country no man, nor no set of men, are forbid to discuss the merits of any question of importance: all were at liberty, soberly and honestly, to enter freely, fully, nay, severely if they liked, and to examine and animadvert upon the conduct of any man, let his station and authority be what it may, and he has the same opportunity of doing so with every institution of the State. No person is prohibited from assembling in a peaceable way to discuss what they may consider a real grievance, which calls for redress;" and in another charge he said: "It is the privilege of every man freely to canvass the conduct of those by whom he is governed. If the assembly should show no symptom of violence, if they come not armed, however strong may be the language of remonstrance, it is not right closely to criticise the language when it is honestly expressed."

But he thought it right also to point out the dangers, because he added: "Were his advice to be taken, he would certainly counsel them to avoid the meeting together in tumultuous assemblies where the danger is great by increasing numbers being brought together. The excitement produced is often very great, while the benefit is small and precarious. The tendency of large assemblies is to excite, and men are apt to be led away by having their feelings warmed by the cheers which usually prevail."[1]

Independently of the discouraging effect of the Newport fiasco, and of the numerous prosecutions and convictions of the Chartists, there were other causes which helped also to influence adversely the cause of Chartism. The people were gradually getting to know that the Corn Laws were the chief cause of the distress they were suffering, and, gradually, numbers of them were falling into the ranks of the Anti-Corn-Law agitators, and suffering themselves more willingly to be led by the middle classes, who were working for that great reform.

Parliamentary reform, not of the advanced Chartist type, but still reform, was being taken up by larger numbers, disappointment at the working of the Reform Act becoming more general, and large meetings were held in different parts of the country to consider the further reforms which were necessary to the adequate representation of the property and intelligence of the country.

Many persons, moreover, had become disgusted by the violence of the Chartist orators, their frequent childish silliness, their incapacity, but, most of all, by the frequent scenes of disorder and the attempt to convert their meetings to the pur-

[1] See *The Northern Liberator*, February 1840.

pose of physical intimidation instead of moral persuasion and discussion.

All these circumstances tended to weaken the Chartist agitation, and with the General Election of 1840, and the accession to power of a new Ministry, Chartism retired for a time from the prominent position it had occupied, and the first crisis of Chartism was passed.

CHAPTER XVIII

THE ANTI-CORN-LAW AGITATION

In the course of the previous chapter reference has been made to the agitation for the abolition of the Corn Laws. It, and the agitation for the Charter, had, for a time, been concurrent, and in some ways had come so much into contact with each other that, in giving a narrative of the one, it was impossible to avoid reference to occurrences which closely concerned the other. In describing the part which the Platform took in the Anti-Corn-Law Agitation, some slight repetition, therefore, or reference to some of the events already mentioned, is unavoidable.

The agitation against the Corn Laws is the most perfect example which our history affords of the action of the Platform as an engine of political warfare.

The laws regulating the importation of corn were an evil under which the people of Great Britain had long suffered. In 1815 as we have seen the Government and Parliament, one House of which was composed entirely, and the other almost entirely of landlords, who used their political power for their own special benefit, rewarded the people of the country for the sacrifices they had made in the great war with France, by what are commonly known as the Corn Laws, and passed an Act which prohibited the importation of wheat until the price of home-grown wheat in the home markets reached 80s. per quarter, high enough protection one might have thought, but not equal to the 105s. a quarter, so shamelessly recommended by a Committee of the House of Commons which had sat in 1813. The agricultural interest was at that period considered by those in authority to be the most important, the predominating interest, in fact, in the country, and therefore the one to be protected and stimulated and fostered at the expense of every other interest. The Act could not, of course, keep wheat at 80s. a quarter, though there were many who wished legislation could have done so, but, by prohibiting importation until it was at that price, it afforded as good a guarantee as was practicable that wheat should be kept at such a price as would keep up the rents to those which landlords had got accustomed to by the high prices during the war.

As a matter of fact, considerable variations in its value took place, for wheat fell to 50s. a quarter in 1821, and then, as we may remember, there had been an outcry of agricultural distress, and petitions flowed into Parliament for further protection.

In 1828 the law of 1815 was slightly modified, and what was known as a sliding scale of taxation was adopted. When the average price of wheat at home was 62s. a quarter wheat could be imported, but the importers would have to pay a duty of 24s. 8d., making the price 86s. 8d. The only improvement effected by this new law was, that when the price reached 72s. a quarter the duty was only 2s. 8d., or a total of 74s. 8d., which was some few shillings less than 80s., plus duty, but practically this sliding scale was nearly as effective protection as was that afforded by the law it supplanted.

This Corn Law had an innumerable train of the most evil consequences. "We plead," said a speaker at one of the Anti-Corn-Law meetings, "against laws that have been enacted to debar mankind here, where God has been most bountiful, from participating in that which He never withheld where He has been least bountiful. Men are starving, yet diamonds are let in duty free; corn is taxed, but turtle is let in free; corn is taxed, but pictures are free; industry is taxed, but that which the rich alone want is free; that, without which the poor cannot exist, and which God, through the bounty of our mother earth, has given for all—*that* is prohibited by the law-making machinations of a sordid few whose rent-rolls to them are more sacred than the primeval charter of man's sovereignty over the globe, and God's ordination that the labourer is worthy of his hire!"

It was, as Cobden said, "A law which took from the poorest of the poor to add to the richest of the rich." The sole class which benefited by it was the class of landowners; it enriched them at the cost of the community. Every other class or interest suffered more or less. The farmers long hugged the delusion that they benefited by it, but even they were to discover their mistake at last. The agricultural labourers even did not profit by it, for the high price of corn brought them no higher wages, whilst they had to pay more for the first necessary of life. But it was upon the manufacturing and operative classes that the worst consequences of the law fell. It was a law which "destroyed our commerce, ruined our merchants, pauperised the population." By enhancing the price of bread, it led to the actual starvation of thousands, and to the misery and semi-starvation of millions and it was the direct and indirect cause of a very great portion of the crime, violence, and agitation which occurred in England during the first half of the present century.

"The Corn Law is, in fact," said Bright, in one of his speeches, "a law of the most ingeniously malignant character. The most demoniacal ingenuity could not have invented a scheme more calculated to bring millions of the working classes of this country to a state of pauperism, suffering, discontent, and insubordination than the Corn Law." [1]

Carlyle, in his lofty impassioned way, burst into contemptuous criticism of it in another direction: "What looks maddest, miserablest, in these mad and miserable Corn Laws, is independent altogether of their 'effect on wages,' their effect on 'increase of trade,' or any other such effect; it is the continual maddening proof they protrude into the faces of all men, that our governing class, called by God and Nature, and the inflexible law of Fact, either to do something towards governing, or to die and be abolished, have not yet learned even to sit still and do no mischief! For no Anti-Corn-Law League yet asks more of them than this:—Nature and Fact, very imperatively, asking so much more of them. Anti-Corn-Law League asks not, Do something; but, Cease your destructive misdoing, Do ye nothing!" [2]

The law, submitted to for long, became at last unbearable. From time to time efforts were made to direct public attention to it, but failed; the mercantile classes, placing too much re-

[1] Bright's *Speeches*, p. 284, 19th December 1845.
[2] *Past and Present*, book iii. chap. viii.

liance on Parliamentary action, without other pressure, and the industrial working classes, mistaking the immediate cause of suffering, seeking remedy for themselves in Chartism. Towards the end of 1836, the price of wheat having become dearer than it had been for years previously, and the evils entailed by the high price of food having become accentuated, an Anti-Corn-Law Association was formed in London, with the view of making some effort to have the law repealed. In the following year an endeavour was made to move Parliament, and a motion was made in the House of Commons for the substitution of a fixed duty of 10s. a quarter instead of the sliding scale. The proposal was, however, rejected by a large majority.[1] In 1838 the question made further progress.

A Petition from Glasgow, for the abolition of the Corn Laws, was presented to Parliament, and a debate took place which elicited from the Prime Minister, Lord Melbourne, the statement that the Government would not take a decided part in the controversy till it was certain that the majority of the people were in favour of a change. Whether his speech was taken as a suggestion of agitation or not, it is certain that soon after—namely, towards the end of September—there was formed in Manchester an Anti-Corn-Law Association.[2] In a little room over the stables of the York Hotel, in Manchester, seven men met together to consider the subject of the Corn Laws. Their consideration resulted in the formation of an association to work for the repeal of the law. Several members soon joined it; and simultaneously, and now quite naturally, the aid of the Platform was invoked. From this on we cannot too closely follow the different steps taken by this Association and its successor, the League, if we wish to understand the inner working of the great system of Platform agitation. With the experience of previous agitations, and with the example of the Roman Catholic Association in Ireland, Platform agitation was being reduced to a highly scientific system. From private meetings the Association progressed to a public meeting, and at the first which was held, the chairman made a public declaration of the object of the Association. "The object was to obtain the free right of the people to exchange their labour for as much food as could be got for it;

[1] 2d July 1837; 229 against 89. [2] Prentice, vol. ii. p. 57.

that we might no longer be obliged by law to buy our food at one shop, and that the dearest in the world, but be at liberty to go to that at which it can be obtained cheapest. It was an object in which men of all political opinions might unite without compromising their principles, and it was a fundamental rule of the Association that no party politics should be mixed up in the discussion of the question."[1]

And now the Platform was further invoked in the form of lectures; and besides the meetings for lectures other meetings were held. Interest in the question grew, and in December the important body, the Manchester Chamber of Commerce, threw its weight into the scale, and adopted a Petition to the House of Commons, in which it said: "Holding one of the eternal principles (of commercial justice) to be—the inalienable right of every man freely to exchange the results of his labour for the productions of other people, and maintaining the practice of protecting one part of the community at the expense of all other classes to be unsound and unjustifiable, your Petitioners earnestly implore your honourable House to repeal all laws relating to the importation of foreign corn, and other foreign articles of subsistence, and to carry out to the fullest extent, both as affects agriculture and manufactures, the true and peaceful principles of *free trade*, by removing all existing obstacles to the unrestricted employment of industry and capital."

Early in January 1839 the Association made an appeal for funds to carry on their plans, money being an essential element in the organisation necessary to give effect to Platform agitation. Several thousand pounds were quickly subscribed, some mercantile men of prominence and wealth having contributed as much as £100 each. Then on the 22d a great banquet took place in the Corn Exchange, Manchester, some 800 people being at it, and a further sum of £600 was subscribed. Next day a meeting of delegates from the various local Anti-Corn-Law Associations, which had been started, was held, and after much speaking a resolution was passed expressing the opinion that, "So long as a plentiful supply of the first necessaries of life is denied by acts of the British Legislature to the great body of the nation, so long will the

[1] Prentice, vol. i. p. 75.

Government and the country be justly exposed to all the evils resulting from the discontent of the people;" and then recording their intentions as to the future, they resolved that "with a view to avert so great a danger by an act of universal justice, this meeting pledges itself to a united, energetic, and persevering effort for the total and immediate repeal of all laws affecting the free importation of grain."[1]

By this time the Platform was getting well to work, and the machinery of organised agitation, already familiar, was being rapidly brought into operation. Numerous meetings against the Corn Laws were held, and delegates selected to proceed to London to supervise the presentation of the Petitions adopted at the meetings. Early in February these delegates met there; the Petitions were presented to Parliament, and Mr. Villiers moved, that evidence be heard at the bar of the House in support of them. His motion was rejected by a large majority.[2] The efforts of the Anti-Corn-Law people were by this time so successful in attracting public attention that they began to meet with opposition from the Chartists, some of whom were evidently beginning to feel that the Anti-Corn-Law Agitation might be a dangerous rival to Chartism.

On the 28th February an Anti-Corn-Law meeting at Manchester was broken up by the Chartists. This conduct evoked a spirited protest from Cobden. He said: "There is nothing I like so much as free discussion, and settling the truth by the test of reason and argument. I shall never flinch from meeting any man, or any body of men, who, as reasonable beings, are disposed to take up the advocacy of the Corn Laws. But I must protest, in the name of the working classes of Manchester, against the conduct of men who will prevent all discussion upon this important question."[3] . . . He went on to show that the abolition of the Corn Laws was emphatically the poor man's question, and said: "We take our stand upon a fixed principle; we say we will have no duty; we will have a total, immediate, and unconditional repeal. We shall go forward in our cause, not turning out of our way to molest others, whatever their object may be, but claiming the right to ourselves, as free citizens, to meet and discuss these questions at all times."

[1] Prentice, vol. i. p. 102. [2] 361 against 172. [3] Prentice, vol. i. p. 118.

A momentous step was taken on the 20th of March 1839, when a great meeting of delegates of the various Associations decided on the formation of a permanent union, to be called the "Anti-Corn-Law League." With the view to secure unity of action, there was to be a central office, which was to be established at Manchester, to which body was to be entrusted the duty of engaging and recommending competent lecturers, the obtaining of the co-operation of the public Press, and the establishing and conducting of a stamped circular, for the purpose of keeping up a constant correspondence with the local Associations.

Thus was the Anti-Corn-Law League launched into the world. "The delegates then separated to agitate the question in all their various localities. . . . Meetings were immediately held in nearly all the great towns which had sent representatives to the London Conference, and the delegates became so many local missionaries to spread the doctrines that had been enunciated in the metropolis. Numerous pamphlets, 10,000 of each, sent everywhere—a free trade newspaper, with a circulation of 15,000, there needed only the vocal denunciation of the Corn Laws in the strongholds of the Protectionists to increase the alarm,"[1] and the lecturers soon followed the tracts and the free trade newspaper. This activity met at first with little Platform opposition or rivalry from the Tory party, for we find a Tory paper, *The Morning Herald*, complaining bitterly that "Lecturers are paid to perambulate the country, and to declaim against the atrocities of landed monopoly. What though these men are empty, conceited blockheads! They are permitted to tell their story day by day, without contradiction, and their uncontradicted falsehoods come at length to be regarded as truths."

By June 1839 "The League was fully organised, and in active operation—no longer a movement of London, Manchester, Liverpool, Birmingham, Leeds, Glasgow, but *National*."[2] Thus early in the existence of the agitation it is evident how large a part the Platform was to take, and how great was the reliance of the leaders on its power to assist them. From this on, for several years to come, the agitation for the repeal of the law was unremitting, and the Platform was seldom silent.

[1] Prentice, vol. i. p. 128. [2] *Ibid.* p. 130.

Prentice, in his *History of the Anti-Corn-Law League*, heads his chapters sometimes as "The Campaign" of such and such a year. It is a not unapt title, for the proceedings of the League, the organisation, the preparation of ways and means, the incursions into hostile districts, partook very much of the character of a campaign.

The campaign in 1840 was inaugurated by a meeting at Manchester of delegates from the different local Associations, and by two great banquets there of several thousand people, at which much speech-making took place in favour of the policy of the League. In March the delegates reassembled in London. Feeling more confident of their position, they came to a resolution which defined their intentions more clearly than hitherto. "Dissociating ourselves," they said, "from all political parties, we hereby declare that we will use every exertion to obtain the return of those members to Parliament alone who will support a repeal of the Corn Laws." It was an important decision, and one to which they steadily adhered. How vigorously the Platform was now working in the cause may be realised from the statement that, during the year, 763 Petitions were sent to the House of Commons, and 22 to the House of Lords, and that the lecturers delivered more than 800 lectures in the principal towns of 32 counties, besides at 49 places in Scotland, and 32 in Wales. Cobden, and many others, members of the Council of the League, had also been holding meetings in furtherance of the objects of the League. Associations had been formed in numerous towns, both large and small, and in each of these the Platform was being constantly used for the purpose of propagating the principles and objects of the League.

Under the influence of this political activity and indirect pressure the Whig leaders had got so far as to pronounce in favour of a moderate fixed duty on wheat instead of the sliding scale. On the Tory leaders, however, no impression was made, nor was any likely, so long as they believed the maintenance of the Corn Laws as[1] "necessary to their salvation."

But neither the tentative compromise of the Whigs, nor the dogged resistance of the Tories, induced the League to deviate one iota from their course. The leaders went on perfecting

[1] See letter from Lord Western, quoted in Walpole's *Russell*, vol. i. p. 367.

and extending the organisation; meetings were added unto meetings, and in ever-widening circles the influence of the Platform extended itself.

One special feature in this movement of the Platform must here be noticed. As I have already had occasion to point out, the Platform must be regarded in a double aspect, as the means of expressing popular opinion, and as a medium for teaching or persuading the public.

Jeremy Bentham, writing in 1820, with considerably less experience of the subject than we now possess, said: "Various are the modifications of which meetings for the purpose of political discussion are susceptible. All of them are more or less contributory to both purposes at once—to instruction and excitation,—but some of them are more particularly suitable to the one purpose, others to the other."

He had not yet realised that the real power of the Platform was its "expression" of the public voice, something far in advance of mere "excitation." The reform agitation had proved once and for ever the effectiveness of the expressive function of the Platform. Again, the whole use, import, and significance of the Platform in the Chartist agitation had been the expressive function. Here, in this Anti-Corn-Law Agitation, however, particularly in all its earlier stages, the Platform is presented to us in its didactic aspect.

The leaders of the movement used the Platform more for the purposes of teaching, and converting, and discussing than it had ever been used before. On no previous occasion in history did the Platform present itself so distinctly, so exclusively, in its didactic aspect as here. The whole system of lecturers which was adopted by the League, the practice of sending what were called "deputations" of the League to towns or country districts to hold meetings and enlighten the people on the subject, and to discuss and argue the matter with the opponents of their plans—all prove that the League thought primarily of the Platform as the most powerful and effective means of educating the people, and of forming the public opinion which the League wished should be formed. The meetings of the Anti-Corn-Law League could not help being in part demonstrations of opinion, but for several years that was altogether their secondary or subordinate characteristic.

The year 1841 was an eventful one for the Anti-Corn-Law League. First came the defeat, then the downfall of the Whig Government. For years doing little more than keeping afloat, Lord Melbourne's Ministry sank at last. On the 4th of June, Sir Robert Peel carried a vote of want of confidence in the Ministers by a majority of one vote;[1] on the 22d, the Queen prorogued Parliament, announcing at the same time her intention of "resorting to the means which the Constitution had entrusted to her for ascertaining the sense of her people," and the following day Parliament was dissolved.

I must suspend for a little the narrative of the Anti-Corn-Law Agitation to give a brief account of this general election. It was the sixth in the space of eleven years (1830, 1831, 1832, 1835, 1837, 1841), almost enough to satisfy the Chartists who asked for annual Parliaments.

In accordance with the new practice of ministerial proclamations of policy from the Platform on the eve of an election, the leader of the Whigs in the House of Commons, Lord John Russell (a fortnight before the dissolution), addressed a public meeting of his constituents, the Liberal electors of the city of London, setting before the country, through them, the issue to be fought for.[2]

"The main question—the question, indeed, which he considered the city of London and the great body of the electors throughout the United Kingdom had to decide upon the approaching occasion—was, whether they would determine to unfetter the industry of the country? It was upon that question that he asked the suffrages of the electors of the city of London." He also said that the precise question upon which appeal was about to be made to the country was: "Whether they would confirm or reject the recent decision of the majority of the House of Commons?"

He spoke again at length on the day of his nomination: "Our object is to diminish, as far as it can be done with safety and prudence, the price of food, give increased employment to the people, and maintain this country in the high station she holds among the nations of the earth.

"Her Majesty's Ministers have proposed a plan to diminish the restrictions on trade and industry, and to lighten the

[1] 312—311. [2] On the 15th June 1841, see *The Times*.

burdens of the people at the same time that they provide for the public service of the country. It is for you now to say that you wish for its adoption."[1]

On the other side, the leader of the Conservative party, Sir Robert Peel, also made a Platform declaration of his policy. Conservative though he was, yet, soon after the passing of the Reform Act, he had begun freely to use the Platform, and had since used it as a means for "building up" the Conservative party after its collapse in 1832, or, as he expressed it at a great banquet given him in May 1838: "My object for some years past has been to lay the foundations of a great party which should diminish the risk and deaden the shock of collisions between the two deliberative branches of the Legislature, which should be enabled to check the too impatient eagerness of the well-intentioned for hasty and precipitate changes in the Constitution and laws of this country, and say with a voice of authority to the restless spirit of revolutionary encroachment, 'Here are the bounds by which thy vibrations shall be stayed.'"[2]

A general election offered the most favourable and impressive occasion for public efforts in this direction, and on the 28th June Sir Robert Peel, at his nomination at Tamworth, spoke at great length. His speech was in the main a repetition of his recent speeches in Parliament. He said: "I think it more respectful when I meet my constituents thus assembled, that, in their presence, I should re-state the opinions I have expressed in Parliament (on the corn duties and on the sugar duties) rather than refer to declarations which I have made in Parliament."

He spoke clearly on the vital point of the Corn Laws: "I cannot consent to substitute a fixed duty of 8s. for the present

[1] It is interesting to contrast the position of Ministers in relation to constituencies at this election and at that of 1818. Then, six members of the Cabinet were members of the House of Commons; of these only one sat for an open constituency—namely, Canning who contested Liverpool—three sat for nomination boroughs, one for a pocket county in Ireland, and the sixth also for an Irish county. In Lord Melbourne's Cabinet there were nine members of the House of Commons. At the election six of them had to contest their seats, and the votes polled were—12,031, 6221, 932, 784, 527, 430. Three were returned without contests for constituencies, with the following number of electors:—6000, 2000, 460.

[2] See *The Times*, 14th May 1838.

ascending and descending scale, and I do not consider that that duty will afford a sufficient protection to the land of this country."

And then, referring to more general subjects, he said: "It was unadvisable, in my opinion, that the Government should continue in power, not possessing the confidence of the House of Commons. I came forward and submitted that question to the test in the House of Commons, and the House of Commons, by a small majority no doubt, but still by a majority of one, declared that the Government had not its confidence. It is now for the people of this country to determine whether they concur in opinion with the majority of the last Parliament, and whether they will give to the members of the present Administration that confidence which was withheld from it by the House of Commons."

The issue was thus clearly put before the electorate by Platform speeches, and practically the leaders of the two great parties agreed as to what that issue was.

The elections went against the Government. The borough elections came first, and a considerable number of seats were lost. In the counties the elections went against the Ministry by an overwhelming majority. Even in the towns and manufacturing districts it was found that the cry of "Cheap bread," which was everywhere raised, met with a formidable rival in the counter cry of "Low wages," which were predicted as the certain consequence of a fall in the staple necessary of subsistence.[1] The landowners and the still unenlightened farmers were alarmed at the progress of the League, and rallied their forces in favour of the party that would oppose it to the utmost, and at this stage of the agitation these two classes were sufficient to return a majority. The number of contests showed some falling off in the public interest in politics, there being only 170 in Great Britain, as against 219 in 1837, and 227 in 1832, but they were quite sufficient to complete the discomfiture of the Ministry.

When the elections were over, and when it was already evident that the Whig Government must resign or be turned out immediately the House met, Sir Robert Peel spoke at a banquet at Tamworth, given to celebrate the election: "I am constantly

[1] See *Annual Register*, 1841.

asked what it is I mean to propose, supposing I am called to the administration of affairs; I will answer that question when I am placed in that position. My advice for the present is, dismiss those who are now in office. They have not the confidence, they had not the confidence of Parliament, and they have not the confidence of the country. Change your physician. The patient has not confidence in him. They found her in health, they leave her in sickness. But it is said, What do you prescribe? I will wait till I am regularly called in."

And "called in" he soon was. When Parliament met, the very first occasion was taken to attack the Ministers; they were defeated by 91 votes, a division which effectually showed the result of the general election; they resigned, and a Tory Government, with Sir Robert Peel at its head, came into office.[1] For the League the most important and encouraging event was the return of their leader, Richard Cobden, as member for Stockport.

While these events were occurring, the Anti-Corn-Law League had been active in a new direction. The useful phase of the Platform, called a Conference, had been had recourse to. A great conference of Ministers of religion, most of them not those of the State Church, it need scarcely be said, was held at Manchester on the 17th August, and three subsequent days. Nearly 700 Ministers attended. The morning meetings lasted four hours, the evening meetings five; Platform speaking the whole time—speaking with effect too, for every auditor would be a missionary, a fresh disciple of the Platform in the cause. The testimony of men so well qualified to speak on the miserable condition of large masses of the people produced considerable effect, and their active intervention gave an element to the agitation which could not but help to elevate its tone, and to impress the public with its justice. Numerous resolutions were passed on the dreadful consequences of the Corn Laws, and a petition to the House of Commons was adopted.

"Your petitioners, convinced of the sinfulness of these laws which violate the paramount law of God, and restrict the bounty of His providence—of their injurious operations on the domestic comforts, and the social, moral, and religious

[1] 30th August 1841.

condition of the people of these realms, of the vast amount of evil which they have already produced, and of the fearful rapidity with which they are driving on their injured and suffering victims to despondency or desperation, and threatening the peace and safety of the Empire—implore your honourable House to devise means for their abolition."

The new Parliament was, however, deaf to implorations. It was prorogued in October. But evils do not cease because Parliament chooses to ignore them, and the distress in the country deepened. How hard to convey the meaning of the phrase "distress deepened." Figures fail to do so—20,000 persons in one place, whose average earnings were only 11¾d. a week; 10,000 persons in another, who were on the verge of starvation; many more thousands in receipt of poor relief—these convey little actual material for realising great widespread distress. Again, to depict one or two cases of poverty and misery as typical cases of hundreds of thousands—that fails still more to convey the meaning. Carlyle has enabled us in a measure to understand it. "So many hundred thousands sit in workhouses; and other hundred thousands have not yet got even workhouses; and in thrifty Scotland itself—in Glasgow, or Edinburgh city, in their dark lanes, hidden from all but the eye of God, and of rare Benevolence, the minister of God—there are scenes of woe and destitution and desolation, such as, one may hope, the sun never saw before in the most barbarous regions where men dwelt. . . . Descend where you will into the lower class, in town or country, by what avenue you will, by Factory Inquiries, Agricultural Inquiries, by Revenue Returns, by Mining-Labourer Committees, by opening your own eyes and looking, the same sorrowful result discloses itself; you have to admit that the working body of this rich English nation has sunk, or is fast sinking into a state, to which, all sides of it considered, there was literally never any parallel."[1]

Over and over again, in the history of this country, one marvels at the patience of the poor. Happily there was at least a prospect of relief, not a near one, but still a prospect, for the Platform was hard at work night and day, arguing, teaching, complaining, remonstrating, demonstrating, proving to

[1] *Past and Present*, book i. chap. i.

all fair-minded men the perniciousness, the iniquity, the injustice of those Corn Laws, and the 700 ministers of the Gospel had sped homewards to work with renewed strength towards the formation of that public opinion which, in the end, is omnipotent, and triumphs over class opinion, however influential and powerful, and meetings were so numerous "that even the names of the places would fill pages."

The opening of the year 1842 found "the whole of the island from Cornwall to Caithness in commotion. To give even a sketch of the meetings held would fill a volume."

With the object of raising money, a great Bazaar was held, and the total sum realised was close upon £10,000.

On the 3d of February Parliament was opened, and early in the same month (8th) a great meeting took place in London of deputies from the conferences and Anti-Corn-Law Associations, nearly 600 persons being present, all with instructions to entertain no proposal for any compromise. This was rather a larger gathering than the meetings of delegates in London in the Economy Agitation of 1779–80, when Mr. Wyvill and some few others met, and the Government of the day trembled.

The Government now, though not trembling, were wavering, the leaders seeing the necessity of making some concession, of giving a little in hope of holding on still to the bulk. The Prime Minister, adhering still to the principle of the existing law, proposed an amended sliding scale.[1] "This new duty," he said, "will cause a very considerable decrease of the protection which the present duty affords to the home-grower." Further than this the Government would not go.

The League, however, were determined not to accept anything less than a total repeal of the duty. The deputies forthwith passed a resolution that the proposed alteration, so far from holding out the slightest prospect of any relief of the

[1] The following table shows the proposed change:—

When Corn is at		Existing Duty.		Proposed Duty.
50s.	....	36s. 8d.	....	20s.
56s.	....	30s. 8d.	....	16s.
60s.	....	26s. 8d.	....	12s.
63s.	....	23s. 8d.	....	9s.
64s.	....	22s. 8d.	....	8s.
70s.	....	10s. 8d.	....	4s.
73s. and upwards			....	1s. a quarter.

distress of the country, was an insult to a patient and suffering people; they recorded their emphatic condemnation of it, and their solemn protest against it. Some subsequent meetings were held, "and then the members separated, each, in his own locality, to aid in the agitation which had been renewed with increased intensity."

A motion in the House of Commons, embodying the principles of the League, was a necessary part of the agitation, and accordingly Mr. Villiers again brought forward a motion that all duties on corn, grain, meal, or flour should cease and determine. But with such a House there was little chance yet of his attaining that object. On this occasion only ninety members voted for it, and in the House of Lords only five were found to support a similar proposition.

Meetings again innumerable were held in opposition to the Government proposal, but the Bill embodying it became law in April.

What strides agitation, and petitioning, and meeting, and Platforming had made since the time of the Economy Agitation may be at once seen by glancing at the figures given by Prentice.[1] "The Anti-Corn-Law Petitions," he says, "presented during the session up to 2d March were:—For repeal, 630; for repeal and freedom of trade, 410; for repeal of corn and provision laws, 1718; against Government proposal, 123; or a total of 2881, with 1,540,755 signatures."

And, in contrasting these figures with the petitions that were presented in 1780 by Mr. Dunning, it is to be borne in mind that they were quite independent of the meetings and petitionings of the Chartist agitation, which just at this time was approaching the crisis of its second great Petition.

In spite of the new Corn Law, the price of bread went on rising, and the distress increased. Another conference of the Anti-Corn-Law League was held in London, and a deputation waited on the Prime Minister. The chairman of the Conference, in addressing Sir R. Peel, stated that since February distress had gone on increasing, capital had still further been diminished, employment decreased, and trade became more depressed. "The population was literally perishing by thousands; they were absolutely starving; the patience of the

[1] Prentice, vol. i. p. 328.

suffering people was nearly exhausted, and a feeling and temper beginning to be manifested which was ominous and dangerous in the highest degree."

The appeal did not, however, move the Government. No further action was taken by Ministers, and on the 12th August Parliament was prorogued. About a week later (on 20th August) the Council of the League held a special meeting, and issued an Address to the people of the United Kingdom, in which, after briefly recounting the proceedings of previous years, they summarised the League's teachings from the Platform: "We declare our unshaken conviction, that the unjust and inhuman Corn Law is the main cause of the evils which afflict the industrial community, destroying the profits of the manufacturers, reducing the wages of the working men, and bringing beggary and ruin upon a large portion of our countrymen; and we desire to record our deliberate opinion that the dense and increasing population of this country cannot be in a prosperous, comfortable, or contented condition so long as they are subjected to the pressure of the Corn Law; and that there can be no guarantee for the peace of society, or for the security of life and property, whilst large masses of the people are sinking into a state of abject destitution." [1]

Their request that Parliament should be reassembled was of course hopeless, and, with such a Parliament, would have been useless. Just at this time a great strike, or "turn-out," for better wages took place in Lancashire and other parts of the kingdom; but both it and the serious riots which followed originated with Chartism and not with the Anti-Corn-Law teaching. The occurrence "made obvious the need of more popular teaching by the League, and increased efforts were made to indoctrinate the people with the principles of free trade."

So far the League agitation had been more or less a middle class agitation.

Cobden pointed this out.[2] He said: "I don't deny that the working classes generally have attended our lectures and signed our petitions; but I will admit that so far as the fervour and efficiency of our agitation has gone, it has emi-

[1] See *Cobden and the League*, by Henry Ashworth, p. 101.
[2] At a meeting at Manchester on 25th August 1842.

nently been a middle class agitation. We have carried it on by those means by which the middle class usually carries on its movements."

The League proceeded to redouble its efforts. "From the termination of the 'turn-out' to the end of the year was one incessant course of teaching on the part of the League. There was the determination that, until the next Parliamentary campaign, every effort should be made to indoctrinate the people with the principles of free trade, and it was carried out with great vigour and perseverance." [1]

The question of money for carrying on the agitation now cropped up; but this was a matter which never troubled the League. By October an expenditure of £100,000 had been incurred and defrayed, and subscriptions were solicited for £50,000 more. Little hesitation was shown in complying with this solicitation. Numerous meetings were held for the purpose, and large sums were promptly subscribed. That the agitation was rapidly gaining ever increasing support from larger numbers of the people was evident; and at the end of the year Bright declared that the League included within its limits "almost the whole of the middle class and of the working population of Great Britain." [2]

Early in the following year [3] the Platform was installed for the first time in a temple dedicated specially to its use—the great Free Trade Hall at Manchester—and there, for nearly four years, a series of meetings were held, "unparalleled in the history of any country for numbers, unity of purpose, determination, enthusiasm, and that constant hope of success which was founded in a deep conviction of the justice of the cause for which all this agitation and all this long course of public instruction was required." [4]

A letter which appeared in *The Morning Chronicle* gives an interesting account of the League itself, and shows us the inner working of that organisation which was at the back of the Platform.

"At the council board of the League Cobden had around him other rich men who make little figure in public, but whose wealth and mercantile operations are known for their vastness

[1] Prentice, vol. i. p. 390.
[2] At Manchester, 29th December 1842.
[3] 1843.
[4] Prentice, vol. ii. p. 8.

throughout the whole civilised world. Several of them who are there every day employ each from 500 to 2000 work-people. . . . All the members being habituated to business they go to their work of agitation with the same precision in the minutest details as they do in their work of cotton spinning. . . .

"By the railways some scores of men issue from and return to Manchester day after day over hundreds of miles of country to address public meetings. By the penny post thousands of letters are daily sent and received, which, without it, would never have been written. By the printing-press, tracts are being distributed to each elector in the kingdom at the rate of three and a half tons weekly—the whole forming an amount of moral power moving from one centre that never before existed in the world, that was never dreamt of as possible to exist."

London, hitherto comparatively silent, was now more vigorously attacked by the League. Between December 1842 and March 1843, 136 meetings were held there. Drury Lane Theatre was taken for a series of weekly meetings, and at the first meeting in it Bright spoke:[1] "There was," he said, "no institution of this country—the monarchy, aristocracy, the Church, or any other whatever—of which he would not say, 'Attach it to the Corn Law, and I will predict its fate.' In this country everything which he held dear was contained. In countries not far off they had seen institutions shaken to their foundations by dire calamities; they had seen crowns and hierarchies shaken to the dust; they had seen ranks, and orders, and parties overthrown; but there was one party which survived all this, and that party was the people. Whatever convulsion might happen in this country, whatever orders might be overthrown, the people would survive. . . . He would now ask the meeting, What was their duty? What was the duty of all their countrymen? He would tell them that the question which they had to decide was, whether this was their country or the country of the monopolists? Were they mere sojourners in the land—mere lodgers—existing in this island, by the sufferance of the monopolists and the owners of the soil? Were the people to sweat at the forge, and to

[1] 15th of March.

toil in the mill, and were they not to eat? The monopolists said 'Yes.' He had attended meetings in the provinces, and the provinces had spoken out and acted as well as spoken. . . . They (the people of London) were the centre of a great empire, the fate of which was trembling in the balance, and which had long been struggling even to faintness with this great iniquity. The provinces, without which they could not exist, and from which they drew all their wealth—all their sustenance—had done that which was the duty of the people of London. He spoke in the name of the numerous meetings which he had attended throughout the country, and he called on them to raise their voices to the Legislature, and to co-operate with those meetings, until that blessed and happy day should arrive when this monopoly should be overthrown, and the blessings which God had provided for the whole of His people should be enjoyed by all." [1]

The usual annual attack was delivered in Parliament by Mr. Villiers, who moved [2] that the House should resolve itself into a Committee for the purpose of considering the duties affecting the importation of foreign corn, with a view of their immediate abolition.

Mr. Gladstone met the motion by a direct negative, and, after five nights' debate, 125 voted in favour of the resolution, and 381 against it, or a majority of 256 for the Government and against the League. The division showed some little progress in the direction of free trade in corn, but the majority was an enormous one, enough to damp the energies and the hopes of the stoutest Anti-Corn-Law Leaguer. So far, however, from being discouraged the League braced itself for further struggles. It made a more determined attack than had hitherto been made on the agricultural districts of the country, and put forth fresh endeavours to convert the farmers and agricultural labourers to its views. Deputations, consisting generally of the members of the Council, visited the market towns and other agricultural centres, and held meetings there. Cobden and Bright, and many others, were ceaselessly engaged in this duty, haranguing—as opponents of the Platform called it—all who came to hear. One thing in con-

1 Prentice's *League*, vol. ii. p. 54.
2 *Parliamentary Debates*, vol. lxix. p. 26, 9th May.

nection with these meetings specially calls for notice—namely, that the Platform was used, not for one-sided speechifying, as it so often now is, but for the *bonâ fide* purposes of discussion. At meeting after meeting persons in favour of the Corn Laws, and persons opposed to them, met, and listened fairly and patiently to the speakers on the different sides of the question, their respective views being only shown by their applause, or when resolutions were put to the meeting for assent or dissent. Nowadays it has become the practice or custom for meetings to be composed almost exclusively of sympathisers with the object of the meeting, the speaking is all on one side, and any one speaking in opposition is scarcely ever given a fair hearing.

In the Anti-Corn-Law Agitation, however, great toleration was accorded to the different speakers, and numerous meetings were held specially and avowedly for the purpose of discussion.

Thus, at Devonport, a public meeting was held in April, to hear a discussion on the Corn Laws between a deputation from the League, and the advocates of monopoly chosen to represent the Conservative Association of the Borough. A clergyman spoke for two hours in favour of protection. Bright spoke for two hours in answer, and then a resolution against the Corn Laws was carried by a proportion of 20 to 1.

At Uxbridge a similar sort of meeting was held. Here Cobden spoke first, and was replied to by supporters of the Corn Law, and resolutions were carried against the Laws.

At Bedford a meeting was held, and Cobden and Moore attended, also speakers from the other side. After the speeches a resolution was proposed by the latter, "That protection to native industry, particularly of the agriculture of the country, is essential to the well-being of the State." It was negatived, and an amendment carried for abolishing all monopolies.

At Rye Cobden and Moore were opposed on the Platform by Mr. Curteis, M.P., who said that "he stood there boldly to contest the ground with Mr. Cobden."

At a meeting at Huntingdon, Bright and Moore spoke on one side, and several landed proprietors on the other, and resolutions were put to the meeting for decision.

At a great county meeting in Essex of some 6000 people Cobden spoke for two hours, and several local landowners spoke against him, and the meeting decided against protection. It is not necessary to give any further instances. Numerous meetings of this sort were held; real genuine discussion was carried on at them; speakers on both sides were usually attentively listened to and given a hearing; there was no rioting or disturbance, and both parties accepted the result with comparative equanimity. Even meetings were held where the question was discussed as between Corn Laws and the Charter, and resolutions carried one way or the other. These instances proved conclusively that a real genuine discussion could be carried on at a public meeting—a point which has, at all times, been strongly contested by those who wish to depreciate the utility and power of the Platform.

In July the Anti-Corn-Law League received great encouragement by the election of Mr. Bright as representative of Durham. The contest was a severe one, being against powerful interests, but the co-leader of the League won, and the triumph was a great one.

Parliament was prorogued on the 24th August 1843, still apparently as resolute as ever against the abolition of the Corn Laws.

Undeterred by want of success so far, the League immediately began a fresh career of action. From the report of the League for the year ending September 1843,[1] it appeared that 650 lectures had been delivered during the year; 140 towns had been attended by its delegates or deputations, many of them twice or thrice; £47,800 had been spent, and tracts and publications innumerable (over 9,000,000) had been issued.

On the 28th September, at a great meeting in Covent Garden Theatre, Cobden announced the plans of the League for the ensuing year. They were important, and showed how well the leaders saw the only way of attaining the realisation of their object. He said:[2] "The League proposes to take another step in giving a direction to the legislative power of this country. We propose to draw the bonds more closely between the League and the electoral body of the country. We

[1] Prentice, vol. ii. p. 119.

[2] See *Speeches of Richard Cobden*, edited by J. Bright and T. Rogers, vol. i. p. 71.

regard the electors of the country as possessing in their own hands absolute dominion within these realms. . . . It is not our fault if the electoral body is not exactly as we should have wished to have found it—we must work with the instruments we have. We are not in fault if the electoral body is so distributed as to give, by its scattered and detached fragments, the greatest advantages to our enemies, who are the enemies of the human race, in meeting us in the field of combat. The plan of the League is to bring the more powerful sections of the electoral body into a union with the more vulnerable portions." He then described the steps proposed to be taken for the registration of voters so as to get a majority at elections, and said that he and his colleagues would visit every borough in the kingdom to urge the people there to petition their members to vote for Mr. Villiers's motion early next session, to supplant every monopolist member, and to have a candidate ready for any vacancy. He then went on: "It is not the intention of the League to recommend any further petitioning to the House of Commons. . . . The Council of the League will recommend the electors not to petition Parliament—of that enough has been done already—but to memorialise the Queen, that she will be pleased to dissolve the present Parliament. . . . As a means of carrying on these proceedings, and to furnish the money for doing so, the Council are resolved to raise the sum of £100,000."

A month later a vacancy arose in the city of London, and the League strained every effort to secure the seat in the person of Mr. Pattison. A great meeting was held at Covent Garden Theatre; a large sympathetic meeting was held in Manchester. The League triumphed, Pattison was returned, though only by a small majority, but it was a great and most significant victory.

The raising of the fund of £100,000 progressed rapidly. "The mode adopted in each place was to originate the subscription at a public meeting. Each meeting was in itself a formidable agitation." At a meeting at Manchester, on the 14th of November, £12,000 was subscribed in an hour and a half, including several subscriptions of £500 each. At Liverpool £4600 was raised before the meeting separated. Glasgow, Leeds, and Bradford each subscribed over £2000; several towns over £1000,—such contributions had never been heard of before in all the annals of agitation.

A curious instance occurred in the autumn of this year of the tenacity of local authorities to old practices. In Worcestershire the High Sheriff refused to act on a requisition signed by Lord Southwell, Sir E. Blount, and Mr. R. Scott, M.P., to call a meeting relative to the Corn Laws.[1] "I decline calling such a meeting for such a purpose," wrote the Sheriff, as if he could still stand in the way of the expression of public opinion, as his predecessors in office had done in the "good old days," now happily long passed. The meeting was, however, called by others and held, and strong resolutions against the Corn Law passed.

Contemporary criticism is often valuable, and the following passage from *The Examiner* of December 1843[2] makes some interesting comments on the actions of the Anti-Corn-Law League. The writer said: "The conduct of its discussions has been acquiring temper, method, and more skilful direction, as it has been getting strength. With the sense of its power has come a higher skill in the direction and wielding of it. The teachers in this great school of agitation have taught themselves many valuable lessons. How admirable have been Mr. Cobden's Addresses to the agriculturists, and what an improvement is to be marked in them upon his previous dissertations, clever as they were; but when he applied himself to the argument for conversion, instead of the invective against error, the higher vein of his powers was opened. By it was swept away at once the mischievous misrepresentation that the advocates of free trade were enemies of the agricultural interest, in the true sense of the word."

The League steadily gained ground. "Meetings in rooms might not be proofs of public opinion," said Cobden, "but open-air meetings in every county, they going perfect strangers and meeting 3000 to 4000 people, all voting in favour of free trade in corn, were decisive and conclusive proofs that the great body of the people were in favour of a repeal of the Corn Laws."

At Covent Garden meeting on 30th November 1843 Cobden said: "Ten or a dozen men commenced the League five years

[1] *The Examiner*, p. 633. [2] *Ibid.* 2d December 1843

ago. We are not men of eminence; we are low-bred, uneducated men if they (the opponents) will; but why have ten such men brought this agitation to its present state? Was it because they agitated for a fixed duty? No; if they had done so, it would have been a rope of sand, and would have been asunder in a dozen places before six months were over. It was proceeding upon the principle that there should be no tax upon bread, no tax in favour of any particular class, that we are what we are now."[1]

That was a perfectly simple, intelligible, and just issue to put before the people, and was one which, in the long run, must ultimately triumph.

The beginning of the year 1844 found the League still hammering away from the Platform. Bright and Cobden were hard at work in Scotland. At a meeting at Edinburgh, on the 11th January, the Lord Provost, who presided, described their labours.

"The champions of free trade, whom we have the honour and pleasure of seeing among us this night, have bearded the lion in his den. They have plainly and affectionately expostulated with the agricultural labourers, the farmers, and the landlords, in the most sottish, the most landlord-ridden, and the most priest-ridden districts; they have instructed and delighted crowded audiences in Manchester, Liverpool, London, and all the great towns. In short, they seem to possess a sort of ubiquity. The papers of the same day record their triumphs in the town and in the country, in the south and in the north. They were in the great commercial capital of the west yesterday—to-day they are in Edinburgh—to-morrow they will be in Perth—the next day in Aberdeen—up through the length and breadth of the land they go, conquering and to conquer. Their labours have been herculean, and they have been cheered with corresponding success."

And at a banquet at Glasgow on the previous night Bright said: "I speak not without authority. We have attended hundreds of meetings. No men in this country have seen the faces of so many of their countrymen as we have. We have shaken by the hand, from our heart of hearts, hundreds of thousands of the intelligent population of this country; and

[1] *The Examiner*, p. 761, 1843.

we have authority for saying, that it is the opinion of the middle classes of this country, who are the intelligent and the powerful, and the electoral classes, that this law is bad, that it originated in injustice, and has been maintained by an unjust exercise of power." [1]

At the end of January we find Cobden declaring that "Our question has been advancing until it has become a great national and a great political question. Our cause has been lifted to the first rank in the senate."

An interesting criticism on the agitation about this period was made by a writer in the pages of *Tait's Magazine*, which is worth quoting, as it conveys a contemporary view of the progress of the League.

"THE LEAGUE AGITATION.—What a fact it is! How it grows, bigger and bigger every week, under all sorts of circumstances. High prices and low prices, bad harvests and good harvests, manufacturing distress and revival of manufacturing prosperity, the inertness of opponents and their virulent antagonism —all help; nothing comes amiss to the League; it can digest and assimilate anything, lives and thrives on anything, and keeps working away with a force, a continuity, a steam-engine precision and regularity, and a progressive expansion of effort, which bring everything within its sweep, and make its eventual and not remote success as sure as though the act for total and immediate repeal were already in the hands of the Queen's printer. This League is doing a great work with a strong heart. It produces the doctrines of Adam Smith on the stage of the patent theatres, preaches them in the market-places of country towns, heads the poll with them at city of London elections, and gets votes of thanks for them from county meetings. It drags the aristocracy of Great Britain down from the seventh heaven of the Upper House, where they sat like Epicurus's gods, to the bar of public opinion, where they are but as men; and makes the proud and lazy culprits acknowledge the jurisdiction, and plead to the indictment like any other criminals."

One important thing the League never lacked—that was, money. It flowed into the League. The £100,000 was being rapidly subscribed. "The League had now the support of the

[1] See *The League*, 20th January 1844.

best part of the Press, both in London and in the provinces. Every speech was reported, and millions of readers looked to the speeches at the Anti-Corn-Law meetings with more eagerness than they did to the proceedings in Parliament." The meetings in London at Covent Garden Theatre were being held every week. "There could be but two or three debates upon the great question in the course of the session, but in the same time it might be discussed thirty times before an audience ten times more numerous."[1]

"If these meetings continue," said Cobden at one of them, "and are carried on with the same numbers, order, and decorum with which they are now, speaking in a voice that is felt throughout Europe, do you think it will be long before their influence will be found in another place whose locality will be nameless, not far from Parliament Street?"[2]

Though the League was thus making most satisfactory progress, the great change in the conduct of the agitation announced by Cobden at Covent Garden in the previous September was inaugurated about this time. I have already remarked that there were two ways in which the Platform could, short of actual revolution, secure the policy recommended by it: the one in influencing in detail the formation of the component parts of the House of Commons; the other in bringing pressure to bear on the representatives when elected.

The League had been trying to act on the second of these courses, and had sought to influence the representatives when sitting. Their meetings had not been formidable enough to appeal to the fears or discretion of some members, nor did the principles of their action at all tend towards intimidation, as the reform agitation had done. They had petitioned Parliament and had gone on petitioning, but every form of remonstrance to the Legislature had been attempted in vain, the petitions of the people had been unheeded, motions in Parliament had been rejected, applications of all kinds had been disregarded.[3]

Petitions with 500,000 signatures had been sent in 1839; as years went on they mounted up to 1,700,000 in 1843, still without effect, and so it was then decided to leave off petition-

[1] Prentice, vol. ii. p. 164. [2] Cobden's *Speeches*, p. 130, 8th February.
[3] See speech of Mr. Villiers, M.P., at Ashton, January 1844.

ing as utterly useless. The leaders of the League decided that the other course should now be had recourse to. As W. J. Fox forcibly expressed it at the Covent Garden meeting:[1] "We are not going to the Legislature this session. No more petitioning. Members of the House of Commons! Members of the House of Lords! do as you please, and what you please —our appeal is *to your masters*. (Tremendous cheering, which lasted for a considerable time.) The League goes to the constituencies, to the creators of legislators, and tells them they have made the article badly, and instructs them how to form it better on the first occasion. Here we carry on the warfare, appealing—not as has been falsely said to calumny, delusion, or to corruption, but calling up in those who possess political power the intelligence and independence which dignify humanity."

And Cobden, speaking in February at Manchester, said: "Now, ladies and gentlemen, your work is not done; it is just about beginning. I don't mean to say that there need be quite so much talking or noise in future as there has been; I don't think there will be any necessity for it. The time is now coming when we people who make so great a show and parade of our labours will become less important in this question, and when the real harvest must be reaped by those men who, in every borough, will content themselves to work strenuously and perseveringly, in secret and in private. *This question must be carried in the registration courts.* It is not in public meetings that this question will be carried. Why, what did Sir Robert Peel say, and what did his party do? Ten years ago, with a large majority against him, such as would have made it almost hopeless that his party would ever again get into power, he proclaimed from the Merchant Tailors' Hall, 'Register, register, register!'[2] His friends set to work; they watched the registration courts; they put men on the franchise whom they could depend upon; and they carried their cause, bad as it was, without a single public meeting or demonstration of any kind. And now, I say, let us, in a good cause—having won our cause in meetings such as this—let us show

[1] 24th January 1844.

[2] The speech referred to was made at Tamworth, not at the Merchant Tailors' Hall. See *ante*, p. 144.

that we can imitate our opponents by attending to the registration courts; let us put men upon the franchise; let us extend the franchise to every man who is a free-trader; and even where you find honest men, who want the franchise, but are not free-traders, put every man you can upon the franchise. Teach yourselves the course by which you are to become enfranchised; learn when you must pay your rates; learn how you must defend your cause in the registration courts. Put yourselves to work in this way, and then this cause may be assuredly won, as the cause of our opponents was; and if it is not won in that way, I solemnly believe it never can be won at all."

Though the League was thus working outside Parliament, it was inevitable that the question now so uppermost in men's minds should, in the course of the session, be brought before Parliament, and on the 12th March Cobden brought forward a motion for an inquiry into the effects of protective duties on the interests of the tenant farmers and labourers, but it was rejected.[1] On the 25th June Mr. Villiers moved that the House do resolve itself into committee for the purpose of considering certain resolutions, the principal one of which was the abolition of the Corn Laws.

Sir Robert Peel, in defending the policy of the Government, declared that "The agriculture of this country was entitled to protection from reasons both of justice and policy. He was not prepared to alter the Corn Law of 1842, and did not contemplate it." And the House of Commons, which shared his opinion, rejected the motion.[2] The division showed some progress, but the progress was marked rather by the decrease of the majority than by an increase of the minority.

In the course of the summer a new element showed signs of movement against the Corn Laws—the labourers in some districts began to have recourse to the Platform, and held meetings to denounce the existing system of protection.[3] *The*

[1] 244 votes against 153. [2] By 330 votes to 142.

[3] Place, in his MSS., 27,821, p. 1, about Chartism, says: "A public meeting was held, January 1839, at Saxmundham, consisting mainly of agricultural labourers. This was the first great meeting of this class of persons. The chair was taken by a shop-keeper, the meeting was opened by a long prayer, to which a thousand voices responded Amen. The most remarkable feature of the meeting was the general reprobation of the Corn Laws, and desire for their repeal."

League, the organ of the Anti-Corn-Law League, very truly remarked that "It is not easy to overrate the importance of such meetings; they are the safety-valves of national distress; our rulers should be glad to find the agricultural labourers stating their grievances in a peaceful and constitutional form, because it shows that the hope of redress is still alive in their bosoms, and that they are indisposed to lend themselves to the frantic suggestions of despair." The occurrence was, however, more significant of the progress of the Platform than any actual addition to the strength of the agitation, for the labourers had no votes, and were unable to exercise any influence on Parliament.

Another occurrence at this time was far more memorable—was, in fact, most momentous—a meeting at which the struggle between Leaguers and Chartists came to a crisis, and which was practically the turning-point in their future destinies. The account given by Gammage, himself a Chartist, can scarcely be improved upon.[1] He said: "The Anti-Corn-Law League had, for some time past, been making a head of their opponents (the Chartists). O'Connor had repeatedly challenged Cobden to meet him in discussion on the subject, which, however, the latter always declined. But on one occasion at Bradford Cobden happened boastingly to ask: 'Where was the man that would meet him in discussion, and maintain that the Corn Law was a just law?' O'Connor at once accepted the challenge thus thrown out; still Cobden fought shy of O'Connor.

"But speedily events so happened as to bring these two chiefs together upon the same platform. A requisition was got up in Northampton to Messrs. Cobden and Bright to address a public meeting in the market square of that town. The Chartists sent a requisition to O'Connor to attend also. . . . The invitations were accepted. At one o'clock on the appointed day Messrs. Cobden and Bright, accompanied by their friends, mounted the hustings amid the cheers of the League supporters. . . . O'Connor, Wheeler, Clarke, M'Grath, and the local Chartist leaders shortly after arrived, amid the applause of the Chartist portion of the audience. A large part of the meeting appeared attached to neither party, but resolved to hear both, and judge for themselves."

[1] Gammage, p. 272.

Mr. Grundy, ironfounder, was elected chairman. "Mr. Cobden was the first speaker. He moved a resolution 'That the Corn Law and all other laws restricting trade for the benefit of a class are unjust, and ought to be forthwith abolished.' And he made out as good a case as it was possible for man to make. Still it was felt that his position was a flimsy one, and that it would soon be dissipated by the sterner facts and reasoning of O'Connor; but those who had formed these expectations were doomed to be disappointed. That he delivered an eloquent speech, one of the most eloquent indeed that he had ever delivered, no one for a moment questioned; but as an answer to Cobden, it was a miserable failure. He skimmed over the surface of every question, but below the surface he never ventured to dive. All the time he was speaking his friends imagined that he was only introducing the question, and when, after a three-quarters of an hour's address, he sat down, there was a look of blank disappointment. Though on rising the cheers of the crowd were long and protracted, when he resumed his seat they were comparatively faint, and speedily died away. What made matters worse, the speech had all the appearance of being well prepared. A smile of triumph sat on the features of the leading men of the League as he concluded. They saw that, so far as O'Connor was concerned, the game was their own."

Some other Chartist leaders also spoke. Bright followed M'Grath (a Chartist orator), "and levelled the most cutting sarcasms at O'Connor, which did not fail to produce their effect. Clarke essayed to speak, but the meeting had become satiated; and the chairman proceeded to put O'Connor's amendment, and the original motion, after which he decided that the latter was carried. It was our firm conviction," says Gammage (evidently endeavouring to console himself) "that the amendment had the majority, but if so, the majority was a small one. Had the subject been properly handled, the majority would have been immense. Thus did O'Connor, on the 15th of August 1844, give the League the greatest victory they ever obtained."

During the autumn the League, in pursuance of its new policy, temporarily abandoned the Platform, and directed almost the whole of their attention to the subject of registration of electors. "The work of instruction had, in a great measure, been done. Opinion had been rapidly becoming right. The great object now was to make it productive of action." [1]

Speaking at Manchester Cobden said: "You cannot carry the abolition of this system unless you are active and energetic in putting yourselves in a position to have the power of carrying out your principles. Talking will not do it. I admit we can show our enemies are wrong, but still we cannot make men do right unless you have the power to compel men to it." From "Register, register, register," he advanced to a further plan, "Qualify, qualify, qualify." "We will cry aloud on every pedestal on which we can be placed throughout the country; we will raise our voice everywhere—'Qualify, qualify, qualify.'"

In disclosing his scheme Cobden said: "The county constituency may be increased indefinitely. It requires a qualification of 40s. a year in a freehold property to give a man a vote in a county. That franchise he regarded as 'merely nominal, and within the reach of every man who has the spirit to acquire it.' I say, then, every county where there is a large town population, as in Lancashire, the West Riding of Yorkshire, South Staffordshire, North Cheshire, Middlesex, Surrey, Kent, and many other counties I could name—in fact, every other county bordering upon the sea-coast, or having manufactures in it—may be won, and easily won, if the people can be roused to a systematic effort to qualify themselves for the vote in the way in which the South Lancashire people have reached to the qualification. We find counties can be won by that means and no other." And he urged the people to acquire freeholds, and therefore votes, in such numbers as would give them the power of returning the members. They could make no better use of their savings.

"The scheme," wrote a writer in *Tait's Magazine*, "is the work of a master-mind in the art and science of agitation, and is plainly destined to exert a most powerful influence, not merely on the particular cause of free trade, but on all cognate questions of popular right and good government."

The Platform was not, however, abandoned by the League

[1] Prentice, vol. ii. p. 249.

for long, as early in 1845 it was again in full work. It was too valuable and powerful an aid to the cause to be neglected for any length of time.

The meetings at Covent Garden Theatre bore testimony to its popularity. Even Cobden was struck by them. Speaking on 15th of January at one of them he said: "Really I who have almost lived in public meetings for the last three years feel well-nigh daunted at this astounding spectacle. . . . But as this is only one meeting of many, and when we look back at the numerous gatherings we have had of a similar kind, and when we remember that not one discordant opinion, violation of order, or even breach of etiquette, has occurred at any of our meetings—why, there is an amount of moral force about these great assemblages which, I think, it is impossible for any unjust law long to resist!"

The movement in favour of purchase of freeholds also gave rise to fresh action on the part of the Platform, a large number of meetings being held to further it, the most satisfactory results following, and thousands of persons purchasing freeholds.

W. J. Fox, speaking at this same meeting, dwelt on some of the incidental advantages of the course: "In this plan there is a moral good beyond, perhaps, what in its original conception was thought of. It tends to act upon the character of the entire labouring population of the country—the working classes—the more toilsome section of the middle classes; it holds out to them a hope, promise, and incitement of the most desirable and elevating description. It says to them, 'Become proprietors of a portion, however small, of this our England; have a stake in the country; be something here.' . . . It gives them a tangible bond of connection with society—a feeling of independence and honest pride. They are put in the position which was deemed necessary to citizenship in the republics of ancient days; and this is adapted to cherish in them the emotions which best accord with consistency, propriety, and dignity of character."

For the purpose of raising further funds to carry on the agitation another great Bazaar was held, this time in London, with the most satisfactory results.

Once more—namely, on the 10th of June—Mr. Villiers

moved in Parliament for a Committee of the whole House to consider his resolutions for the abolition of all restrictions on the importation of foreign corn, and once more he was defeated.[1]

About this time Cobden appears to have discovered that he was committing one mistake—namely, that he had not been making as much use of his position in Parliament for pushing the agitation as he might have done. Agitation in Parliament had ever been a most useful stimulus to the Platform; a great debate there gave a great impetus to discussion out of doors—in fact, as we have seen, Petitions were often sent to Parliament in such a form as would necessarily raise a debate there. A debate in Parliament sometimes kept a question alive out of doors; a successful division there gave enormous encouragement and incentive to whatever the cause was which the Platform was agitating, or a disastrous division there often damped the energies of the Platform. The two institutions are so closely interwoven, and so interdependent, that any violent action in the one almost instantly affects the other. Perhaps Cobden's appreciation of this principle was somewhat quickened by the fact that the last harvest had been a very good one, and there was some little slackening of the enthusiasm for the abolition of the Corn Laws.

Speaking in London, a few days after the rejection of Mr. Villiers's motion, he said: "The House of Commons is not such a bad place after all, especially for agitation. Last year we made a little mistake at the beginning of the session; we laid our heads together, and came to the conclusion that we could employ ourselves better out of doors in visiting some of the counties and rural districts, and agitating a little in the country; this year we have changed our tactics, and we thought that Parliament, after all, was the best place for agitating. You speak with a loud voice when speaking on the floor of that House; you are heard all over the world, and if you have anything to say that hits hard, it is a very long whip, and reaches all over the kingdom." But his avowal of the efficacy of speech in Parliament must not be considered as clashing

[1] On the division there were for the motion............ 122
Against.. 254
Majority against.............................. 132

with his opinion of the efficacy of the Platform, for in the same speech he said: "I think we ought to feel deeply indebted to such meetings as this, which have stood by this question, which have cheered on public men in its advocacy, which have aided in disseminating the knowledge that has gone forth from this vast building, in which we have brought the public mind on both sides so far to defer to the expression of public opinion as to show that they are bound to acknowledge the justice of our principles."[1]

It would be an interesting speculation as to how much more time would have elapsed before the League would have attained its object had affairs continued to progress as they had been doing the last few years. Would the continued efforts of the leaders have resulted at the next general election in a sufficient Parliament majority to have carried the abolition of the Corn Laws? The question must remain for ever undecided, for before that election came a great event happened which completely altered the whole aspect of the case. Early in July anxiety was felt as to the prospects of the coming harvest. The month passed with alternating hopes and fears. August found men in a state of trembling suspense. Before the end of the month it was seen that the harvest could not be a good one; in another month it was clear that the harvest was a disastrously bad one. From Ireland, with its 8,500,000 of persons, nearly 5,000,000 of whom lived on potatoes, came the appalling intelligence that the potato crop had failed, suddenly and completely, and that famine must inevitably ensue. The probability, almost the certainty that thousands would be starved to death, loomed close and awful.

With the deepening crisis the energies of the League were redoubled. On the 28th October a great meeting of the members of the League was held in the Free Trade Hall at Manchester, some 8000 persons being present.

"What is the remedy?" asked Cobden, in the course of his speech. "You would say, open wide the ports, and admit the bread of the whole world to feed the people. That is the obvious and natural remedy" . . . but, he went on: "What I wish to impress on you now is this, that it is not the opening of the ports alone we want, but we want to set our backs

[1] See *The League*, 5th July, p. 642.

against them, to prevent them from ever being shut again. . . . I for one believe that the day of our redemption draweth nigh. But we must not relax in our labours; on the contrary, we must be more zealous, more energetic, more laborious than we have ever yet been. When the enemy is wavering, then is the time to press upon him. I call, then, upon all who have any sympathy in our cause, who have any promptings of humanity, or who feel any interest in the wellbeing of their fellowmen, all who have apprehensions of scarcity or starvation, to come forward with their efforts, to avert this horrible destiny, this dreadfully impending visitation."

Mr. Ashworth also spoke: "I therefore implore you, as you would spare the people around you from impending famine, to bestir yourselves, and act forcibly as one man, and the sliding scale and fixed duty are for ever done with."

Bright also made a long speech: "We have no change of tactics to offer you. We have no sudden blow to propose by which we hope to abolish the Corn Law. Seven years' work, and the results of seven years' work, have shown how far we have acted wisely. There must be no faltering for the future; everything that is past stimulates us to go on in the same course."

Once more the *Memoirs of Sir Robert Peel* let us into the innermost recesses of the minds of the Government. On the 27th October Sir J. Graham wrote a warning note to Sir Robert Peel: "The Anti-Corn-Law pressure is about to commence, and it will be the most formidable movement in modern times. Everything depends on the skill, promptitude, and decision with which it is met."[1]

On the 1st November we find Peel's views set forth in a Cabinet Memorandum: "I cannot disguise from myself that the calling together of Parliament on account of apprehended scarcity—the prohibition of export in other countries—the removal of restrictions on import (sanctioned, as in the case of Belgium, by a unanimous vote of the Chambers)—the demand for public money, to be applied to provide sustenance for a portion of the people—will constitute a great crisis, and that it will be dangerous for the Government, having assembled Parliament, to resist with all its energies any material

[1] Peel's *Memoirs*, vol. ii. p. 136.

modification of the Corn Law. . . . We must make our choice between determined maintenance, modification, and suspension of the existing Corn Law."[1]

On the 6th November he proposed to his colleagues "To issue forthwith an Order in Council remitting the duty of grain in bond to one shilling, and opening the ports for the admission of all species of grain at a smaller rate of duty until a day named in the Order." This proposal did not, however, meet with the approval of his colleagues.

About this same time a dissolution of Parliament was suggested to him as a possible course to be pursued, but, he says in his *Memoirs*, "It appeared to me that there were grave objections to the proposal that we should notify to the constituent body on the eve of a general election the intention to repeal the Corn Laws for the express purpose of inviting an expression of their opinion on that particular subject. I thought such an appeal would ensure a bitter conflict between different classes of society, and would preclude the possibility of dispassionate consideration by a Parliament, the members of which would probably have committed themselves by explicit declarations and pledges, and would approach a discussion which could not be deferred, with all the heat and animosity engendered by severe contests at the hustings."[2]

On the 13th November a public dinner was given at Birmingham to Mr. Villiers, and was made the occasion for a great Free Trade demonstration. Mr. Villiers made a long speech.

"Gentlemen—Government have decided on nothing; they wait for you to suggest what their decision shall be. There never, in my opinion, was a time when the people of this country were more called on to speak out. I was convinced that it would be a libel on that character which you have honourably acquired, if at such a time you were found lagging behind the rest of the community, and that you would, by your silence, give evidence of wanting public spirit. In a cause of justice and humanity you would be never found wanting, and I am sure that you would not descend to notice the humble efforts of an individual like myself if you did not intend to rise up yourselves and accomplish the work. Gladden the hearts then, cheer the courage of millions by calling

[1] Peel's *Memoirs*, vol. ii. p. 146. [2] *Ibid.* p. 166.

on Government to strike down at once and abolish for ever their selfish and mischievous obstacle to the supply of food for the people. And if Ministers should resist that appeal, or Parliament should sanction their refusal, call on them to put the electors on their trial, and try whether they are the proper depositaries of power, or faithful guardians of the interests of those unenfranchised millions who earn their bread by the sweat of their brow."

As the month went on and anxiety deepened, meetings became more and more numerous. At all of them the remedy urged and asked for was "open the ports." Deeper and deeper was the gloom of coming disaster settling down on the nation. The voice of the Platform became more earnest and imploring. Towards the end of November the necessity of opening the ports for the free importation of corn as the only possible means of saving the country, having already reached the Prime Minister, at last reached the leader of the opposition in Parliament, Lord John Russell. Though it was the eleventh hour, he was gladly received by the Leaguers. "I confess," he said in an Address to the Electors of the City of London,[1] "that on the general subject (of a tax upon corn) my views have, in the course of twenty years, undergone a great alteration. I used to be of opinion that corn was an exception to the general rules of political economy; but observation and experience have convinced me that we ought to abstain from all interference with the supply of food. Neither a Government nor a Legislature can ever regulate the corn market with the beneficial effects which the entire freedom of sale and purchase are sure of themselves to produce. I have for several years endeavoured to obtain a compromise on this subject. . . . It is no longer worth while to contend for a fixed duty. . . . The imposition of any duty at present, without a provision for its extinction within a short period, would but prolong a contest already sufficiently fruitful of animosity and discontent. . . . Let us then unite to put an end to a system which has been proved to be the blight of commerce, the bane of agriculture, the source of bitter divisions among classes, the cause of penury, fever, mortality, and crime among the people. But if this end is to be achieved, it must be

[1] 22d November 1845.

gained by the unequivocal expression of the public voice. . . . The Government appear to be waiting for some excuse to give up the present Corn Law. Let the people by petition, by address, by remonstrance, afford them the excuse they seek."[1]

One would think from this letter that the people had not been doing these things. The people had been petitioning until they found it useless to do so any more; they had been addressing and remonstrating to the extreme limits of such practices. If that were all that were required they had afforded the Government ample excuse for abolishing the Corn Laws. And now, without requiring any invitation from the Whig leader, the Platform, from one end of the country to the other, was resounding with prayers, and advice, and implorations, the more impressive from being imbued with the intense earnestness begotten by a great and impending danger. The orators of the League were unceasingly active—active with a sort of herculean strength. In the course of three weeks we find Cobden and Bright speaking at meetings at Sheffield, Leeds, Wakefield, Bradford, Gloucester, Stroud, Bath, Bristol, Nottingham, Derby, Stockport, and many other places. Great meetings were held too in London, Edinburgh, Glasgow, and numerous other great towns; and *The League* of the 6th December wrote: "We cannot here speak in any detail of the public meetings of the past few days. There is no keeping pace with them. Nor is it necessary to attempt it. These expressions of national feeling and opinion are, with variations of a merely local and circumstantial kind, of a substantial similarity—we might almost say, of a sameness—that renders it needless to notice them individually. The history of one is the history of all. . . .

"Such an agitation as that which now stirs this country is a novelty in the history of popular movements. The world has seen nothing like it before. An agitation on the basis of the truths of economic science; an agitation to arrest the progress of national calamity, in its first stages, by removing its primary cause; an agitation whose objects and principles command the respect both of philosophy and of statesmanship,—this is really a new fact, as it is also one in the highest degree honourable to the people by whom it is exhibited."

[1] Peel's *Memoirs*, vol. ii. p. 177.

While the Platform was thus in full work, the Prime Minister was again advising the suspension of the existing Corn Laws for a limited period; but not being supported by all the Cabinet, he went to the Queen at Osborne, on 5th of December, and asked leave to resign.

The Queen accepted his resignation, and sent for Lord John Russell; but he, not feeling himself able to take office, Sir Robert Peel was, on the 20th December, required to withdraw his resignation, which he did, and the Cabinet was reconstructed. In the meantime, in the face of ever-deepening anxiety, the voice of the Platform was becoming minatory.

Bright, speaking on 19th December, said: "Two centuries ago the people of this country were engaged in a fearful conflict with the Crown. A despotic and treacherous monarch assumed to himself the right to levy taxes without the consent of Parliament and the people. That assumption was resisted. This fair island became a battlefield, the kingdom was convulsed, and an ancient throne overturned. And if our forefathers two hundred years ago resisted that attempt, if they refused to be the bondmen of a king, shall we be the born thralls of an aristocracy like ours? Shall we, who struck the lion down—shall we pay the wolf homage? Or shall we not, by a manly and united expression of public opinion, at once, and for ever, put an end to this giant wrong? Our cause is at least as good as theirs. We stand on higher vantage ground; we have large numbers at our back; we have more of wealth, intelligence, union, and knowledge of the political rights and the true interests of the country; and what is more than all this—we have a weapon, a power, and machinery which is a thousand times better than that of force, were it employed—I refer to the registration, and especially to the 40s. freehold, for that is the great constitutional weapon which we intend to wield, and by means of which we are sure to conquer; our laurels being gained, not in bloody fields, but upon the hustings, and in the registration courts." [1]

On the 15th December a great meeting of the citizens of London was held in the Guildhall. "Never was there a more important, a more enthusiastic, or a more influential assemblage collected in the metropolis." On the 17th some 20,000 per-

[1] Bright's *Speeches*, vol. ii. p. 287.

sons met at Wakefield to petition the Queen to call Parliament together with a view to the repeal of the Corn Laws. Perth, Bradford, Rye, Hull, and other places, almost innumerable, held meetings, and from the north of Scotland to the south of England the cry which rang from the Platform was, "Open the ports."

On the 23d of December a great and crowning meeting, in one way the most remarkable meeting ever held in this or any other country, was held by the League in the Manchester Town Hall. It was attended by many of the leading merchants and manufacturers of Manchester and the surrounding towns. An account was rendered at it of the £100,000 which had been subscribed to the League, a resolution was passed rescinding the existing resolution against petitioning, and recommending that Petitions be again sent, and then a resolution was passed that, "in order to enable the Council of the League to make renewed and increased exertions for the repeal of the Corn Laws, a subscription in aid of the great fund of £250,000 be now commenced." Whilst the speeches were being made, the subscriptions flowed in. Twenty-three persons and business firms gave in their names for £1000 each, twenty for £500 each, and at the close of the meeting the chairman announced that the amount subscribed was £59,165.

At a meeting soon after at Leeds, £34,000 was subscribed; at one at Liverpool, £12,000; at one at Glasgow, £10,000. Within one month £150,000 was subscribed. These remarkable facts speak for themselves.

One meeting, however, of a totally different character, but none the less instructive, must be mentioned, the more particularly as it is such an admirable illustration of the "expressive" function of the Platform. This was a meeting of agricultural labourers at Goatacre in North Wilts.

The Times of 7th January has given a graphic report of it: "The chairman was a labourer; the speakers, with the exception of two, were labourers; and the object in view was to call public attention to the present condition of the labouring population in this part of the country, and to petition her Majesty and the Legislature to take decisive steps for the speedy relief of their extreme distress. The meeting was to have been held in a large booth erected in a field, but the great expense of providing such accommodation was beyond the combined contributions which these poor people could spare from their very scanty means; and, therefore, they were compelled to assemble together in the cross-road of the village, and to endure the inclemency of a winter night while they talked over their common sufferings. The whole of the arrangements and proceedings were strikingly characteristic of the occasion. A hurdle, supported by four stakes driven into the ground beneath a hedge on the roadside, formed a narrow and unsteady platform, capable of supporting only the chairman and one speaker at a time. Below this rustic erection were placed a small deal table and some rushbottom chairs, borrowed from a neighbouring cottage, for the accommodation of reporters. Four or five candles, some in lanthorns, and others sheltered from the wind by the hands that held them, threw a dim and flickering light upon the groups on this spot, before and around which were gathered nearly 1000 of the peasantry of Wiltshire, some of them accompanied by their wives and their children, who, thus collected, presented a wild and painful appearance. In the shadows of the night the distinctive garb of their class was everywhere discernible, but when the flitting clouds permitted the moon to shine brightly in their faces, in them might be seen written, in strong and unmistakable lines, anxiety, supplication, want, hunger, ever responsive in expression to the sentiments and statements delivered by speakers, who merely described in plain unvarnished language the miseries of their rural auditors.

"The chairman said: To all who are here present, and to my poor fellow-labourers in particular, I call your attention to a subject of the utmost importance—a subject which demands very serious consideration. You know by painful experience that we are suffering under distress and poverty; and we are met here this evening on purpose to make known that distress to her Majesty and to her Ministers, to pray them to open the ports and to repeal the unjust Corn Laws, so that we and our families may enjoy the bounties of Providence. . . . I say, then, let us unite together to advocate the cause of Free Trade. . . . God Almighty in His providence caused the earth to produce abundance of provisions for man, and what one nation could not produce another could; therefore everything should be so managed as to have free commerce throughout the world. (Hear, hear.) The labouring classes were in a most distressed condition at the present time. Those who were in distress should come forward and manfully make their distress known; that would show the necessity for Free Trade, which he believed to be the only remedy. (A voice—'It can't make us worse.')

"Charles Vines, in seconding the resolution, said: Friends, I wish the moon was a little brighter just now, that I could see better who is here; but I see enough to find that here is a good many people, and almost all of 'em weart smock-frocks and poor old hats as I do. Some of us heard from a pulpit a short time ago that the mind of man is like to be dissatisfied. I believe it. Dissatisfied minds have brought all these men here to-night. (A woman's voice—'Ay, and women too.') . . . I don't come here to talk politics; I don't know nothing of 'em. But I don't know much of the Corn Laws, only that they ha'nt done we labourers much good. It is a long time till July next before we get new potatoes; and unless something turns up for we poor creatures, starvation stares us in the face on both hands. But I sincerely hope 'long looked-for' will come before July next. (Hear, hear.) To obtain our rights effectually, we must all, with one heart, lift up our cry and petition her Majesty to remove the restrictions upon trade and commerce, so that the poor labourers may have bread and cheese and good table-beer, to enable them to do the work which their present scanty food never can. (Hear, hear.) May that cry meet with a reply from our gracious Queen. God save the Queen! (Cheers, and responses of 'Amen.') Friends, every man who is born and bred a labourer has for his birthright a living from the soil, to be obtained without being restricted by any laws—unjust laws I might call 'em—enforced by our Legislature. (Cheers.)

"Another speaker said: There was nothing left for them now but starvation or Free Trade. He believed that Free Trade would give them good beef and bread to eat, instead of potatoes and no meat or bread. Bad living had made the agricultural labourers physically weaker; he hoped also that it would now have the effect of making them wiser. It had made them wise enough to attend that meeting. They must speak out their distresses, or they could not expect relief."

After a closing speech from the chairman, urging them to abstain from violence or disorder, the meeting dispersed.

One other extract from a speech I give, as disclosing much of the idea prevailing in some men's minds as to the principles of Government: "But I do think the time will come when every labouring householder will have the privilege of sending men to Parliament. When every man comes under the power of every law that is made, ought not every man to have a voice in making that law?"

All through the early part of this month of January the tide of Platform oratory flowed on. On the 15th a great League meeting was held at Manchester; and then, on the 19th, Parliament was opened by the Queen in person. In the debate on the Address in reply to the Queen's speech Sir Robert Peel stated that, on the question of the Corn Law, his opinions had undergone great change, but he postponed until the 27th making a statement of the extent to which they had changed. On that date he propounded his scheme for dealing with the Corn Laws, and one fresh triumph was added to those already won by the Platform. He then proposed that the admission of Indian corn and buckwheat should be duty free, and that all British Colonial wheat should be admitted at a nominal rate of duty. As regarded other wheat, a considerable reduction should be made, and should commence at once.[1] At the end of three years, or to be more exact, on the 1st of February 1849 grain of all kinds should be admitted into the country subject to only a nominal duty for statistical purposes.

There is no need to enter on any detail of the discussions on these proposals.

Mr. Villiers, consistent to the last, moved that all duties on imported corn should forthwith cease, but with a Government scheme in rivalry it was of course rejected. The third reading of the Government Bill was moved on the 11th May, and carried by 327 votes to 229, and the Lords, with the experience derived from the reform agitation still comparatively fresh in their memory, accepted the Bill, and on the 26th June read it a third time, and passed it.

[1] When the average price of wheat was under 48s. a quarter the duty was to be 10s., the duty falling by 1s. with every 1s. of rise in price, till, on reaching 54s. a quarter, it should be a fixed one of 4s. a quarter.

Once more then the Platform had triumphed; once more gained the point for which it had agitated; once more had it won a great and splendid victory.

With the enactment of the Government measure the work of the League was accomplished. "Our task is concluded," wrote *The League* newspaper in its farewell address; "our labours are at an end. We have seen the great principles for which we have struggled through seven years of doubt and difficulty brought to a triumphant issue, and permanently established in the legislation of the Empire. The records of Parliament are the evidence of our services; the freedom for which wise men wrote, and good men sighed, and brave men struggled, has been won peacefully, honourably, and completely. Laws devised by a jealous, monopolising, and ungrateful spirit to restrain the bounties of Providence, and fetter the energies of an industrious, a brave, and a loyal people, have been swept from the statute book to take their place in the records of unhonoured history."

Fitting was it then, once the need for the Platform in this cause had ceased, that the great organisation at its back should cease also. Accordingly, on the 2d July, the Council of the League held a meeting, which was to be the final meeting of that celebrated body. "It was to die in the midst of its strength, in the very hour of its triumph." Mr. George Wilson, the chairman of the League, presided, and in his speech gave a history of the League.

Elihu Burritt,[1] who was present, and subsequently described the proceedings, said: "The chairman opened with deep emotion at the first chapter of that existence. It read like the first chapter of every great moral reformation that has changed the condition of the world. It began substantially with 'they met in a little upper room.' Every enterprise that has blessed humanity has originated in some 'little upper room,' where men who dared to make themselves of no reputation for the good of their race have met to pray or to plan."

And then, after a full history of the League had been given, a resolution was proposed by Cobden, and seconded by Bright —"That an Act of Parliament having been passed providing for the abolition of the Corn Laws in February 1849, it is

[1] See *The Last Hour of the League*, by Elihu Burritt.

deemed expedient to suspend the active operation of the Anti-Corn-Law League."

In proposing this resolution, Cobden referred to his own labours, and those of his friend's colleagues, and said: "Many people will think that we have our reward in the applause and *éclat* of public meetings; but I declare that it is not so with me, for the inherent reluctance I have to address public meetings is so great, that I do not even get up to present a petition to the House of Commons without reluctance."

His labours for the abolition of the Corn Laws were now happily at an end, and after the resolutions had been passed, the chairman announced that it was his duty to say that "the Anti-Corn-Law League stands conditionally dissolved."

But though the labours of the League were closed, and though most of the men who took part in it have now passed away, its career remains for ever instructive in many matters of the depest import. Latest born of popular movements, the League profited by the good in previous agitations, shunned the evil, and placed the art of agitation, so to speak, on a scientific basis; and most conspicuous of all among their actions is the prominence they accorded to the Platform. Essentially, the triumph of their agitation was due to the Platform. It is true that millions of tracts were distributed, that pamphlets, and articles, and leaflets were scattered broadcast throughout the land; it is true that portions of the Press afforded the movement invaluable aid, and that debates in Parliament advanced the cause; but, over and above all this, it is true that the main burden of the battle fell on the Platform—that it was by the spoken word to the assembled masses that the cause was most effectually advocated. It was by the thrilling eloquence of powerful orators, and the convincing arguments of skilful speakers, that the minds of the masses were swayed far more than by all the printed statements sent forth from the Press. "Knowledge is the power," said Cobden once,—"knowledge alone—by which we shall bring this foul system to the dust;" but in no way was knowledge more effectually spread than from the Platform, not merely spread, but driven home at white-heat into the hearts and minds of the hearers, by the power of the orator, and by the enthusiasm of great public meetings.

The Platform could not, however, have been as effective as it showed itself in this Anti-Corn-Law agitation had it not been for certain circumstances which must be remembered.

First of all, it had a powerful and most effective organisation at its back—a central body, composed of men of wealth, position, and of the highest business capacity—men so devoted to the work they had taken in hand that, sacrificing other claims and duties, they attended 600, 800, 1000, or even 1300 meetings of the Council of the League. From the central office at Manchester issued the lecturers, and the deputations, and the speakers, to preach the great principles held by the League. There too were devised the plans, the tours, the campaigns, which were to spread the tenets of the League, and to win converts to the cause.

Contrasted with the organisation of the Catholic Association it was inferior in one respect, and necessarily so—namely, in the ready-made network of organisation which the co-operation of the Roman Catholic clergy, and the organisation of that Church, at once gave the Irish movement; but in other respects it was in no way inferior, and in many superior. Local associations, local sympathisers, and local workers there were in abundance, but though they were not under the control of the League, they were none the less energetic and efficient.

Another important element in the success of the League was the fact that the Council had never been restricted in their operations for want of money. There was practically unlimited money for the furtherance of the agitation. £10,000 was subscribed at one time, then £50,000, then £100,000, and finally £250,000 was in course of collection when the need for more ceased. Not any agitation could boast of so much financial aid, and without financial aid agitation is uphill work. When one contrasts these sums with the few pounds that Hardy and the London Corresponding Society had at their disposal, or with the £967 which the Chartist Convention with difficulty succeeded in scraping together, one can understand the enormous additional strength such a fund would give the League, and the great additional resources which were at the disposal of the League. Money, which has been called the "sinews of war," is equally the sinews of agitation.

Another important cause of the strength of the League was the singleness of its aim. There were no "six points" of the Corn Laws such as there were of the Charter, to obtain any one of which would have required an agitation all to itself; there was no trimming to catch this or that support, no succumbing to the expedient. The total abolition of the Corn Laws—that was the one object steadily, unswervingly adhered to during the seven long years of agitation. *The League* newspaper, the organ of the League, laid this down very clearly: "The League, as the League, has no opinion on any other than one question—is precluded, by the fundamental principle of its constitution, from so much as thinking of any other than one question. The total and immediate repeal of the corn and provision monopolies is the one object for which we are associated; and for this object we invite and accept the co-operation of every one who, on whatever ground, is willing to co-operate with us, with no more solicitude as to his opinion on any other."[1]

W. J. Fox, speaking at Covent Garden meeting in January 1844, said: "It is appropriate and desirable to reiterate the League principle, the one aim and object of this association, that for which we are banded together—without which we will never be content, till we attain which our organisation and exertions will continue—the one broad simple principle of Free Trade; and, as applied to the greatest practical case, the total, the immediate, and the unconditional abolition of the Corn Laws. That is the star by which we steer; to that single point we bear right on, heedless of all other considerations. We care not for parties; we care not for demarcations of faction, new or old; we care not for the consistencies or inconsistencies of this or that leader of any portion of the House of Commons—the total, the unconditional, and the immediate abolition of the Corn Laws is what we ask, and all we ask."

And Cobden said: "The single and undisguised object of the League is to put down commercial monopoly."[2] And speaking within sight of the end of the agitation, he said: "I am anxious, not merely that we should all of us understand each other on this question, but that we should be considered as occupying as independent and isolated a position as we did

[1] See *The League*, 26th April 1845.

[2] September 1843.

at the first moment of the formation of the League. We have nothing to do with Whigs or Tories; we are stronger than either of them; and if we stick to our principles we can, if necessary, beat both. And I hope we perfectly understand now that we have not, in the advocacy of this great question, a single object in view but that which we have honestly avowed from the beginning."[1]

And over and above this singleness of aim in the movement there was complete unanimity among the leaders. Not from the time that the League was founded until the final dissolution took place was there any difference or dissension among the leaders; there was no rivalry for leadership, there was no division into a physical force party and a moral force party, no splitting off of this section or that to found some society that never more would be heard of. Absolute unanimity prevailed. The rock upon which many an agitation had been wrecked in the past, and on which many would be wrecked in the future, was successfully avoided by the Leaguers. But no amount of unanimity among leaders, nor singleness of aim, nor unlimited funds, nor powerful organisation, could have triumphed if the object which was being striven for had not been a just one. Here lay the real secret of the success of the agitation. This it was which armed the Platform with such invincible power, this it was which, as knowledge spread, steadily won men to the cause.

Bright, speaking at Manchester in October 1844, said:[2] "If you feel despondent upon this question, think for a moment what it is you are fighting for. It is for no paltry triumph of a faction; it is not to elevate this man or that man; or to set waving this flag, or to pull that flag down. No; but you are fighting for one of the greatest and the noblest causes which ever united the exertions of any body of men; you are fighting for the liberation of the industry of 27,000,000 of your fellow-countrymen, and not for the liberation of their industry only; but, as everything that is established here becomes a fashion for the world, you are also working out the liberation of the industry of the whole human race from all the tyranny which monopoly in every clime and in every age has inflicted upon it."

[1] Cobden's *Speeches*, vol. i. p. 362, 15th January 1846.
[2] See *The League*, 26th October 1844.

The law which was being striven against was distinctly and palpably a most unjust law, working wide evil for the advantage, one can scarcely call it the good, of the few.

The real interest of the agitation, in regard to a history of the Platform, the real instruction to be derived from it, centre in the means resorted to by the leaders of the agitation for winning their cause.

Bright, speaking at Manchester in January 1845, said:[1] "Our object is to create public feeling, and to array public feeling against this law to such an extent that the law shall be virtually repealed, that the triumph shall be consummated; and then the Act of Parliament, the mere sanction of the Legislature, will be but the formal acknowledgment and ratification of that which public opinion has already decreed. (Cheers.)"

But this could not be realised all at once. There were steps in the process, slow and laborious, but none the less essential for the success of the cause. Platform speaking alone could not do it, though Platform speaking could and did incite to the necessary measures.

"As the League depended for success solely on constitutional means, it was necessary, as the combat deepened, to investigate the means which the Constitution had placed at their disposal;"[2] and as force was not alone out of the question, but was never for a moment dreamt of, the only means remaining was the one I have already mentioned as the usual method of Platform influence—namely, influencing the composition of the House of Commons. That was the idea which had also shown itself in the agitation for Roman Catholic emancipation; indeed, *The League* newspaper of 8th June 1844 avowed that "The means by which religious exclusion was overthrown are a precedent to guide us in our great struggle for the removal of commercial restrictions." But the precedent was an incomplete one, and the agitations were not parallel cases. Platform agitation in Ireland and in England have ever been two totally different things, and the difference, I think, accounts, to a certain extent, for much of the extreme form which Irish agitation has taken. It was always easy in Ireland to whip up a Platform agitation—the Roman Catholic emancipation agitation and the agitation for the repeal of the Union proved

[1] See *The League*, 25th January 1845. [2] *Ibid.* 4th July 1846.

this conclusively. The greater proportion of the people in Ireland wanted little argument to move them to either of these objects—the great majority of them were of that opinion already—no argument was necessary, no discussion of any converting use. But the action of the Platform on Irish subjects was limited to Ireland. That is a most noteworthy fact. The most the Platform could do in Ireland was to influence a certain number of the constituencies in that country; and therefore there was no possibility ever of its converting a a majority of the House of Commons to the object of the particular agitation of the time being; indeed, with but few exceptions, no effort was made in Great Britain by the Irish leaders to persevere in the work of converting the British electorate. Thus limited in its power of convincing, the Platform in Ireland quickly, almost instantaneously, passed on to demonstrations of physical force, and these were far more relied on than constitutional action which, so far as Ireland was concerned, was practically an impossibility. It was the demonstrations of physical force disclosing the certainty of civil war in Ireland which frightened the English Government into conceding Catholic emancipation, and not the creation or conversion of a majority in the House of Commons by the steady convincing action of the Platform; and the main difference between the action of the Platform in this case—in which it succeeded—and in that of the agitation for the repeal of the Union—in which it failed—was, that in the latter case the English Government risked the alternative course of refusing the demand.

In Great Britain it is different. Here it is ever within the possibility of the Platform to decisively influence the majority in the Imperial Legislature by other means than physical demonstration of the strength and numbers of the votaries of the particular cause. There is nothing to prevent any cause being so advocated as to win over such a majority of the electorate as would give a majority in the representative body, and thereby secure the realisation of the cause. That is the means of effecting great reforms which the Constitution has left open to the people. The means were scarcely possible even here before the Reform Act of 1832; they have become ever easier with the enactment of the successive Reform Acts.

This great principle, then, of securing the object of agitation by influencing the constitution of the House of Commons had been clearly recognised by the leaders of the Anti-Corn-Law agitation. *The League* expressed it clearly when it wrote:[1] "To transform an electoral, and through that a representative minority into a majority is the very end and aim of our exertions." That was first attempted by carrying out Peel's recommendation to register. But the existing voters to be registered were not numerous enough to effect the change, and so the farther step was taken of creating voters. Numerous meetings had been held with this object, thousands of freeholders had been created, several constituencies had been secured, when the failure of the potato crop and the bad harvest introduced other elements into the question. It cannot, however, be doubted that even had no such dreadful catastrophe happened as the failure of the potato in 1845, the agitation for the repeal of the Corn Laws would, in the course of time, have been successful.

This great agitation will ever be remarkable for the manner in which it was conducted. It has been distinguished above all others by its peaceableness. Here was no question ever of prosecutions for incitement to violence. Never once did Platform speech call for such notice; never once did the agitation violate or exceed the most rigid letter of the law. As *The League* truly wrote in its "Farewell Address"—"Our march has been stained by no blood—our success is sullied by no tear."

Now and then, in the earlier days of its existence, a League meeting would be disturbed or even broken up by some of the more extreme Chartists, but that was not the fault of the Anti-Corn-Law agitators.

Cobden, speaking so far back as 1843, said truly: "Never was there a great public question agitated for four years with so few of those acts of violence and indiscretion which, from the nature of things, must belong, in a greater or less degree, to all subjects of public excitement."[2]

And Ashworth, one of the historians of the League, reviewing the whole agitation, wrote: "I think I may safely affirm that there never was in this or any other country so extensive,

[1] *The League*, 17th August 1844. [2] *The Examiner*, 1843, p. 121.

so energetic, so long continued, and so peaceful an agitation upon any other political subject."[1]

The peaceableness of the agitation was directly due to the counsels and inculcations of the principal leaders of the movement. In speech after speech the imperative necessity of order and decorum and peaceful conduct was insisted on.

Bright spoke strongly at Covent Garden in December 1844 on this point:[2] "Our past policy," he said, "has been peaceful. Slanderers and monopolists have said that we have instigated to sedition and to rebellion. The statement is false, like all the grounds upon which they base the maintenance of their monopoly. We never did instigate to sedition or rebellion. We appealed to the reason of our countrymen, and to their sense of justice; and that appeal has been answered in a wonderful manner. . . . We will go on with moral means for the future. The assertors of great national rights should be the very last persons to commit wrong. We hold ourselves to be the advocates of such rights, and we will gain them, if possible, by the peaceful policy which we have hitherto adopted. Recollect that it is only by a peaceful course like that which we are pursuing that a good cause can have any vantage ground. If you come to force in any matter of this description, why, then, it is decided by physical power, or by the chapter of accidents, and in the field both are upon a level; but keep to reason, to the sense of justice, and the consciences of men—appeal to this great and, in the long run, unerring tribunal, and then your great and good cause is everything. Every blow you give tells; every speech you make, every article you print, and every fact you bring forward, is a blow which your opponents can neither parry nor return, and thus you go on conquering and to conquer, and nothing can prevent it."

A speech of another orator of the League[3] clearly laid down the moderation of their demands—revolution was no part of its aim: "We understand not the doctrine of tolerating a certain portion of robbery, iniquity, and oppression upon the community, and on individuals. We take up our position on

[1] *Cobden and the League*, p. 118.
[2] See *The League*, 14th December 1844.
[3] W. J. Fox, see *The League*, 27th January 1844.

the *right* and the *wrong* of the case—for property of all sorts, as realised by human skill and labour, and as sanctioned by human laws and institutions. We avow our respect for, and we hold in sacred veneration, the property of the class which has most opposed itself to our claims. The broad acres of the landowner are his; we mean not to touch them; we set up no scramble for their division. We interfere not with his regulations of that which, by inheritance or by purchase, belongs to him. Let him do as he will with his own; he is amenable to opinion if he violates decency and morality; but so far as he keeps within the limits which the great objects of human society prescribe, we respect his rights even there. We meddle with nothing whatever of this—let him have his whole rights. The land is his, the produce of the land is his, or theirs to whom he hires out that land; but there is one thing which is not his, and that is, the industry of other people, their labour, their skill, their perseverance, their bones and sinews, their daily toil; and the bread which they earn by that toil and work he has no right to diminish by taxation. They are his fellow-countrymen and not his slaves. The labourer's bones and muscles are his own property, and not the landlord's."

And then, further, there had hitherto never been an agitation in which the language of attack had been so moderate. Even if we select some of the strongest expressions, there was not much that was so very reprehensible. Cobden spoke of his opponents as "a most narrow-minded, leaden oligarchy," as "bigots and monopolists," as "a vile and wicked set of taskmasters," as "a bankrupt and profligate portion of the aristocracy." Possibly the strongest passage in any of his speeches is to be found in a speech at a meeting at Drury Lane Theatre, referring to the landed aristocracy: "Let them go on, and in a short time they would find themselves like the French nobility, previous to the revolution, an isolated, helpless, powerless class—a class that, in their own inherent qualities, in their intellectual and moral powers, were inferior to any other classes of society. They not only clung to the feudal abuses, but they actually tried to put a restraint upon the supply of food for the people. They were warring against the progression of the age. They fancied that their feudal system was necessary to the existence of the community. Why, their feudal system had gone in France; it had gone in Germany; in America it had never existed. The question now was, Whether the feudal system in this country was to flourish beside an advancing and progressive manufacturing and commercial community? There were manufacturing and commercial communities in other countries where feudalism did not exist. They would exist here by the side of feudalism, if feudalism would allow them; but if not by the side of feudalism, feudalism would not be permitted to stop the progress of civilisation, if not by the side of it, then the manufacturing and commercial interests would flourish upon the ruins of feudalism."

These, however, are only occasional blemishes, scarcely calling for notice in a series of almost innumerable speeches, but impartiality demands that the blemishes of the Platform should be noticed as well as its virtues. And, as a set-off on the other side, it may be affirmed that never yet, in the history of the Platform, had the level of teaching been uniformly so high, so noble, or so moral; never yet had the language of the speakers been so free from the taint of violence, exaggeration, or incitement to ill-feeling. One illustration may be given of the height which was attained in the language used from the Platform.

It is a speech of Cobden's delivered at Manchester in January 1846. He said: "I have been accused of looking too much to material interests. Nevertheless, I can say that I have taken as large and great a view of the effects of this mighty principle (of free trade) as ever did any man who dreamt over it in his own study. I believe that the physical gain will be the smallest gain to humanity from the success of this principle. I look farther, I see in the free trade principle that which shall act on the moral world as the principle of gravitation in the universe—drawing men together, thrusting aside the antagonism of race, and creed, and language, and uniting us in the bonds of eternal peace. I have looked even farther; I have speculated, and probably dreamt, in the dim future—ay, a thousand years hence—I have speculated on what the effect of the triumph of this principle may be. I believe that the effect will be to change the face of the world, so as to introduce a system of government entirely distinct from that which now prevails. I believe that the desire and the motive for large and mighty empires, for gigantic armies and great navies, for those materials which are used for the destruction of life, and the desolation of the rewards of labour, will die away. I believe that such things will cease to be necessary, or to be used when man becomes one family, and freely exchanges the fruits of his labour with his brother man. I believe that, if we could be allowed to reappear on this sublunary scene, we should see, at a far distant period, the governing system of this world revert to something like the municipal system; and I believe that the speculative philosopher of a thousand years hence will date the greatest revolution that ever happened in the world's history from the triumph of the principle which we have met here to advocate."[1]

Nearly half a century has passed since these words were uttered; there is but little sign yet of gigantic armies, and great navies, ceasing to be necessary, yet one cannot but admire the lofty ideal which was thus expressed to the world; one cannot but feel how great a moral force must flow from conduct dictated by such principles. Contrast language such as this with the language of the Platform in previous agitations, and how great, how wonderful is the improvment. Contrast it with that of the agitation running side by side with the Anti-Corn-Law agitation, and how vast the difference. How violent and even bloodthirsty were the speeches of Stephens and Oastler, and others of the leading Chartists. How coarse and vituperative the speeches of Hunt, and sometimes of Cobbett. How bombastic and absurd the speeches of Gale Jones and his contemporaries compared with the speeches of the prominent men of the Anti-Corn-Law League. Even the speeches of the reform agitators of 1830 stand on a lower level.

And yet one other matter remains for mention in which this agitation showed a marked superiority over any previous agitation—namely, in the personal character of the leaders. There was a complete absence of self-seeking on their part, of ambition, or of vanity. Different was it in the other agita-

[1] Cobden's *Speeches*, vol. ii. pp. 362, 363.

tions. Feargus O'Connor's main incentive to agitation was the gratification of his personal vanity, the love of taking the lead at meetings, the love of popular applause.

Attwood's speeches betray time after time that frequently his uppermost thought was of himself. In one speech he assured his audience that, "but for their great prudence, they would have been destroyed like the reformers of old, and he picked out from among them, and in all probability lodged in a dungeon."[1] In another: "I rejoice in the course of conduct I have pursued more and more under the awful circumstances which I see approaching, and I have now only to say that whenever I die I wish no other inscription to be placed upon my tomb than 'Here lies the founder of Political Unions.'"[2]

The love of popular applause was to Hunt the very breath of his nostrils.

One seeks in vain for any egotism or vanity in the speeches of the leading orators of the League, and Mr. Morley, in his *Life of Cobden*,[3] says: "I cannot find a trace or a word in the most private correspondence betraying on the part of any prominent actor in the League a symptom of petty or ignoble egotism. They were too much in earnest. Never on a scene where the temptations to vanity were so many was vanity so entirely absent."

It is a feature of the agitation which not alone deserves to be recorded, but to be brought into the most prominent notice as showing the high level which the Platform can attain.

In all these respects then, in the character of the leaders, in the moderation of their language, in the complete absence of incitement to violence or disorder, this agitation distinguished itself above all that had gone before, and showed a progress in the methods of popular movement which might well have been deemed impossible.

Many and of the vastest importance were the lessons to be deduced from this great agitation. One of the speakers of the League[4] thus described what by some would be considered the most important of all: "When men shall inquire in what way they may overthrow some hoary abuse, protected by power,

1 Attwood's *Life*, p. 140, 17th May 1830.
2 *Ibid.* p. 152, 13th December 1830. 3 Vol. i. p. 279.
4 G. Thomson at Covent Garden. See *The League*, 22d February 1845.

surrounded and defended by wealth, rank, and corruption—when they would learn whether they may venture to hope that, by exertion, toil, and sacrifice, they can bring such an abuse to the ground—they shall then turn to the pages which record the history of the Anti-Corn-Law League; they shall therein learn that voluntary association will work greater miracles than the hands of them who reared the Pyramids; that bloodless revolutions may be brought about by the agitation of men's minds; that there are weapons that cannot be struck down in the warfare; that there is a power which, though impalpable and invisible, is yet universal and irresistible, and will outlive Ministers, and Governments, and States, and rule the world when man is man indeed."

Bright, at the final meeting of the League, drew attention to other lessons derivable from it: "If a thinking and philosophic mind were asked what the League has done, I am of opinion that his answer would include many other points and many other things beyond the repeal of a particular statute. We have taught the people of this country the value of a great principle. They have learned that there is nothing that can be held out to the intelligent people of this kingdom so calculated to stimulate them to action, and to great and persevering action, as a great and sacred principle like that which the League espoused. They have learned that there is in public opinion a power much greater than that which resides in any particular form of Government; that although you have in this kingdom a system of government which is called 'popular' and called 'representative,'—a system which is somewhat clumsily contrived, and which works with many jars and joltings—that still, with a great principle, and with great labour, and with great sacrifices, all those obstacles are overcome, and out of a machine specially contrived for the contrary, justice and freedom at length is achieved for the nation; and the people have learned something beyond this—that is, that the way to freedom henceforward is not through violence and bloodshed. I take it that there is no better lesson for the people to learn from it than this,—that by persevering effort—that by no infraction of moral law—by strict obedience to the principles which we believe to be enjoined by the Christian code, they can obtain so great and signal victories, and victories which are not tarnished in the gaining, victories which can never be lost—more great and more glorious than any other nation ever achieved by force of arms."

But not less important than these lessons was the fact that from its inception to its end the agitation had been to the people one continual educational power—one long course of training in the amenities of public discussion—a seven years' apprenticeship—at the end of which the Platform, from whatever point of view regarded, had reached a higher level than ever before; it had shaken off its earlier vices and deformities, and shown to the world that they were excrescences, and not a necessary part of its being; it had set a standard of dignity, gravity, and composure in public discussion, which future generations in their troubles might advantageously imitate; it had weaned great numbers from those violent courses which Chartist orators were accustoming them to, and in so doing practically drew the sting of Chartism, and turned into a constitutional direction that which otherwise threatened to become a revolutionary movement.

CHAPTER XIX

THE SECOND CRISIS OF CHARTISM

How great a change had come over English life in regard to the Platform during the quarter century that had elapsed since the "Six Acts" had been in force, is evidenced by the remarkable fact that not only one but two great Platform agitations were being carried on simultaneously over a prolonged course of years. While the Anti-Corn-Law agitation had been running its course to its successful conclusion, and while the Platform was taking the prominent part in it which has just been described, the Chartist agitation, of which much more was still to be heard, had also been moving along, with somewhat chequered fortunes, and had also been continuing to employ the Platform for its purposes.

Incidental mention has been made in the last chapter of the doings of the Chartists, but to complete the account of the proceedings of the Platform in connection with them, it is necessary to resume the story of the agitation which has been interrupted by the narrative of the Anti-Corn-Law agitation.

But, in reverting once more to the history of the Platform as used by the Chartists, we pass back to a Platform disfigured by all the vices which had characterised it up to 1840. We step down from the eminence to which the Platform had been raised by the leaders of the Anti-Corn-Law agitation. We pass to a Platform remarkable for the absence of all those qualities which have just been praised, to an agitation with an ever shifting, ever varying organisation, and with leaders ever quarrelling among themselves. We pass to the frothy utterances of restless self-seeking adventurers, working without cohesion of purpose, ignorant of definite aim, and unwilling to sink their individual idiosyncrasies for the sake of the general object.

It must not, however, be inferred that the working of the Platform in this Chartist agitation is one whit the less instructive—very far from it. The instruction to be derived is pregnant with the most important lessons and conclusions. The teaching, it is true, is in great part in the negative form, showing the weak parts of the Platform and its worst side; but the conclusions are none the less valuable.

Some ten months or so after the dissolution of the National Convention in September 1839 a new plan of organisation was devised. A meeting was held at Manchester in July 1840, and the resolution was arrived at to merge all the local bodies into one association to be called "the National Charter Association of Great Britain."[1]

Soon after this, some of the Chartist leaders began to emerge from prison, on the expiration of their sentences of imprisonment. Several of them were given public receptions, at which numerous speeches were made, and Chartism began to revive. Thus, on the 27th July,[2] a great demonstration came off in Birmingham in honour of William Lovett and John Collins; and at Glasgow "an imposing demonstration of the people" took place, at which "it was computed that not less than 200,000 people" were present, in honour of other of the Chartist leaders.

Lovett was not very long out of prison before he gave to the world, in an "Address to the Political and Social Reformers of the United Kingdom," some of the conclusions which he had formed in his retirement. "Brethren," he said, "in addressing you as fellow-labourers in the great cause of human liberty, we would wish to rivet this important truth on your mind. You must become your own social and political regenerators, or you will never enjoy freedom. For true liberty cannot be conferred by Acts of Parliament or decrees of princes, but must spring up from the knowledge, morality, and public virtue of our population. . . .

"Though revolution were to follow revolution, and changes were to be continually effected in our constitution, laws, and government, unless the social and political superstructure were

[1] Speaking in the House of Commons in May 1842 Mr. Duncombe said: "There are about 600 of these Chartist Associations in England and Scotland." —See Hansard's *Parliamentary Debates*, vol. lxiii. p. 20.

[2] 1840.

based upon the intelligence and morality of the people, they would only have exchanged despotism for despotism, and one set of oppressors for another."[1]

An interesting passage in this Address is his frank criticism of Chartist meetings. "Our public meetings," he said, "have on too many occasions been arenas of passionate invective, party spirit, and personal idolatry, rather than public assemblies for calmly deliberating and freely discussing national or local grievances; or as schools for the advancement of our glorious cause, by the dissemination of facts, and inculcation of principles; as it is by such teachings that our population will be prepared *to use wisely* the political power they are now seeking to obtain."

And in another Address, issued about the same time, he said: "It is not the mere possession of the franchise that is to benefit our country,—that is only the means to a just end—the election of the best and wisest of men to solve a question which has never yet been propounded in any legislative body—namely, how shall all the resources of our country be made to advance the intellectual and social happiness of every individual?"

Lovett's counsel, however, fell on unheeding ears. The process he recommended was not rapid enough to suit the more impetuous leaders of the Chartists.

The General Election of 1841 afforded the Chartists an opportunity of showing their strength. Their action was, however, in strong contrast to the action of the Anti-Corn-Law League in its efforts to influence the composition of the House of Commons, and in holding severely aloof from parties, was the action of the Chartists at the General Election of 1841. Their efforts at influencing the composition of the House of Commons were confined almost altogether to bringing forward candidates on the hustings, to explain and defend the principles of Chartism, and to there getting a show of hands in their favour—a performance far short even of the scheme of which they had so often boasted, of sending the persons so chosen to claim their seats in Parliament. In the few cases, where they had votes, their leader, Feargus O'Connor, persuaded them to vote for the Tory candidate, so as to show their

[1] *The Life and Struggles of William Lovett*, p. 245.

detestation of the Whigs—a policy which, according to Gammage,[1] "brought endless division into the ranks, worse even than was introduced by the discussion of moral and physical force."

It was this "endless division" which ultimately wrecked Chartism.

Gammage, in his History, frankly describes the numerous errors which went to deprive the Chartist movement of much of its power. Their one abiding error was want of union. The leaders lived in a state of perpetual quarrel. Lovett and Collins published a work entitled *Chartism*, which contained a plan for the organisation of the Chartists throughout the kingdom. "It met with a howl of denunciation." Vincent, on his release from prison, went in for the advocacy of temperance, and recommended Temperance Chartist Associations. He too was jeered at. Some Scotch Chartists established Christian Chartist churches, where political sermons were preached. They fared no better. All and every one of these actions met with the vehement denunciations of O'Connor, who, according to Gammage,[2] "never sought to raise the Chartist body from its position by enlightening its members. He had no wish for that body to be anything more than a mere mob to conclude every meeting with three cheers for Feargus O'Connor and *The Northern Star.*"

Late in the autumn of 1841 O'Connor was released from prison. While in prison he had announced that, when released, he would appear in a suit of fustian, to show how completely he identified himself with the working classes, and accordingly, when he was released, a procession took place in York, with O'Connor, in his fustian suit, seated in a triumphal car (specially made for the occasion), followed by thousands cheering the "Lion of Freedom."

Once again at large he was quickly at daggers drawn with large sections of the Chartists: differences were perpetually cropping up, or quarrels occurring—quarrels unnecessary now to refer to, except as explaining one of the causes which neutralised the power of Chartism. Quarrels among leaders naturally extended to quarrels among their followers, and meetings of one section of the Chartists were disturbed by

[1] Gammage, p. 210. [2] *Ibid.* p. 213.

Chartists of another section. After describing some uproarious proceedings at Leicester, Gammage says: "The same folly which reigned at Leicester pervaded more or less the Chartist body generally. Reason was trampled under foot, passion, led by the spirit of demagogueism, was rampant, and no man stood the slightest chance, who had courage enough to diverge from the path marked out by O'Connor and *The Northern Star*. . . . One section of the Chartist body could not tolerate a different policy from its own. Hence the strife and bickering, hence the dwindling down of the Chartist party from powerful bodies to comparatively insignificant units.

All through these proceedings the Platform was kept hard at work. Meetings here, and meetings there, meetings by one section of the Chartists, meetings by another section. Lecturing tours by this man, and receptions for another man, but the Platform spoke with many voices, inaudible now at this distance of time, in the jarrings and jinglings of uncertain contradictious sound.

One result, however, emerged from the chaos of dissension —a second great petition for the Charter. With much labour of meetings, and Platforming, and by the aid of another specially elected Convention, it was compiled; and it was signed—it was said—by "3,315,752 of the industrious classes."

On the 2d of May 1842 it was escorted to Parliament by a large procession of working men, and presented to the House of Commons. Its bulk was so great that the doors were not wide enough to admit it, and it was necessary to unroll it to carry it in.[1]

The Petition is completely lacking in the pathos of the first great National Petition. The petitioners began their petition by saying, "That Government originated from, was designed to protect the freedom, and promote the happiness of, and ought to be responsible to, the whole people." They impugned the authority of the House of Commons; they protested against the existing system of representation; they complained of the National debt, of the operation of the Poor Laws, of the "disparity between the wages of the producing millions, and the salaries of those whose usefulness ought to be questioned," instancing the daily income of the Queen at £164:17:10, and

[1] Hansard, vol. lxii. p. 1373.

of thousands of workmen at 3¾d. They complained, further, of an unconstitutional police force, of a vast and unconstitutional army, of the constitution of the House of Commons, of the "existing monopolies of the suffrage, of paper money, of machinery, of land, of the public Press, of religious privileges, of the means of travelling and transit, and a host of other evils too numerous to mention."[1] They contended that the people of Ireland were fully entitled to a repeal of the Legislative Union, and they wound up by "demanding" the House immediately, without alteration, deduction, or addition, to pass into a law the document entitled "The People's Charter."

It was presented to the House by Mr. T. Duncombe, who, on the following day, moved that the petitioners might be heard at the bar of the House by themselves, counsel, or agents, in support of the allegations of their Petition.[2] The Government opposed the motion as giving rise to hopes which were certain to be disappointed; the Home Secretary believed a compliance with the demands of the Petition would tend more directly to lead to the increase of the sufferings of the people than any other cause. Mr. Macaulay opposed it, as he believed "universal suffrage would be fatal to all purposes for which Government exists, and for which aristocracies and all other things exist, and that it would be utterly incompatible with the very existence of civilisation."[3]

Mr. Roebuck, while supporting the motion, begged the House not to judge of the people of England by the language of the foolish and malignant and cowardly demagogue[4] who had written the Petition; and Lord J. Russell, while expressing his respect for the petitioners, declared his abhorrence of the doctrines set forth in the Petition.

Sir Robert Peel expressed his sincere sympathy with the sufferings of the people, but his firm resolution not to consent to those momentous changes in the Constitution which could yield no relief, but rather produce an aggravation of the evils

[1] For a copy of this Petition, see Hansard, 1842, vol. lxii. p. 1376.

[2] Hansard, vol. lxiii. p. 32, 3d May 1842. [3] *Ibid.* p. 46.

[4] Sir R. Peel referred in this debate to Feargus O'Connor (not by name, but by unmistakable reference) as "a man who has perverted to his own evil purposes the minds of the respectable, intelligent, industrious, honest, labouring classes of this country."—*Ibid.* p. 78.

complained of. The Petition, he said, was altogether an impeachment of the constitution of this country, and of the whole frame of society, and he had come to the conclusion that those demands, if complied with, would be mischievous to the petitioners themselves. Forty-nine voted for the motion, and 287 against it, giving a majority of 238 against it, and thus ended the episode of the second great National Petition.

The prospect of gaining the Charter having thus, by the rejection of the motion, receded into greater distance, the more restless Chartists, availing themselves of the widespread distress in the manufacturing districts, directed their attention to the more feasible measure of a strike, or turn-out for higher wages. The movement began early in August; large meetings were held at Manchester and in other places, and vehement Platform speeches were made. Once more the Platform was showing how easy it is to excite ignorant and uneducated men to violent courses when they are in poverty and distress.

The pitiable confidence in the immediate success of the Charter is illustrated by the proceedings at a meeting at Mottram Moor on the 7th August, where it was resolved never to resume work until the Charter should become the law of the land. It was said that at this meeting the extensive outrages which were committed on the following days were discussed and agreed on. In Yorkshire and Lancashire large numbers of men left their work, and moving about in large mobs compelled others to do so too, in many cases using very great violence, and destroying a considerable amount of property.

Factories were invaded, and the machinery disabled and brought to a standstill. At Ashton a public open-air meeting was held, and straight from it went the people to "turn out" the workers in factories, and to disable the machinery. At Preston a meeting was held on the night of the 12th of August. As early as five o'clock the next morning a crowd assembled at the same place and moved off to stop some factories working; subsequently a serious riot ensued, the military fired, four persons were shot dead, and many wounded. Nor was this by any means the only occasion where there was loss of life. At numerous other places meetings were also held, and the nature of the speeches can be inferred from the fact that the persons present immediately proceeded on a tour of intimidation and violence. In Staffordshire Thomas Cooper, a noted Chartist, was holding meetings, which thousands attended, and was "working masses up to a perfect fury against the richer classes,"[1] and soon after serious disturbances occurred.

Here, indeed, the Platform had reached its lowest depths. Avoiding discussion, shunning an appeal to Parliament, or even to the general public, the people passed at one step to action. They met, speeches were made, and they proceeded at once on their illegal courses. There is nothing to be said in defence of the Platform when turned to such purposes as these. Its misuse so can only be deplored; happily, however, it is not often so misused.

The excitement ran so high in all the manufacturing districts that the Government issued a Proclamation cautioning persons against taking part in the riotous scenes that were enacted. The law was energetically put into force, numerous arrests were made, not alone there but also in London. Special Commissions were issued for the trial of the rioters, and large numbers were punished, many being sentenced to transportation. Feargus O'Connor and some other leading Chartists were also arrested, and committed for trial.

The proceedings of the people in connection with the strike evoked from John Bright an "Address to the men of Rochdale," which contains an interesting opinion on the Chartist Platform speakers.

"Your speakers talk loudly. They tell you of your numbers and your power, and they promise marvellous results if you will but be firm. They deceive you; perhaps they are themselves deceived. Some of them contrive to live on this deception, and some are content with the glory of their leadership. They flatter you grossly, and they as grossly calumniate your employers. They pretend to be working out your political freedom; they know that that freedom can only be obtained through the electoral body and the middle classes, and yet they incessantly abuse the parties whom it is your interest to conciliate and convince. For four years past they have held before your eyes an object at present unattainable, and they have urged you to pursue it; they have laboured

[1] Gammage, p. 243.

incessantly to prevent you following any practical object. They have vilified the substance and extolled the shadow. They have striven continually to exasperate you against those who alone will or can aid you to overturn the usurpations of the aristocracy. They have succeeded in creating suspicion and dissension, and upon that dissension many of them have lived."[1]

The Chartists were thrown into considerable confusion by the conviction of several of their leaders. Funds too were very limited, and though a great deal of Platforming was carried on by O'Connor and others, no progress in the cause was made. The failure of the strike, moreover, brought discredit on the Chartist leaders who had aided and abetted it—many of the working men feeling disgusted at the way in which they had been misled, and the proceeding generally "produced an effect upon the interests of Chartism from which it took years to recover."

The history of the movement, and of the use of the Platform in connection with it, present but few topics of interest in the course of the next few years. A great conference took place at Birmingham in December 1842, some 400 to 500 delegates being in attendance from all parts. First one section and then another section retired from it. The remainder decided on a new organisation, with an annual Convention, the members to be elected by public meetings in their respective localities.

In the following spring[2] the proceedings against O'Connor and several other Chartists came on at Lancaster Assizes, and resulted in his conviction, but a writ of error was moved for, and he was never called up for judgment.

The Convention met in September 1843, when, at O'Connor's suggestion, a "Land Scheme" was adopted, which was to renew the face of society, and to ensure social happiness for all, and for a considerable time afterwards O'Connor's principal energies were devoted to its realisation.

In the summer of 1844 the Chartist cause received the severe reverse, which has already been described, at the hands of the Anti-Corn-Law League. Nothing is to be gained by pursuing in any detail the proceedings of the Chartists in these and the

[1] See *Cobden and the Anti-Corn-Law League*, by Henry Ashworth, p. 108.
[2] 1843.

next few years. Quarrel succeeded quarrel. Gammage, who is delightfully frank, says: "It is by no means a pleasant task to wade through the mass of treachery, falsehood, and folly, that engrafted itself on one of the noblest movements that ever engaged the energies of a people."[1]

One form of organisation followed another, and with such rapidity that none of them was carried out, and scarcely could any one make out at any particular time what the organisation actually was. The Platform was kept going through it all—at conferences, conventions, and meetings of all sorts—doing nothing worthy of mention, and nothing redounding to its credit. For some years, in fact, Chartism dragged itself along, surviving more upon its name and its earlier history than upon anything it was doing to promote the cause or secure the objects of the Charter. In 1846 it received a severe blow in the triumph of the Anti-Corn-Law League and the repeal of the Corn Laws. The Chartist leaders had originally set themselves against that agitation, declaring that the object was as difficult to attain as the "six points" of the Charter, but now it was attained, and all their prognostications were shown to be false. Moreover, the success of the management of the Anti-Corn-Law agitation contrasted forcibly with the non-success of the management of the Chartist agitation, a non-success which had been attended with the actual ruin of thousands, through imprisonments, loss of employment, and other injuries. Large masses of the people too were, by the abolition of the Corn Law monopoly, detached from the ranks of the discontented, and a powerful leverage for dissatisfaction was taken from the Chartists.

In August 1847 there came a general election, the old Parliament having been dissolved on the 23d of July, owing to the efflux of time. The election "was probably the most quiet"[2] which had ever occurred. Chartism attained one triumph, in the election of Feargus O'Connor for Nottingham, but except his return, and that of a few others who were Radicals rather than Chartists, Chartism made no impression on the constitution of the House of Commons.

The election over, the Chartist energies were directed to obtaining signatures to the third great National Petition,

[1] Gammage, p. 287. [2] *Annual Register*, 1847, p. 95.

which was now decided on. A great petition seemed to be regarded by O'Connor and the leading Chartists as a sort of pastime for their followers, something to keep the people occupied with, something that would stave off actual ulterior measures, whilst it afforded themselves unlimited opportunity of Platforming, and keeping themselves prominently before their followers. This Petition was destined to exceed in renown either of its predecessors, being carried into notoriety on the crest of a great wave of revolutionary excitement, which had its centre in Europe, and which reacted, as had invariably been the case hitherto, on the United Kingdom, hurrying large masses of the people into violent political excitement. It was the second great climax of the Chartist agitation, the result or product of all the meetings that had been held, and of all the speeches that for years had been poured forth by the voluble leaders of the movement.

The new Parliament was soon called on to deal with matters of the gravest importance—an autumn session was deemed necessary, and Parliament met on the 18th of November.[1] The political atmosphere of Europe was charged with electricity, and the first drops of a coming storm were already falling. At home the country was still in the throes of a commercial and, financial crisis, with consequent distress among the industrial population; whilst the state of Ireland was lamentable, verging on ruin, owing to the repeated failure of the potato crop; verging on rebellion, owing to the misery of the people, and the incitements to violence of certain of the Irish agitators. There was thus ample material for excitement, and the Chartist leaders set themselves to work to avail themselves of it.

"Towards the latter end of December large gatherings took place in London and many of the provinces."[2] "Scotland began to move," and there was a great meeting at Edinburgh. Early in the new year—the memorable 1848—O'Connor visited Birmingham, where a large meeting was held, and numerous other meetings also took place.

Suddenly the clouds of revolution burst in France. At the end of February Paris was once more the scene of a revolution. The populace rose, the tumult and excitement increased, colli-

[1] 1847. [2] Gammage, p. 312.

sions took place between the people and the half-hearted military, the people triumphed, the King abdicated and fled, the monarchy fell, and a Republic was established. "The news filled the democrats with hope," writes Gammage.[1] "M'Douall passed rapidly through Scotland haranguing large meetings; Kydd traversed Yorkshire; and West was rousing the democrats in the neighbourhood of Newcastle-on-Tyne."

On the 2d March "a tremendous gathering" took place at Lambeth. Stepney Green, Clerkenwell Green, and Bethnal Green "were the scenes of immense gatherings of the metropolitans."

On the 6th March a meeting was held in Trafalgar Square, after which there was considerable rioting. In some of the principal manufacturing towns throughout the country there was also rioting. At Glasgow the people marched through the streets crying "Bread or revolution"; serious rioting ensuing the military had to fire, and several persons were killed. O'Connor went to Hanley in the Potteries, and addressed a great meeting of some 7000 persons.

"Newcastle, Dumfries, Sunderland, and a host of towns were roused at the summons of the people of Paris. Public meetings were held, and the spark of democracy seemed to light up every breast."

On the 12th March there was a meeting at Peep Green, in Yorkshire—"The flag of the Republic was exhibited, and resolutions were passed pledging the meeting to stand by the Charter."

Meetings were also held at Manchester, Bradford, Ipswich, Sheffield, and many other places. On the 13th what Gammage calls "a great meeting," and what the *Annual Register*[2] calls "a most despicable affair," was held at Kennington Common. On the 15th there was a meeting at Blackheath, and at Birmingham "a large meeting" in favour of the Charter. On Sunday, the 19th, a meeting was held at Oldham Edge. "O'Connor estimated the gathering at a quarter of a million."

"That was a sacred day," he said, "and a sacred cause, and let each man swear with him to high heaven, uncovered, with his hat off, never to abandon the cause until freedom had been obtained," and the whole multitude uncovered.

[1] Gammage, p. 313. [2] *Annual Register*, 1848, p. 38.

The example set by France sent a shock of excitement throughout Europe, and deeply stirred and excited popular feeling in every European country. The middle of March saw the overthrow of Prince Metternich in Austria. A little later the King of Bavaria was forced to resign. In Saxony, Hanover, and Baden popular Constitutions were forced from the Governments. Italy was in a ferment of revolution. Milan was captured by the people, and the Austrian troops driven from it. In Sicily the people revolted, and exacted concessions from the King of Naples. Even the Papal States were in a state of agitation, and the Pope was compelled to grant a new Constitution to his subjects.

As the intelligence of these events successively reached the Chartists, the news "appeared to increase their determination to win the long-cherished principles for which they had struggled." Meeting after meeting was held, and the Platform was kept in full operation, in its most loud-mouthed style. A speech made by Ernest Jones at a meeting in London on 27th March is a good illustration of the style then in vogue: "I believe the people are prepared to pronounce the mighty fiat to ring the inevitable knell of slavery! I should be a guilty man, did I say so without a well-grounded conviction. For the evil that might come, I should in part be responsible. The widow and the orphan would have a right to curse me. But, before heaven, I believe that we stand upon the threshold of our rights. One step, were it even with an iron heel, and they are ours. I conscientiously believe that the people are prepared to claim the Charter. Then I say take it, and God defend the right. . . . We'll steer the right course. We won't be intemperate and hot-headed, but we will be determined. We'll respect the law, if the law-makers respect us; if they don't, France is a republic."

It was with language such as this that the Platform now resounded.

Gammage, in his account of this period, says: "Reports continued to arrive of the march of democracy in the provinces. Newark, Plymouth, Northampton, Dudley, Dundee, Exeter, and other places met, elected delegates to the Convention, adopted the Petition, and passed resolutions to have the Charter." Ten thousand persons were addressed by Dr. M'Douall in Nottingham. At Loughborough, Coventry, Southampton, and Macclesfield meetings were held; also at Aberdeen, Blackburn, and "even at Newport, where Chartism had never lifted its head since the unfortunate riots. . . . From scores of other places signatures to the Petition poured in. Meeting upon meeting was held, speech after speech was delivered, and no means were left untried to fan the immense excitement that seemed to threaten the existence of the Government."[1]

Once more—namely, on the 4th April—another National Convention assembled in London, the members having undergone the usual process of election, that of being nominated by public meetings. Its very first proceedings revealed the old split between the advocates of physical force and of moral force. The delegates proceeded to give reports of the state of feeling in the districts for which they had been elected. One said that "there was no use in preaching patience to the starving masses." Another said his constituents were ready to try one more Petition, but if that were rejected, they would "go to work," let the consequences be what they might. Another, that his constituents were tired of meeting. Another, that so long and so continuous had been the misery that the people were beginning to feel reckless. Several said that their constituents wished to attain their ends without physical force, but they wished for the Charter at all risks. Ernest Jones said that his constituents were ready, if necessary, to fight to a man; and a delegate, named Reynolds, declared that: "A few drops of blood were as nothing in the scale, and if moral means failed, the people were prepared for any means."

Feargus O'Connor said: "He looked on that Convention as a fair and faithful representation of the people. Chartism was increasing, and to be increased. He believed that he would have 5,400,000 signatures to the Petition. The events in France had given an impetus to the movement. Thrones were crumbling and tumbling on the Continent, and was it to be expected that England would remain in slavery under such circumstances? On Monday they would go down to the House. He was not prepared to destroy the movement he had been mainly instrumental in raising by precipitation, nor was he prepared to allow the people to remain in bondage one moment

[1] Gammage, p. 322.

longer than they could obtain their freedom. . . . If the Petition were rejected, he recommended simultaneous meetings all over the country to address the Queen to dismiss the Ministry, and call to her Councils men who would make the Charter a Cabinet question. If that were unavailing he would never flinch, but would sooner die than not win the Charter He meant to wait no longer than the time when the majority of the people demanded it, and were prepared to establish their rights. He thought they now had power to obtain it."

Gammage, referring to these reports, says: "It will at once be seen that the country was suffering under an enormous load of misery; that such misery had given rise to a vast amount of discontent, which, together with the excitement on continental affairs, had produced a very threatening state of things. But these were not alone the elements necessary to carry a successful revolution. They might have been auxiliaries, but for the groundwork it required something more. It required a well-grounded, intelligent, public conviction—formed in the moments of deliberation—of the truth, the justice, the value, and necessity of the people's political and social rights. That intelligent conviction was, after years of agitation, yet to be achieved."

Monday, the 10th April, was the day appointed for the presentation of the third and last great National Petition. It was very much like its predecessors, only not quite so elaborate. After complaining of the system of representation the petitioners asked that "the Charter" might be enacted, with its "six points"—universal suffrage, equal electoral districts, the ballot, payment of members, abolition of property qualification, and inasmuch as septennial Parliaments prevented "for six years out of seven those who are annually arriving at maturity from exercising the right of suffrage" annual Parliaments were asked for.

To give full effect to the solemnity and importance of the occasion, the Convention decided that a great meeting should be held at Kennington Common, and that there should be a procession from there to the House of Commons to present the Petition. It having been stated that half a million of people would assemble at Kennington, the Government and large numbers of the peaceable and orderly classes began to take the necessary measures for the preservation of peace, and for preventing the intimidation of Parliament. The Government on the 6th April issued a notice through the Police Commissioners.

"Whereas the assemblage of large numbers of the people, accompanied with circumstances tending to excite terror and alarm in the minds of her Majesty's subjects, is criminal and unlawful; and whereas not only those persons who take an active part in such assemblage, but those also who, by their presence, wilfully countenance it, are acting contrary to the law, and are liable to punishment," the Police Commissioners directed public attention to the Act of Charles II. against tumultuous petitioning. The notice continued, "All persons are hereby cautioned and strictly enjoined not to attend or take part in or be present at any such assemblage or procession. And all well-disposed persons are hereby called upon to aid in enforcing the provisions of the law, and effectually to protect the public peace, and suppress any attempt at the disturbance thereof."

The Home Secretary informed[1] Parliament that "The Government endeavoured in this notice to state what was the common law of the country, and what was the statute law with respect to assemblages, for whatever purpose convened, when those assemblages were attended by circumstances calculated to strike terror and alarm in the minds of her Majesty's loyal and peaceable subjects."

A large number of troops were moved up to London, every preparation was made to suppress any attempt at an outbreak, such as had occurred in foreign capitals; but what was most remarkable of all was the fact that some 170,000 persons enrolled themselves as special constables throughout the metropolis for the defence of their own districts, or as movable bodies to co-operate with the soldiery and the police in the preservation of peace and order. Such a sight as an armed populace determined to preserve order had never been seen in England before.

The ever memorable 10th of April arrived. The Convention, having assembled at their usual place of meeting, started from thence for Kennington in a large and profusely decorated car drawn by six horses, and another car conveying the Petition.

[1] Hansard, vol. xcviii. p. 6, 1848.

Numerous other processions also converged from different parts of the city—the thousands, variously estimated from 15,000 to 150,000, met at Kennington Common—the apotheosis of Chartist Platforming was reached.

All the high hopes of the Chartists, however, were to be quickly dashed, and the disillusionment was to be rapid and complete. No tamer or more humiliating ending could, by any possibility, have been imagined.

On arriving at the scene of the meeting Feargus O'Connor, as leader of the Chartists, was sent for by the Commissioner of Police, who was in a tavern near, and was informed that, though the meeting would not be interfered with, no procession would be allowed. So little fight was there in O'Connor that he promised that the procession should be abandoned. He then had before him the difficult task of persuading the meeting to abandon their triumphal march to the House of Commons. He returned to the meeting and addressed it. He implored them not to injure their cause by any act of folly. He would go down on his knees to implore of them not to do so. He pointed to the Petition which, he said, contained the voices of 5,700,000 of their countrymen, who would be looking for good conduct from them that day. He then told them that the Executive would accompany the Petition, and urged on them not to accompany it. He called on those who were determined to act like prudent, sensible men, and to see the Charter speedily the law of the land, to hold up their hands—when a forest of hands were raised. "So help him God, he would die upon the floor of the House, or get their rights for them. He loved them better than his own life. If you want to kill me," he continued, "my life is at your command, but to others I will not surrender it without a struggle. Then there is another thing I wish you to remember. I do not think you could well spare me just now. I will go on with you steadily, and peacefully, and resolutely, and I will present your Petition to-night. On Friday there will be a debate on it, and nothing can prevent our success if the people do not destroy themselves by intemperance and folly." He called upon those who thought the Convention had acted wisely in preventing a flow of bloodshed among the people to raise their hands, and again a forest of hands were raised. He congratulated them again and again on their good sense, and repeated his exhortations respecting the procession, and concluded by saying that, "though he might be stretched on the rack, he would smile terror out of countenance. Go on conquering and to conquer until the People's Charter had gloriously become the law of the land."

Several other speakers addressed the meeting, and then, instead of the Petition, on its decorated car, being escorted by an irresistible multitude to the Houses of Parliament amidst the roars of an applauding populace, it was placed in three "crazy cabs," and, accompanied by Feargus O'Connor and the Executive of the Convention, was carried in this humiliating way to Parliament.

On the return of the general Chartist crowd towards the north side of the river, they found the police drawn up on the bridges and approaches in deep ranks, and all passage denied them. There was much struggling and violent endeavour to force a crossing; "But," says Gammage, "the masses did not risk a collision with the police." Some slight combating ensued, and in a few instances heads were broken; but after a time the crowd were turned back, and manœuvred into detached masses, and then small parties of not more than ten each were allowed to pass. Soon after three o'clock the great mass of processionists and spectators dispersed, and all further anticipation of trouble was at an end.

"Thus ended," says the writer in the *Annual Register*, "amidst scorn and ridicule, a demonstration which was well calculated to overthrow all the existing institutions of the State, and reduce this country to the anarchy of the continental States."

"Considering the excitement previously existing," says Gammage, "the day passed off singularly peaceful." In every quarter, except by the Chartists, general satisfaction was expressed at the collapse of the proceedings.

Lord Lansdowne, speaking in the House of Lords on the part of the Government, said that "Her Majesty's Government had received the most unequivocal support from the great body of the people, not only in the metropolis, but in all the neighbouring parts of the country. All showed themselves ready to make the greatest sacrifices, if necessary, in support of law and order. And he would say, that if there was any circumstance which imparted to her Majesty's Government more than another that degree of confidence which they possessed, and which was necessary in order to enable them to act as they had done, it was the certainty which they had acquired within the last forty-eight hours, that there was no class on whom they might have occasion to call for support, from whom they would not have received it."[1]

The result of this culminating effort of Chartism, and of popular movement in Great Britain, was not confined merely to this country. "The event of this day," wrote the *Annual Register*, "produced a most powerful effect not only in England but throughout Europe."[2] The novelty was that "the dangerous assemblage was put down, not by the troops, nor even by the police, but by the people themselves—by the zealous and almost unanimous determination of all classes that such proceedings should not be permitted."

But if we go deeper than this view of it, and ask why it was that the people themselves had taken so decided a part in opposing and suppressing the threatened disorder of Chartism, the answer is, that it was because the bulk of the people had already passed the boundary or dividing line which affords the true test of the stability of a State—the line which divides those who would profit by vast and forcible changes in the Constitution, and those who would not. To the great bulk of the people more would have been lost in the turmoil that would have followed a Chartist revolution than could possibly have been gained. They were already in possession of great privileges, and they were unwilling to see them imperilled. The great rights which the Platform had striven for in the days gone by—free speech, public discussion, and free criticism of Government,—all that it had been then so remorselessly abused for, all that it had been crushed for, and all which it had subsequently won, had proved to be the salvation of England in the crisis of her fate. There can, indeed, be no question but that it was solely owing to the Reform Act of 1832, and the repeal of the Corn Laws in 1846, that the "batons of the citizens" were directed against the minority of their fellow-citizens rather than against the Government

[1] Hansard, vol. xcviii. p. 72, 1848.

[2] *Annual Register*, 1848, p. 53.

authorities. Had these two great measures not been passed, the Chartist agitation must have had a widely different issue from that which it had,[1] for they had detached vast numbers from the opponents of the Government, and had enlisted and enrolled them in the ranks of those interested in preserving order in the country, and maintaining the fundamental rights of society, and of government.

Sir Robert Peel, writing some time after, takes comfort to himself for his policy in 1846: "Many of the men," he says, "who had been the loudest in the condemnation of the measures of 1846, and the least scrupulous in imputing dishonesty and treachery to the advisers of them, openly rejoiced on the 10th of April 1848 that provision had been made for the total repeal of the Corn Laws."[2]

The finishing blow to the Chartist demonstration was given when, on the 13th April, the Select Committee on Public Petitions brought up a special report on the great National Petition of the Chartists. The Committee reported: "That in the matter of signatures to the Petition there had been a gross abuse of the privilege of petitioning. Instead of 5,700,000 names, as stated by Feargus O'Connor, the number had been ascertained to be 1,975,496. It was further evident to the Committee that on numerous consecutive sheets the signatures were in one and the same handwriting; that the names of distinguished individuals were attached to it, such as Victoria Rex, Duke of Wellington, Sir Robert Peel; that numbers of names were fictitious, such as 'No Cheese,' 'Pug Nose'; other signatures obviously belonging to the name of no individual, and others which your Committee do not hazard offending the House and the dignity and decency of their own proceedings by reporting."

So condemnatory a statement dealt a stunning blow to those who had got up the Petition; indeed, so much was this the case that though, on previous occasions, when a great mass of petitions were presented on some particular subject, Parliament usually took the subject of the petitions into consideration at a more or less early date, no move was now made by those who were most interested in the matter to bring the

[1] See speeches by J. Hume and Lord John Russell in House of Commons on 21st June 1848.

[2] *Memoirs*, vol. ii. p. 313.

subject under discussion in Parliament—a tolerably conclusive proof that they felt the full weight of the blow. Many a Friday passed without even the debate which O'Connor promised at Kennington—many a year before any one of the "six points" of the Charter was actually realised.

The short debate which took place in the House of Lords on the evening of the Chartist meeting at Kennington is worth referring to for two views expressed on public meetings and the Platform—the one by the Duke of Wellington, the other by Lord Brougham.

The Duke of Wellington said: "I do think no great society has ever suffered such a grievance as this metropolis has suffered within the last few days from the error of this great meeting, which was to have consisted, it was said, of 200,000 persons. God knows how many thousands really did attend, but still the effect was to place all the inhabitants of the metropolis under alarm, paralysing all trade and business of every description, and driving individuals to seek for safety by arming themselves for the protection of the lives of themselves and of their neighbours, and for the security of their property." He expressed a hope that by legislation "meetings might be limited to the numbers that could properly discuss the questions that are to be considered by the individuals who think proper to discuss them."[1]

The other view was that expressed by Lord Brougham, he who had been so strong an advocate for freedom of speech and discussion. "I hold it," he said, "to be an absolutely essential condition to the exercise of the right of public meeting for discussion, and to its existence as a matter of right, that the meeting should be for discussion alone. Whenever it is a mere assemblage of numbers, too large for any possibility of discussion, it becomes an assemblage of numbers merely for the display of physical force, and can only have the intention of overawing the Government, and of forcing measures on the Government and on the Parliament. . . . I have ever held that those meetings that are called, whether in England or Ireland, 'monster meetings' are in themselves essentially illegal. They are mere exhibitions of physical force, and it is only by a perversion of language that they can be affected or

[1] Hansard, vol. xcviii. p. 71, 1848.

pretended to be meetings for that which becomes an impossibility at them—discussion. All never dream of speaking; but all, if they do not dream of acting, place themselves in a position that, without any will or intention of their own, they may be driven, before they know it, into illegal courses."[1]

In dealing with the revival of Chartism in the acute form in which it had presented itself, the Government did not confine its action merely to precautionary measures against a disturbance of the peace in London. Once more, and so far as Great Britain was concerned, for the last time, did the Legislature endeavour to interfere with the Platform.

The proposal of the Government was brought forward in the House of Commons by Sir G. Grey, Home Secretary, a few days[2] before the Kennington meeting.[3] He said: "I deeply regret that the spirit that has recently manifested itself in some parts of the United Kingdom—that the seditious and treasonable designs which have been openly avowed by too many persons, at least in one part of the United Kingdom, have rendered it necessary for her Majesty's Government to come to Parliament to ask for an alteration in the law applicable to these extraordinary circumstances. . . . He stated that there was nothing further from their intentions than placing the slightest restriction upon the free, full, and indisputable right which the people of this country possess, and ought to enjoy, of discussing public affairs and deliberating upon every political matter, still less with the right to petition Parliament. Those rights had long been enjoyed, and he felt that their legitimate exercise constituted the best security for the continued preservation of our institutions, that to those rights we are indebted, under Providence, for those constitutional liberties which we prize so highly, and upon which so much of the greatness and happiness of this country depends. . . . It is owing to the free exercise of those rights that we are enabled to maintain our ground, and occupy that happy position which England at present holds—that England has not bent beneath the storm that has swept over the continent of Europe, has shaken the most powerful and despotic thrones, and disturbed what were considered the most firmly established institutions in the world. . . .

[1] Hansard, vol. xcviii. p. 70. [2] 7th April. [3] Hansard, vol. xcviii. p. 20.

"Highly, however, as we may esteem those rights, I doubt not it will be universally felt that the exercise of them has its limits, and that recently those limits have been passed; no man forming the decision of a dispassionate judgment can doubt that those limits have, to a very great extent, been transgressed; that under a pretence of discussing grievances, language of the most seditious description has been held; and that the law is, in some respects, insufficient for the repression of proceedings thus dangerous and exciting."

Sir G. Grey referred for proof mainly to speeches delivered in Ireland, then approaching the crisis of the Rebellion of 1848: "There was," he said, "a difference in the laws in force in England and Ireland on the subject of high treason, and it was desirable to assimilate them." Into the details it is unnecessary to enter. It was now proposed to reduce several of the offences hitherto treated in both countries as high treason from the crime of high treason to that of felony. But there was another proposal in the Bill which affected the Platform. It appeared that if a person openly and publicly excited others by speech to certain treasonable acts he was exempt from any penalty except that which attached to sedition. This was a bailable offence, and persons who were indicted for sedition were able to continue their designs precisely in the mode which had already subjected them to prosecution. It was therefore proposed to make the compassing or promoting of certain treasonable designs by "open and advised speaking" a felony, and consequently an unbailable offence.[1]

The proposed alteration was not a very formidable limitation

[1] As the proposal became law, it is convenient to give the section of the Act which enacted it.[1] "If any person whatsoever after the passing of this Act shall within the United Kingdom, or without, compass, imagine, etc., or intend to deprive and depose our Lady the Queen, her heirs, etc., from the style, honour, or royal name of the imperial Crown of the United Kingdom, or to levy war against her, in order by force or constraint to compel her to change her measures or counsels, or in order to put any force or constraint upon, or in order to intimidate or overawe either House of Parliament . . . and such compassings, intentions, etc., or any of them, shall express, utter, or declare, by publishing any printing, or writing, or by open or advised speaking, or by any overt act or deed, every person so offending shall be guilty of felony, and shall be liable on conviction to transportation for life, or for any time not exceeding two years' imprisonment with hard labour."

[1] Sec. 3, 11 and 12 Vict. cap. 12, 22d April 1848.

on freedom of discussion—very different, indeed, from those which had been proposed by Pitt in 1795, and by Lord Castlereagh in 1817 and 1819; but it was met by the most vehement opposition from a small section of the House of Commons. On the motion for leave to introduce the Bill Hume declared that "The interference with the freedom of speech on political matters was to impose a power which was neither wise nor just," and he dubbed it a "gagging law."

W. J. Fox, now a member of Parliament, said: "That which, in his eyes, gave to the Bill its peculiar character, was the infringement it proposed upon that liberty of speech which had hitherto been the boast of Englishmen, and one of the great safeguards of our liberties. Once let it become the law of the land that spoken words—not words only tending to the destruction of the Sovereign, and to the promotion of rebellion, but words which may be construed as tending to impair the freedom of discussion in either or both Houses of Parliament, or may be interpreted as tending to overawe their deliberations—may subject the speaker to transportation for seven years or for life; and it seemed to him that no man would be safe in addressing a public meeting in times of political excitement. It was in such times, when men were roused by some invasion of their privileges, or were stimulated by a strong desire to extend them—when multitudes were gathered together, and when mind and feeling were glowing and ardent with popular aspirations—that it became morally impossible to weigh and measure every word and syllable, so as to stand secure against the misrepresentation of an ignorant reporter, or the perversion of a malignant spy." [1]

Lord J. Russell, the Prime Minister, defended the proposal: "I admit that there is danger in extending penalties of this kind to words spoken; but at the same time we have to consider that the penalty of high treason has frequently been awarded for words spoken—often a very few words—when they were supposed to express treasonable sentiments. At the present time—especially of late—instead of secret conspiracies and counsels in the dark to overthrow the monarchy, it has become a common means of compassing treason to address speeches to large masses of people, and to use words exciting to the levy-

[1] Hansard, vol. xcviii. p. 51, 1848.

ing of war and to the use of arms for the purpose of overbearing all legitimate authority in the country, and thereby of compassing mischievous and dangerous ends. When the mode of overturning the Government is changed, it is necessary to change the punishment."

Quite in the older style of not losing much time over such measures, the second reading was moved on the 10th of April, the day of the Kennington meeting. Hume again opposed it: "While he did not think it right or becoming that a Convention should be sitting in judgment over the acts of the House, he had always considered the freedom of speech in public meetings as the palladium of the liberties of this country, for it was there where a community of feeling was established, and where violent spirits evaporated. . . . Every agitation, however constitutionally, and however peacefully conducted, must be more or less for the purpose of overawing Parliament."

Mr. Wakley regarded it as a gagging Act, and not less gagging than "the Six Acts" passed in 1819.

The second reading was carried by 452 to 35. Yet so decided was the opposition, though supported by such small numbers, that Sir George Grey was again called on to defend the Bill. He said the Bill proposed to alter the law with respect to speeches which now only amounted to sedition.

"It was justly said that words written were usually employed with more deliberation than words spoken; but although this was the case in some instances, yet when, day after day, they saw persons repeating the same advice, making use of the same exhortations, and holding out the same guilty objects, he could not but consider the speeches as made deliberately, and as designed to instigate to the commission of crime. The Government thought that this offence should be treated as something more than misdemeanour—in fact, it ought to be a felony. If it were so treated, the party could not prosecute his designs as before, because he would be immediately subject to arrest, and the offence would not be bailable." [1]

Feargus O'Connor said: "The prosecutions which had taken place in 1839–41 were quite sufficient to show that the existing laws required no strengthening. Let them pass the Bill, and

[1] Hansard, vol. xcviii. p. 171.

that which was the safety-valve of the Constitution being fastened down, discontent would at once explode; there would no more be an opening for the expression of public opinion. . . . Let them pass that law on that day, and that day week hundreds of secret societies would be organised throughout the kingdom, which sooner or later would result in a storm that would swamp the Government and shake the Empire to its foundations." [1]

Lord J. Russell also spoke. "I believe," he said, "that, according to the spirit of the Constitution, great latitude of discussion should be allowed; that inflammatory language should be permitted; that language which may incite to alienation from our Constitution, from our monarchical Constitution, should be permitted to proceed to great lengths, because I know that, without the allowance of some abuses of this kind, the free liberty of discussion cannot be maintained.

"There is now an Act on the statute book by which, if any person in this country prints and publishes any writing with intent to cause the levying of war, he may be found guilty of high treason, and may be capitally punished. I ask, Is it fit that one person who sits down and writes a newspaper, afterwards published, in which he commits this offence, should be capitally punished; and that others, his confederates and allies, should advisedly and with preparation make, day after day, speeches, with reporters from the newspapers before them, who will, they know, repeat every word they say; that these words shall be of equal or of greater malignity than those published by his confederates and allies; and that the one shall be found guilty of high treason, and capitally executed, while the other can only be brought up on a charge of seditious language, may get bail, and then be tried for a misdemeanour? Is that equal or fair justice?" [2]

In opposition to Government views, it was alleged that the Bill was a dangerous innovation; that it was for the first time doing away with the difference between words spoken and words written, in opposition to all authority, and in defiance of all precedent. And in support of this view Judge Foster was quoted, who, in his *Discourse on High Treason*, wrote: "Mere words are always liable to great misconstruction. . . .

[1] Hansard, vol. xcviii. p. 230. [2] *Ibid.* p. 236.

Words are transient and fleeting as the wind; the poison they scatter is, at the worst, confined to the narrow circle of a few hearers; they are frequently the effect of a sudden transport, easily misunderstood and often misrepresented."

Blackstone was also quoted as an authority against the Government. "For they (words) may be spoken in heat, without any intention, or be mistaken, perverted, or misremembered by the hearers; their meaning depends always on their connection with other words and things, and they signify differently according to the tone of voice with which they are delivered."

As a matter of fact this argument was not correct, as may be seen by referring to the Act of 1795, where the penalty was imposed for writing, printing, preaching, or other speaking, expressing, publishing, etc. etc., thus putting speaking and writing on the same basis. The opposition to the proposal was, however, sufficient to shake the Government from their purpose; and Lord J. Russell announced that the Government were ready to propose that those parts of the Bill which were new, and which referred to advised speaking, should have only a temporary operation, and come again under the consideration of Parliament. Those parts were accordingly limited to two years.[1]

The subject did not come under the consideration of Parliament when the two years expired, and thus ended the last effort made by any Government to legislate in any way against the Platform in Great Britain.

I have quoted Wakley's absurd statement that the measure was not less gagging than the "Six Acts" passed in 1819, just to draw attention to the enormous difference between the legislation of 1848 and the previous legislation. Pitt's legislation in the last decade of the last century absolutely silenced the Platform. Lord Liverpool's "Six Acts" almost did so. The Act of 1848 had no effect whatever on the use of the Platform, no visible effect on its language.

The day after the collapse of the meeting on Kennington Common, and the presentation of the National Petition, the Convention reassembled. O'Connor, unabashed by failure, declared that 400,000 to 500,000 persons had been present the

[1] The clause thus amended was carried by 242 votes to 50.

day before. But his ridiculous exaggerations could not conceal the reverse Chartism had suffered.

Gammage, the Chartist historian of the agitation, in reviewing the crisis of the movement, said: "O'Connor was right in the course he took in abandoning the procession; the people were anything but prepared for a physical encounter with the Government. O'Connor was wrong, not in abandoning the procession, but in having encouraged so long the empty braggarts and enthusiastic but mistaken men of the Convention, and in inducing them almost to the last moment to believe that he would head the procession to the House of Commons. The boasting which took place on this subject, and the miserable result, inflicted a wound on Chartism from which it has never recovered. O'Connor's power declined from the 10th of April. As men reflected, they perceived that he was not the man they had fondly imagined him to be, and step by step they withdrew their support."

From this turning-point in the Chartist agitation we are slowly let down deeper than ever into a chaos of divided counsels, of purposeless and contradictory meetings, of jarrings and discords, of frothy, vacuous Platformings.

The Convention continued its sittings for some little time, making arrangements for simultaneous meetings, at which delegates were to be elected to a National Assembly, and a National Memorial to the Queen was to be signed asking her to dissolve Parliament, and call to her Council such Ministers only as would make the People's Charter a Cabinet measure, and then it dissolved itself.

A large number of meetings continued to be held. At Aberdeen a meeting of 6000 persons passed a resolution in favour of forming a National Guard. At Manchester a meeting, "said to be attended by 100,000 persons," was held in support of the Charter. At many other places "large and spirited meetings" were also held, and "the utmost enthusiasm was manifested." Then came a week "famous for meetings." On Easter Monday O'Connor visited his constituents at Nottingham, where, seated in a triumphal car, he was drawn to the meeting by four horses, with postilions dressed in green silk and velvet jackets and caps. At Liverpool "an immense assembly" met; at Glasgow a large gathering took place; at

Skercoat Moor, near Halifax, "an immense concourse" assembled; at all of which, and many others as well, there was almost no end of speaking and passing resolutions.

The election of delegates to the National Assembly having taken place, that Assembly met on the 1st of May—some 60 members or so, instead of the anticipated 100, being present; but when it met, the delegates seemed to have no settled policy. Their first proceeding was to give reports from their respective constituencies. "It was evident from these reports," says Gammage, "that a great majority of the districts were opposed to physical force." Several, however, were in favour of it. This crucial question came at once under discussion, but so little agreement was there on it, that ultimately a motion was adopted "That all discussion on the subject was highly impolitic." Then it was resolved to call upon the country to raise £10,000 for purposes of agitation, but there is no record of that sum, or indeed any considerable part of it, having ever been got, and we may rather infer the contrary.

A provisional Executive was chosen by the Assembly, a sort of Chartist Cabinet, the members of which were to have £2 weekly, and when travelling, second-class fare and 2s. 6d. a day.

On the 10th a discussion took place as to the appointment of paid commissioners, "and considerable ill-feeling was manifested"—one member expressing a hope "that when they went out to lecture they would confine themselves to plain common sense, give themselves no airs; and if they had any sarcastic powers, would keep them at home, carefully locked up." Numerous other discussions took place. During one of them we read: "No very amiable feeling was manifested;" of another, "It was a long, wrangling discussion, in which almost every delegate found fault with somebody else." Then the adjournment of the National Assembly for six weeks was moved. One, Ernest Jones, supported the motion, and said: "He did so with peculiar feelings because they had now heard the funeral oration for that Assembly pronounced by its own members. Several members had joined their eloquence for that purpose; there was a division amongst them. When that Assembly met, it was then that the Chartist body saw the elements of popular power gathered together and concentrated.

It was then that that power might have been wielded for the mightiest objects, but, amid the desertion of friends and the invasion of enemies, the fusee had been trampled out, and the elements of their energy were scattered to the winds of heaven."[1] The motion was carried, and, says Gammage, "thus ended the Assembly."

In one thing only did the Assembly represent the Chartist body truly—namely, in its want of unity. But besides the split between moral and physical force men, a new source of division was appearing among them, weaning many away from the Chartist chiefs—this was a movement for a moderate measure of Parliamentary reform. Several large meetings on the subject were held, and petitions presented to the House of Commons; and in June 1848 Hume moved that the elective franchise should be so extended as to include all householders, that votes should be taken by ballot, that the duration of Parliament should not exceed three years, and that the appointment of members to population should be made more equal. The motion was of course rejected,[2] but it served the purpose of presenting a possible for an impossible measure of reform.

There was another cause tending towards the disintegration of the Chartists. The Government was again putting the ordinary law of the country vigorously in force. Prosecutions were launched against them right and left. From Platforming the more reckless or foolish had passed on to violence or preparations for violence. The contagion of Irish agitation and rebellion excited them; drilling was practised in parts of the north of England; riots occurred: in one place a police constable was shot dead; and arrests followed by the score—arrests for illegal drilling, for seditious speeches, for attending illegal meetings, for riot and rescue, or riot and assault, for seditious conspiracy, for conspiracy to levy war against her Majesty; and convictions followed, and then sentences—sentences of twelve months' imprisonment, eighteen months, two years, transportation for life. Thus between failure, and divisions, and punishments, the life was gradually being crushed out of the Chartist agitation.

At length, on the 3d July 1849, just fifteen months after the presentation of the great National Petition, O'Connor brought

[1] Gammage, p. 353. [2] By 351 against 84.

a motion before the House of Commons, "That this House adopts the principles embodied in the document entitled the People's Charter." Lord J. Russell opposed it, "conceiving that if adopted it would tend to produce the greatest evils, and that they were in the enjoyment of benefits which, if they lightly parted with, they would deserve to be deemed the most foolish and unwise nation on the face of the earth." So little Parliamentary support had the Chartists now, that only 15 members, including tellers, voted for the motion, whilst 224 voted against it. "Such was the result of this motion after all the bluster of 1848."

Again, in 1849, did Hume bring his motion about Parliamentary reform before Parliament, and again was it rejected. After this debate, and after the rejection of the motion of 3d July, relative to the Charter, the Chartists practically lost their chief, as "O'Connor drew towards the Hume school of reformers."[1]

A little later Gammage adds: "The Chartist party became more divided than ever, in consequence of the attempted union with middle class reformers."[2] And gradually the sands of the Chartist agitation ran lower and lower. Towards the end of 1851 "disaffection began to be manifested at the Executive for the apathy of the Chartist body." A little later "the Executive grew weaker every day;" then a new Executive was what was called "elected," which followed the steps of its predecessor; and then, at last, "the National Charter Association ceased to exist."

I have dwelt in some detail on the later history of the Chartist agitation, the more clearly to explain the failure of the Platform to win that success which had crowned its efforts in other agitations. It is easy now, after the lapse of years, to see the causes of that failure; and the experience of the Anti-Corn-Law agitation affords a most efficient standard for testing the proceedings of the Platform in the Chartist agitation. In the Anti-Corn-Law agitation success, as has already been stated, was due to the singleness of the object agitated for, to the abilities of the leaders, to the complete harmony of all workers in the cause, to the thoroughness of organisation, to the practically unlimited financial support, and to the argu-

[1] Gammage, p. 372. [2] *Ibid.* p. 376.

mentative power of the Platform consequent on the provable and proved goodness of the cause. Each and every one of these circumstances was notably absent in the Chartist agitation.

The "six points" of the Charter, each point a great reform in itself, could most certainly not be designated "singleness of object," could only loosely give even the most superficial unity of purpose. Universal suffrage, annual Parliaments, equal electoral districts, the Ballot, one and all were questions of vast and complicated character, upon each and every one of which there were the widest differences of opinion. Yet all these—and some others besides—were to be embodied in one programme which was to secure the general assent of the great mass of the population of the United Kingdom; and the realisation of this vast programme was the herculean task which the leaders of the agitation undertook. Had they been united and at one, and had the spirit of union permeated the whole people over whom they set themselves up, the agitation might have been more formidable, though it scarcely could have had a different end; but neither they, nor the people who followed them, were united, and it was this particular circumstance which led, more than any other, to the collapse of the agitation. Then there was no commanding leader among them. The most notorious of their leaders, the erratic and eccentric Feargus O'Connor, "the Chartist Chief," "the Lion of Freedom," "the Lion of the North," raised himself at one time to such prominence as to evoke the expression, "Chartism narrowed itself into O'Connorism," but he held a disputed leadership; he had many rivals who either never acknowledged his authority, or quarrelled with him, and then separated from him, taking with them some section or another of the Chartists; and then among the self-appointed leaders there were endless jealousies, and rivalries, and bickerings, and quarrellings. Nor was there even among the people themselves much union. Union was not their forte; nor, indeed, under their circumstances was much union to be expected. So recently as 1837 Place wrote: "Why has it happened that the working people who compose an immense majority of the nation have never yet done anything on a large scale to advance any of their interests? Why have they never adopted any plan to advance their own respectability?

The answer is Want of union. If it be asked why have they not been united? The answer is, The want of knowledge of their condition in relation to society. This ignorance has all along been their bane; it is still their bane."[1]

So long as the movement merely took the form of large meetings the want of unanimity was not apparent, but once organisation was attempted, the want of union became apparent. Thus it happened that from the very first of the numerous National Conventions down to the very last of them, discord was their prevailing characteristic, and the record of their proceedings is the record of perpetual differences of opinion.

Another cause of their failure is explained by Place, who makes a very acute comment on popular movements in general. "There has long been," he says, "and still is, a strange notion among small as well as large bodies of working men who frequently meet together, that *they* are *the* working people. They always succeed in persuading themselves that whatever project they take up will be adopted by the whole body, and no number of disappointments has the least effect upon them calculated to induce them to disabuse themselves."[2]

The same "strange notion" beset the members of the successive Conventions. They persuaded or deluded themselves that they were the representatives of the people, with all the moral and physical power of the people at their back. They did not, would not, recognise that even their section of the people were as much divided in opinion as they were themselves.

Under these circumstances a powerful or compact organisation was practically impossible. Very little organisation indeed was attempted, except through the system of Conventions, constituted of persons nominally elected by different large towns, and except when these Conventions were sitting, there was no central organisation at all.

Of financial support too the agitation had little,—the people agitating being too poor to be able to give much aid of that sort. Feargus O'Connor spent a good deal of his own money, but it went more in support of his own personality in the cause than to the cause itself, and, all told, formed but a very

1 Place, MSS., 27,819, p. 224.

2 *Ibid.* 27,791, p. 343.

trifling sum in comparison with such sums as were at the disposition of the Anti-Corn-Law League.

Thus, in all these important respects, it is apparent how disadvantageously circumstanced the Chartist agitation was to secure success.

All these defects, however, were relatively unimportant in comparison with the greater question—the goodness or justice of the cause; and here, though the Platform had a true and just cause to champion—namely, the condition of large masses of the people—the Chartists, by the extreme nature of their programme, neutralised the arguments which might have been urged in favour of that great object. Of the "six points" of the Charter, Universal Suffrage was the chief. In the then condition of the great bulk of the labouring population, ignorant, ill-educated, and utterly untrained, Universal Suffrage would have led the country to certain ruin; indeed, if the successive National Conventions afforded a fair example of the sort of Parliament which Universal Suffrage would have produced, there was not a vestige of ground for even a hope, much less a belief, that the interests of the country would have been safe in such keeping, or that the condition of the people would have been permanently ameliorated under a Parliament elected by Universal Suffrage.

But extreme as was this demand, a great number of the Chartists in reality meant what, in the then condition of the people, would have been tantamount to a revolution—a revolution not of progress, as that of the Reform Act had been, but of confusion, anarchy, and retrogression. Place, writing about 1843, affirmed that the common people in hundreds of thousands openly avowed their hostility to the Government, and declared their determination to pull it down by main force. "A thin veil," he says, "easily seen through, was thrown over their intentions; but no one was ignorant either of the course they were taking, or to what they intended it should lead, or of what the mass anticipated."[1]

This character of the movement was not altered as it continued its career, for the Platform, in the later stages of the agitation, rang with sentiments as defiant as any that had previously been given expression to. There can,

[1] Place, MSS., 27,820, p. 2.

indeed, be little doubt that the Chartists put before themselves objects which, if realised at the time, would have been a dangerous revolution. Other classes of the people, whose opinion was more likely to be right, and who practically constituted the nation, saw how disastrous such an event as the realisation of the Chartist plans would be, and no amount of Platform eloquence, no arguments that the Chartists could have used, could have persuaded the middle and upper and governing classes to comply with the Chartist demands. They would have fought first, believing that the lesser evil. And it was, happily, just this which the Chartists, as a body, were not prepared to do. A portion of them were for having recourse to force—at least the most blatant of their leaders boasted that they were—but most of them, especially in the later stages of the agitation, thought the cause should be won by moral force, and they would not adopt other means for winning it. In this divided state of Chartist opinion the Platform gave a divided, uncertain voice.

Nor was the style of the Platform at this period at all such as to win adherents to the cause. Instead of the closely argumentative speeches which gained numerous converts to the Anti-Corn-Law League, there was frothy, uncertain declamation, and meaningless generalities; and instead of the advice to agitate by peaceful, constitutional means, there was a continual, covert, at times, indeed, an open incitement to force and violence. Rather more was it of a style to alienate support than to secure sympathy.

And so from all these united causes the Platform, in this instance, failed to extract from Parliament at the time any one of the "six points" of the Charter.

But though it thus to all outward appearance failed, we should err greatly were we to conclude that it really failed. Rather was its failure like that of a seed sown in the ground, which for a time is apparently dead and gone, but soon brings forth a new life. Of the "six points" of the Charter three have since been engrafted on the Constitution—vote by ballot, equal electoral districts, and no property qualification; whilst in household suffrage we have approached very closely to the most important of the "six points"—"Universal Suffrage."

I must, however, refer more specifically to the results of the agitation so far as the Platform is concerned. Reprehensible as its language too often was, with its blatant, bombastic, and frequently criminal ravings, yet, through all, it fulfilled one great function, the greatest to discerning statesmen—the informing function.

In the Anti-Corn-Law agitation the most prominent feature of the Platform was its didactic character. Here its equally prominent feature was its informing character, for it laid bare the evils under which masses of the population were suffering, and disclosed, indistinctly and confusedly it is true, some of the ideas which were passing through, or were forming themselves in the minds of the masses of the people. Through its medium the inarticulate voice of great masses of the people became more or less articulate; through it that most difficult of all problems to rulers, What are the thoughts of the people? was solved; through it men became aware of the direction in which the masses were moving.

These are services the value of which it is impossible to overrate. Parliament, though nominally a representative body, did not do it. The representative system was not perfect enough for that. No royal commission or committees could have elicited the drift of popular desires or ambitions in the manner the Platform had done, or have disclosed more thoroughly the condition of the people. Nor could the Press have done it either, for no special correspondents or newspaper articles would have given the information with such an impress of truth as the Platform did, or have enforced it with such weight. From the Platform the truth frequently came first hand.

The Platform, despite all its faults, had, during the Chartist agitation, done a vast service for the people. Once more it voiced their feelings, and depicted their condition as no other organ of public expression could have done. It drew public attention, far more emphatically than any agitation hitherto, to the social and material condition of the industrial population of the country. It crashed, like the reverberations of a huge bell, into the ears of the governing classes of the kingdom, and told them in unmistakable tones that a new order had arisen in the State, with wants which must be regarded, with needs which must no longer be ignored, with feelings which must no longer be trampled on. It forced on the assembled body of the representatives of the electors, and on the House of Peers, the consideration and adoption of measures for the social, material, moral, and intellectual improvement of the masses. It revealed to Parliament a wholly new sphere of duty and action—one which up to this had been resolutely ignored or neglected,—and it opened out to statesmen new vistas of contingencies which could only be disregarded at the vastest peril to the State.

Nor was its voice without effect. A marked change took place in the conduct of Parliament and in the attitude of party leaders to the questions thus forced on their attention by the Platform. Several Commissions of Inquiry into matters affecting the condition of the people were issued. In 1842 an Act was passed prohibiting the employment of women and children in mines and collieries. In 1843 an Address to the Queen was adopted[1] by the House of Commons, praying her Majesty would take into her instant and serious consideration the best means of diffusing the benefits and blessings of a moral and religious education among the working classes of her people; and in the following year an Act was passed regulating the employment of women and children in factories. The administration of the Poor Law was softened and improved, and measures for promoting education were adopted. Then in 1846 the Corn Laws were repealed, and in 1847 the labour of women and young persons in factories was limited to ten hours a day. Any enumeration of measures, however, but imperfectly conveys the great change which soon became evident in the whole tone of Parliament, and of the speeches of Ministers or members, and in the increased attention given to the social and material improvement of the people. The leader of the Opposition—Lord John Russell—avowed, in 1844, the pressure being put on them. "There is," he said, "another topic which, I think, must force itself upon our attention, in some shape or other, before a very long period elapses—I mean the condition of the people of England." And Sir Robert Peel, speaking in 1847, said: "I do feel that the point at which we ought all to strive is to improve the condition and elevate the feelings of the great labouring class.

[1] On Lord Ashley's motion.

I tell you it is not safe unless you do it. You are giving these classes intellectual improvement, and unless you remove every law inconsistent with that intelligence, the institutions of the country will be in danger, especially in the event of a calamity occurring in this country such as is now desolating Ireland."

Though there was so much that was reprehensible in the Platform during these long years of the Chartist agitation, and though so many illustrations have been given of the depths to which it at times descended, it would be wrong to infer that all the speeches were equally bad, that no striking thoughts were eloquently expressed, that no good counsel was ever given by the Chartist speakers, that none of the leaders ever rose above the level of the claptrap eloquence of a demagogue. One passage from a speech of Vincent may be quoted as an illustration of something better than most of the Chartist speeches hitherto referred to: "The world," he said, "is up against aristocratic institutions. True, the battle is fought on various fields. One day it is seen in the struggle of Dissenters against the dominion of a law-made Church. Another day it is heard in virtuous efforts to free the black slave. Another time it speaks in the exertions of our oppressed Catholic brethren. One moment in the cry against the Corn Laws, and at another moment in the erection of a school. These are but indications of a great and noble spirit. Higher principles are the springs of action; the belief in the brotherhood of humanity—a desire to realise Christian institutions. It is a mental and moral rebellion against the prejudices of ages. And, gentlemen, why should you fear this indication of a new power? For myself I rejoice at it. I see with Channing that this is an age pregnant with events. I behold this rise of mind, and the tremulous pulsations of the democratic heart, with the greatest joy. Hail it, gentlemen, I beseech you. Do not despise it; encourage it; help it on. Look on this multitude; God is their and your common parent. He made them, as He made you in His own image. Sin and aristocratic institutions have marred that image; and just in proportion as the religious, intellectual, moral, political, and social elevation of the masses are secured, so in proportion will the image be restored to its original beauty. Do not wonder why the multitude reason on abstract rights, instead of clamouring for bread; there's a nobility in it beyond all praise. To my mind it is one of the sublimest spectacles to see a ragged and hungry people pondering over nice abstractions, and saying: True, we want bread; but we demand rights long withheld. This is true magnanimity. It shows that a spark from the Deity has entered their souls. It is a proclamation of the Christian truth—'Man shall not live by bread alone, but by every word that proceedeth out of the mouth of God.'"

This is not a solitary instance of striking utterance. Numerous speeches are to be found containing passages inculcating good and true principles, peaceable and orderly conduct; many of them display a true appreciation of what was really for the welfare of the people; many advocated reforms of the most irreproachable character. But, on the whole, it must be acknowledged that the examples the Platform set in this Chartist agitation were—to borrow Gammage's simile—beacons to warn successors off the rocks on which the cause was wrecked. Still, despite all, the Platform had the great virtues or merits that it afforded a comparatively harmless outlet or escape for many evil passions which would otherwise have found a more violent and disastrous form of expression, and that it expressed and conveyed to the governing authorities and classes what was passing in the minds of the people, and thus, in the most trying and dangerous crisis of the national fate, rendered the most invaluable services towards the peace and welfare of the country.

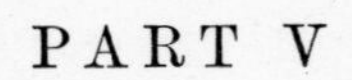

PART V

CHAPTER XX

THE SECOND REFORM ACT AGITATION

The history of the Platform during the fifteen or sixteen years that followed 1848 may be passed briefly over. There was no great Platform campaign to compel a Government to adopt a particular policy, or to make some special concession to popular wishes; there was no upheaval of the working classes such as that of which the Chartist demonstration of the 10th April 1848 was the culminating display; there was nothing specially notable in the period. Nevertheless it was one of steady progress for the Platform. Ministry succeeded Ministry, and Parliament followed Parliament, general election followed general election, and each change or event served ever more and more to strengthen the position of the Platform as a great political institution. We find ourselves no longer recording as important incidents in the history of the Platform the outpourings of men like Gale Jones and Henry Hunt; no longer noting as memorable the speech of a member of Parliament outside Parliament, or as still more eventful, the speech of the one Minister or ex-Minister who ever spoke outside Parliament in the early times—Charles Fox. Those days were passed, and the nearer we approach more recent days, the greater becomes the difficulty in finding space even to enumerate the speeches outside Parliament from the Platform of Prime Ministers and ex-Prime Ministers, of Cabinet Ministers and ex-Cabinet Ministers. Everything that had been contemned and legislated against before—public meetings, great demonstrations, peripatetic orators, harangues—have become in the progress of years common occurrences; even the greatest statesmen descended from the lofty seclusion of Parliament to take part in the more robust and less constrained publicity of the Platform.

And what had been also adding so immensely to the power

of the Platform as time went on was that every step which the House of Commons gained in authority was also so much gained for it, for the Platform was ever exercising a growing power over the House of Commons. Even in 1849 we find complaints of the change that had occurred as regards representatives and their constituents.

"Every one," says a writer in *The Quarterly Review* of 1849, "who observes closely the proceedings of individual members, is well aware of the unconstitutional thraldom in which many of them are held by their constituencies. We are not here renewing the general argument as to the use and abuse of close boroughs; we only note how much the reduction of their number has added to the subserviency of public men to democratic influence. One of the advantages promised by the advocates of the Reform Bill was, that it would put an end to the illegal associations and other popular demonstrations which, as was alleged, only arose out of, and were irregular compensations for, the injustice of the old system of representation; and that when Manchester and Birmingham had legitimate organs in the Legislature, the voice of seditious agitation would be no longer heard. Has such been the result? Have not, on the contrary, the excitement on public questions, the demonstrations in populous districts, the riots, the disturbance, the whole system of agitation—that is, *intimidation*—become much more constant and audacious, and especially in the very districts to which the pretended panacea of representation had been applied—Birmingham, Manchester, Stockport, etc.? Has not agitation become a kind of chronic fever among us of the same kind as that which assumes an acute character in France under the form of *émeutes?* They are both the heavings of the democratic deep." [1]

If the frequent intercourse of constituents with their representatives was a chronic fever, and if popular meetings and demonstrations were a "heaving of the democratic deep," they were things that were likely to be permanent.

That the constituencies were claiming and asserting more direct control over their representatives is, I think, evident from the fact that Mr. Bright felt it necessary to make a protest and declarations of independence on the subject in 1851.

[1] Vol. lxxxv. p. 291.

In an Address to his constituents (in May) he said: "Notwithstanding that there is not a man in England with a higher idea of the exalted position of any one who, at all worthy, should occupy the place of your representative, yet, when I speak of a vote in Parliament, I endeavour to shut out from my mind any idea of controlling influence down here or elsewhere. I am most happy, when I can, to agree with you; but I think there is a higher, loftier, purer standard for a representative than even the influence of those whom he may represent; and that standard is his own intelligent, conscientious convictions of duty on the question which is before him."

Yet, while thus asserting his independence, he claimed later that he had acted in accordance with the principles on which he had been elected. In his Farewell Address of March 1857 to the electors of Manchester, he wrote: "I believe that slander itself has not dared to charge me with having forsaken any of the principles, on the honest support of which I offered myself twice, and was twice accepted as your representative."

The actual progress of the Platform during the years that succeeded 1848 is best to be gauged by examining in some detail its action during the agitation which resulted in the Reform Act of 1867, for in a period of comparative repose, such as those intervening years were, there is little sufficiently distinct or definite to record as marking the progress of the Platform; and it is only by contrasting its state at one period with its state at another that we can comprehend the change which has taken place, and realise the position which, in progress of years, it attained.

The question of Parliamentary reform slept, or, rather, had been used as the plaything of parties in Parliament until the autumn of 1858. Hume's motions in Parliament and the meetings outside, which had exercised a disintegrating influence on Chartism, had produced little definite effect in other ways. The country had taken no pressing interest in the subject. Various Bills had been introduced in a half-hearted sort of way, and nothing had come of them.

When, in the early months of 1858,[1] the Tory Government came into power, Disraeli, in his speech to the electors of Buckinghamshire, on his re-election on accepting office, an-

[1] 8th March 1858.

nounced that it was totally impossible that the question could any longer be "trifled with"; but he proceeded at once to trifle with it by declaring that the time when the Bill for reform was to be brought forward was quite another thing. Much remained to be done before a great domestic question like this could be attacked.

"We have, if possible, to effect a reconciliation with our great ally (France); we have other tasks before us most difficult to fulfil; we have to put down a revolt in India; . . . we have to carry a Bill through Parliament for the government of that country; we have to introduce financial measures of no ordinary gravity." These things would have to be got out of the way first, but the Government would give to the subject their most earnest and serious consideration.

It is evident from this that the Government was not very keen about reform; but a Government cannot always prevent a question being forced into prominence, and in the autumn of 1858 the country was once more stirred into life on the subject by the Platform. Bright, who thought it desirable to put some pressure on the Government to keep them up to the collar, proceeded to awaken the country from the Platform.

His first speech was an address to his constituents at Birmingham.[1] The main argument was that the House of Commons did not satisfactorily represent the nation. Once more, owing to the growth and progress of the nation, the nation had outgrown its constitution—the House of Commons no longer represented "equitably or even honestly the population of the country."

"There are in the House of Commons at present 330 members (more than half the House) whose whole number of constituents do not amount to more than 180,000, and there are at the same time in Parliament 24 members whose constituents are upwards of 200,000 in number."[2]

Moreover, "there is this great significant fact, that wherever you go in Great Britain or Ireland, five out of every six men you meet have no vote." He urged the reduction of the franchise, the adoption of the ballot, and a redistribution of seats. "The question of Parliamentary reform is a great and serious question. . . . Why should reformers not have their own

[1] On 27th October 1858. [2] Bright's *Speeches*, vol. ii. p. 13.

Reform Bill? Why should we not, by public meetings, by petitions, and when the proper time comes, by presenting ourselves at the polling booths, do everything in our power to pass that measure into law?"[1]

The Platform stood now in a vastly different position from what it did when the last Reform agitation took place. Now a great orator like Bright addressed not merely the 5000 or 10,000 people who listened to him, but addressed the whole nation. His speech was reported in every newspaper, and newspapers, if not ten times as numerous as they were in 1832, were ten times more widely read. He declared this himself when speaking in December 1858 at Manchester. "From this platform," he said to the large meeting he was addressing, "I do not speak to you only; I speak to all my countrymen." And then he added a tribute to the efficacy of Platform agitation: "If they wish for reform—if they think me honest, informed, capable on this question—if they have any confidence in those with whom I am associated—then let them meet in their cities, their towns, their villages,—in country parishes even, where free speech is not forbidden,—let them meet and speak; let them resolve, and let them petition. If they do this, I think I can promise them that before long they will be in full possession, and in free exercise of those political rights which are not more necessary to their national interests than they are consistent with the principles of their boasted Constitution."[2]

From Manchester he went on to Scotland, where he spoke at Edinburgh and Glasgow.[3] "When I look upon these great meetings, at several of which I have been permitted recently to be present, I cannot help asking myself, What is the question—what is the matter—which appears to be stirring to their very innermost depths the hearts of my countrymen? Is it some sudden frenzy, some fanaticism which wise men must rather be sorry for than rejoice over? Judging by the looks of expectation and hope—even of assurance of success—which light up the countenances of so many before me, I must believe you have at least some great and worthy object which has brought us together. I believe no more worthy object can assemble the citizens of any free nation; for here we are met

[1] Bright's *Speeches*, vol. ii. p. 26. [2] *Ibid.* p. 52. [3] 21st December 1858.

to discuss the great question of Constitutional Reform, and to consider how far it may be possible to confirm and give greater permanence and security to whatsoever portion of liberty we have derived from our forefathers." [1]

Early in the following year he addressed great meetings at Bradford and Rochdale, and then Parliament opened.

The Queen's Speech had informed Parliament that its attention would be called "to the state of the laws which regulate the representation of the people in Parliament." And on 28th February [2] Disraeli introduced the Bill of the Tory Government. "Parliamentary reform," he said, "had become successively a public question, a Parliamentary question, and a ministerial question." The chief characteristics of the Bill were the proposal of the principle of identity between the county and the borough franchise, and the introduction of certain new borough franchises. The second reading of the Bill was rejected by a majority of 39—mainly on the ground of the inadequacy of the proposal—and thereupon Parliament was dissolved (23d April).

The general election which took place did not, however, result in a majority for the Conservatives, and on the night of the 12th of June they were defeated in the House of Commons by 323—310 on a vote of want of confidence. They resigned, and were succeeded by a Liberal Government.

It is a most interesting fact that the formal announcement of the resignation of Ministers was not reserved for Parliament, but was made from the Platform—namely, at a banquet on 13th June at Merchant Tailors' Hall. Lord Derby, the Prime Minister, in replying to the toast of her Majesty's Ministers, announced that they had that day placed their resignations in the hand of the Sovereign, and he briefly described what would be the policy of the Conservative party once they were again in opposition.

Parliament, apparently, no longer afforded sufficient opportunity for making great party manifestoes, for at a banquet given about a month later at the same place, Disraeli, ex-Chancellor of the Exchequer, and practically leader of the Tory party, availed himself of the occasion to make a great party speech "formulating his position and policy."

[1] Bright's *Speeches*, vol. ii. p. 53. [2] 1859.

"I can truly say that, from the earliest moment when I gave attention to public affairs, I have ever had it as one of my main objects to restore the power and repute of the great party to which we are proud to belong, and which I believe to be intimately bound up with the welfare and renown of this country. My connection with that party has existed in days of trial and comparative adversity, but I have never ceased to have faith in its destinies, because I believed it was founded on principles to which the great body of the nation responded. In attempting, however, humbly to regulate its fortunes, I have always striven to distinguish that which was eternal from that which was but accidental in its opinions. I have always striven to assist in building it upon a broad and national basis, because I believed it to be a party peculiarly and essentially natural—a party which adhered to the institutions of the country as embodying the national necessities, and forming the best security for the liberty, the power, and the prosperity of England."

It is interesting proof of the growing appreciation of the Platform by the Conservative party to find the ex-Prime Minister still further using it for the purpose of a declaration of the policy of the party of which he was leader.

On the 29th October 1859 a great Conservative banquet was given to Lord Derby and his colleagues in the late Ministry. Lord Derby made a long political speech, and in the course of it said: "We meet here to testify and declare our adherence to the principles and doctrines of true Conservatism . . . that conservatism which loves the interests of the people at large, but will not be led away by noisy denunciations of violent and blustering demagogues, either to shrink at the voice of menace, or timidly to concede rights and privileges to large bodies of men for the purpose of obtaining some amount of temporary popularity, when in our hearts we believe that the concession of those very coveted boons would be injurious rather than beneficial to the classes whom it is sought to benefit."

He said that the conduct of Sir Robert Peel in 1845 "completely and entirely for the moment shattered the Conservative party in this country," and that the Duke of Wellington had exhorted him to assume at once the leadership of the party. He had accordingly done so. He now announced his present policy as leader, and declared that he had no desire for the immediate overthrow of the existing administration.

Disraeli also made an interesting speech on the same occasion. Referring to the policy of the leaders of the party during the preceding ten years, he said: "It has been our wish to put an end to that which I may describe as 'the monopoly of Liberalism,' which, in our opinion, has exercised a very pernicious influence on the course of public proceedings, and on the character of public men. Now for more than a quarter of a century, by this theory of the monopoly of Liberalism, half the public men in England have been held up as individuals incapable and unqualified to attempt any measures which might improve the institutions or administration of the country; while, on the other hand, the other half were, in order to sustain this monopoly, perpetually pledging themselves to changes and alterations, injudicious in almost every case, and in many impracticable, and when they were in power they expended all their resources in inventing evasions by which they might extricate themselves from the fulfilment of their previous promises. . . . I believe we have brought about a healthy state of political parties. Men will now be judged by the policy which they recommend, and the measures they bring forward, not by traditions which are generally false, not by promises which are seldom fulfilled."

Though a Liberal Government had come into office the agitation for Parliamentary reform was doomed to disappointment for a time. Other events and circumstances pushed the subject aside, and it was not until 1865 that it again became a burning question. In Parliament it had been of course several times raised, but came to nothing, and that there was no Platform agitation for it appears to have been used as an argument against it.

In 1864 a Bill was introduced by Mr. Baines for lowering the borough franchise, and Mr. Gladstone made some important remarks on popular agitation: "We are told that the working classes do not agitate for an extension of the franchise; but is it desirable that we should wait until they do agitate? In my opinion, agitation by the working classes upon any political subject whatever is a thing not to be waited for, not to be made a condition previous to any Parliamentary movement, but, on the contrary, it is a thing to be deprecated, and, if possible, anticipated and prevented by wise and provident measures. An agitation by the working classes is not like an agitation by the classes above them, the classes possessed of having leisure. The agitation of the classes having leisure is easily conducted. Every hour of their time has not a money value, their wives and children are not dependent on the strictly reckoned results of those hours of labour. When a working man finds himself in such a condition that he must abandon that daily labour on which he is strictly dependent for his daily bread, it is then that, in railway language, 'the danger signal is turned on,' and because he feels a strong necessity for action, and a distrust in the rulers who have driven him to that necessity. The present state of things, I rejoice to say, does not indicate that distrust; but if we admit this, we must not allege the absence of agitation on the part of the working classes as a sufficient reason why the Parliament of England and the public mind of England should be indisposed to entertain the discussion of this question."

The winter of 1864–65 saw the recommencement of Platform agitation for reform. Bright addressed his constituents at Birmingham on the 18th January 1865. Presenting the subject in the simplest and therefore most striking manner, he said: "An Englishman, if he goes to the Cape, can vote; if he goes farther, to Australia, to the nascent empires of the New World, he can vote; if he goes to the Canadian Confederation, he can vote; and if he goes to those grandest colonies of England not now dependent upon the English Crown, there, in twenty free, and, in the whole, in thirty-five different States, he can give his free and independent vote. It is only in his own country, on his own soil, where he was born—the very soil which he has enriched with his labour and with the sweat of his brow—that he is denied the right which, in every other community of Englishmen in the world, would be freely accorded to him. . . . I demand then this, which is but the right of our Constitution, that the House of Commons shall be made freely and fairly to represent the Commons and the people of the United Kingdom. . . . I claim for these millions, for whom I am now pleading, the right of admission, through their representatives, into the most ancient and the most venerable Parliament which at this hour exists among men; and when they are thus admitted, and not till then, it may be truly said that England, the august mother of free nations, herself is free."[1]

The question did not yet, however, make much way, and early in July Parliament, having nearly reached the term of its existence, was dissolved, and a general election took place. On the electoral Platform it was given due prominence. The Prime Minister, it is true, in his election at Tiverton, said nothing about it, but his example was not followed by others, and scarcely a candidate but referred to it as a measure not much longer to be deferred.

Disraeli was returned without a contest for Bucks, and in returning thanks he made a speech which was practically a party manifesto. After praising Lord Derby's reform proposals of 1858 he dwelt on the desirability of the people having opinions on the subject of the distribution of power in the State. He gave no pledge, however, to deal with the question of Parliamentary reform, which he defined as the question of the distribution of political power. He referred to the State Church, and said he was "the uncompromising and conscientious upholder of that great constitution"; and he avowed himself in favour of "a Conservative foreign policy."

Mr. Gladstone, defeated at Oxford, sought the suffrages of South Lancashire. "At last, my friends," he said at a great meeting at the Free Trade Hall at Manchester, "I am come among you; and I am come—to use an expression which has already become very famous, and is not likely to be forgotten —I am come among you 'unmuzzled.'"[2] It is a not inapt description of the Platform, and it is that freedom from restraint which has made the Platform so attractive to so many statesmen. In Parliament members of all ranks and parties are more or less "muzzled," tied down, quite necessarily, by the forms of debate, limited to the particular subject under discussion, and restrained by the traditions and proprieties of the House. On the Platform they are "unmuzzled," and can range unchecked over the whole field of political life and requirements, from imperial questions of the gravest magnitude, down to matters of purely local interest or concern.

[1] Bright's *Speeches*, vol. ii. p. 112. [2] See *Daily News*, 19th July.

This phrase of Mr. Gladstone's is of interest for another reason—namely, as being in great measure prophetic of his future career as a great—possibly with one exception the greatest—Platform orator of our, or indeed of any age.

Ever since the first Reform Act the impetus which the electoral Platform at a general election could give to a subject was enormous, if it was one which commended itself to the judgment of the electorate. Hundreds of platforms, attended by thousands of people, resounding day after day with statement and counter-statement on a particular topic must of necessity bring home to men's minds its true aspect, and leave impressions which are not apt quickly to fade. And so it was at this election with the question of Parliamentary reform, and the elections resulted in considerable gains for the Liberal party.

Shortly after the elections were over Lord Palmerston, the Prime Minister, died. Earl Russell succeeded him, and Mr. Gladstone became leader of the House of Commons.

The new Parliament met on the 6th February,[1] and on the 12th March Mr. Gladstone brought forward in the House of Commons the Reform Bill of the Government. Its main proposals were that the right of voting in boroughs should be conferred on persons occupying houses of the annual rental of £7; and in counties the right of voting was to be reduced from a tenancy of £50 annual value to a tenancy of £14 annual value. By these and some other proposals, which need not be here referred to in detail, it was estimated that some 400,000 voters would be added to the electoral body.

At first the Bill was received with comparative indifference in the country. The Platform was silent. "There is no applause," wrote *The Times* on the 20th March, "not even an echo. We have listened in vain for the faintest note of approval, or the contrary, or bare recognition from the provinces."

On the same day, however, the first stir was made. The National Reform Union held a meeting "in a drawing-room" at Manchester, and passed a resolution "That the executive of the Union be requested to recommend to all branch associations to hold town's and other public meetings in favour of the Bill, and to prepare petitions in favour of the same."

[1] 1866.

On the 26th March a town's meeting was held at Birmingham to consider the Bill, and it was resolved "That the members for the borough be requested to support the Bill."

On the 27th March a conference of reformers from various districts of Manchester was held, and from that time on a considerable number of meetings were held, and the Platform expressed a general approval of the measure.

At Edinburgh, after resolutions had been adopted approving of the Bill, one was adopted directing "That a copy of the resolutions be transmitted to the members for the city, with a request that they will give the Bill their earnest support."

At Leeds an open-air meeting of the West Riding of Yorkshire was convened by the Lord Lieutenant of the Riding, and Lord Houghton and Mr. Forster spoke at it.

At Rochdale a great meeting of some 10,000 to 11,000 people was held. Bright spoke at it. "We are for peace and for justice," he said, "and for the safe and gradual advance of freedom. We believe that the time has come when the middle classes, who are mainly liberal, shall unite and can unite with the great body of the working class, who are aspiring for something higher and better than they have hitherto had; and we say that, united together, we can gain from our Government and Parliament whatever is necessary for us."

The most important of the public meetings took place at Liverpool, where Mr. Gladstone and the Duke of Argyle were present. It was held in the Amphitheatre,[1] and a resolution was passed "That this meeting agrees that the Bill proposed by her Majesty's Government, and now before the House of Commons, deserves general and hearty support as an honest and practicable proposal towards an amendment of the laws relating to the representation of the people."

Mr. Gladstone took the occasion to make from the Platform an announcement which he had not made in the House of Commons. He said: "We stake ourselves, we stake our existence as a Government . . . and we stake our political characters, upon the adoption of the Bill in its main provisions. You have a right to expect from us that we shall tell you what we mean. You have a right to ask that the trumpet, which it is our part to blow, shall give no uncertain sound.

[1] On the 6th April 1866.

We have passed the Rubicon; we have broken the bridge; and we have burnt the boats behind us. We have advisedly cut off from ourselves the means of retreat."

The second reading of the Bill was moved on the 12th April, and Mr. Gladstone, in winding up the debate, disclosed how important an element the proceedings of the Platform had come to be regarded. "I counted the meetings," he said. An Opposition member here interrupted with the words "Got up!" "The meetings are 'got up,' are they?" replied Mr. Gladstone; "then you have your remedy. Do you get up meetings against the measure. It will then be seen whether it is or is not an easy matter to get an expression of public sentiment on which to found your operations.[1] I counted the petitions presented from public meetings, and signed by the chairmen of these meetings individually, and I found that between the 11th and 17th of April there were 187 such petitions, besides 500,000 to 600,000 signatures from individuals in favour of this Bill."

The second reading was only carried by five votes.[2] The Government, nevertheless, proceeded to produce to the House of Commons[3] the second half of their scheme of reform in a Bill for the redistribution of seats. It too was read a second time, but neither it nor the Representation of the People Bill were destined to be read a third time, for on the 18th June an amendment to the latter, moved by Lord Dunkellin, that the principle of rating should be adopted as the basis of the borough franchise rather than rental, was carried in opposition to the Government,[4] and the Government resigned. Lord Derby became Prime Minister, and Mr. Disraeli Chancellor of the Exchequer.

The acceptance of office by the new Cabinet necessitated a large number of elections. It is worth carrying one's mind back for a moment to some of the elections in previous times to contrast the difference between the conduct of Ministers in relation to the electoral Platform then and at this period; it is necessary to do so to enable us to realise the huge strides that the Platform has made.

1 *Parliamentary Debates*, vol. clxxxiii. p. 144.

2 318 voting for it, and 313 against it.

3 On the 7th May.

4 By 315 votes against 304.

Take the election of 1818 which I have described, when all the principal Ministers except one sheltered themselves in the intrenched position of nomination boroughs, and the style of oratory deemed sufficient for the constituencies of the time was illustrated by Lord Castlereagh's "recollecting in a particular manner that the wheat on a farm which was occupied by his father was then covered with snow," and declaring that nothing could exceed the beautiful verdure of Ireland. Go back still farther to the celebrated election of 1784—Pitt's great triumph, when eight Cabinet Ministers out of the nine were peers, and Pitt, the sole commoner, contested the University of Cambridge, where speaking was not permitted. How different was it here in 1866!

The Secretary for War made a long speech from the Platform in Huntingdonshire; the First Lord of the Admiralty one at Droitwich; the Chief Secretary for Ireland spoke at Cockermouth—several columns of *The Times*[1] were taken up with reports of their speeches;—the Secretary for India spoke at Stamford; the President of the Board of Trade in Devonshire; the Secretary of State for Foreign Affairs made a long and exhaustive speech to his constituents at King's Lynn. All their speeches were reported, at length, in nearly every newspaper, and read by the great mass of the population.

"The new Foreign Secretary," wrote *The Times*, "has not been an hour in office before he is invited to assist in reforming the map of Europe. (It was just after Prussia's triumph over Austria.) This, however, he must put off, though hours now count for armies and sovereignties, till he has delivered and justified himself to the tradesmen of a small port somewhere between sea and land down on our eastern coast."[2]

Disraeli, the new Chancellor of the Exchequer, and in everything, except name, the leader of the party, spoke at Aylesbury, on his re-election for Bucks. "It must be a very exacting opponent," wrote *The Times*, "who will complain of his reticence. Though he does not descend to details, he lays down principles on a variety of subjects, and indicates how the affairs of the country ought, in his opinion, to be conducted as regards both foreign and domestic policy."[3] He

[1] See *The Times*, 12th July 1866. [2] *Ibid.* 13th July 1866.
[3] *Ibid.* 14th July 1866.

said: "We are sometimes taunted with not having a policy. . . . But our policy, to our own minds, is definite and distinct. It is to uphold our constitution in Church and State. It is to bring in all those measures, and pursue in every respect that policy which will secure for this country a continuance of prosperity and peace."

We have the authority of *The Times*[1] for saying that "something of the principles of the party" was learned from these speeches; but the really remarkable fact about them was, that they bore startling testimony to the vast change that had passed over political life since the Reform Act of 1832 had been passed; they were the most convincing tribute which could be paid to the position and power of the Platform. That every Minister who had to undergo re-election had felt himself compelled to appear on the Platform before his constituents, and to take them, and, through them, the country, into his confidence, was such a recognition of the Platform as had in earlier times never even been dreamed of.

The fall of the Ministry apparently imperilled the prospect of reform, and the Platform at once gave evidence of animation. Meetings were promptly held in London and throughout the country. It is only possible to mention some of them, and to give a few extracts from the more important of the speeches, adding such comments as were made on them as will show the views held on the Platform generally by the leading statesmen of the day.

The first meeting was of an unfortunate character. It took place on the 2d July[2] in Trafalgar Square; some rioting ensued, and disorderly crowds proceeded through some of the wealthier and more fashionable streets of the west. The riot can scarcely be considered as having much connection with the Platform, yet, for the sake of damaging the Platform, every riotous meeting is put down by its opponents as due to the objectionable practice of holding public meetings. The proceedings on this occasion were totally unorganised; the persons assembled were bent on other amusements than listening to speeches; there was no order in the proceedings; the few men who endeavoured to speak were unable to make themselves heard. It was nothing more, in fact, than an assembly

[1] *The Times*, 16th July 1866. [2] 1866.

of people: the electors of London were not there; the men to be enfranchised by the Reform Bill were not there; the working men of London were not there; some leaders of the Reform League, and a fortuitous concourse of the waifs and strays and roughs of a great city composed the assembly. The meeting evoked a severe censure from *The Times*.[1]

"A public meeting in such a place, at such a time, constitutes in itself a breach of the peace. It is an annoyance to peaceful people and a disturbance of the public convenience. Moreover, by their professed character, such meetings are acts of intimidation. They are not meetings for the exercise of legitimate powers of persuasion, and for publicly urging in reasonable statements the views of the working class; they are menaces, intended, if possible, to raise alarm in the Legislature by a display of numbers and passions. . . . Such 'demonstrations' are an abuse, and a mischievous abuse, of a valuable privilege, and if they do not cease of themselves they must be put a stop to. The right of public meeting does not mean the right of public annoyance and private insult."

A short time after—namely, on the 23d July—the subject of public meetings in the metropolis came up in a far graver and more acute form.

A great demonstration was announced by the Committee of the Reform League to be held in Hyde Park in favour of the extension of the franchise. The authorities, disapproving of such use of a space devoted to the public recreation, and apprehending a disturbance of the peace in case such a gathering were permitted, determined to close the gates of the Park, and to prevent the multitude attending the meeting. Great crowds collected outside the Park. When the leaders of the demonstration, at the head of a large procession, came up, they attempted to enter the Park, but were refused by the Police. They did not press their request but endeavoured to persuade their followers to proceed to Trafalgar Square. The mob, however, tore down the railings of the Park in several places, and so rushed in; there was some fighting between the Police and the rougher elements of the crowd, the aid of the military was invoked, a considerable number of arrests were made, and several persons were injured but no life was lost.

[1] *The Times*, 3d July 1866.

By the time it was dark most of the people had left the Park.

The occurrence naturally led to a debate in Parliament on the following day. The Home Secretary, on the part of the Government, while declaring that they had no desire that any public meeting should be prevented when held in the proper place, and at the proper time, for the most free discussion of any subject whatever, thought that the Parks were not the places in which such meetings ought to be held. . . . He acknowledged that "the disturbance did not begin with the leaders of the meeting. It had its origin with persons who came to the Park with very different purposes from that of free and open discussion." [1]

On the other side Mr. J. Stuart Mill maintained that if the people had not the right of meeting in the Park they should have it, "for, if not, what other place was there that could suit them?" [2]

In the House of Lords Lord Derby, the Prime Minister, expressed his firm belief "That those who desired to make a great demonstration had no intention of causing any breach of the public peace. But, he said, on the other hand, I think it is idle to contend that what they desired was to afford a fair opportunity for public discussion. It was impossible to believe that any such fair discussion could take place under such circumstances; and I cannot but think that the object was, not by a breach of the peace, but by a demonstration of physical force, to overawe the Legislature, and give a false impression of public feeling upon the subject of Parliamentary reform." [3]

Lord Granville said: "I am as strongly as possible in favour of the right of public meeting. . . . At the same time I believe that for the purposes of real discussion these monster meetings are valueless . . . in these very large meetings numbers make discussion almost impossible."

The Trafalgar Square meetings and the Hyde Park riots both did considerable damage at the time to the reputation of the Platform.

[1] Mr. Walpole's speech, *Parliamentary Debates*, vol. clxxxiv. p. 1395.
[2] *Ibid.* p. 1414.
[3] *Parliamentary Debates*, vol. clxxxiv. pp. 1370, 1371, 24th July 1866.

"The Reforming host," wrote *The Times* on the 24th July, "have shown conspicuously how useless such gatherings as these are for political discussion, and how easily they might produce serious danger to the public peace;" and the following day, reverting to the subject, it wrote: "The most conclusive proof has been given that such gatherings, which can serve no useful purpose whatever, cannot be sufficiently reprobated."

Outdoor meetings having been somewhat discredited in London by the Trafalgar Square and Hyde Park meetings, the next great meeting was held indoors, at the Agricultural Hall, Islington, on the 30th July 1866. Some 20,000 people were said to have been at it; there was a great deal of noise and interruptions, and the speakers could scarcely make themselves heard. The most notable speech was made by J. S. Mill, then Member for Westminster, in the course of which he said: "His object was not to talk to them about reform; no words of his were needed to stimulate their zeal on that point; their presence that evening was a sufficient answer to those who supposed that such appeals were necessary. Reformers had been much attacked for holding these large meetings, because it was said that they were inconsistent with discussion. But discussion was not the only use of public meetings, one of their objects was demonstration."

On the 8th August 1866 a meeting, convened by the Reform League and the London Working-men's Association, was held in the Guildhall, London. Here again the subject of popular meetings was spoken about. The Lord Mayor presided, and in an introductory speech he said: "Public meetings such as that he had the honour to address were convened for the purpose of giving expression freely, temperately, and independently to certain views, and interchange of opinions; but there were three things essential to the satisfactory attainment of that object—the first was good temper, the second good judgment, and the third moderation."

Mr. Beales, who was one of the principal speakers, said: "What had led to such demonstrations (as those just passed)? Invective after invective had been poured forth against the working classes. They had been characterised as so venal, so ignorant, and so vicious as to be unfit to be admitted to the exercise of the franchise. The working men had assembled in their halls in the first instance to protest against such a falsehood, but their meetings thus held were either ridiculed or ignored, and they then deemed it their duty to meet in larger numbers out of doors. Acting upon that view, they selected Hyde Park as a place where those assemblages might have the effect of at last bringing conviction home to the minds of their opponents. In doing so they had no wish to have recourse to brute force"—a sentiment which was endorsed by a Mr. Conolly, who said: "The working men of the present day, under the direction of O'Connell, Cobden, and Bright, had learnt to see that the greatest political changes could be effected without resorting to violence, and without shedding one drop of blood."

Parliament was prorogued on the 10th August 1866, and the Platform was left in undisturbed possession of the great question of reform for the autumn and winter.

The first really great meeting of the recess was held at Birmingham on the 27th August. "If the presence of an immense host," wrote *The Times*, "is to be taken as an earnest of enthusiasm and of devotion to a cause, the gathering was a decided success. The 'demonstration' also partook of as much of the character of spontaneity as anything in its way can do. The people themselves organised it and carried it out; it was essentially a working men's movement." The procession consisted of six divisions; the people behaved admirably; they preserved regularity and decorum themselves. The distance traversed to Brookfield was about $2\frac{1}{4}$ miles. Throughout that entire space, and every avenue leading to it, was one dense mass of people; every window, and parapet, and balcony was crowded; there were scores of banners, numerous bands of music playing, and every accessory to produce a scene which it would not be easy to describe.

There were six platforms, the speaking did not last very long, and three resolutions were passed—the principal one: "We hereby pledge ourselves to demand, agitate for, and use all lawful means to obtain registered residential manhood suffrage as the only just basis of representation, and the ballot to protect us from undue influence and intimidation in elections." The enormous crowd quietly dispersed.

In the evening there was a large meeting in the Town Hall. Here Bright was the principal speaker. "There are times," he said, "when I feel no little despondency at the small result of many years of public labour; but to look upon a meeting like that assembled here, and to look upon that vast gathering which your town has exhibited to the country and to the world to-day, is enough to dispel every feeling of fear or of despondency, and to fill the heart, and nerve the arm to new and greater labours for the future. During the last session of Parliament, in the debate on the second reading of the Franchise Bill, I took the opportunity of offering a word of counsel and of warning to the powerful party in the House which opposed that Bill. I asked them to remember that if they should succeed in defeating that Bill and overthrowing the Government, there would still remain the people of England to be met, and the claims of the great question of reform to be considered and settled. We have not had to wait long before that which I foretold has come to pass.

"In London we have seen assemblies of the people such as for a generation past have not been witnessed. In many other parts of the country there have been meetings greater than have been seen for thirty years, and notably to-day there has been a voice given forth from the very centre and heart of England which will reach at least to the circumference of the three kingdoms.

"At this moment I am told that outside there is an audience far greater than that I now address, whilst to-morrow morning there will be millions of an audience throughout the whole of the United Kingdom, anxious to know what has been done and what has been said on this 27th day of August in this great town of Birmingham. . . .

"In this England 5,000,000 of grown men, representing more than 20,000,000 of our population, are to be permanently denied that which makes the only difference between despotism and freedom all the world over. I venture to say that this cannot last very long. . . . Let us do as our fathers did thirty-four years ago—let us have associations everywhere. . . . Let us rouse the spirit of the people against the slanderers of a great and noble nation. There will soon come another election. The working men may not be able to vote, but they can form themselves into a powerful body, and they can throw their influence in every borough on the side of the candidates who pledge themselves to the question of reform. If they do this, you may depend upon it they will change many seats, and give a certain majority for reform in the next Parliament."[1]

Mr. Gladstone, not yet the ardent devotee of the Platform which he has since become, descended only once into the arena during the struggle, and spoke at a meeting at Salisbury on the 7th September. He promised that a fair consideration should be given to any well-digested scheme of reform brought forward by their successors in office, provided it was introduced promptly, and showed a spirit of moderation and justice.

The real tide of Platform power, however, swept along in other places than this quiet south of England city, and under other leadership than Mr. Gladstone's.

On the 24th of September 1866 a great meeting was held at Campfield, Manchester—some 80,000 to 100,000 persons of the working and middle classes were present; there were processions, and bands, and banners, and there were six Platforms, and resolutions were passed, the principal being the same as that adopted at Birmingham.

In the evening a meeting was held in the Free Trade Hall, which was crowded. Mr. Potter, M.P., who presided, said: "This meeting and the demonstration of the morning showed that the men of Lancashire were prepared to take their part in the coming struggle for reform."

Bright also spoke. "Great as is this meeting, and transcendently great the meeting which was held in the middle of the day, the question which has brought us together is worthy of our assembly, and of every effort we may make. We are met for the purpose, as far as lies in our power, of widening the boundaries and making more stable the foundations of the freedom of the country in which we live."

The next evening he spoke again at a banquet. "I am not in favour of manhood suffrage as against household suffrage. . . . These great meetings, as Mr. Mill very justly said, were not meetings so much for discussion, as they were meetings for demonstration of opinion, and, if you like, I will add for exhibition of force. Such exhibitions, if they are despised and

[1] Bright's *Speeches*, vol. ii. p. 185.

disregarded, may become exhibitions of another kind of force. . . .

"I think that the question was settled in 1832 whether the changes which may be necessary in the Government of the United Kingdom can be accomplished by peaceable means, or whether force will be necessary for their completion." [1]

And here, as it appeared just at this very time, I must quote some extracts from a most interesting article in *The Times* containing an elaborate examination of the position and province of the Platform. It is, with one exception, the only effort I have come across by any writer to assign a position to the Platform as a political institution, and to compare it with other institutions affecting public opinion. *The Times* said: "The Platform has its proper and natural vocation, very different from that of the statesman, or the Legislature, or the Press, or the pulpit, or the man who writes pamphlets and books. . . . A public meeting consists of men who, whether speakers or listeners, feel a general agreement, and expect to hear only one side, and that maintained on fully recognised principles. It would be impossible to hold a public meeting except on these conditions, for no debate would be possible in three short hours in the presence of a multitude. The speakers must suppress even minor differences and express only the points which they hold in common. The immediate object is to bring to a common opinion men who can hold opinions and do nothing more, unless it be to give a vote which they have often given before, and which will not signify much. . . .

"The public meeting really has more affinity with the pulpit or the writer of books and pamphlets than with Parliament, or the daily press, or any institution affecting a deliberative and a governing character.

"The battles of the Constitution are in Parliament, and compared with them, all the public meetings in the country, though good in their way, and with their use, are but holiday-making, mere parades, scenes on a prepared stage. Our own relations must be much more with the Legislature than with any such system of one-sided demonstrations. We appreciate them, and hope ever to do full justice to them. . . . We reverence them as a national institution. But we can never

[1] *The Times* Report.

see more than they claim, and what they claim is only the one-sided utterance and recognition of sentiments and facts occupying either very debatable ground, or cumbering the mere approach to the grand argument before us. We should doubt whether it be at all possible for the platform ever to gain a more deliberative and Parliamentary character, nor is it necessary. We have a free Parliament and a free press, and can well allow the platform to retain its old one-sided character. In the lines it has chosen for itself, it has still much to do; it may contribute materials and foster opinion, and even hasten the settlement of reform."[1]

This estimate of the Platform is by no means an appreciative one, nor is it quite accurate in its conclusions, for the Anti-Corn-Law agitation had shown conclusively that discussion could take place at public meetings. But accepting the estimate as a fairly correct description of the status of the Platform when the article was written, the description only serves to heighten the effect of the progress which the Platform has made since then. "The battles of the Constitution," may have been fought in Parliament then—they are fought on the Platform now,—one-sided argument may have distinguished the Platform then, but the Platform has since attained to a "more deliberative and Parliamentary character," inasmuch as Platform discussion is no longer one-sided, but is effectively waged now by the two great parties in the State; whilst over and above this progress in power the Platform has become the means of and instrument for imposing the will of the constituencies on their representatives.

All through the autumn the agitation for reform went on. On the 8th October 1866 a great meeting of the working classes took place at Leeds; there was a huge procession 4 miles long, and not less than 70,000 persons; there were five Platforms. "It is no exaggeration to say that the whole concourse numbered little less than 200,000 persons," women and children included. At each Platform there was a chairman and speakers. "A flourish of trumpets was the signal for silence, and then, after a few words of admonition with a view to good order and respectful attention, simultaneously at all the five Platforms, the first resolution was moved as follows: 'That this meeting

1 *The Times*, 25th September 1866.

enters its solemn protest against, and its denial of, the charges of venality, ignorance, drunkenness, and indifference to reform, brought against the working classes during the last session of Parliament; and hereby pledges itself to advocate for the future registered residential manhood suffrage and the ballot as the only just and proper basis of representation.'

"In answer to a trumpet call, a show of hands took place in its favour, which was one of the most decided attestations of unanimity the most ardent and uncompromising manhood suffrage devotee could possibly have desired."

After some other resolutions the enormous meeting quietly dispersed. "Everything passed off in an orderly manner, notwithstanding that the enthusiasm was at a high pitch."

In the evening a great meeting was held in the Town Hall —Bright spoke, and declared, in the course of his speech, that "the few meetings which had been held since the close of last session of Parliament had had a prodigious effect."[1]

On the 16th October a great meeting was held on Glasgow Green; a great procession preceded it; about 150,000 were present; there were six Platforms, flags and banners by thousands; the principal resolution passed was for "manhood residential suffrage"; and in the evening a great meeting in the City Hall, and Bright spoke: "Gatherings of scores of thousands of men, extending from south to north, must have some great cause. Men do not leave their daily labour—the necessary occupations of their lives—thus to meet, unless they believe that there is some great question submitted to them in which they have a deep and overpowering interest. And the question is this—Whether in future the Government and the legislation of this country shall be conducted by a privileged class in a sham Parliament, or on the principles of the Constitution of the nation, through its representatives, fairly and freely chosen?

"What we charge against the Parliament is this: That it is chosen from constituencies not only so small that they do not and cannot adequately represent the nation, but from constituencies so small as to be influenced by corruption, and by all kinds of motives that are neither national nor patriotic. . . .

[1] *The Times*, 9th October 1866.

Out of every hundred grown men in the United Kingdom eighty-four have no votes."

It is unnecessary to enumerate all of even the principal meetings during this autumn and winter. There was no slackening of energy as the winter went on; the Platform was kept fully occupied. On the 3d of December there was a great demonstration in London of the Trades Societies in favour of Parliamentary reform, and "the working men of the metropolis, like the working men of other parts of the country, expressed their opinion upon the reform question." They did so in the best temper and in the most orderly spirit.

The Times, in a leader, stated that "a more orderly set of people never came together," and summed up the effect of the meeting by remarking that, "What was done yesterday was amply sufficient to show that a large number of the artisan class desire the franchise, and that there is no reason to believe they will abuse it." [1]

There was a very large procession of all the trades, with bands and banners (about 30,000 persons). They assembled in the Mall, St. James's Park, and proceeded to Beaufort Grounds, in Brompton. There were several Platforms, and some short speeches were delivered, and then the meeting dispersed. There was no disturbance of any kind.

Beales, who spoke, said: "It was a demonstration worthy and honourable to the men of London, as a continuance of the great national protest against the libellous charges brought against the working classes of indifference to reform and unfitness for the franchise, and a continuance of the national movement in favour of manhood suffrage, protected by the ballot, as the only franchise commensurate with the rights of the people. That national movement commenced in July last in Trafalgar Square and at Hyde Park, and had been increasing in volume, in intensity, and in enthusiastic unanimity throughout the length and breadth of England, Scotland, and Ireland."

In the evening of the following day (4th December 1866) a great meeting was held in St. James's Hall, London; Bright was among the speakers. Nearing the end of the recess, and within view almost of the end of the agitation on this partic-

[1] See *The Times*, 4th December 1866.

ular question, his speech assumed somewhat of a retrospective character, and enables us to see what he thought had been accomplished by the Platform. He said: "It is about eight years since that I took the opportunity of giving (in a speech) what I thought was somewhat wholesome counsel to the unenfranchised working men of this country. I told them that the monopolists of political power in this country would not willingly surrender that power or any portion of it. . . . I said that if the working men wished for political power, they had only to ask for it in a manner to show the universality of their desire, and the union and the power which they were able to bring to bear upon it; and I recollect particularly making a suggestion that involved me in a good deal of unfriendly criticism—namely, that I had thought the time had come, or would soon come, when it would be the duty of the working class to make use of that great organisation of theirs, which extends over the whole country,—the organisation of trades' and friendly societies for the purpose of bringing to bear upon the Government the entire power of their just demand. I said, further, that I believed one year only of the united action of the working class through this existing organisation would wholly change the aspect of the question of reform. Now it appears that the wholesome counsel which I gave eight years ago has become the counsel of all those who are in favour of the enfranchisement of the working man, and that counsel has been adopted recently to a large extent, and every man in the kingdom feels that the aspect of the question has been wholly changed." And a little further on he referred to "the noble exhibition, the orderly and grand exhibition of opinion which has been made by the working men of England and Scotland during the past three months."[1]

An autumn and winter of agitation such as this had been, with its almost numberless meetings and speeches, would, less than half a century earlier, in the time of Lords Liverpool, Sidmouth, and Castlereagh, have inevitably resulted in Royal Messages with sealed green bags, in Secret Committees of both Houses of Parliament, in Suspensions of Habeas Corpus Act, in Seditious Meetings Acts, with a death penalty for infraction of its provisions, in prosecutions for high treason.

[1] 4th December 1866.

But times had changed. The Platform had become too powerful to be suppressed, the right of free public discussion had been irrevocably established, and the nation was showing itself ever more and more disposed to discuss and settle outside Parliament great national issues, leaving only the carrying out of its decisions and behests to Parliament.

Meetings and demonstrations continued up to the very meeting of Parliament on the 5th February 1867, and that they had had their effect even on the Tory Government was shown by the prominence which was given in the Queen's Speech to the subject of reform, and the early date on which Ministers declared their intentions. But that they had not had a great effect was evident when the Government disclosed their first scheme of reform. It is unnecessary to refer in detail to the abortive scheme of proceeding by resolutions. In the Bill subsequently introduced it was proposed that, as regards the boroughs, every householder who had occupied a house for two years, and been rated to the relief of the poor, and paid his rates personally, should enjoy the franchise. As regards the counties the franchise was to be reduced from a £50 occupancy to a £15 occupancy; certain new franchises were also proposed. As regarded redistribution, thirty seats were to be taken from certain constituencies and given to others.

When the Easter recess came, and Parliament was silent for a brief period, discussion was at once transferred to the Platform, and some large and important public meetings were held with reference to the proposed measure of reform. "The object insisted on at most of these meetings was that of removing or diminishing some of the restrictions by which the Bill proposed to limit the borough franchise, especially the requirements of personal rating, and of two years' residence, and also to promote the insertion of clauses enabling lodgers to exercise the franchise."[1]

The largest of these gatherings was held at Birmingham on the 22d April, some 50,000 persons being present, and resolutions were passed in favour of registered residential manhood suffrage. In the evening a great meeting was held in the Town Hall, at which Bright spoke, and a resolution was passed "That this meeting regards the limitations of the

[1] *Annual Register*, 1867, p. 64.

borough franchise in the Government Bill as wholly inconsistent with an honest and sufficient extension of the franchise, and declares its opinion that the measure, now before Parliament, inasmuch as it requires the personal payment of rates by every occupier, and a residence of two years, and does not include any clause for the enfranchisement of lodgers, is a virtual denial of the claims of the working classes to their rightful or any real share of political power."

On the 23d April—Easter Tuesday—a great reform demonstration was held at Leeds. There were five Platforms, at each of which there was a chairman and a set of speakers. The speeches were chiefly condemnatory of the Reform Bill because of its restricted character; and resolutions were passed in favour of "registered residential manhood suffrage, protected by the ballot, together with such a redistribution of seats as will place the representation in accordance with the wealth, population, and intelligence of the nation."

In addition to these meetings, conferences were held at Birmingham and at Newcastle. Whether it was the effect of these meetings or not, the fact is that, as will be presently seen, the Bill underwent several important modifications.

About the end of April 1867 the Reform League announced its intention of holding a public meeting in the forbidden territory of Hyde Park in favour of reform.

With the events of 1866 still fresh in memory, the Government issued the following notice or proclamation:—"Whereas it has been publicly announced that a meeting will be held in Hyde Park on Monday, the 6th May, for the purpose of political discussion, and whereas the use of the Park for the purpose of holding such meeting is not permitted, and interferes with the object for which her Majesty has been pleased to open the Park for the general enjoyment of her people; now all persons are hereby warned and admonished to abstain from attending, aiding, or taking part in any such meeting, or from entering the Park with a view to attend, aid, or take part in such meeting."

In spite of this proclamation the Reform League resolved to hold the meeting. At the eleventh hour the Government decided that the meeting was not to be opposed, but great preparations were made for the preservation of order. On the appointed day the great meeting came off, "and passed off with the quietness and good order of a temperance meeting," —some 40,000 to 50,000 persons were present. Ten Platforms, or rather sites, were chosen from which to speak, and crowds collected round them.

"Generally, the addresses may be characterised as being rather 'strong,' and what is termed 'full-flavoured,' in their expressions of delight at the victory of the Reform League over the Government on the Park question. All, however, inculcated more or less strongly the necessity of maintaining the most perfect order throughout the whole of their proceedings, even until every man had reached his own home." [1]

Beales, the President of the Reform League, said he might congratulate them and himself upon the fact that their work was finished as regarded the Parks and the right of the people to hold political meetings. . . . The meeting before him was constituted in accordance with all the appeals which he had made, and was a complete and honourable refutation to the slanderous imputations so shamefully promulgated, and the unwholesome fears so recklessly expressed that it could not be held without riot, disorder, and injury to person and property. Such attacks were unworthy of the country, and disgraceful to its national character.

A resolution was passed, urging the House of Commons to make the Reform Bill a more full and honest measure for the extension of the franchise, and equalising the borough and county franchise on the principle of household suffrage.

And here an interesting interlude in the general movement of the Platform must be referred to. Mr. Gladstone, in consequence of certain adverse divisions on amendments proposed by himself, wrote a letter, on the 18th April, which was taken as meaning that he was determined to relinquish all further efforts to amend the Bill. Forthwith a series of public meetings were held, at which resolutions were passed expressing confidence in him, and encouraging him in his opposition. Between the 22d April and 7th May over fifty such public meetings were held. [2] On the 11th May certain deputations, consisting of seventeen members of Parliament, a large num-

[1] *The Times*, 7th May 1867.

[2] *A History of the Reform Bills of* 1866 *and* 1867, by Homersham Cox, M.A.

ber of wealthy manufacturers, and some clergymen, waited on Mr. Gladstone to present him with a large number of addresses and copies of resolutions which had been passed at them.

In reply to the speeches made by the deputations, Mr. Gladstone made a long speech himself, in the course of which he said that he considered it "his duty to use every effort, and to avail himself of every remaining opportunity to strike at the odious principle of inequality and injustice involved in the Bill, and if we fail, as we probably shall fail . . . to decline to recognise or be parties in any measure to it as a settlement of the question, and to continue to maintain by every constitutional means in our power the principles on which we have acted."

This proceeding evoked, a couple of days later, a severe reproof from Disraeli. "I regret much that the old stages and antique machinery of agitation should have been readjusted and reburnished, and sent up by Parliamentary train to London, and that we should have been threatened with an agitation of a most indefinite and incoherent character, for at this moment I am at a loss to know whether the proposed agitation is to be in favour of manhood suffrage or of a £5 rating. I regret very much that these spouters of stale sedition should have come forward to take the course they have. It may be their function to appear at noisy meetings, but I regret very much that they should have come forward as obsolete incendiaries to pay their homage to one who, wherever he may sit, must always remain the pride and ornament of this House."

As the Bill progressed through Committee, one change after another enlarging its scope was made in the Government scheme. The first important alteration was the substitution of "twelve months" for "two years" as the term of residence required with respect to the new voters in boroughs. Then a fundamental alteration was made—the proposal as regarded personal payment of rates fell to the ground, and the Government accepted the great principle of household suffrage pure and simple. Then the proposed county franchise of £15 was reduced to £12. Then the number of boroughs which were to surrender one member was increased.

Ultimately, on the 15th August, the Bill received the Royal Assent. Its general effect may be briefly stated. In counties it reduced the qualification for voting to £12 occupation franchise. In boroughs it reduced the franchise from a £10 occupancy to the occupancy of a house; in other words, all occupiers of houses or tenements in towns who had resided in them for twelve months, were given the right of voting, provided they were not disqualified by certain specific disqualifications. By these alterations the number of electors in counties was increased by about 300,000, and in boroughs by 850,000 or a total increase of 1,150,000 in Great Britain.[1] As regards the distribution of seats, the Act semi-disfranchised 38 constituencies, and as there were 7 other seats available, having been disfranchised for other causes, there were 45 seats made available for distribution. Of these 25 were allotted to counties, 13 to towns hitherto unrepresented and having a large population, 1 to the University of London, and the remaining 6 were given as additional members to certain of the largest towns.

How vast a change had passed over the country since the first Reform Act was passed, is shown by the calm manner in which this Act was received by all classes. In 1832 a very widespread anxiety existed that the existing order of things would be quickly subverted. In 1867 no fear of sudden change existed, and the general feeling was that certain reforms, none very wide-reaching, would be more quickly attained.

It remains to state how far the Platform can claim to have constrained Parliament to pass this measure, and also what were the effects of the measure on the Platform.

With the ever-growing complexity of political forces and influences it becomes more and more difficult to discover how much of the cause of great measures of reform is attributable to the Platform.

Disraeli, when accepting the amendment which imported into the Reform Bill its principal feature—that of household suffrage,—declared that the Platform, or, as he called it, the meetings, had no effect on the Government. He said: "Whatever may be the influences that regulate the conduct of others, I can assure the House that her Majesty's Government, in the course they are taking, are not influenced by the terrors

[1] The total number of electors in Great Britain in 1868 was 2,220,000.

which have been depicted, and the agitation with which we have been threatened." He could not, however, have admitted their influence.

Mr. Gladstone expressed an opposite opinion. He said: "It appears to me to be entirely beyond dispute that assemblages of the people for discussion and manifestation of their opinion regarding the question of reform have had an important, I will venture to say, a vital influence and effect in bringing that question to its present position."[1]

A review of the history of the different abortive attempts to extend the Reform Act of 1832 proves, I think, quite conclusively that the Platform had a decisive effect in bringing about the Act of 1867. The Platform stirred in the autumn of 1858, and in the very next session of Parliament the Tory Government made an attempt to deal with the question. The Platform awoke to action in the autumn of 1865, and first the Liberal Government, and then the Tory Government, seriously took up the question, and, under the watchful attention of the Platform, had to settle it. Other influences doubtless cooperated in this direction, but the real impelling, decisive influence was that which came from the great gatherings of the people in all parts of the country, speaking by and from the Platform.

The effect of this measure on the Platform can be briefly summarised.

Unlike its great forerunner of 1832 it neither originated nor brought into action any new phase of the Platform. It only accentuated and developed those which were already in existence. It gave a larger audience to the Platform; it extended somewhat the sphere of its action; and it rendered more frequent the practice of personal communication between the leading statesmen and the people, and between representatives and their constituents. In this latter respect, therefore, it drew closer the bands between the electors and the representatives, and thus brought the latter in an increased degree under the direct control of their constituents.

It is desirable, before proceeding further, to revert to the Bill of 1866 relative to meetings in the Royal Parks, as it evoked the expression of opinions on the subject of public meetings

[1] Hansard, vol. clxxxviii. p. 1973.

from several of the leading statesmen in the House, which are both interesting and important.

On the 3d May 1866, before the meeting in Hyde Park came off, Mr. Bright drew attention to the subject in the House of Commons. He said: "It may be said, and with a certain show of reason, that a great meeting amidst a great population may be attended with, or may sometimes be attended with, danger to the public peace. . . . Where English people, English blood, and English-speaking people are found, whether in our colonies, in the United States, or in the United Kingdom, great meetings have never been found productive of breaches of the peace. I defy you to find anything in history to show that, as a rule, great public meetings have been attended with breaches of the peace in this country." He referred to Manchester, but there the fault of disturbance lay with the magistrates and the yeomanry.

Referring to the proposed meeting, he said: "I take the liberty of asserting that a meeting of this nature, whether in London or in any great town, in a crisis of this nature, if I may use the phrase, is an important and useful event."

He very pertinently asked what difference there was between the people in the large towns where meetings had been held, and the people in London, that the latter should not be allowed to meet in the Parks. "I maintain that the character of the English people is guarantee for a peaceful issue on a day like that."

Disraeli, somewhat later, expressed his opinion. "Having had a good opportunity of observing the turbulent among the people who form these meetings, I am bound to say that they are not of the working classes, and that they are very different from the sensible and well-meaning subjects of her Majesty whom they taint. But the tendency of those meetings is to give an occasion for all the scum of a great city to take advantage of the circumstance, and to conduct themselves in the manner which has unfortunately taken place. I repudiate, then, the views imputed to us, as to our being opposed to public meetings of the working classes on subjects in which they take an interest. On the contrary, I believe public meetings, properly held, at the proper time, and in the proper place, to be most desirable. I regard them, under such circumstances, as one of the great political safety-valves to which we should trust. So far from discouraging them I would allow of no impediment to public meetings of the working classes at the right time and place on political subjects, confident as I am that it is to the advantage of society that they should take place. But I am confident that, unless they are held at the proper time and place, they give the opportunity for riot, tumult, and disturbance, and what has occurred proves the soundness of my view."[1]

Mr. Gladstone also expressed his opinion. He said: "I must say that if there be those who question either the lawfulness or the usefulness, in given circumstances, of great assemblies of the people for political purposes, I am not among such persons. . . . I can conceive nothing more legitimate in general than the principle of such meetings."[2]

The Government were not, however, satisfied with the existing state of the law as regarded meetings in the Parks; and on the 3d of May the Home Secretary (Walpole) moved for leave to bring in a Bill for the more effectually and better securing the use of certain royal parks and gardens for the recreation and enjoyment of her Majesty's subjects. He said that the object of the measure was to enable the law to be better enforced, not to alter it excepting as to the remedy. The Bill provided that no meeting of a public character should take place or be held without the permission of her Majesty in any of the royal parks within the metropolis; and that any person convening, or assisting in convening, any public meeting in contravention of that Act, or any person joining or taking part in such a meeting, should be liable to be arrested, and summarily convicted on application before one of the police magistrates, and on his conviction should be liable either to a penalty not exceeding £10, or to be imprisoned for a term not exceeding two months.

This Bill led to several debates. On the motion for its second reading John Stuart Mill expressed at length his views on the subject of the Platform: "I see no reason why we should at present discuss all the purposes for which the Parks should or should not be allowed to be used. All I am anxious

[1] *Parliamentary Debates,* vol. clxxxiv. p. 1414.
[2] *Ibid.* vol. clxxxvi. p. 1973.

about is that political meetings should be allowed to be held there. And why do I desire this? Because it has been for centuries the pride of this country, and one of its most valued distinctions from the despotically-governed countries of the Continent, that a man has a right to speak his mind, on politics or on any other subject, to those who would listen to him, when and where he will. He has not a right to force himself upon any one; he has not a right to intrude upon private property; but wheresoever he has a right to be, there, according to the Constitution of this country, he has a right to talk politics to one, to fifty, or to 50,000 persons. I stand up for the right of doing this in the Parks. . . .

"There is no decent argument for the interdiction of political meetings in the Park which does not proceed on the assumption that political meetings are not a legitimate purpose to apply a public place to, and that it is, on the whole, a desirable thing to discourage them.

"Honourable gentlemen opposite say that these multitudinous meetings are not held for the purpose of discussion, but for intimidation. Sir, I believe public meetings, multitudinous or not, seldom are intended for discussion—that is not their function. They are a public manifestation of the strength of those who are of a certain opinion. It is easy to give this a bad name, but it is one of the recognised springs of our Constitution. Let us not be intimidated by the word 'intimidation.' Will any one say that the numbers and enthusiasm of those who join in asking anything from Parliament, are not one of the elements which a statesman ought to have before him, and which a wise statesman will take into consideration in deciding whether to grant or to refuse the request? We are told that threatening language is used at these meetings. In a time of excitement there are always persons who use threatening language. But we can bear a great deal of that sort of thing without being the worse for it in a country which has inherited from its ancestors the right of political demonstration. It cannot be borne quite so well by countries which do not possess this right. Then the discontent, which cannot exhale itself in public meetings, bursts forth in insurrections, which, whether successful or repressed, always leave behind them a long train of calamitous consequences."

The Bill was read a second time, but the Government, apparently not knowing its own mind on this important subject for two consecutive weeks, subsequently introduced an amended Bill, increasing the penalties and proposing to make participation in any meeting in any of the Parks for political, religious, or other public discussion, a misdemeanour; and again, a little later on, they came forward with fresh proposals; finally, on the 15th August, abandoning them all, and leaving the law in exactly the same state as it was.

In the course of the debates Disraeli once more expressed his opinion on public meetings: "I think," he said, "that any Government which sets its face against public meetings, especially on political subjects, would do an unwise act. They are the safety-valves of a free country, and I do not know that anybody benefits more by these public meetings than those responsible for the government of the country. . . . I do not agree that public meetings must necessarily and generally be held in the open air. I admit that meetings are not always called for discussion. Sometimes they are held to make demonstrations of the opinions prevalent among the people. . . . I still believe that the proper mode by which these expressions of opinion, which are to my mind highly salutary in a society like ours, would be within a building or covered place."

Here, then, with the withdrawal of the Parks Regulation Meetings Act, and the passing of the Reform Act of 1867, might be ended the account of the part which the Platform took in the Reform agitation of 1866–67. There are, however, two incidents which occurred soon after which must be briefly referred to, illustrating as they do the growing use made of the Platform by the leaders of the Conservative party, for the purpose of explaining their policy, or justifying their past actions, with the view of winning popular favour.

The Reform Act of 1867 was claimed by the Tories as a great party triumph, and in the course of the Parliamentary recess a grand banquet was given to the Prime Minister, Lord Derby, on the 17th October 1867 by the Conservative party at Manchester, some 900 persons or so being at it, and five Cabinet Ministers, in addition to the Prime Minister. It was a great party celebration, and he—Prime Minister and Tory chief—

made an elaborate political speech. He recognised that the gathering was "essentially a political meeting"; he gave a long review of the Reform Act, and of the numerous abortive Reform Bills which had preceded it, and then entered on an elaborate eulogy of the working classes. Referring to his imprudent phrase used in debate in the House of Lords that the Bill was a "leap in the dark," he said: "It was, it is, but I thought that in this case boldness was safety, and I will add that the experience I had in the period of the cotton distress of the many excellent qualities of the working classes, more especially in this district, led me to form such an opinion of their intelligence, their reasonableness, their sound sense, and their absence from personal and social prejudice, to believe that they could, without danger, be intrusted with that share in the representation of the country which the recent Act has largely intrusted to their hands. I believe that they are sound at heart and core. I have the greatest possible confidence in their loyalty as a body to the throne and the institutions of the country."

But an even more remarkable party function in which the Platform was availed of was that at Edinburgh, where Disraeli, Chancellor of the Exchequer, was entertained at a great banquet on the 29th October by the Conservatives of Scotland, and delivered a memorable speech.[1] The chairman (Sir W. S. Maxwell), in proposing Disraeli's health, said: "Until reform was undertaken by the Conservatives the question was regarded as a joke." In his speech of thanks Disraeli, after giving a very party-perverted history of the question of reform, expressed his opinion that the question was one for the Tory party to deal with if they thought proper, and after referring to the numerous attempts that had been made both by Tory and Liberal Ministers to deal with it, he said: "I had to prepare the mind of the country, and to educate—if it be not arrogant to use such a phrase—to educate our party. It is a large party, and requires its attention called to questions of this kind with some pressure. I had to prepare the mind of Parliament and the country on this question of reform." And then he proceeded to detail the points which, in his opinion, it was his duty to impress upon Parliament. For seven

[1] 5¾ columns in *The Times*.

"weary and toilsome years" he was engaged in this process. . . . Then there was a change of Government; Lord Derby came into power; and it was his opinion that it was necessary to bring in a Reform Bill. "Well, we brought in a Reform Bill. We passed a Reform Bill. . . . And then I am told that we have done nothing—that it is our opponents who have carried the Bill."

Proceeding then to refer to the adoption of "household franchise," which, it is to be remembered, was at first opposed by him, and only adopted when proposed by some one else, he observed: "I say in brief that Lord Derby could not have fixed upon any other solution of the borough franchise question than that which we arrived at. . . . When you try to settle any great question of this sort there are two great merits which the statesmen should not forget. First of all, let the settlement be founded on some principle, but that is not enough; let it also be a change that is in harmony with the manners and character of the people that you are dealing with. . . . There was a principle in saying that a man who has a house, and by his residence and by his contribution to the taxation, has shown that he is an individual interested in the welfare of the community of which he is a member, and the kingdom of which he is a subject—there was a principle in saying that that was a man whom you could trust in preference to the migratory pauper."

It is most interesting finding the two great leaders of the Conservative party thus utilising the Platform. On the day after this speech Disraeli made a long speech in reply to an address from the working men of Edinburgh. "If the working men are not influenced by wise Ministers," wrote *The Times*, "they will be liable to the control of demagogues."

The Reform Act passed and out of the way, the Irish Church question sprang into prominence. A very large number of meetings were held throughout the country urging the disestablishment of that institution, but though it was made the test question at the General Election of 1868, it was a small matter in comparison with the reform of the Parliament of the kingdom.

The general election showed how greatly the position of the Platform had altered. Mr. Gladstone, fighting South-West

Lancashire, availed himself freely of it. On the 12th October he spoke at Warrington; on the 14th at Liverpool; on the 18th at Newton; on the 20th at Leigh; on the 22d at Ormskirk and Southport; on the 23d at Wigan.[1]

Bright too was freely using the Platform. On the 26th and 30th October he spoke at Birmingham; on the 3d of November at Edinburgh, where he was presented with the freedom of the city. Here he gave an eloquent description of the election which is worth quoting. "There is a great battle going on at this moment, and without exaggeration one may say that it is a battle with confused noise, although it is not a battle which the prophet described 'with garments rolled in blood,' but there is a confused noise throughout the country from John O'Groats to Lands End. All over Great Britain, and all over Ireland, men are discussing great questions. . . . Well, I say then, let us in this battle and in these discussions bear our part; let us avoid heat of passion as much as we can; let us strip from all these questions that which does not belong to them; let us grasp with all our might the pith and kernel of them; and let us honestly endeavour to find a true solution for whatever difficulties beset the nation."

The Conservative Government were less energetic. The Prime Minister was silent. Disraeli, secure of the affections of the electors of Buckinghamshire, contented himself for some time with the usual written address to the electors, and it was not till the 9th November, at the Lord Mayor of London's banquet, that he broke silence.

Speaking on the eve of the dissolution of Parliament, he said: "Under any circumstances the dissolution of Parliament is the most important event in the life of Englishmen. But on the present occasion there are circumstances which give to that event a greater importance than any it could otherwise possess, because in dissolving that Parliament, her Majesty will appeal to the sense of that largely increased constituency which is the consequence of the late Reform Act. . . . We have a perfect confidence that the great body of the people

[1] The difference in the length at which speeches were now reported may be judged by the fact that the Liverpool speech occupies five columns of *The Times;* the Newton speech four columns; the two speeches on the 22d seven columns.

who will now be called upon to exercise their suffrages, will elect a wise and patriotic Parliament. . . . It has been said of her Majesty's Ministers that they have no policy. But their policy is a very simple one. It is to maintain the Constitution of their country."

Parliament was dissolved on the 11th. On the 19th the nominations for Bucks were made. There was no contest; and when Disraeli was declared duly elected, he made a long speech to his constituents, "whom he has been known to take more freely into his confidence than the House of Commons itself." He said: "No one knows better than myself that in the course of an agitated, and now, I am sorry to say, a long political career, I have done many things which I regret, and said many things which I deplore; but a man's career must be judged of by its whole tenor and character. I can say this for myself with the utmost sincerity—that I have always sought to maintain the greatness of my country; that I have never had one thought of a base or sinister character, or of self-interest; and that there is no reward which I more desire, and which I more prize than the good opinion of my fellow-countrymen in whatever political party they may be ranged.

"I say that what we have seen during the half of the general election that has as yet transpired has been such as completely to vindicate the people of England from all those charges made against them, and from all those fallacious dangers that were alleged and imputed during the progress of the great Act to which I have just referred. And I have no doubt that, whatever may be the general opinion of that Parliament about to be assembled, it will be a wise and patriotic Parliament, and will do its duty to the country. And why have the people of England exercised, and why will they exercise, their suffrage in this manner? It is because the people of England are proud of the country to which they belong; they are proud of the monarchy, which, although limited, is a real monarchy; they are proud of their Parliaments; they are proud of their laws; they are proud, above all, of the administration of the law in this country, which they know is singularly perfect and pure; they are proud of the personal liberty which every Englishman enjoys, and which the native of no other country in the world enjoys in the same degree; they are proud of the deeds of their ancestors, and of the heroic exploits of those who preceded them in this country; and they are proud of belonging to an ancient and a famous land. And it is with the responsibility of all these feelings that they have exercised, and will exercise, the suffrage which, by the great Act of last year, was accorded to them."

The general elections went, however, decisively against the Conservative Government, and on the 2d December 1868 Lord Derby resigned.

CHAPTER XXI

THE BULGARIAN ATROCITY AGITATION

After the passing of the Reform Act of 1867 eight years elapsed before any such abnormal activity as calls for special notice was shown by the Platform. Those years were not, however, a period of quiescence with it; but such had been the growth of the Platform, and so closely had it been woven into the political life of the country that proceedings, which would have been most memorable and noteworthy half a century previously, had become so common, and so much a matter of course, that they can be passed over without comment.

One event in this period of eight years must, however, be specially mentioned, as it was the attainment of an object long agitated for by the Platform, and therefore a triumph for it, though a tardy one. In 1872 the system of the ballot, or secret voting at Parliamentary elections, was enacted by Parliament. Long anterior to the first Reform Act, and when electors were few, the ballot had been agitated for as the sole means of escaping the intimidation and cruelty which the system of open voting enabled landowners or other persons of power to exercise. The question was essentially a Platform question and not a Parliamentary one, for the people who profited by open voting were members of Parliament, the people who smarted under it were the electors. Naturally, therefore, the electors were the first to complain of it, and to demand the protection of secret voting. But one of the very last things an unreformed Parliament, bent upon maintaining its own power, would concede, was any reform which rendered the electorate less dependent on them, and so the demand for the ballot made little way. In 1830, on the third reading of the East Retford Bill, the first attempt was made in Parliament to introduce the principle that the votes of the electors should be given by ballot.[1] The proposition came from O'Connell, and twenty-one members voted for it. In the first drafts of the Reform Bill of 1831 the adoption of the ballot had been suggested, but it was abandoned.

The intimidation used by the Tories at elections prevented the question from falling into abeyance. "The late election," wrote Lord John Russell [2] to Lord Melbourne in September 1837, "has converted many to the ballot." Lord Melbourne, however, "hardly felt justified in giving the question such a lift as would be given by making it an open one" in the Cabinet. Nearly every year a motion was made in the House of Commons in its favour, but, of course, without result.

As one of the six points of the Charter it was urged from the Platform and agitated for at nearly every Chartist meeting. "The suffrage, to be exempt from the corruption of the wealthy, and the violence of the powerful, must," said the first great National Petition, "be secret. The assertion of our right (of the franchise) necessarily involves the power of our uncontrolled exercise. We ask for the reality of a good, not for its semblance—therefore, we demand the ballot." Association with Chartism, however, instead of serving the cause only rendered it more obnoxious than ever, and with the defeat of Chartism it receded again into the background. Even the reformed Parliament was unwilling to concede it. In the Reform agitation of 1866 it had again been brought forward and coupled with reform.

But it was not for some years after the reformed Reform Parliament had been sitting that the ballot was finally carried, and that the measure long agitated for, long striven for by the Platform, was conceded by the Legislature. With this exception, there is, in this period, nothing of sufficient interest to record relative to the Platform.

In 1874 Parliament was, quite unexpectedly, dissolved, and a general election took place. The Platform played a prominent part therein—all parties vied with each other in the extent to which they used it, from the Prime Minister and ex-Prime Minister down to the newest candidate for Parliamentary honours. The elections resulted in a majority for the

[1] See *Annual Register*, 1830, p. 94. [2] See Walpole's *Russell*, vol. i. p. 286.

Conservative party, the Liberals resigned, and the Conservatives were forthwith installed in power under the leadership of Mr. Disraeli.

For a year affairs jogged quietly along, then a cloud, the size of a man's hand, appeared on the eastern horizon. An insurrection broke out in Herzegovina against the Turkish Government; the movement spread to Bosnia. Strange and remote as the cause of provocation might seem, yet from it there ensued one of the most startling outbursts of Platform agitation ever witnessed in this country.

From the very outset the insurrectionary movement evoked sympathy in England. At the instigation of Earl Russell a meeting was held in Willis's Rooms in London on the 9th September 1875, and resolutions were come to to assist in every legitimate way to obtain the removal of the wrongs suffered by the Christians of Bosnia and Herzegovina, and to appeal for aid on behalf of the destitute fugitives. The outbreak, "slight in the first instance, not encouraged by foreign Powers, and which might easily have been put down by prompt action, was neglected until it grew into a serious insurrection." The financial collapse of Turkey occurred just at this time, and the insurrection gained ground. In December[1] Lord Derby, the Secretary of State for Foreign Affairs, speaking at a meeting of Conservative working men at Edinburgh, avowed that "The eternal Eastern question is before us again," and as months went past it assumed an accuter form.

Reports of Turkish cruelties reached England from time to time; and the *Daily News*, in a leading article on the 20th June, wrote: "The Moslem population of Turkey seem intoxicated with the idea that England is with them, and the belief that with her help they may defy Russia is only too likely to slide into the conviction that thus protected they may do as they please with the insurgents and the Christians."

Three days later the first real report of atrocities in Bulgaria was published in the same paper in a letter from its correspondent dated 16th June: "Dark rumours have been whispered about Constantinople during the last month of horrible atrocities committed in Bulgaria. . . . One of the most fertile and productive provinces of the Turkish empire is thus

[1] 15th December 1875.

being laid waste. An intelligent Turk estimates the number of killed at 18,000. Bulgarians speak of 30,000, and of the destruction of upwards of 100 villages. In one town 1500 persons, mostly women and children, have been massacred."

"Even now it is openly asserted by the Turks that England has determined to help the Government to put down the various insurrections. England, says a Turkish journal, will defend us against Russia while we look after our rebels."

At the end of June, Servia and Montenegro began war against Turkey; and about the same time a considerable portion of the English public began to fear that the Government, with its traditional jealousy of Russia, and the idea that the maintenance of the Ottoman Empire was the only guarantee against the advance of Russia to the Dardanelles, would insist on Turkey being left to settle her own internal disturbances, and that thus the country might become involved in a war for the maintenance of the integrity of the Ottoman Empire. By degrees the terrible details of the Turkish cruelties in suppressing the rising in Bulgaria became public.

On the 8th July the *Daily News* published another letter on the Moslem atrocities in Bulgaria. On the 27th July a meeting, convened by the League in aid of the Christians in Turkey, was held at Willis's Rooms. Lord Shaftesbury presided, and said: "We are here to-day to take a line of action that will elicit an expression of the feeling throughout the country which we believe to be universal." It was resolved "That this meeting desires to express its emphatic opinion that no moral or material support should be afforded to the Turkish Government as against the insurgent provinces.

"That this meeting expresses its deep abhorrence of the cruelties committed by the Turkish irregular troops upon the women and children and unarmed inhabitants of Bulgaria, and calls upon the Government to use its utmost influence, whether alone or in co-operation with the other great Powers having treaty engagements with the Porte, to require the Turkish Government to put a stop to practices revolting to all civilised nations.

"That the notorious abuses of the Turkish rule in Europe, and the repeated failure of the Sublime Porte to fulfil its solemn obligations, render it hopeless to expect that any settlement of the Eastern question will prove permanent which does not confer upon the inhabitants of the insurgent provinces the full rights of self-government."

Parliament was still sitting, and it might have been thought that Parliament would have been active in the matter; but the Government had no reliable information, they said, to give, and one way or another succeeded in staving off the question, without any definite announcement of a policy, until the 15th August, when Parliament was prorogued.

On the very next day another letter was published by the *Daily News* from its correspondent, with further information as to the Turkish atrocities in Bulgaria. Fifteen thousand people were killed in four days. "You cannot increase or diminish the horror of the thing by mere statements of round numbers. Twenty thousand crimes, each one of which is infinite in itself, are not less horrible than a hundred thousand."

"Bodies of men cut up and flung to the dogs;" "the hacking to pieces of helpless children, and spitting them on bayonets;" "little children of both sexes maltreated and brutalised until they died;" "thousands of women outraged with every circumstance of brutality."

Here was provocation enough for the rising passion of Englishmen, fuel enough for any agitation, and the extra sting was added that these infamies were being perpetrated by the Government for whom Englishmen had wasted thousands of precious lives, and spent nearly eighty millions of money. The heart of the country thrilled with horror at these infamies, with wrath against the Turkish Government, in whose name and interest they were perpetrated, and with the determination to shake England free from any association with that Government. Familiar now with the Platform, ever good-at-need in the popular cause, the people turned to their old, their trusted, their unfailing friend. First one meeting, and then another, and then, as an extra incentive, came a detailed account of the destruction of Batak. A public meeting at Battersea Fields expressed indignation at the Turkish atrocities; another at Darlington protested against any support being given to Turkey. On the 26th August there was a meeting at Liverpool. On the 29th the working men of

Hackney met, and a resolution was passed "That it is imperative on the people to at once repudiate the representation of a Government which, by its policy, is compromising the honour of the nation, and making England a participator in crimes which are an outrage upon humanity and a lasting reproach to civilisation." The same day a meeting was held at Glasgow. On the 31st large meetings were held in six large towns. On the 1st of September several meetings were held. Among the number, one at Sunderland, where one of the speakers admirably expressed the purport of the movement. "The people must declare," he said, "that England would never wield a weapon in defence of torturers, violators, and assassins." Gradually the daily number of meetings increased. A meeting at Birkenhead "regretted that so much blood and treasure should have been wasted in defence of Turkey, and earnestly requested the Government to withdraw its countenance and support from that corrupt and moribund State, which is a disgrace to Europe and to civilisation." A meeting at Rochdale "earnestly urged on her Majesty's Government promptly to withdraw all semblance of support to the Turkish Government by such measures as shall not permit our policy as a nation to be construed into connivance with Turkish misrule and oppression." "They must agree with him," said a speaker at Sheffield, "that these Christian provinces should never be handed over again to Ottoman rule."

On the 4th September there were meetings in nine large towns in different parts of the country. On the 5th there were meetings in seventeen towns. On the 6th in twenty towns.

Contemporary criticism on these proceedings throws valuable light on the agitation.

"The large public meetings that are now being held all over the country," wrote the *Daily News*,[1] "show unmistakably that the English people will no longer accept the false excuses which have been made for the support given by their rulers to the abominable Government of Turkey.

"The demonstrations which we are called to report day by day are nobly distinguished by this peculiarity, that men of all political opinions and religions are taking part in them.

[1] 6th September.

. . . Not for many years has been seen so powerful and resistless a movement of public opinion determined to assert its rights against those who were misrepresenting it.

"Far above every other requirement this demand is heard, that the populations which have suffered such cruel wrongs at the hands of the Turks—those of Bosnia, Herzegovina, and Bulgaria—shall have governments of their own, tributary indeed to Constantinople, but free from all administrative interference by the Sultan and his Pachas. This demand, which is too intelligible to be misunderstood, is made at meeting after meeting."

Lord Hartington, speaking at "The Cutlers' Feast" at Sheffield, said (on 7th September 1876): "Since Parliament rose an agitation and excitement has risen in the country which, for its earnestness, its suddenness, and its intensity surprised all of us. It is an agitation which has been perfectly spontaneous. I have not heard a whisper that it has been fomented, or that it has been excited by the leaders of any particular party. I have scarcely even heard a whisper respecting those professional agitators to whom so much of these matters is generally attributed."

And *The Times*, in a leading article on the 8th September, wrote: "There is no mistaking the voice of the people, and it is the voice of the people that speaks now in every variety of expression and tone, from the energetic remonstrances of the provincial meeting to the elaborate argument of the ex-Premier."

Mr. Gladstone, in his celebrated pamphlet on *The Bulgarian Horrors*,[1] described how it had come about "that the nation, deprived of its most rightful and most constitutional aids, has been called upon at the season when the task would under ordinary circumstances be impossible, to choose between leaving its most sacred duties unperformed, and taking the performance of them primarily into its own hands."

After referring to the refusal of the Government to discuss the question of the events in the East, or to give any information on the subject, he wrote: "The state of the case then is this: The House of Commons has in the main been ousted from that legitimate share of influence which I may call its

[1] Dated 5th September 1876.

jurisdiction in the case. A subject of paramount weight goes before the people at the time when the classes having leisure, and usually contributing most to form and guide public opinion, are scattered as disjointed units over the face of this and other countries. In default of Parliamentary action, and a public concentrated as usual, we must proceed as we can with impaired means of appeal. But honour, duty, compassion, and I must add shame, are sentiments never in a state of *coma*. The working men of the country, whose condition is less affected than that of others by the season, have to their honour led the way, and shown that the great heart of Britain has not ceased to beat. And the large towns and cities, now following in troops, are echoing back, each from its own place, the mingled notes of horror, pain, and indignation.

"Let them understand that the importance of their meetings, on this occasion at least, cannot be overrated. As Inkerman was the soldiers' battle so this is the nation's crisis. The question is not only whether unexampled wrongs shall receive effectual and righteous condemnation, but whether the only effective security shall be taken against its repetition. In order to take this security the nation will have to speak through its Government, but we now see clearly that it must first teach its Government, almost as it would teach a lisping child what to say. *Then* will be taken out of the way of an united Europe the sole efficient obstacle to the punishment of a gigantic wrong."

On the 9th of September Mr. Gladstone addressed a great open-air meeting at Blackheath, and though the weather was most unpropitious, 10,000 persons or more were at it.[1] Three resolutions were proposed. The first, recording the sense of horror and disgust at the terrible outrages committed by the Turks, and expressing the opinion that the British Government had failed to exhibit sufficient promptitude in discovering those outrages, and energy in regard to the adoption of the measures which they render necessary. The second, urging the Government to adopt certain measures in concert with the other Powers of Europe to provide effectually against the recurrence of such atrocities. And the third, approving of an Address to the Queen praying her to adopt the measures referred to.

[1] See *The Times*, 11th September.

Mr. Gladstone spoke from a covered platform or hustings. He said: "I have lived long in public life, I have witnessed many vivid movements of the popular mind, but never one to compare with that which, during the last fortnight, has taken its commencement, and has swollen with such immense rapidity, and such legitimate rapidity to the dimensions of a national movement. . . . It is idle to deny or disparage the character of this movement. It is absurd to connect it with the mere action of any political party, however powerful. . . . As it has been a national movement in contradistinction from a party movement, so it has been a popular movement in contradistinction from an autocratic movement . . . the working men in the first instance raised this flag under which we are now marching."

Clear as was the expression of the popular voice, and distinct enough in its main features as was the popular policy, the difficulty was to compel the Government to carry out the wishes of the people. The Government were, in fact, completely masters of the situation. Parliament, the executive of the Platform, was not sitting; pressure upon representatives was useless except as to pressing them to get the Government to assemble Parliament; meetings could pass resolutions, but could not give effect to them. One device alone remained for bringing the popular views formally and directly before the Government—a deputation to Ministers. On the 11th September Lord Derby received two large deputations at the Foreign Office—one from the London Trades Unionists, and leading representatives of the working classes; the other from the Working-men's Peace Associations. In reply he made two speeches, which, as Mr. Gladstone said, "undoubtedly constitute a ministerial manifesto."[1]

They showed that the Government were slightly shifting their ground, coming slightly round to the policy desired by the people. But the country was not disposed to be content with such a slight change. The meetings of indignation continued. On the 11th there were about thirty meetings; on the 12th there were some sixteen or so; on the 13th there were over twenty-five; on the 14th there were over twenty-eight; on the 15th there were over fifteen,—over a hundred meetings

[1] See his letter in *Daily News* of 16th September 1876.

in five days. With such a turmoil of voices the Government were forced at last to take some action.

On the 16th September 1876 Sir S. Northcote (Chancellor of the Exchequer) addressed a meeting at Edinburgh of the Conservative Working-men's Association. He said: "I felt that it might not be inopportune that I should, on behalf of myself, and perhaps, to some extent, on behalf of other members of the Government, express our sentiments on the topics which, at the present moment, create so much anxiety and so much interest in the country. . . .

"These meetings which have been held throughout the country, the strong language which has been used at them, here and there, may have run into excess, yet they have their use. They have their advantage by showing that England is actuated by no feeling of mere selfishness. These meetings cannot fail, if they are properly turned to account, to strengthen the voice of England in the councils of Europe in this same matter; but, on the other hand, if the language, if the mere excited language, there used is really to be taken as expressive of distrust of the policy of your Government, if it is intended to weaken their hands, and to embarrass them rather than strengthen them in their action, I fear, whatever may be the consequences to this Government, or the political consequences to this country, the consequences to the peace of Europe and the interests of humanity abroad will be worse still."[1]

On the 18th September "a large and imposing meeting of the citizens of London," convened and presided over by the Lord Mayor, was held at the Guildhall. An Address to the Queen was adopted, praying "That her Majesty's Government would do all in its power to secure the separation from Turkey of the provinces inhabited by the Slavonic race, and their independence of a Government which has proved itself unworthy to rule them;" and further praying that it might please her Majesty "to convene Parliament at an early date to take these grave matters into consideration."[2]

In the evening Exeter Hall was crowded with working men who had been invited to attend "in the name of humanity to express their horror at the diabolical outrages of the Turks in

[1] *The Times.* [2] *Ibid.* 19th September 1876.

Bulgaria, and proclaim to the world their indignation that the Government of England should be found supporting so foul a system."

Mr. Fawcett, M.P., presided, and made a powerful speech: "I believe you have gathered together here not simply to express your deep indignation at the fearful atrocities which have been committed in Bulgaria. You have a more practical object in view. You are determined that as far as in you lies no Government shall adopt with regard to the Eastern question a policy unworthy of the English nation. . . . It will of course be said that the Eastern question is surrounded with complexities, and that it is not at an excited public meeting that we can frame a policy on a difficult and complicated subject. . . . Of course we know what will be said in certain quarters about such meetings as these. We shall be described as demagogues, but remember this: Such meetings as these have won for England some of her greatest triumphs, and have certainly saved her from some of her greatest perils. Twelve years ago, if the working men had not assembled as they are now assembling, why, England would have had to bear the lasting shame of having sympathised with the slave-owners of the South." After referring to the fact that Mr. Gladstone had propounded a policy, he said: "It is for you, a meeting like this, to decide whether you will accept the clear, the distinct, the precise, and the noble policy of Mr. Gladstone. . . . If you like, and if meetings like this choose, you can confer sooner or later on him power to carry out this policy."

On the 20th September the Prime Minister himself descended into the arena at Aylesbury, and there made a most important speech. It showed plainly enough that the arrow of popular agitation had hit its mark. He said that the Foreign Secretary has two most important ends to accomplish. "He has at the same time to secure permanent British interests of the highest importance, and he has to secure the maintenance of peace in Europe. Under ordinary circumstances a British Minister so placed, whatever might be his difficulties, would have the consolation of knowing that he was backed by the country. It would be affectation for me to pretend that this is the position of her Majesty's Government at this moment. Unquestionably there is a large party, a large portion of her Majesty's subjects, whose thoughts and sentiments are attracted and absorbed by other things than the maintenance of the permanent interests of this country or the maintenance of peace. These are matters which require and are receiving the most earnest and constant attention of the Government. But, unhappily, a great portion of the people of this country, prompted by feelings which have drawn their attention to extraneous matters, have arrived at a conclusion which, in the opinion of her Majesty's Government, if carried into effect would alike be injurious to the permanent and important interests of England, and fatal to any chance of preserving the peace of Europe. . . . The next step is for Lord Derby, on the part of the Government, to recur exactly to the position which he occupied before the Servian war.[1] What was that position? It was an attempt to settle, with the concurrence of all the powers of Europe, the relations, the future relations, that should subsist between the Christian subjects of the Porte and the Turkish Government. Why are we to be opposed, why are we to be attacked because such is our object and such is our aim? The country in some of its exhibitions has completely out-Heroded the most extravagant conceptions."

This speech, says Mr. G. Carslake Thompson in his most interesting and excellent work on this period,[2] was a direct blow in the face of public opinion. "It challenged both the correctness of its judgment and the legitimacy of its power, and it is impossible to say that the self-confidence of public opinion was not staggered on both points. . . . A new element was introduced into the situation by the shock which the speech gave to the confidence of public opinion in its own power to determine the course of the country in the last resort—that is to say, in its own sovereignty. Public opinion began to be dimly conscious that, in addition to a problem in foreign affairs, it might have a constitutional question to consider before long."

The meetings continued. On the 25th September the *Daily*

[1] That war was before the massacre at Batak.

[2] *Public Opinion and Lord Beaconsfield*, 1875–80, vol. ii. pp. 19, 25, by G. Carslake Thompson.

News gave a list of them. "Since the publication of the *Daily News* telegram of 7th August, meetings in 262 places have been reported in London papers. This does not include duplicate meetings in the same town, nor merely preliminary or committee meetings."

And in a leading article of the same date it said: "We publish to-day a list as complete as we are able to make it of the places at which public meetings have been held to express the national indignation at the horrors which have been perpetrated in Bulgaria. . . . We publish this concise account of what has been done, in order that the Government and people generally may be better able to understand the meaning, and estimate the value of the movement which suddenly made itself felt all over England.

"The movement is inspired by no motive of a merely personal or even a merely national character. . . . Though the political chiefs have followed the movement they did not originate it."

And *The Times* of the 26th September wrote: "The agitation has done good work in manifesting the change in the national view of the Eastern question."

On the 27th September the Lord Mayor of London and an influential deputation waited on Lord Derby at the Foreign Office to present the Address adopted at the Guildhall meeting.

"They desired," said one of the deputation, "certainly to have from his lordship a clear, frank exposition of the policy of the Government."

But that was what the Government was not disposed to give. The Government could not apparently recognise the right of the Platform to ask for it. Lord Derby point-blank refused the demand for the immediate summoning of Parliament.

"The Government have no measures of urgency to propose in Parliament." As to its being called for the purpose of approving or disapproving what had been done by the Government, it seemed to him that that might be as well done in January or February as in November; and as regards summoning it to give an influence or direction to negotiations in progress, the earliest date would very likely be too late. . . .

"It is quite possible while rejecting the idea of political autonomy, to accept the idea of local or administrative autonomy. I do not particularly like the phrase. I much prefer the plain English phrase of local self-government. But I take the word as I find it, and I think in that direction we may look for a possible and practical solution. . . .

"I do not at all wish to disguise the fact that what has happened in Bulgaria has, to a certain extent, changed the position, not only of our own Government, but of every European Government in regard to Turkey and the east of Europe."

Gradually, as September went on, the number of meetings decreased. In the last week of the month some thirty or so were held. The *Daily News* wrote on the 2d October in a leading article: "The pretence is made that the public meetings have not expressed the deliberate and permanent convictions of the nation, but have merely given vent to a gust of sentiment sweeping across it.

"We are told that the public feeling has been cowed by Lord Beaconsfield's defiance at Aylesbury, and that, among other symptoms of feebleness and decline, public meetings began to die away. This surely is an absurd statement. When public meetings have been held all over the country, the country cannot be expected to begin and hold them all over again; the more have been held, the fewer remain to be held. The country, through its local organisations and communities, has given distinct expression to its convictions and feelings. To ask for more is to ask for incessant agitation and protracted tumult.

"There are people who cannot be convinced without being terrified; who cannot be persuaded, but who give way when they are threatened."

Up to about the 12th October meetings went on; after that date there are few reports of any, at least properly belonging to the character of "indignation meetings." They had said their say, and therefore ceased.

Bright, in a speech at Manchester, admirably summed up the position.[1] He said: "The Ministry heap ridicule and contempt on the proclamation of change of opinion and policy which more than 300 public meetings have announced to the whole world. The fact is, that the nation looks one way, and the Government looks another. There has been nothing like

[1] On 2d October 1876.

it, I believe, in this country since the time of the Reform Bill, when the Duke of Wellington was endeavouring to form an anti-reform movement.

"There has been no such demonstration against the policy of the Government as there has been within the last two months. . . . A year ago there were scores of meetings condemning their conduct with regard to fugitive slaves. . . . And now, twelve months later, we find ourselves in a perfect hurricane of condemnation of this Government."

The nation having expressed its opinion, further discussions, for the time at least, were continued by members of the existing or of the late Government, or by members of Parliament addressing their constituents.

"There is silence for the moment," wrote *The Times* in the following month,[1] "because the speakers have said what they wanted to say, and because the Government is believed to be making earnest exertions in the cause of peace."

Here, then, may be examined the first stage of this remarkable Platform movement. Its beginning was entirely free from any party motive—men of all parties joined in it. It was a purely spontaneous movement, arising "from the uncertainty which prevailed respecting the Ministerial policy, and the uneasiness lest the country should be suddenly and unawares committed to a great war."[2] It was for a time devoid of leaders; it was throughout practically devoid of any organisation, though an attempt was made to give it one. No incitement came from above; no communication passed from place to place as to the expediency of holding a meeting. As Parliament was not sitting, the movement had the most remarkable and altogether novel character of being an attempt to influence the policy and actions of the Government or Executive directly.[3] Hitherto the Platform had exercised its influence on the Government through the House of Commons; now, as Parliament was not sitting, it endeavoured to influence it without such intervention. There was no effort made to oust the Government; the one prevailing idea was to induce, to compel, it to change its policy.

1 25th November. 2 *The Times*, 25th November 1876.

3 See *Public Opinion and Lord Beaconsfield*, by G. C. Thompson, vol. ii. p. 33.

"Thus considered, the agitation was an attempt to assert its sovereignty independently of the machinery of party."[1]

The next most notable thing in connection with the movement was its universality. In every part of the country meetings were held: in the north, in the south, in the east, in the west, in the great central cities, in remote seaside watering-places—all joined in one chorus. It was "a veritable insurrection of public opinion"; or, as Mr. Lowe expressed it,[2] "The people of England have taken this matter into their own hands."

And there are certain features about these meetings which deserve notice. They were all local meetings—generally indoor meetings—in the largest hall of the city or town—most of them were convened by the Mayor, or some local persons of importance. And what is very interesting to remark is, that not one of them was a county meeting. That old institution seems to have been swept aside in the progress of political life; the time-honoured formula—"The nobility, gentry, clergy, and freeholders of the county"—appears to have completely fallen into desuetude.

It is further to be remarked that the meetings were in no ways demonstrations of physical force. Thorough and wholesale as was the condemnation of the policy of the Government, there was not the haziest idea of subverting the Government; they were peaceable, and orderly, and men of all ranks, and classes attended them.

Of this form of influencing the Government or Executive various opinions were, and may be held. *The Times*, writing on the 14th September, said: "The public meetings which have been held throughout the country have instructed Lord Derby, and with the utmost jealousy of the rush and impulse of democratic movement, we cannot regret them. . . . We have more than once confessed that we do not regard the multiplication of meetings throughout the country with unmixed satisfaction. Government by impulse is of necessity to a large extent government by chance, and those who would have our national policy inspired by reason as well as feeling must needs be jealous of any course which tends to subject the con-

[1] See *Public Opinion and Lord Beaconsfield*, by G. C. Thompson, vol. ii. p. 35.

[2] At Croydon, 13th September.

trol of public affairs to the hazards of popular ebullition. But the meetings which have been so numerously held have been and remain a necessity, for both reason and feeling have been outraged by the policy pursued in the East, and we must use the only means in our power to correct the errors that have been committed."

Once Mr. Gladstone took part in the general expression of opinion, some people's minds were influenced more hostilely than they probably otherwise would have been. Thus a writer in *Blackwood's Magazine*[1] of November 1876 declared "The country has been delivered over to the most pernicious agitation ever set afloat within the memory of its oldest inhabitants. . . . This year, under the auspices of a great statesman . . . public speakers have been heard upon nearly 500 platforms, arousing the warlike fury of the people, demanding the expulsion of a numerous race from the territory which they have inhabited for centuries, denouncing their own Government for moral and material, if not purposed complicity with massacre, spoliation, and rape, etc. etc." . . .

Another remarkable fact in connection with this agitation—indeed, the most remarkable of all—was, that it was an incursion by the Platform into a sphere of politics from which it had hitherto held more or less aloof. Hitherto most of its action had lain within the sphere of home politics, the reform of Parliament, the abolition of abuses, the increase of the popular control over Government,—these had been its main objects and desires. It is true that in the questions of the Civil War in the United States, and of the Crimean War, it had taken a certain part, and given evidence of an active watchfulness which the Government might advantageously heed; but never, until this Bulgarian atrocity agitation, had the Platform so unequivocatingly asserted its intention of taking up the reins in matters of foreign policy, and of entering the sacred precincts of foreign diplomacy which hitherto had been kept as the exclusive, the sacred, preserves for kings, statesmen, and diplomatists. That, above all others, was the lesson to be learned from the agitation.

Sir Stafford Northcote, in his speech at Edinburgh on the 16th September 1876, showed that the Government felt the point

[1] P. 632.

and the sting of the agitation. He said: "I desire to say a few words to you as to the attitude which the people of this country have held in times past, and do generally hold, and the attitude which at the present moment they hold, in regard to questions of foreign policy. Now, I think I may say this in regard to the general attitude which the people in this country hold with regard to foreign policy—as a rule they do not understand it. (A voice, 'A thousand times better than the Government.') I say that not by way of reproach to the people of this country, I say it merely as a matter of fact, and because it is almost impossible that it could be otherwise."

The argument is one which is very familiar to students of English political history. From the very first claim put forward by the people to participate in their own Government, they were consistently told by Tory statesmen and Tory Parliaments that they did not understand how to govern, and their demands were resisted. Time and the Platform tolerably well knocked that argument on the head as applied to home affairs; and, so far, experience has proved that the people are much better able to govern than those who kept the government from them. But the argument was revived when the people, having advanced in political education and intelligence, came to claim their right to participate in government as regarded foreign affairs. And yet their claim to the one is as clear and as indisputable as it is to the other, for the foreign relationships of the country are of every whit as much importance to them as are home affairs. Even now the claim to keep the people in ignorance of their exact relationship with foreign Powers is sometimes stretched so far that Parliament even is kept in the dark while negotiations are being proceeded with, or measures are being taken, most materially, possibly vitally, affecting the welfare or existence of the nation. It may occasionally be a matter of convenience that it should be so; but, if so, the reasons should be made plain to the people, and the recognition of their right to know them must be conceded. The foreign policy of the country is of such vital consequence to the people that they will, quite rightly and naturally, insist more and more on having the real decision about it. The Bulgarian atrocity agitation was the first plain unmistakable monition to the Government and the world, that henceforth the Platform would concern itself ever more and more with foreign affairs, and would, as far as was in its power, exercise decisive authority.[1]

It would be taking a narrow and circumscribed view of this agitation were we to consider that its effect was confined to this kingdom. The effect of the Platform is no longer so circumscribed. Very far from it. Its proceedings were watched with the keenest interest abroad, more particularly in those countries whose interest, possibly whose fate, were involved in the vast issues at stake. While Parliament was not sitting, it was to the Platform that foreign Powers had to look for English opinion—not merely to the Platform speeches of Ministers but to the Platform generally. Mr. Forster and Lord Hartington, on their return from visiting the East, both described in their speeches how anxiously the Platform was watched by the Turkish Government, whilst the appreciation by the Russian Emperor of the value of public opinion in England was proved by the request he addressed to the English Government, that the details of a conversation of his with the English ambassador should be made public in England.

The effect of the agitation at home was by no means as decisive as might have been expected. Mr. Gladstone, subsequently referring to the agitation, said:[2] "It was admitted by the Government themselves to be the expression of the country. That national feeling produced its effects; it produced the Conference at Constantinople."

But it did something more than that; for though the Government, with its philo-Turkish and anti-Russian feelings, and with a large and submissive majority in the House of Commons, was not very easily to be moved, it was certainly checked in its warlike tendencies to support the integrity of the Turkish empire, and was forced back on the policy of non-interference between Russia and Turkey unless British interests were actually threatened or compromised.

It is unnecessary to follow in detail the successive outbursts of Platform activity in the ever-varying phases of the Eastern

[1] "The extra-Parliamentary debates have done more to spread knowledge and promote the growth of opinion than anything that has taken place in the assemblies of either Lords or Commons."—*Weekly Times*, 1st April 1877.

[2] See his first Midlothian speech, 25th November 1879.

question, for there came in this period frequent accesses of activity and then a lull. The most notable suffice to display the meaning and moral of the whole agitation.

The Platform, not having quite answered the expectations of its followers, it was deemed desirable to give it, if possible, some form of organisation; and early in the winter of 1876–77 an "Eastern Question Association" was started. A "National Conference" was convened and held in St. James's Hall, London, on the 8th December.[1] "It was a representative meeting in a very broad sense." The Duke of Westminster, who presided, stated the object of the Association. He said: "As this country has already emphatically decided that on no account whatever will the English nation go to war for Turkey as against Russia or against any other Power, we ought to disabuse the Turkish mind of all idea of obtaining assistance from this great country."

The Times, in a leading article criticising the meeting, observed: "Were Parliament sitting, the real situation of the Porte would be made clear to it in twenty-four hours by an unequivocal display of national opinion. In the absence of Parliament public meetings may do the same kind of service in an imperfect way, and that is, perhaps, the best plea for the Conference."

Parliament met on the 8th February 1877, and to it was in great measure transferred the discussion of the Eastern question. But the Conservative majority in Parliament leaned more to the Government policy than to the Platform policy, and the public opinion expressed by the Platform received no fresh accession of strength by the transference of the discussion to another arena. The Government, however, after several debates had been raised, avowed their intention not to interfere in the war which had broken out between Russia and Turkey, so long as Turkish interests alone were involved. They, however, declared that should British interests be imperilled England would not be indifferent. The declaration of this "charter of neutrality" satisfied public opinion for a while, and actual agitation was suspended. The Eastern question, nevertheless, continued "the all-absorbing topic of

[1] 1876.

public interest. Public men were expected to allude to it every time they opened their mouths."[1]

Mr. Thompson, in his work on *Public Opinion and Lord Beaconsfield*, referring to this particular period, says: "Comparing the summer of 1877 with the state of things a year before, public opinion had suffered a disappointment in its reliance on Parliament—at all events on the sitting Parliament,—and had lost much of its self-confidence in its own power to control the Executive."[2]

All through the autumn of 1877 there were meetings and speeches. Bright, Gladstone, Forster, Lord Salisbury, Lord Beaconsfield (at the Guildhall), Sir S. Northcote, and several other Ministers and ex-Ministers, all spoke, some of them several times. The fall of Plevna in December raised fears of England's intervention to save Turkey, and agitation again became very marked, the Platform was again had recourse to, and a very large number of meetings were held. Of this agitation *The Times* of 16th January 1878 wrote: "We receive from all sides reports of public meetings held in view of the momentous issue on which the representatives of the nation may very shortly be asked to pronounce. The result almost everywhere is the same. The nation is declaring itself for peace, and it expects with confidence that its representatives will give effect to its unmistakable wishes. If we could trust outward signs the difficulty would be to discover from what quarter any opposition to the national will is to be looked for. The language of Liberals and of Conservatives is in agreement on the main point."

But though the meetings had "made clear the meaning of the country," yet when Parliament met, on the 17th January, the action of the Platform was brushed aside as a matter of little consequence, Ministers, with but little delay, proceeded to take measures indicative of war. A special vote of £6,000,000 was asked for naval and military purposes, and the fleet was ordered to enter Turkish waters. It was evident the Platform had failed to carry its point, and Mr. Gladstone practically acknowledged this in his speech at Oxford[3] when he said: "By the vigorous action of public opinion which began in the autumn of 1876, we have to a great extent controlled

[1] Thompson, vol. ii. p. 247. [2] *Ibid.* p. 220. [3] 30th January 1878.

the action of the Government. But though we have controlled it we have not got to the root of the mischief. We have by pressure from without kept down the action of the power whose influence we fear. But that power is still there. The disposition and the direction are unchanged, and the best proof that within the Cabinet it is supreme is in the vote which has just been submitted to Parliament." The approval of the vote was not come to without some anxiety on the part of some of the supporters of the Government, as they urged expedition in the matter, fearing to get communications from their constituents on the subject, "for," said they, "there has grown up in these modern times a most abominable practice of getting up meetings by wire all over the country, and sending back to Parliament the resolutions of those meetings."

In the imminence of war, agitation against war became more difficult. When the Government had progressed so far, had practically committed themselves to a course from which they could not recede, it was hopeless to expect to check the Government by agitation. Meetings to denounce opposition to the Government as unpatriotic began to be held, and Government supporters broke up the meetings of those who were opposed to the Government policy—notably one in Hyde Park.

"It is hardly too much to say," remarks Mr. Thompson in the work above referred to, "that out-of-door agitation was *put down*."

With a freer hand the Government proceeded more rapidly. The vote of credit was passed; the Reserves were called out; Indian auxiliary troops were brought to Malta; the secret convention with Turkey was made. For a long time England was on the very verge and brink of war, but, ultimately, terms of settlement were agreed to; the Berlin Treaty was signed; "Peace" was assured; "with honour" said those who had made it.

Reviewing the home political history of these most critical and exciting years, the principal question which presents itself is—How far the Platform was successful in directing or influencing the Government? There will doubtless ever be a great difference of opinion as to the answer. That it materially influenced the Government for some time, and in some ways is, I think, clear; but undoubtedly in other and more important ways the Platform failed to assert its authority, or even its influence, over Parliament.

Having regard to the result of the general election two years later, it must be acknowledged that the Platform did during these years truly represent the majority in the country, and spoke its voice. It failed, however, to make its influence decisively felt in the House of Commons, owing to the existence there of a majority, elected on other issues, which was obedient to the leadership of a Minister who was not too susceptible to the voice of the Platform.

The failure proved that the Platform was not omnipotent—that it had not the power of at once controlling the policy of the country. The lesson was a most instructive one to a people anxious above all things to have the whole government of the country—that is to say, its foreign, as well as its home affairs—under their own absolute control. The causes of the failure are plainly visible. In the first place, the Platform, though it represented a majority in the country, represented but a comparatively narrow majority. Had it represented a really large majority, such as it did in the Reform agitation of 1831–32, the Government must have at once bowed to the storm. In the next place, it more or less wasted its energies in endeavouring to do directly what it should have done indirectly. Had the Platform, instead of passing resolutions to be forwarded to the Government, which did not care about them, put in each constituency direct, persistent, and imperative pressure upon the Parliamentary representatives, its action would have been more effective. Even that, however, might not have completely succeeded, especially then, when the franchise was on a narrower basis than it is now. Manifestly a weak place in the system of Platform government was disclosed. But as a set off against a certain degree of weakness here, it is to be borne in mind that influencing the representatives in the House of Commons is but one of the two means which the Platform possesses of making its power felt. The other is that of influencing the composition of the House of Commons by influencing the electorate. To that task the leaders of the Liberal party soon addressed themselves, and the results of the General Election of 1880 afforded ample proof that if the Platform could not make its authority felt at all times, it was determined to secure for itself a House of Commons which would submit to that influence should the occasion arise for its exercise.

CHAPTER XXII

THE PLATFORM AT THE GENERAL ELECTION OF 1880

It is, indeed, a most remarkable phenomenon of modern times, and one of which this General Election of 1880 gives a most interesting example, that the issues upon which a general election is fought are for months, even for years in advance, placed before the people of the country, more by the Platform than by Parliament.

In the earlier part of the reign of George III., indeed all through his reign, his Majesty's speech dissolving Parliament was deemed quite sufficient declaration of a programme for the electorate to express their opinion on. Ministers troubled themselves not at all as regards elections except as to how to manipulate the funds and the prizes of patronage at their disposal so as to secure the largest number of seats. Whatever of political discussion was carried on at a general election came from the Opposition. The Reform Act of 1832, however, as we have seen, introduced a new system, and compelled a departure from that haughty reticence with which Ministers loved to shield themselves. Other manifestoes were required than royal speeches, and Ministers had to address themselves to the electorate. And when another half-century had passed over the revolution was complete. Even Parliament had ceased to be the arena of the preliminaries of the electoral contest, and the Platform defined the issues on which the election would be fought. It was found to be a greater force for influencing the people than any action in Parliament.

So long before the General Election of 1880 as July 1878, we find Mr. Gladstone on the Platform at Southwark beginning to prepare the ground. "I must say, that if I can form a judgment, there never has been a period when the differences between the two parties have been more broadly pronounced, and more clearly declared. If a man cannot see that now, he is blind indeed. . . . It is quite time that the people of this country should, on the earliest convenient opportunity, be consulted as to the mode in which they are being governed."

In November 1878 Mr. Gladstone spoke at Greenwich: "At the next general election," he said, "the people would have to deal with a question so large as to include all other questions—the question of the manner in which this country is to be governed. 'Personal government' was not a happy phrase, and he protested against its being interpreted to mean that the Sovereign desired to depart from the traditions of the Constitution; but he charged the present advisers of the Crown with having insidiously begun a system intended to narrow the liberties of the people of England." Then, taking as his text the injustice of the Afghan war, he brought home to his audience in the most striking way the principle and meaning of self-government: "But the responsibility (for that war) which at this moment is an undivided responsibility resting upon ten or twelve men, will next week, or the week afterwards, very likely be divided between them and the two Houses of Parliament, and within no long period—it may be within a very short period—the people of England will have to say whether they will take upon themselves their share of that responsibility. And remember that if they do, their share will be the largest of all. They are the tribunal of final appeal. Upon them, upon every constituency, upon every man in every constituency who gives his sanction to an unjust war, the guilt and the shame will lie."

Early in the following year[1] the official leader of the Opposition, Lord Hartington, spoke at Liverpool: "The record upon which this Parliament and this Government will have to be judged, and upon which they will appeal to the constituencies, will be upon their foreign policy, upon the results of that policy on the security of our own empire, and upon its effects on the temper and character of the nation. . . . Up to the present time the country has never been consulted, and upon such vital and important questions we, the Opposition, decline to treat those matters as past and done with. We

[1] 6th February 1879.

shall not cease to bring them before the consideration of the country. We shall try to bring phrases to the test of truth, and induce the people, if it may be, to look these facts in the face, and to decide intelligently whether they wish to be governed by a foreign policy such as it has been during the last few years."

The Easter recess of this year, and again the Whitsuntide recess, were crammed with speeches from leading politicians on both sides, delivered at meetings or demonstrations in various parts of the country, in all of which the issues upon which the constituencies would have to decide were kept in the foreground. Lord Salisbury, Lord Hartington, Mr. Gladstone, Mr. Chamberlain, Mr. Smith, Cabinet Ministers, and ex-Cabinet Ministers, spoke several times, asserting and replying, charging and denying. When the recess came the campaign was renewed with greater vigour than ever, and with large accessions of numbers on each side.

At a meeting at Newcastle-on-Tyne on the 19th September Lord Hartington expressed the weight which lay on many men's hearts: "We are met to-day," he said, "at the period of a very grave crisis; but at the same time I must confess that we meet under a certain sense of powerlessness and of impotence."

Numerous were the meetings and speeches which followed. On the 9th October Sir Stafford Northcote spoke; on the 11th the Home Secretary; and on the 17th and 18th Lord Salisbury spoke at a great Conservative demonstration at Manchester. There is a most valuable passage in a speech made by Lord Hartington at Manchester shortly after Lord Salisbury's visit there, which bears strong testimony to the position which the Platform had attained.

Lord Hartington, speaking at Manchester,[1] said: "I think it cannot have escaped the observation of any who have paid the slightest attention to public affairs how great is the contrast between the languid interest which has lately been excited by the debates in Parliament, and the intense interest now being raised by great public meetings such as this, which are being constantly held in all parts of the country in the interest of one or other of the political parties. Now, what

[1] 24th October 1879.

is the cause of this contrast? It is not that political interest in the country is flagging. The excitement and interest which are shown in these meetings are a proof that that is not the case. But undoubtedly it is the fact that, during the last two or three sessions, comparatively little interest was taken in the debates in Parliament. Is not the cause to be sought for in this, that the nation is beginning to feel that Parliament has ceased practically to control the issues of our policy? Long experience—the experience of five years—has proved that the Government has only to decide and to act, and that it is absolutely certain that whatever decision or action the Government resolves upon will be confirmed by the present House of Parliament. Well, I think that in this transfer of interest from Parliament to the country there is reason to give us hope, and there is every reason to stimulate our exertions."

The principal feature of this autumn Platform campaign was Mr. Gladstone's visit to Midlothian—the constituency which he had decided on contesting at the approaching general election. On the 24th November [1] he left Liverpool for Scotland. He spoke at several stations on the way where the train stopped. At Carlisle he said: "In eleven former dissolutions and elections it has been my fortune to take an active part, but in no one of those eleven, although they have extended over very nearly half a century, have I known the interests of the country to be so deeply and so vitally at stake as they are upon the dissolution that is now approaching."

In this his first campaign in Midlothian, his first speech was delivered in Edinburgh on the 25th November. It and his subsequent speeches constitute a good-sized volume in themselves, and cannot therefore be referred to in detail here; but a few extracts must be given from them, which testify in the most striking manner to the position to which the Platform had attained. In these Platform speeches there was not one subject which Parliament had treated during recent years that was reserved from mention; just as if it was not just as much the province of the Platform to deal with them as it was of Parliament itself. Peace, war, home affairs, foreign affairs, colonial affairs, Indian affairs, the prerogatives of the Crown—one and all were not merely referred to, but treated

[1] 1879.

in the fullest detail. Never had a more striking tribute been paid to the status and dignity of the Platform, never had its position been so fully recognised and acknowledged, not merely in word, but in act, as the superior, and ultimate arbiter of Parliament.

"Gentlemen, I have come into this county to repeat, with your permission, the indictment which I have to the best of my ability endeavoured to make many times elsewhere against her Majesty's Government. It is a very serious indictment. It is well in these things that men should be held to the words that they utter, should be made to feel that they are responsible for them, and therefore you will perhaps allow me to read a sentence which I embodied in the letter written in reply to your most flattering and most obliging invitation. My sentence was this: 'The management of finance, the scale of expenditure, the constantly growing arrears of legislation, serious as they are, only lead up to still greater questions. I hold before you, as I have held in the House of Commons, that the faith and honour of the country have been gravely compromised in the foreign policy of the Ministry; that by the disturbance of confidence, and lately even of peace, which they have brought about, they have prolonged and aggravated the public distress; that they have augmented the power and influence of the Russian empire, even while estranging the feelings of its population; that they have embarked the Crown and people in an unjust war (the Afghan war), full of mischief if not of positive danger to India; and that, by their use of the treaty-making and war-making powers of the Crown, they have abridged the just rights of Parliament, and have presented prerogative to the nation under an unconstitutional aspect which tends to make it insecure.' Not from one phrase, not from one syllable of that indictment, do I recede. If, gentlemen, in addressing this constituency there be any part of it upon which at the close I shall not seem to have made good the original statement, most glad shall I be to attend to the legitimate appeal of those who may think fit to challenge me upon the point, and to bring forward the matter—alas! only too abundant—by which every one of them can be substantiated before the world."

Almost more remarkable than the acknowledgment to the

rightful sphere of the Platform was the way in which the Platform was used, as it were, to indict Parliament. "I really have but one great anxiety. This is a self-governing country. Let us bring home to the minds of the people the state of the facts they have to deal with, and in Heaven's name let them determine whether or not this is the way in which they like to be governed. Do not let us suppose this is like the old question between Whig and Tory. It is nothing of the kind. It is not now as if we were disputing about some secondary matter; it is not even as if we were disputing about the Irish Church, which no doubt was a very important affair. What we are disputing about is a whole system of government, and to make good that proposition that it is a whole system of government will be my great object in any addresses that I may deliver in this county. It is no longer the Government with which you have to deal. You have to deal with the majority of the House of Commons. The majority of the House of Commons has completely acquitted the Government. Upon every occasion when the Government has appealed to it, the majority of the House of Commons has been ready to answer to the call. Hardly a man has ever hesitated to grant the confidence that was desired, however outrageous in our view the nature of the demand might be. Completely and bodily the majority of the House of Commons has taken on itself the responsibility of the Government—and not only the collective majority of the House of Commons, gentlemen. If you had got to deal with them by a vote of censure on that majority in the lump, that would be a very ineffective method of dealing. They must be dealt with individually. That majority is made up of units. It is the unit with which you have got to deal. And let me tell you that the occasion is a solemn one, for as I am the first to aver that now fully and bodily the majority of the House of Commons has, in the face of the country, by a multitude of repeated and deliberate acts, made itself wholly and absolutely responsible in the whole of these transactions that I have been commenting upon, and in many more; and as the House of Commons has done that, so upon the coming general election will it have to be determined whether that responsibility so shifted from an Administration to a Parliament, shall again be shifted from a Parliament to a nation. As yet the nation has had no opportunity, nay, as I pointed out early in these remarks, the Government do not seem disposed to give them the opportunity. To the last moment, so far as we are informed by the best authorities, they intend to withhold it. The nation, therefore, is not yet responsible. If faith has been broken, if blood has been needlessly shed, if the name of England has been discredited and lowered from that lofty standard which it ought to exhibit to the whole world, if the country has been needlessly distressed, if finance has been thrown into confusion, if the foundations of the Indian empire have been impaired, all these things as yet are the work of an Administration and a Parliament; but the day is coming, and is near at hand, when that event will take place which will lead the historian to declare whether or not they are the work, not of an Administration and not of a Parliament, but the work of a great and a free people. If this great and free and powerful people is disposed to associate itself with such transactions, if it is disposed to assume upon itself what some of us would call the guilt, and many of us must declare to be the heavy burden of all those events that have been passing before our eyes, it rests with them to do it. But, gentlemen, let every one of us resolve in his inner conscience, before God and before man, let him resolve that he at least will have no share in such a proceeding; that he will do his best to exempt himself, ay, that he will exempt himself, from every participation in what he believes to be mischievous and ruinous misdeeds; that, so far as his exertions can avail, no trifling, no secondary consideration shall stand in the way of them, or abate them; that he will do what in him lies to dissuade his countrymen from arriving at a resolution so full of mischief, of peril, and of shame. Gentlemen, this is the issue which the people of this country will have to try."

On the 26th Mr. Gladstone spoke at Dalkeith. On the 27th he spoke at West Calder. On the 29th he made a long speech in the Corn Exchange, Edinburgh, and then went on to a meeting at the Waverley Market, where some 20,000 persons were present. "There is nothing that I can say, or that much better and wiser men could say, to this meeting that is one-half as remarkable as the meeting itself. It is no light cause that has brought together—that has called off from their usual occupations to stand in such compressed mass before me—this great ocean of human life." . . .

On the 1st December, in the course of his journey farther north, he spoke at Dunfermline, Perth, and Aberfeldy Railway Stations. On the 5th December he spoke at Glasgow (6000). "Well, gentlemen, what then is the general upshot of this review in which I have been engaged since I came to Scotland? Let us look at it together. I will use the fewest words. We have finance in confusion; we have legislation in intolerable arrear; we have honour compromised by the breach of public law; we have public distress aggravated by the destruction of confidence; we have Russia aggrandised and yet estranged; we have Turkey befriended as we say, but mutilated, and sinking every day; we have Europe restless and disturbed; Europe, which, after the Treaty of Paris, at all events so far as the Eastern Question was concerned, had something like rest for a period approaching twenty years, has, almost ere the ink of the Treaty of Berlin is dry, been agitated from end to end with rumours and alarms, so that on the last 10th of November we were told that the Prime Minister thought that peace might be preserved, but on the previous 9th of November—namely, four months after the Treaty—it had been much more doubtful. In Africa you have before you the memory of bloodshed, of military disaster, the record of 10,000 Zulus—such is the computation of Bishop Colenso—slain for no other offence than their attempt to defend against your artillery with their naked bodies their hearths and homes, their wives and families. You have the invasion of a free people in the Transvaal; and you have, I fear, in one quarter or another,—I will not enter into details, which might be injurious to the public interest,—prospects of further disturbance and shedding of blood. You have Afghanistan ruined; you have India not advanced, but thrown back in government, subjected to heavy and unjust charges, subjected to what may well be termed, in comparison with the mild government of former years, a system of oppression; and with all this you have had at home, in matters which I will not now detail, the law broken, and the rights of Parliament invaded. Gentlemen, amidst the whole of this pestilent activity—for so I must call it—this distress and bloodshed which we have either produced or largely shared in producing, not in one instance down to the Treaty of Berlin, and down to the war in Afghanistan,—not in one instance did we either do a deed or speak an effectual word on behalf of liberty. Such is the upshot, gentlemen, of the sad enumeration.

"Gentlemen, I wish to end as I began. Is this the way, or is this not the way, in which a free nation, inhabiting these islands, wishes to be governed? Will the people, be it now or be it months hence, ratify the deeds that have been done, and assume upon themselves that tremendous responsibility? The whole humble aim, gentlemen, of my proceedings has been to bring home, as far as was in my power, this great question to the mind and to the conscience of the community at large."

During the fortnight he spent north of the Tweed Mr. Gladstone addressed on various occasions personally upwards of 75,000 people, and were the vast crowds who assembled in various places to do him honour computed, it may fairly be said that something like a quarter of a million of persons took some part in the demonstrations everywhere evoked by the mere announcement of an intended visit.[1]

Even a hostile critic bore testimony to the extraordinary character of this performance.[2] "As a personal achievement it is as marvellous as anything in his whole career. The mental and physical energy, the powers of endurance, the unfailing resources of rhetoric which sustained and animated the whole course of his "campaign," amply account for the enthusiasm of his supporters; and displayed by a veteran statesman nearly seventy years old, must extort the respect and admiration even of his opponents."

The opening of the new year saw the Platform in full swing again—Minister after Minister and ex-Minister after ex-Minister carrying on the political war by Platform speeches. Up to the eve of the meeting of Parliament the strife continued.

"It was estimated that in the course of this recess more speeches had been made by Cabinet Ministers than in all the recesses of other Parliaments put together."[3]

Parliament met on the 5th February. On the 8th of March,

1 See the volume of Mr. Gladstone's Midlothian speeches.

2 See *Blackwood's Magazine*, January 1880.

3 *Annual Register*, 1880, p. 5.

quite suddenly and unexpectedly, the announcement was made that on as early a date as possible her Majesty, with the advice of her Ministers, would dissolve Parliament. It came as a great surprise, and caused great excitement throughout the country. The issues chosen by the Government for the decision of the country were set forth by Lord Beaconsfield—not in the Queen's Speech, as was the fashion in pre-reform days, not in Parliament, not from the Platform, but in a letter to the Lord Lieutenant of Ireland. One issue was the inevitable question of Ireland, and the other was the foreign policy of the Government—on which a vote of confidence was asked for.

The first ex-ministerial speech was made by Mr. Gladstone at a meeting at Marylebone on the 12th March, where he spoke "as an elector." "That on which I have long insisted," he said, "is, that upon the present occasion all the separate questions are swallowed up and absorbed in one question, and that question is—Does this nation approve or does this nation condemn the manner in which the Government of this country has of late been carried on?"

He announced Lord Derby's accession to the Liberal party. . . . He expressed the hope that whatever the answer of the country might be, it should be clear and unequivocal. . . . "I also hope the answer will be right. We stand here in the cause of law—in the cause of liberty. We stand here to maintain the institutions of the country against men falsely called Conservatives, who have handled them worse, and in some respects have brought them into greater insecurity than I have ever known them in. We are here in the cause of law—in the cause of liberty, of order, of prosperity, and of prudence at home. We are here in the cause of faith, honour, and peace abroad."

Lord Hartington, the official leader of the Opposition, began his campaign in North-East Lancashire on the following day, with a speech to a large meeting at Accrington. On the 16th Mr. Gladstone left London for Scotland, speaking on the way at Grantham, York, Newcastle, and Berwick to several thousand people. On the 17th he resumed his campaign in Midlothian with a long speech.

"The battle of the elections," wrote *The Times*,[1] "may be

[1] 18th March 1880.

considered to have commenced in earnest when we have to report an opening speech of five columns by Mr. Gladstone, as well as a mass of meetings in other constituencies, with addresses by minor lights of both parties.

"It may be to a good many candidates a rather unwelcome truth, but it had better, we think, be told. It is that at this stage of affairs it matters comparatively little what is said on either side. We have practically had the electoral campaign fought out beforehand during the past year."

The Ministers were prevented taking very energetic action on the Platform by the fact of their having still to attend in Parliament to wind up the business before the dissolution. Some of them, however, began their election campaign about this time—Mr. Smith speaking on the 17th, and Mr. Cross at Warrington on the 18th. On this same day Mr. Gladstone made two long speeches, and on the following day another. On the 21st he made three speeches, on the 22d two. Two Ministers also spoke on the 22d, also Lord Hartington. On the 23d no less than five Ministers spoke and three ex-Ministers.

On the 24th Parliament was dissolved. The next day the Chancellor of the Exchequer, Sir Stafford Northcote, thus put the issue before the country at a meeting in Devonshire: "I venture," he said, "to ask you to which party is it safer to entrust our interests—to the party who will be always apologising for what has happened, to the party who will be always endeavouring to explain away their position, or who will only defend it with that half-heartedness which necessarily belongs to a belief that they have a bad case? Or will they consider it safer to entrust your interests to those who are firmly convinced that in all they have done, and in all that England has supported them in doing, they have acted from pure hearts and pure consciences, and who will be prepared to maintain the position which they hope they have won for England, not only with thorough and unbroken courage, but with thorough and unbroken confidence in the justice of that position?"

The first nominations were made on the 30th March, when some few unopposed seats were filled. The first pollings took place on the 31st. From the outset the Liberals were successful.

It has been stated[1] that during the campaign Mr. Gladstone made no fewer than fifteen great speeches, Lord Hartington twenty-four, Mr. Bright six, Mr. W. H. Smith six, Sir Stafford Northcote six, Colonel Stanley nine, and Sir William Harcourt six, besides speeches innumerable on lesser occasions. This, however startling a phenomenon it may be on account of the high position of the speakers, represented but a fraction of the actual amount of platforming. In every one of the 658 constituencies in the United Kingdom, contested or uncontested, the Platform was used. In the contested constituencies it was used nearly daily by all candidates, several times daily by some, and there was a larger number of contests than ever before. Over a thousand candidates for Parliamentary honours, all speaking at the same time, asserting and denying, arguing or entreating, speaking not merely for days, but weeks, to audiences of hundreds and thousands—some even, through the Press, to the audience of the nation—to this, from the small beginnings chronicled in this work—the eighteen contested elections for the first Parliament of George III.'s reign—had the election Platform come in the year 1880.

When the election was over the Liberals were found to be in a large majority, and the Platform had its revenge for the refusal of the Executive to regard its voice. Foiled in its efforts to influence as it wished the conduct of the members of Parliament, it had recourse to the slower and more arduous but more effective alternative of endeavouring to influence the electorate. That it succeeded in that endeavour the General Election of 1880 afforded the most irrefragable proof.

[1] See *The New Parliament*, 1880, by William Saunders, p. 38.

CHAPTER XXIII

THE THIRD REFORM ACT AGITATION

The Liberal triumph at the General Election of 1880 led up to the last great display of Platform activity which remains to be chronicled—the agitation of 1884, for the extension of the franchise to the county householder.

The nearer we approach the present time, the more difficult it is to assign exclusively or definitely to the Platform the initiation of any great reform; the forces of political life have become so much more closely interwoven, and act and react on each other so rapidly that it is hard to separate them.

On this occasion, however, the really interesting and important point of the matter is, not so much as to how far the Platform originated and forced to completion this last great constitutional reform, but the proof which the agitation affords of how completely and thoroughly the greatest and highest statesmen of the day have adopted the Platform for the purpose of the discussion of measures actually before Parliament, and how completely the Platform has been incorporated into the governing institutions of the country.

The identity of the borough and county franchise had long been regarded as a desirable object to be attained. The Reform Act of 1867 had made the distinction between the two more marked and anomalous than before, and many years did not elapse until the anomaly began to engage active consideration. In 1872 the subject was brought before Parliament by Mr. Trevelyan, who moved: "That this House would be more likely to devote due and adequate attention to the wants and interests of our rural population, if householders outside the boundaries of Parliamentary boroughs were in possession of the franchise; and that it is expedient to extend to counties the occupation and lodging franchises now in force in boroughs." The motion was rejected.

Year after year the subject was again raised in Parliament. In 1876 the redistribution of seats—"so as to obtain a more complete representation of the opinion of the electoral body"—was tacked on to it, but equally ineffectually.

In 1877 the Platform began definitely to take up the question. On the 16th May in that year a conference of delegates from all parts of England was held in Exeter Hall, London. Mr. Bright, who took the chair, pronounced that there had been, to his mind, no more remarkable public meeting or conference held in his time. More than thirty members of Parliament were on the Platform, and the audience included upwards of 2500 representatives of the unenfranchised county householders from every quarter of England.

The more exciting topic of the Eastern Question prevented any immediate progress being made, but the advent to power of a Liberal Government in 1880 was a guarantee that the subject would be dealt with. The Platform waited patiently, but as year after year slipped past, and still no sign was made by the Government, it began again to move.

In May 1883 a meeting was held in London of the National Liberal Federation, and a resolution passed urging the Government to introduce a Bill extending the franchise to householders in counties. It was then resolved that in order to ascertain and formulate the opinions of the Liberal party on this question, a conference of representatives of all Liberal organisations throughout the country should be called.

Accordingly such a conference was called, and met at Leeds on the 17th October 1883. It was attended by representatives from about 500 Liberal Associations from all parts of the country. Mr. J. Morley presided. "The present Conference," he said, "was a proof of the conviction which was growing in the Radical party, that it was not enough for them to be the helpless exponents of excellent ideas, but that they must organise, they must unite, and they must co-operate. Their starting-point was that reform was necessary; their discussion was to be as to procedure and details."

After considerable discussion as to the question of the precedence of Parliamentary Reform, London Government Reform, and Local Government Reform, it was decided, while leaving the decision to the Government, to recommend the

Government to give the precedence to Parliamentary reform, and a resolution was passed "That this Conference, believing that the extension of the franchise is a matter of paramount and urgent importance, is of opinion that it is the duty of her Majesty's Government to introduce a Bill dealing with the question in the next session of Parliament."

A resolution was also carried that a franchise Bill having been passed, a measure should follow for the redistribution of seats, such as would give as nearly as possible an equal value to every vote, and secure a true expression of the will of the nation.

In the evening of the 18th a great meeting (5000) was held in the Town Hall, at which Mr. Bright presided; and a resolution was passed approving of the action of the Conference.

In a subsequent criticism on this Conference *The Times*[1] wrote: "It marked an epoch in the history of the present movement for reform; it first gave substance and purpose to the popular demand for the extension of the franchise, and probably determined in no small measure the mode adopted by the Government in dealing with the question."

On the 29th February 1884 Mr. Gladstone moved in the House of Commons for leave to introduce a Bill assimilating the county and borough franchise, or, in other words, extending the franchise to every householder in counties. The measure proposed would, it was estimated, add 2,000,000 of voters to the electoral body. A measure for the redistribution of seats would follow the next session. The Bill passed the House of Commons by large majorities. In the House of Lords, however, the Bill was, on the 8th July, what some called "hung up," others "rejected," by the adoption of a resolution not to assent to its second reading until their Lordships had knowledge of the Government scheme of the redistribution of seats.

Lord Salisbury, the leader of the Conservative party, speaking in the House of Lords,[2] announced the policy of his party. "In the presence of such vast proposals," he said, "we appeal to the people. . . . We do not shrink from bowing to the opinion of the people, whatever that opinion may be. . . . But now that the people have in no real sense been

[1] 31st July 1884.

[2] *Parliamentary Debates*, vol. ccxc. p. 469.

consulted, when they had at the last general election no notion of what was coming upon them, I feel that we are bound, as guardians of their interests, to call upon the Government to appeal to the people, and by the result of that appeal we will abide."

Instantly, on the rejection of the Bill by the Lords, the Platform was appealed to to decide the strife between the two Houses of Parliament. All through the winter and spring it had been by no means idle, and the Conservative leaders had been freely using it; but its action was little more than that normal state of activity to which we have become accustomed in these later days. Now it entered on one of those great crises which prove its vast utility, and demonstrate its tremendous power.

It is impossible to go into details of the speeches, nor is it necessary to show how the subject was threshed out to the last straw by the Platform. I wish rather to bring into prominence the actions of our leading politicians as regards the Platform, and to cull from their speeches such passages as reveal their views on the Platform.

The Platform led off with a great reform demonstration in Hyde Park on the 21st July, and, to emphasise its import, the day selected for it was a week-day, when attendance at it meant the loss of a day's wages to most of those who attended. A huge procession of some 25,000 to 30,000, which took three hours to pass a given point, marched through the streets of London to Hyde Park. There were representatives from endless numbers of political and trades organisations, and clubs, and associations; there were banners innumerable, and numerous bands of music. "We will have the Bill." "The Franchise for every working man." "The Government for the people." "Give us the vote." "We demand the vote." "The people's will—the Franchise Bill and the reform of the House of Lords." "Shall the peers rob the people of their vote?" These were some of the mottoes on the banners. The streets were crowded with spectators. The procession was not barred out of Hyde Park as in 1866, but was given unrestricted admission. Tens of thousands had assembled in the Park, and seven platforms had been constructed for the speakers. One identical resolution was proposed at all of them.

"Resolved—That this vast assembly, consisting of seven enormous meetings, . . . emphatically protests against the rejection of the Representation of the People Bill by an irresponsible and unrepresentative House of Lords, notwithstanding its almost unanimous acceptance by the people, and the people's accredited representatives; and it approves Mr. Gladstone's action in advising her Majesty to summon an autumn session of Parliament, and his determination to send up the Bill again to the peers; and further expresses its opinion that the continued existence of an unchecked power of impeding and obstructing the popular will at present exercised by the House of Peers is not conducive either to the welfare of the people or the peace and prosperity of the country. That a copy of this Resolution be sent to the Prime Minister."

At five of the platforms members of Parliament presided, and from all seven numerous speeches were made, most of them animadverting in strong language on the action of the Lords. At the close of the proceedings the huge meeting peaceably dispersed.

"There was some talk of demonstrating against the houses of Conservative peers, but the leaders of the demonstration gave it clearly to be understood that any persons who did so would be regarded as public enemies, and would be delivered up to the police." [1]

The Times' criticism on the demonstration is very valuable as showing the manner in which such occurrences had come to be regarded.

"Yesterday London witnessed a great and imposing spectacle. . . . It was a demonstration made by the people and for the people, and it exhibited every sign of spontaneity and enthusiasm. . . . These men were no roughs paid to shout at the word of command; they were no idlers gathered together to enjoy a holiday or an outing. They gathered spontaneously for a special and legitimate purpose, and they fulfilled that purpose with perfect good humour and good sense, and with as little interference as possible with the convenience of their fellow-citizens. . . . If the demonstration was to be permitted at all—and after the experience of 1866 no man in his senses would have dreamt of forbidding it—the only prudent course

[1] *The Times*, 22d July 1884.

for the authorities to take was to leave it to organise itself. This course was taken, and its prudence was amply justified by the issue.

"It is impossible to praise too highly the good conduct of the people. There was no violence, no confusion . . . all was spontaneous, all was orderly, all was good-humoured. . . . Demonstrations of this magnitude are not frequent in this country. It is not at all expedient that they should become frequent, or that they should be resorted to on light occasions. But their very infrequency is the measure of their significance, and the test of their sincerity, and their moral effect is, therefore, the greater in proportion as their occurrence is rare. . . . There was absolutely nothing revolutionary; there was not even an approach to disorder in yesterday's proceedings."

Parliament was still sitting, but the leader of the Tory Opposition in the House of Lords, and of the Conservative party in the country, Lord Salisbury, Prime Minister designate, descended from the Olympian heights, dragging his colleagues after him, to plunge into the battle on the plains. It was a very striking incident—a great change from the unbroken silences of the Tory leaders in the days not so very long past.

A great Conservative demonstration was held at Sheffield on the 22d July. Here Lord Salisbury spoke from the Platform. He insisted that as the two Houses of Parliament were at variance, the Government should dissolve Parliament and appeal to the country to decide between them. "The House of Commons was elected upon issues that have passed away; its life has been nearly spent; it is the most servile House of Commons —servile to the Minister, servile to the caucus—that the Palace of Westminster has ever seen; and we are denounced because we will not allow this House of Commons, so discredited— discredited by every circumstance, discredited by every by-election that takes place—to settle upon an unsound, partisan, and inequitable basis the Constitution which we are appointed to protect.

"The Government set up all sorts of shams and counterfeits; they descend into the streets; they call for processions; they imagine that 30,000 radicals going to amuse themselves in

London on a given day expresses the public opinion of the country. That is not the way in which a progressive, cultured, and civilised State determines the opinions of its citizens. Nothing can have been more good-humoured as yet than the multitudes of their own partisans whom they have summoned into the streets to keep them in countenance. But they appeal to the streets; they attempt legislation by picnic —but that has its dangerous side. There is no more hopeless condition in which a popularly governed State can be plunged than when its policy is decided by demonstrations held in the streets of the metropolis; and to that end, I am afraid, the Government would be very sorry to come. At all events, they will resist to the best of their power the legitimate appeal. But we must keep the truth in this matter clearly before our eyes. If they do not want the opinion of the people, if they are content to go on with the ordinary constitutional powers of the two Houses of Parliament, it is open for them to do so, and I have no doubt that the business of the country will not seriously suffer. . . . A party can speak by processions and demonstrations, but the nation can only speak at the polling booth, and any attempt to substitute the counterfeit voice which is manufactured by the caucus, will assuredly not lead to a true ascertainment of the feelings of the people, and will be bitterly and indignantly repudiated when the people have their voice."

"We, at all events," he said, "will not consent to be guided by the public opinion of the streets."

Whilst the leader of the Opposition in the House of Lords was thus making use of the Platform for his party's ends, his first lieutenant, the leader of the Opposition in the House of Commons, was simultaneously using it in a different part of the country.

The next night the discussion was taken up by Mr. Chamberlain, who spoke at the Devonshire Club, commenting on Lord Salisbury's speech—point by point—as closely as if he were in the same House of Parliament as Lord Salisbury, or Lord Salisbury were in the House of Commons, and speaking to him across the table of the House. Lord Salisbury proclaimed the policy of the Conservative party in the struggle; Mr. Chamberlain proclaimed the Liberal. "We have, with all the calmness of conscious strength, in the assurance of certain victory, to pursue the constitutional issues which he has raised; and we have to sweep away obstacles which now cut off this vast multitude of unenfranchised men from the political rights to which, by universal consent, they are entitled. We have also to assert—and we shall not shrink from the task—the supremacy of popular rights and representative institutions over personal authority and hereditary privilege."

And now the fight waxed hot and furious. To the perpetual accompaniment of minor meetings all over the country, Ministers and ex-Ministers debated, discussed, asserted, and denied, almost without intermission at public meetings, north, south, east, and west. On the 25th July Mr. W. H. Smith spoke in London. On the following day two great Liberal meetings were held at the Pomona Gardens, Manchester, in support of the Franchise Bill, Lord Hartington and Mr. Bright speaking at them. Lord Hartington said: "I will endeavour to state as briefly as I can the main objects for which I conceive that this and similar meetings have been called. If I am not much mistaken, before the month of October next there will be meetings, not so large, but similar in character to this, in every town, in every district, and in every village in the north of England, and they will, in the main, be actuated by the same objects as have called us here to-day.

"I take those objects to be, in the first place, to show the strong determination which animates all classes in this country, the enfranchised and the unenfranchised alike, to secure the enfranchisement of the householders in counties. Secondly, I take it that we are met together to express our confidence in the Government of Mr. Gladstone, and in the procedure which that Government proposes to adopt in order to carry into effect the object we have in view; and thirdly, I take it that we intend to protest against the unprecedented, and, as we consider, the unconstitutional action of the House of Lords, or a majority of the House of Lords, to dictate to the Government when, and at what time, a dissolution of Parliament shall take place."

The next day Sir Stafford Northcote was again platforming; and the day after that—namely, on the 28th July—Lord Salisbury and Sir S. Northcote addressed a large meeting of the representatives of the Conservative Associations of the metropolis and of the home counties, held at Cannon Street Hotel. About 1000 persons were present, and the Lord Mayor presided. Nearly 300 associations were represented.

Lord Salisbury's speech was a criticism on Mr. Chamberlain's, Mr. Bright's, and Lord Hartington's speeches, just as if he had actually heard them all delivered in Parliament; but it is interesting also as containing an acknowledgment of the advantages of Platform discussion—an avowal which few of his predecessors, Sir R. Peel or Canning excepted, would have thought of making. "It is one of the advantages of the thorough discussion which I hope this question will receive before November that all false pretences and all hollow pretexts will be repudiated, and the cause which logically and constitutionally has the right will be triumphantly established."

Sir Stafford Northcote's speech was even more interesting. He said: " . . . We shall be told that we are saying the same thing over and over again. But it is not a question of what the speeches are, but a question of the audiences to whom they are delivered. If the same speeches are delivered at Manchester, Sheffield, Newcastle, or Liverpool, the question is, Who are the audiences to whom they are addressed, and what is the effect upon these audiences, and whether we are bringing these matters home to them by meeting them face to face and encouraging them in the battle which they have to fight ?"

But it was mainly interesting as being a defence of that very caucus-organisation which, when employed by the Liberals, was so heinous an offence. "There is nothing common about the meeting we are addressing to-night," said Sir S. Northcote. "It is no mere gathering of some 1000 or 2000 persons representing some particular constituency. It is a representative meeting of those who are charged to come here on behalf of those metropolitan constituencies which, whatever Mr. Gladstone and his friends may say about them, are at the centre of knowledge and power. . . . One of the battles we have to fight is the battle of the metropolis and of the metropolitan counties, and we are fighting it in the best possible way—not through some casual mass meetings, not through organised processions at 8s. a head, but by calling together our chiefs of the staff, our working committees, our representatives of the associations all round, to give them the word, which in turn they are to pass to those behind."

On the 30th July Lord Northbrook spoke at Hull, Sir M. Hicks-Beach at Stroud, and Mr. W. H. Smith at Shoreditch.

The 4th of August was another great day. Sir Stafford Northcote and Mr. W. H. Smith spoke at Hughenden, while Lord Hartington spoke at Birmingham, after a great reform demonstration which was held there in the day—a demonstration of which *The Times* wrote: "It may fairly be questioned whether any previous demonstration there could compare in point of magnitude, organisation, and imposing effect with the monster procession and open-air gathering of to-day."

The 10th of August was even more prolific in speaking. The ex-War Secretary spoke at Lancaster, whilst a great Conservative demonstration took place at Pomona Gardens, Manchester—a counter-demonstration to that of the Liberals. The meeting was announced as one "to protest against the dictation of the caucus, and to support the demand of the House of Lords for a complete Reform Bill." Sir R. Cross presided. There was also an "overflow meeting," and Lord Salisbury and Sir M. Hicks-Beach spoke at both of them.

Lord Salisbury, who was so averse to the opinion of the streets, gloried in the opinions of the gardens. "I believe that the numbers assembled for the present demonstration exceed anything of which we have had experience before, and that as many as 120,000 tickets have been taken for this demonstration." Lord Hartington's, Mr. Bright's, and Mr. Chamberlain's speeches were commented on and replied to.

It is specially worthy of note that all these meetings were held, and all this speechifying, or "haranguing," as it used to be called, took place while Parliament was actually sitting, for Parliament was not prorogued until the 14th August. Never, in fact, in the whole history of the country so far had the discussion of a great public measure been so completely taken out of the hands of Parliament, while Parliament was actually sitting, and transferred absolutely and entirely to the Platform.

Never had the use of the Platform for the purposes of discussion been so palpably and incontestably proved. It is still a part of some people's political creed that the Platform cannot discuss questions. One may reasonably ask what more or what greater discussion could any topic have received than the discussion this one received by the Platform? What more convincing proof could there be of the belief held by our greatest statesmen as to efficiency of Platform discussion than that, while Parliament was actually sitting, they should desert Parliament for the Platform.

A week later Parliament was prorogued. Sir M. Hicks-Beach spoke at Portsmouth, and a couple of days later—namely, on the 23d August—there was a great Conservative meeting at Nostell Priory, where Sir S. Northcote spoke twice.

A week later the Prime Minister, freed from Parliamentary cares, went down and addressed his constituents. His speech was awaited with the keenest anxiety. Following somewhat the lines of the Reform agitation of 1831–32, the agitation had been assuming—ever more decidedly—the form of an agitation against the House of Lords. The special measure of the extension of the franchise to a certain extent sank, or was merged into the greater question of the continuance of an hereditary Upper Chamber of Parliament. That House was again standing in the way of a great measure of right and justice, and ominous murmurs were plainly audible—murmurs best preçised in the formula, "Bend them, mend them, or end them," each of which three courses had countless advocates and supporters. For the Platform was not occupied alone by Cabinet and ex-Cabinet Ministers, but the whole rank and file of Parliament were orating and "haranguing" on the subject in speeches too numerous even to calculate, and there was an air of deep substantial meaning in the agitation which had scarce been visible since 1832.

When the Prime Minister's speech was delivered, it absorbed the attention of the Empire. No more momentous speech has been delivered in recent times. A few words from the speaker, of one sort, would have fanned into a consuming flame the agitation against the House of Lords; a few words of another sort would soothe and still the rising passions of the people. The future trembled on the utterances of the speaker. Just as in the great crisis of the Reform agitation of 1832, when Attwood had described the people of England as standing "like greyhounds on the slip," so now they were straining to be let go. But the signal was not dropped. The moderation of the speech was its great characteristic.

"What is the purpose with which I have come among you?" . . . said the Prime Minister. "It is to promote, by every legitimate means in my power, the speedy passing of the Franchise Bill. . . .

"The rejection of that Bill has already drawn in its train other questions of the gravest kind, and has suggested to the minds of a vast portion of the people the inquiry, Whether the time has come when it will be necessary to study the means of introducing an organic change into the constitution of the House of Lords? Now, gentlemen, into that question it is not my intention on this occasion to enter. The controversy now before us with regard to the Franchise Bill is sufficiently weighty, and the field sufficiently wide. Should the passing of that measure be delayed, I have no doubt that the field of that controversy will become wider still. But my duty as a Minister of the Crown—speaking for myself, and I believe expressing with tolerable fidelity the opinions of my colleagues—my duty as a Minister of the Crown is not to look into the far future while the work of the day demands every energy, and more than every energy, that we possess. What we want is a national expression of opinion in the constitutional modes familiar to this country upon this great question—Whether two millions of your fellow-subjects are to be admitted to a share in political and Parliamentary power? That is enough for me to put before you. Others are more free to enter into what may or may not happen in the ulterior stages of this great conflict. But for my part I seek to avoid them. It may be the timidity of age—it may be the indolence from which none of us are altogether free,—but I own to you, gentlemen, that I look with reluctance to entering upon questions of organic change in the constitution of this country, unless and until the moment comes when I can no longer deny their necessity. I believe that the House of Lords has not yet placed itself in a position of irretrievable error, I believe it is possible it may go back, and may go back with dignity and with honour. . . .

"There is another point upon which I will not endeavour to touch to-day, which is the allegation that the House of Lords is not willing to give way to the House of Commons, but it is willing to give way to the people. Perhaps I may be able to refer to that matter more at length upon another day. But I will venture to say this: the doctrine that it is the function of the House of Lords to point out the time of dissolution, and to determine when the country is to be referred to, is a doctrine which has no place whatever in our history or our Constitution. To tamper with that doctrine, to give it the smallest countenance, to admit one jot or tittle of it, would, in my opinion, be treason to British liberty; and I tell you fairly, I would far rather abandon my share in the Franchise Bill, and that which would go with it, my share in political life, than for one moment cease to raise the loudest protest in my power against the introduction of this, the grossest innovation which, either in a reformed Parliament or in an unreformed Parliament, was ever heard of, by a majority of the House of Lords. . . .

"I have said that I shall avoid all discussion on the future constitution of the House of Lords. I will go one step farther, and I hope you won't consider it a sign of weakness. I know that Scotch politics, as they are distinguished by great firmness, are also distinguished by great forbearance and great tolerance; and I hope you will extend to me that forbearance when I tell you that I am not at all averse to the intermixture of the hereditary principle in the constitution of the House of Lords. In a mixed society, in a mixed Government, it has many merits as qualifying the action of many other principles which would be more unchecked without it. But, in my opinion, the worst enemy of the hereditary principle is the man who places it in direct conflict, brow to brow, with the elective and representative principle. If the hereditary chamber deliberately involves itself in that conflict and perseveres in it, it is treading the pathway which leads to an issue that I will not describe, but it is not that of safety or of honour."

Reporting the incidents of the meeting, *The Times* reporter said: "It was noteworthy that Mr. Gladstone's declaration of his personal adherence to the principle of an hereditary House was received in silence, broken only by a few faint murmurs of dissent. When, however, he proceeded to warn the peers that they were placing the hereditary principle in jeopardy by provoking a contest with the representative House and with the people, he was cheered to the echo. Tremendous cheering also followed his declaration that the doctrine that the House of Lords had a right to fix the time for the dissolution of Parliament was a doctrine that had no place in our history or our Constitution, and was foreign to British liberty."

On the 1st September Mr. Gladstone again addressed a large meeting at the same place, and in the evening he addressed a meeting of the working men of Edinburgh in the Waverley Market.

Mr. Gladstone said: "In the crisis at which we have arrived, what we, the Ministers of the Crown, desire is to hear the voice of the nation. I thank you for enabling me to meet this vast assemblage, which, vast as it is, I chiefly rejoice in, because its gathering together is perfectly spontaneous. It is not under the command of any organisation. It is not collected by the use of the long purse of a wealthy party. It has not been assembled by providing gratuitous tickets by railway for the purpose of bringing together the population of many counties, or at least that portion of the population which can be induced to come. These are not the means, gentlemen, by which you have been brought together. It has been by your own personal and conscientious impulse, and the request made to me to receive your address has been prompted from yourselves. . . .

"Gentlemen, you see how wide is the difference between our opponents and ourselves; but let me tell you that the decision of this question does not rest with us. It rests with the nation. It is the voice of the nation that will prevail. We, the Ministers of the Crown, have scrupled to assume a great activity in stirring up the people, because we consider that the expression of opinion which we desire and invite ought to be their act and not ours. Consequently, though I have come here to address my friends and constituents in Midlothian, neither I nor the Ministers in general have gone scampering about the country, first to this place and then to that, in order to make a sort of show of opposition to the

House of Lords in this important matter. No, gentlemen, we look to you for your support, for a full, free, natural expression of opinion and conviction."

Some little time elapsed before the Conservatives renewed the Platform combat. On the 9th September, however, Sir R. Cross spoke near Liverpool, and the day after at Kilmarnock. On the 15th Sir Stafford Northcote spoke twice, and the ex-Postmaster-General once, at Edinburgh, and the next day Sir S. Northcote again spoke at Edinburgh.

The day following (17th September) Mr. Gladstone, while travelling in Scotland, received several addresses, and, in replying to one from Montrose, he said: "I rejoice in these local manifestations, because what is desired by the Ministers upon this occasion is to know whether they are acting in conformity with the views, the fixed convictions, and the reasonable desires of the nation; and although we see with great satisfaction large and spontaneous assemblages of men, such as took place in Manchester and in London, where the working classes, prompted by themselves, sent their deputations from great distances to take part in a very remarkable demonstration, yet I am still better pleased with their purely local manifestations."

And replying on the same day to an address from the Brechin Liberal Association, he said: "We, I trust, shall do our parts, but it is to the sober and deliberate manifestation of public opinion throughout the land that we trust. You, I am bound to say, are doing yours. These local declarations are the very thing that we want; they express the true sentiment of the people; they do not proceed from central agency; they do not represent the accumulation of men swept from vast distances into one spot to make a show of public opinion. What I see is the fruit of the soil upon which I stand."

On the 18th September two Conservative ex-Ministers "platformed." On the 21st the Prime Minister again found occasion to use the Platform: "I am of opinion," he said at Coupar Angus, "that these local meetings in places comparatively small are, in some respects, more remarkable even than the great assemblages in the large towns. They afford a proof that it is not only in those places where political intelligence circulates rapidly and powerfully that there is a feeling on this matter, but that it pervades the whole of the land; it descends into the minutest channels of social influence."

On the 23d Sir Stafford Northcote spoke twice at Newcastle; and on the 24th Mr. Gladstone was again doing what used to be called "haranguing." On the 24th September he spoke at Perth. "The nation cannot live in a daily agitation of politics. It is only upon these occasions that it can be roused to act. The calls of your private and individual lives are far too urgent to enable you from day to day to be considering as a nation what is done by one or the other House of Parliament, and forming opinions on one or the other of the thousand questions continually before them. It is only in these great crises that it is possible to address a call to the heart and mind of the country sufficient to bring about anything of the manifestations that are now so abundantly before our eyes."

Two days later, on his way home, he made a final speech at Carlisle. But scarcely had the Prime Minister gone into retirement than the Prime Minister designate took up the running.

On the 30th September Lord Salisbury arrived in Scotland. Imitating Mr. Gladstone's example, he spoke at different places in the course of his journey—to this had a Conservative Prime Minister designate come.

It may be thought that the activity of the Platform up to this in this agitation was sufficiently remarkable; but what had hitherto taken place was as nothing to its activity in this month of October 1884.

On the 1st Mr. W. H. Smith spoke at Newport, in the Isle of Wight; and on the same day Lord Salisbury addressed the Conservative Associations of the west of Scotland in Glasgow. He said: "The doctrine that you can determine the wishes of the people of England by demonstrations, or processions, or meetings, or addresses on railway platforms, is utterly new and utterly untenable. . . . It is not from demonstrations of that kind that you can gather what the opinions of the people are. The truth is, that there is no way of ascertaining who are on one side and who are on the other, except by the elementary process of counting them. There is no other way of ascertaining it save by summoning them to the poll where they can be constitutionally counted. . . . I reject as utterly unconstitutional and new the idea that, by those who come out in processions or who come to meetings, the opinion of the people can be discerned. . . . Now putting aside the evidence of demonstrations, which are very useful for bringing the party together, for inducing men to work for a common cause, for assuring them that they have co-operation, but which are not useful as a substitute for the constitutional process of election, let us inquire, etc."

On the 3d October Lord Salisbury delivered another long speech in Glasgow, and a shorter one at an overflow meeting; and the next day Lord Hartington addressed two meetings of his constituents in North-East Lancashire.

On the 6th the "National Liberal Federation" held its annual meeting at Stoke, and Mr. Chamberlain was present. "The question which is before us," he said, "is, Whether this country is to be governed by its people or by the peers, whether popular rights are to prevail, or whether arbitrary authority and privilege are to rule?" There was a large procession and a demonstration of some 30,000 people, and there were five platforms at the place of meeting, and in the evening more than a dozen meetings were held in the neighbouring towns.

The following day Mr. Chamberlain spoke at two meetings at Hanley. "Every now and again, at rare intervals, the whole country seems to be stirred by some deep and common impulse. The voice of the nation rises and swells until it drowns the feeble notes of faction, and pronounces in unmistakable terms a nation's will. Something of that sort occurred when there was a feeling of horror and indignation evoked by the outrages in Bulgaria. . . . And again the same thing happened when Mr. Plimsoll roused the conscience of the nation to the iniquity of sacrificing brave men's lives to the supposed necessity of commercial enterprise. . . . The agitation in which we are engaged is rapidly assuming a similar character. A great wave of excitement has passed over the country. The torrent is still rising. Yesterday it was Scotland; to-day it is the Midland district; to-morrow it will be Wales; and everywhere it is not a party agitation—it is something like a real uprising of the people. . . . Up to the present time we have had at least five times as many meetings as our opponents have had, and our meetings have been ten times as numerously attended; but that is not the most important distinction. Our meetings have been, as far as I know, in almost every case open meetings—true assemblies of the people. Our opponents have not dared to hold one single free and open meeting in the course of this agitation except one at Darlington, where they were defeated by a large majority, and one at Bournemouth, where they attempted a procession which was incontinently broken up. . . . How long is this state of effervescence and agitation rapidly degenerating into irritation to continue? These great gatherings are only held at considerable inconvenience. They effect a great disturbance of ordinary business, and they involve much personal sacrifice."

On the same evening Sir M. Hicks-Beach was speaking at Bristol.

On the 9th the Home Secretary spoke at Derby, and the ex-Home Secretary at a meeting near Liverpool.

The 11th was a memorable day. Lord Hartington addressed a great meeting or demonstration of some 15,000 at Chatsworth. "I fear I must admit that we have hardly come here to-day for the purpose of discussion. Discussion can be conducted more conveniently at meetings less vast than the present. We have come essentially to demonstrate, and to show that in the opinion of the vast mass of the people of this country there does exist a strong and an earnest desire that the household vote should be extended to the county householder."

Sir William Harcourt also spoke at the same meeting. And on the same day Lord Salisbury spoke at Kelso, and Sir Richard Cross at Wigan. Thus, on the one day two Cabinet and two ex-Cabinet Ministers were utilising the Platform. What a contrast to the time when a single speech from Canning was the sum total of Ministerial Platform oratory in a whole year, and was thought a most noteworthy and memorable event, or even those darker ages when the voice of a Minister was never heard from one year's end to another except in Parliament.

On the 13th October Sir Stafford Northcote spoke at Birmingham, and here, unfortunately, the meeting was broken up by some of the Liberals, and there was considerable disturbance. "A scene thoroughly disgraceful to English politics," wrote *The Times;* "a conpicuous offence against public liberty."

In the course of the three following days no less than ten Platform speeches were made by Ministers or ex-Ministers. Sir Stafford Northcote spoke twice at Birmingham, twice at Warrington, twice at Liverpool; Sir Charles Dilke spoke at Oldham, Manchester, and Stockport; and Sir R. Cross spoke once at Liverpool. On the 19th Sir R. Cross spoke at Chester, and Mr. Chamberlain spoke twice at Newtown, in Montgomeryshire. "This demonstration," he said, "forms part of an agitation which has been unparalleled in our time. It has been for the most part a great and orderly demonstration, gradually developing itself, testifying to the intelligent interest which the people take in public affairs, and conclusive to the mind of every honest and impartial man as to the evident determination of the great mass, at all events, of the people of the United Kingdom that the foundations of liberty should be at once extended."

On the 20th three Cabinet Ministers spoke—Sir Charles Dilke, Mr. Childers, and Mr. Chamberlain. The next day there was even a greater display of Platform oratory. One Cabinet Minister and three ex-Cabinet Ministers spoke. Among the latter Lord Salisbury, who made a most interesting speech reviewing the "autumn campaign."

"It has," he said, "given the country an opportunity of hearing both sides of the question, and of forming their deliberate judgment thereupon." After referring to Liberal accusations, he said: "I do not in the least admit the error which they impute to us (of bringing the question of the House of Lords before the country), because the imputation of that error rests upon the assumption that the people of this country must be treated rather like lunatics, and that it is dangerous to mention any matter in their hearing, lest it should set up a perilous and destructive line of thought. I do not believe in the policy of plastering over difficulties and trying to avoid dangers by reticence. The only chance we have in this country is fair, free, open discussion; and if I am told that we have brought before the attention of the country subjects which, but for us, would not have been brought before them, I say all the better. The sooner that they discuss them the better they will be able to judge upon them. The only thing we have to fear is a hasty uninformed judgment, and the longer they are able to discuss them, the more thoroughly these questions are agitated in their view, with the more perfect confidence we may assure ourselves of the sound judgment that will ultimately be arrived at."

Here ended this great autumn Platform campaign, for Parliament met on the 23d October, and Ministers and ex-Ministers and members of Parliament had to be back in their places.

I have gone rather into detail in this matter, because I have been anxious to bring into full prominence the position to which the Platform had attained. I have only referred to the speeches of actual members of the Cabinet at the time, and members of Lord Beaconsfield's Cabinet when it was dissolved in 1880, because I wanted to show to what an extent the Platform has been adopted by the actual party leaders of the day. I cannot say that the list is absolutely complete,[1] but it is very nearly so, and is, at any rate, sufficiently so to prove how enormous a change has come over the political life of the country since the Platform gradually struggled into being.

That, in the course of about three months, the Prime Minister should have made important Platform speeches on nine occasions, and several other less important ones, that the Prime Minister designate should have spoken eight times, that in addition to these speeches Cabinet Ministers should have spoken thirty times, and members of the preceding Cabinet thirty-eight times, or a total of some eighty-five speeches, is indeed the most remarkable testimony to the position which the Platform has attained.

How strangely, under such circumstances, do all the old jeers against "peripatetic agitators" sound. How funnily does Canning's speech, which I have already quoted, now read about "ambulatory tribunes," whose rostrum was pitched, sometimes here, sometimes there. With what language would Lord Liverpool and Lord Sidmouth have characterised such conduct in their successors.

The general effect might be increased were I to add to this

[1] The speeches of ex-Liberal Ministers are not included. Mr. Bright spoke several times, Mr. Forster a few times.

list an enumeration of the speeches of many statesmen of great eminence, abilities, and experience, who also took an active part in the agitation; and below them again of the great mass of members of Parliament whose constituents had to be enlightend or wooed,—but space does not permit.

The *Annual Register* of 1884 contains a summary of the meetings held: "Judging from party meetings, the balance of numbers has been enormously in favour of the Liberals, who claimed to have held 1277 public gatherings in England, and 235 in Scotland (a total of 1512), against 184 in the former, and 11 in the latter country (195), in support of the House of Lords."

Thus it is computed that over 1700 public meetings were held in Great Britain in the course of this agitation. "The attendance at these meetings," continues the *Annual Register*, "varied considerably, for which one set of estimates gave 3,500,000 for the Liberals, and 300,000 only to the Conservatives. Another calculation raised the numbers of the latter to 671,000, and reduced those of the Liberals less than 1,500-000."

The effect of the agitation is known to all. Within less than two months the Franchise Bill became law, and in the following session of Parliament the almost greater measure was passed for the redistribution of seats. The one added over 2,000,000 of voters to the electoral body; the other practically realised one of the "six points" which had been demanded by the Charter—equal electoral districts.

Indirectly these measures established the Platform more firmly than ever as a political institution; for the multiplication of polling places, and the enlargement of the constituencies, created demands on representatives and candidates which can only be met by a constant resort to the Platform.

One final fact will enable us still further to realise the enormous progress which the electoral Platform has made. In 1761, at the first general election in George III.'s reign, there were 18 contests. In 1885, at the general election, the first under the new Reform Acts, for the 567 seats allotted to Great Britain, there were 522 contests.

PART VI

CONCLUSION

CHAPTER XXIV

CONCLUDING CONSIDERATIONS

SUCH, then, has been the history of the Platform, in its main features, from the time of its entrance into the field of English political life—a history of brilliant progress, and of vast achievement, of a successful struggle for the valuable rights of free speech, of public meetings, and of self-government.

Once the events of the life of the Platform are put into the consecutive form of a narrative, one understands how simple and natural has been the growth of this great institution, and by what natural transitions it passed on from one stage to another of progress and power.

Springing from germs in the Constitution itself, and in the character of the people or race, it first had a long and desperate fight for free speech. Speech was not free so long as men were prevented criticising the institutions of the country, the actions of the Government, or even the iniquities of public officials. Speech was not free when the suggestion that Parliament did not fairly represent the interests of the nation might be construed into an attempt to bring the Government of the King and Parliament into contempt, and might lay the speaker open to an indictment for high treason. But freedom of speech was not beloved in those times by governing authorities.

Time after time in the one place where it existed—namely, in Parliament—it had been the last stronghold of liberty against the aggressiveness of monarchy and despotic principles. It was submitted to there only out of necessity, and was hated and abhorred and discountenanced by those who were anxious to reserve to themselves the authority and advantages of government. But if submitted to in Parliament, there was no such imperative necessity for submitting to it outside Parliament. There it was clear, to their minds at least, that indulgence in free speech at public meetings could only imperil the existing order of things, and be an unmitigated evil.

The great bulk of the people, however, were determined to have the liberty of expressing their opinions. Thought was free, language should be free also. Were people to suffer and not to complain? How could existing abuses be made evident to the country at large if they were not to be exposed? How could the machinery of Government be improved if a perpetual bar was to be put on criticism? And so the people strove for free speech. The strife was long and arduous, but it was won, definitely, and finally in 1825, when the Seditious Meetings Prevention Act of 1819 expired,—not yet three-quarters of a century ago. The right of meeting where the people liked, and when they liked, was then established, once for all; the magisterial censorship of the Platform came to an end; thenceforward the people could say what they liked, could discuss what proposition they wished, subject only to those moderate restraints of the ordinary statute, or of the common law, which cannot be considered as interfering with freedom of discussion. It was a splendid triumph—the shackles on speech were knocked off, and the Platform could give the whole of its efforts unimpeded to the great work that lay before it.

The history or narrative of the life of the Platform brings out too into clear light its various functions, and shows when they began to operate. The earliest, and at the same time the great fundamental function or use of the Platform was what may be called the "expressive" function;[1] or, to put it in another way, the Platform was first used by the people for the purpose of describing their condition or circumstances, or expressing their feelings. When men are oppressed by particular laws, or when their condition is rendered miserable by particular circumstances, their first natural instinct is to seek redress. In the ruder states of society, or by the more ignorant classes, redress is ordinarily sought by violence.

On all occasions, however, in this country, violence was

[1] This phrase is used by Mr. Bagehot in his work on *The British Constitution*, p. 133, as one of the functions of the House of Commons.

found to be the most disastrous form of seeking redress, resulting in imprisonment or transportation, sometimes even in an ignominious death on the scaffold, and the alienation of all public sympathy. There are, indeed, few more pathetic scenes in the more recent history of this country than the trials of many of these ignorant and mistaken men who sought redress by violence, and the agony and suffering entailed on their wives and families by their transportation or death. But as the people progressed towards education, and gained even the crudest ideas of government, they sought redress by meeting together, by formulating their complaints, and informing the public and the Government of the country of their condition.

The Platform was thus, in its first and earliest function, an informing voice admonishing the Government of the condition and needs of sections of the people; and happy was the country to be able to hear this voice, for the worst evils of Government are in a fair way for removal when they are discovered and protruded on the public gaze.

Time after time in each of the agitations which have been chronicled in this work have we seen how the people at their meetings avowed that their object was to inform the Government and the Legislature of their condition and wants. One resolution, which pointedly shows this, may be quoted as typical of or summing up the spirit of countless others: "Resolved—That we, at this meeting assembled, have met to make known our distress and our wants, trusting that our statements may meet the public eye, and reach the hearts of our legislators, to the end that they may pass such measures as shall secure to industry its full reward, and thus improve the condition of ourselves and our fellow-countrymen."

It was a hopeful and not, as so many Tory statesmen imagined, an alarming sign, once the great toiling masses, hitherto dumb and not willing nor able to speak, began to find their voice through the Platform, and to appeal to the Legislature and to the public for redress, instead of taking the remedy into their own hands. This was a distinct step towards progress, the first towards a removal of the evils which affected them. Violence could only be met with repression; an appeal to reason and humanity could not fail, in time, to produce some alleviation.

It may at first sight seem somewhat strange that we should find this first function of the Platform constantly recurring in later years after the nation had made great progress, and when, in some ways, the Platform had already advanced beyond the merely expressive function; but the function is an abiding and not merely a transient one. As years went on new masses were constantly growing up who used the Platform in its primary and most primitive function, at the same time that other classes of greater education and experience had passed beyond this initiatory stage, and were employing it in the more advanced functions of discussing remedies or suggesting them to the Legislature. It was foolish, it was almost criminal conduct on the part of the statesmen of the pre-reformed Parliament to prevent the people petitioning or complaining.

As wave after wave of population rolled into the already teeming cities, as the great ebb and flow of manufacturing prosperity and adversity swept backwards and forwards, as industry became revolutionised by the introduction of steam and the unending improvements of machinery, the condition of the people underwent vast vicissitudes. The industrial population felt to its extremest limits every pulse-beat of change, and any adverse change fell with the most fatal force on the poorest and most helpless. And surely those who suffered were those who were best qualified, I do not say to suggest the remedies, but to depict their condition and to enumerate their sufferings. The Parliament of the pre-Reform Act period failed lamentably in representing the interests of the poorer, more distressed portions of the nation,—in fact, not merely did not represent them at all, but ignored them and acted against their interests—and the Parliamentary representatives then were almost the last persons who could tell aught or cared aught about the condition of the people. Indeed, there are very few more remarkable phenomena in the earlier Parliamentary history of this century than the ignorance, sometimes recklessness, that prevailed in Parliament as to the social, material, moral, and intellectual condition of the great bulk of the people of the country.

It was quite necessary, therefore, that the Legislature should be vividly and forcibly informed of the state of the people; and the Platform taught Parliament much; but not till the informing voice of the Chartist Platform hammered the information into the mind of the governing classes, and these classes found themselves standing on the brink of an abyss, or, as it were, looking down into the crater of a volcano of human miseries and passion, did even a reformed Parliament begin really to grapple with the great "condition of England" question, or fully understand that that was, for England, and for them, the question of all others.

From the "expressive" function—the describing and voicing of grievances—it was a simple and perfectly natural step in an upward direction to the discussion or consideration of remedies, and this "discussing" function must be regarded as the second function of the Platform in order of growth, and also, like the expressive, an abiding function.

As soon as men passed from mere statements, or complaint, on to the discussion of remedies, it is plain that they had advanced a stage both in education and reasonability. Much discussion could be, and was, carried on in and by the Press, both by newspapers and other publications; but it was cold and ineffective in comparison with verbal discussion on the Platform, where antagonistic opinions had often to be defended and supported by combatants face to face, and in the presence of the people, who, by their vote or resolution, awarded the victory. Moreover, this form of discussion was a new method of considering public affairs, for it was in addition to the discussion carried on in the Press, and to the discussion in Parliament; it brought large numbers of men into mental and political activity, who otherwise would have been passive or indifferent; and it laid open, as it were, a wholly new vein of political opinion and intelligence.

It is perfectly true that in the earlier stages of Platform discussion, such discussion as there was, was not of a high character, nor of any appreciable value. One would have no justification for expecting otherwise. Platform discussion could not, in fact, in its incipient stage, compete with discussion in Parliament. The bulk of the men who attended the meetings were ill-educated and ill-informed; the speakers too often were not much better. The conclusions arrived at by large bodies of the people in public meetings were often unwise, and showed gross ignorance; but as time went on, and the political education of the people advanced, a vast improvement in this respect took place.

The Anti-Corn-Law agitation affords a perfect example of this function of the Platform, for it was mainly by Platform discussion and hard matter-of-fact reasoning and argument that the public mind was converted to the abolition of the Corn Laws. From the very infancy of the movement its promoters pressed the Platform into their service, and trusted implicitly to public discussion to gain converts to their cause. The meetings were usually specially designed for the purposes of discussion—persons holding views in favour of the Corn Law being invited to come and discuss the question, and at meeting after meeting it was thrashed out on the Platform in speeches of the closest argument by the champions of opposing views. The agitation was an uphill one—hopeless, apparently, at the outset, when all obstacles to its success were contemplated; but, in the end, those obstacles were overcome by sheer force of discussion, and the Act which abolished the Corn Laws stands in the statute book as a permanent and most striking testimony to the successful use of the Platform for the purposes of discussion and conversion.

The unsuitability of the Platform for the purposes of discussion has often been insisted upon. Whenever any exceptionally large meeting or series of meetings took place anywhere, the argument was generally revived. Lord Brougham, in his work on *The British Constitution*,[1] has stated the argument very well. He said: "It is never to be lost sight of that such meetings[2] as we have been speaking of, and indeed all popular assemblies, are convoked, not for deliberation or for discussion, but for very different purposes. They are attended by men all of one opinion; all engaged heart and soul in the pursuit of one object. They meet to excite and influence each other; to give vent to feelings which they have long entertained and cherished, or declare opinions which they, or some person for them, have already formed. They bear no contradiction; they listen to no reason. They are bodies of men assembled for action, not for consultation; their

[1] Chap. ix. sec. 2.

[2] He had been referring to the meetings in Ireland in 1828, but he specifically includes "all popular assemblies."

real objects are to prepare for some violent act, and to impress the Government with fear."

Numerous other writers have given expression to much the same opinion, and there is a certain amount of truth in the argument which gives it an air of plausibility. It was, in the main, true of the great meetings to which Lord Brougham, in the first instance, referred: they were more demonstrations of opinion than for argument or discussion; it was true of the great meetings in Ireland in the Repeal agitation; it was in the main true of some of the huge meetings in England at different times. But the fallacy of the argument lies in limiting the idea of the Platform to its purely "discussing" function; and to allege it as true of "all popular assemblies" is both incorrect and misleading. Meetings innumerable, or, to use Lord Brougham's words, "popular assemblies," have been convoked and held for the purposes of deliberation and discussion, and very effective discussion has taken place at them. The whole Anti-Corn-Law agitation is a standing contradiction to Lord Brougham's argument.

But the subject has undergone a vast change since then, and what apparently had not dawned on his mind, and what others who use a similar criticism are blind to, is the larger aspect of the modern Platform discussion which is so marked a feature in the present time, and of which so striking an illustration has been given in the last chapter. It is true that in recent years meetings have assumed a very one-sided character, so far at least as the speaking is concerned, and that it is not often a speaker opposing the object for which the meeting is held can obtain a hearing. The old system of the rival candidates at an election speaking from the same hustings has ceased to exist; each now holds his separate meetings. Likewise, in times gone past, as I have narrated, at numerous county and other meetings, opposing speakers discussed the question in the presence of the meeting. Now, such a practice scarcely obtains. But there is no diminution of Platform discussion on this account, nor is Platform discussion one iota less valuable. Rather has it reached a more enlarged, a more impressive form. The rival candidates in an election contest hold their separate meetings, and argue and discuss with each other on the questions of the hour, quite as much if not more than they did when they both stood upon the same Platform. And in the higher ranks of politicians, as I have shown, the leaders of the rival parties do the same. The Prime Minister and ex-Prime Minister, Cabinet Ministers, and ex-Cabinet Ministers, argue with and answer one another from separate Platforms, just as thoroughly and effectually as if they met on one Platform, and there argued with each other, and presented their respective policies to the arbitrament of those assembled to listen to them.

If the speeches made on the Platform were not reported in the public Press, then there would be much cause to lament that the older practice of rival speakers addressing a meeting, and of the meeting being more strictly deliberative and consultative was not continued, but no great party leader now makes a speech which is not reported at full length in almost every newspaper in the Empire, and no one of local importance or ability makes a speech which is not reported in the local newspapers. Thus the discussion is as thorough as if it took place at a meeting, and thus all men are given the materials for forming an opinion on the points at issue.

It is true that the Platform is thus dependent on the Press for the fulfilment of the "discussing" function, but it has ever been more or less so. The same, however, may be said of Parliament, for if the debates in Parliament were not reported in the Press, a vast amount of the influence of Parliament would be gone, for a very small proportion of men would read the volumes of the Parliamentary debates as they from time to time appeared. The suitability of the Platform for discussion is indeed so manifest, and is now so generally acknowledged, that I need not dwell further on this function of it.

The transition from this to the third great function of the Platform was again quite a natural one. From discussion as to remedies, and decision as to the most desirable, it was quite a natural step to the adoption of means for attaining the object fixed on, or enforcing the conclusions come to. This, I think, may best be described as the "controlling" function. This control was exercisable in two ways—one by putting the candidate through a public political examination on the Platform, and exacting pledges from him as to his future conduct in Parliament if elected; the other by bringing pressure to bear on the representatives in Parliament.

The essence of the problem which the growing democracy of the United Kingdom had to solve was the one I have already stated—namely, how, consistently with the existence of the Crown and of the Upper House of Parliament, could it secure absolute self-government and supreme control in the government of the nation, both as regarded its internal affairs and its external relations? The impossibility of a community in a body carrying on a regular government is manifest to a person of any understanding. A people or community is accordingly forced to entrust their own powers, or at least a portion of them, to some individuals, or set of individuals, to exercise in their behalf.[1] The problem then is, how and upon what terms and conditions, and by whom are the persons to be chosen who are to stand, as it were, in the place of the people? As a general solution of this problem, all modern democracies have adopted in one form or another a system of representative government. Each national democracy, however, has adopted the special form which it thought most desirable or most feasible. The system which had come down from the past in England has been already described. In most respects the system of representation was little more than nominal. Down to the time of the first Reform Act, by far the largest proportion of the members of the House of Commons were wholly independent of the people; whilst of the others the majority went to Parliament absolutely free from any pledges or conditions whatever as to their future conduct in Parliament. Even in the cases of those who did give some sort of pledge, the pledges were only morally binding, nor do they appear to have been looked on at all seriously.

Once the democracy of England had grown so powerful as to force from the Government a revision of the Constitution, and once the first Reform Act was passed, an immense impetus was given to the enforcement of the principle of responsibility of representatives to their constituents. It is curious how strongly even some Liberals held to the independence of action of the representatives. Thus Lord Brougham, in his

[1] See *Essay on Government*, by James Mill.

work just referred to,[1] went so far as to lay down the canon that "The people's power being transferred to the representative body for a limited time, the people are bound not to exercise their influence so as to control the conduct of their representatives, as a body, on the several measures that come before them;" and in his work on *Political Philosophy* he wrote: "The most serious risk to which the representative principle is exposed in a democracy arises from the impatience of the people, and their disposition to take back a portion of the power which they have entrusted to their deputies, by controlling them in its exercise on questions of a peculiarly interesting nature. The peculiar importance of any measure, either of general legislation, or of adminstrative policy, affords no excuse for this interference."[2]

But the people could scarcely be expected to remain passive spectators of the actions of their representatives, and to take no part in politics except once in every septennial period. For many long years they had suffered under their so-called representatives. They accordingly set themselves to remedy the evil—to do exactly those things which Lord Brougham said were inconsistent with the principle of representation; and they worked out the remedy by making the Platform the instrument of their controlling power.

John Stuart Mill, in his treatise on *Representative Government*,[3] has explained the feasibility of making this control effective. He wrote: "Let the system of representation be what it may, it will be converted into one of mere delegation if the electors so choose. As long as they are free not to vote, and free to vote as they like, they cannot be prevented from making their vote depend on any condition they think fit to annex to it. By refusing to elect any one who will not pledge himself to all their opinions, and even, if they please, to consult with them before voting on any important subject not foreseen, they can reduce their representative to their mere mouthpiece, or compel him in honour, when no longer willing to act in that capacity, to resign his seat."[4]

[1] *The British Constitution*, chap. vii.

[2] Brougham, *Political Philosophy*, vol. iii. chap. xii.

[3] J. S. Mill, *Representative Government*, chap. xii.

[4] Mill was not in favour of this being carried to an extreme. "The electors will not do wisely if they insist on absolute conformity to their opinions, as the condition of his retaining his seat."

Once the first Reform Act was passed, a very much larger number of constituencies were in a position to exercise a stricter examination of those seeking to represent them. The candidate was obliged to appear before the electors, and to make from the Platform a public avowal of his political creed. If he neglected aught, he was liable to be questioned as to his opinions, and to have pledges exacted from him. From that time down to the present the practice of exacting pledges from candidates has steadily been on the increase. Candidates have now to stand the test of one Platform examination after another, on this subject and on that. Electors insist now on knowing all the views of the candidate who seeks to represent them. Vague promises or ambiguous declarations no longer suffice. An elected representative now goes to Parliament pledged up to the eyes on almost every conceivable subject. That complete independence of action which members of Parliament claimed for themselves in pre-reform times has practically become a thing of the past. Within certain limits, and in the cases of some public favourites, a certain degree of latitude is allowed; but on the whole, the position of a representative has within the last century undergone a complete and entire change as regards his independence of action.

But this is very far from satisfying now the exigencies of electors, or being a sufficient control over a representative by his constituents. Numerous events happen which require suggestions from them to him, or a great crisis arises on a subject not dreamt of at the election time, and on which the electors may have strong views as to what should be done. Meetings are held at which he is or is not present, the voice of the Platform is invoked to express the opinions of the electors on the political question of the hour, or even on the action of their representative in respect to it, and the expression of opinion is conveyed to him, if not actually as a direct instruction which he must follow, at any rate as an intimation, which, experience teaches him, can only be disregarded at considerable risk, or for some very good reason to the contrary.

Nor are the requirements of the electors any longer satisfied with seeing their representative merely at election time, nor with the rendering of the account of the stewardship at the end of the Parliament—possibly a period of six or seven years. They expect now and require from their representative at least an annual rendering of such account; the Platform is had recourse to as the best and most satisfactory, indeed, the only means of obtaining it face to face, and the verdict is given in the resolution of approval or disapproval which is passed by the meetings which he addresses.

In large constituencies one meeting does not suffice, and the representative has to make a tour of his constituency, addressing meetings in all populous centres, and giving all the electors the opportunity of hearing him.

A representative has, in fact, in the present day to live under the scrutinising gaze of his constituents, and in public communication with them. Thus the choice of representatives is supplemented by a never-ceasing control over them, and the power of the people becomes unceasingly effective.

This method of controlling the representative does not remove the fundamental defect in the system of representative government—namely, an actual surrender of power in electing a representative. But it has a moral force which is sufficient, which is, in fact, so powerful that no representative could venture to defy it for any length of time. The limited period for which a representative holds his trust, and the certainty of a day of reckoning when the life of a Parliament comes to an end, act as very sufficient deterrents on the independent conduct of representatives. It is true that were they to combine, they could—as has been once done already—prolong the life of Parliament, and postpone the day of reckoning; but in these times there is no danger of this.

Indeed, so far from members endeavouring to keep their seats in defiance of the wishes of the bulk of a constituency, several instances have occurred of members resigning their seats in consequence of what they considered as vital differences between them and their constituents. The resignation by Sir Robert Peel of his seat for Oxford so far back as 1829, which has been already mentioned, set an example in this, and since then other instances have occurred of members resigning their seats, because they could not conscientiously carry out the wishes of their constituents.

The occurrence is not, however, very common, for, as a rule, the representatives now chosen are in thorough accord with opinions of their constituents, and being of the same way of thinking in so many things, with the same cast of thought, the same interests, and the same principles, the probability is that the representative on the one hand, and the constituents on the other, will regard in the same way any new question that suddenly arises.

The long-increasing tendency on the part of constituencies to keep a tight control over their representatives received considerable accentuation after the passing of the Reform Act of 1867, in the formation in many constituencies of local Associations established with the view of selecting candidates, carrying on electoral contests, and of uniting the party. The representative system was closely followed in the election of the members of these Associations. The theory of these institutions was, that the Association, having been elected by the members of the party at large, was representative of them, and that all the members of the party should, therefore, place their votes at the disposal of the Association, to be used for the benefit of the party as the majority of the Association might decide.[1]

In 1877 the farther step was taken of federating the various Liberal Associations together, so that delegates from them might formulate the policy which was to be adopted by the Liberal party as a whole, and this central body was called "The National Liberal Federation." The first conference of the delegates took place at Birmingham, and the occasion was celebrated by a great meeting there on the 31st May. In 1880 the Federation had over 100 branches connected with it. Mr. Chamberlain claimed that it had organisations in 67 boroughs, and 10 counties, and out of these, at the general election, 60 had returned Liberals.[2]

The serious consequences which its opponents anticipated—namely, that the effect of this central body would be "to transfer all power from Parliament to this self-constituted Committee,"—have, however, hardly been realised. So far,

[1] See *Public Opinion and Lord Beaconsfield*, vol. i. p. 21.

[2] See "A New Political Organization," by J. Chamberlain, *Fortnightly Review*, July 1877; *The Nineteenth Century*, 1882, p. 959, "The Birmingham Caucus," by W. T. Marriott; also the same magazine, May 1882, "Town and Country Politics," by Rev. J. Guinness Rogers.

the local constituencies have been too independent to be willing to submit to much dictation from any central body, nor is it desirable that the Platform in this sphere of its duty should be ruled by a Central Association, for that would be substituting one tyranny or form of personal rule for that from which, with much difficulty, they have emancipated themselves, and would be destructive of that self-government which the independent action of the Platform in each constituency gives.

Viewing this action of the Platform as a whole, it is not, I think, too much to say that the Platform has, by the exercise of its "controlling" function, effected what practically amounts to a revolution in the system of representative government. Technically, members of Parliament are as free as ever they were; the people's power is legally surrendered into their hands on election; practically, however, they are not free; and though the new system has not the force of law, it is rapidly acquiring almost equal stability by the force of custom. The uncontrolled powers of members of the House of Commons have, in fact, been brought under the direct control of their constituents. Constituents are able to sway them to their will, and members go to Parliament no longer to act just as pleases themselves, or, as the euphuism was, to act according to their consciences, but more as delegates from the constituencies.

And in the larger and more important aspect of the case the Platform is able, by its controlling function, when collectively employed, to impose its will on the House of Commons, and therefore on the Government of the country. In gaining this authority over the House of Commons it has, as I have before remarked, simultaneously profited by the increasing authority which the House has been acquiring to itself from the Crown, from the House of Lords, and generally from the feudal aristocracy which so long exercised such sway over the fortunes of the country.

Just as the House of Commons has been becoming ever more and more the executive of the Constitution, so Parliament has been becoming every year more and more the executive of the Platform.

Mr. Bagehot, in his work on *The British Constitution*, has

pointed out that "The ultimate authority in the English Constitution is a newly-elected House of Commons. No matter whether the question upon which it decides be administrative or legislative; no matter whether it concerns high matters of the essential constitution, or small matters of daily detail; no matter whether it be a question of making a war or continuing a war; no matter whether it be the imposing a tax, or the issuing a paper currency; no matter whether it be a question relating to India, or Ireland, or London,—a new House of Commons can despotically and finally resolve.

"The House of Commons . . . when sure of the popular assent, and when freshly elected, is absolute—it can rule as it likes and decide as it likes. And it can take the best security that it does not decide in vain. It can ensure that its decrees shall be executed, for it, and it alone, appoints the executive; it can inflict the most severe of all penalties on neglect, for it can remove the executive. It can choose, to effect its wishes, those who wish the same; and so its will is sure to be done."[1]

But the power outside which makes and unmakes the House is greater than the House. The people have chosen the Platform as the principal means of expressing themselves. It speaks their voice at election time, and it speaks their voice to their representatives when seated in Parliament, and it is from it, and by it, that their voice reaches and controls the Government of the day.

It is by thus making the Platform a controlling power, that the English people have so far worked out the problem how they, as a democracy, could, consistently with the existing form of the Constitution, take to themselves the government of the country and keep it under their own direction.

The Platform has, in fact, been the instrument by which a liberty-loving people have won their freedom, without bloodshed or disorder, such as stained the revolutions in other countries. It has been the means by which England has "set an example to the world of a great nation passing from an aristocratic domination to a wholly democratic government without civil war."[2] And it has won the victory by reason and conviction—a far more permanent and enduring victory than any won by violent and forcible revolution.

[1] Bagehot, p. 227. [2] Place, MSS., 27,819.

One service more which the Platform has rendered can best be described in the words of De Quincey, who, in a work written some sixty years ago, has given, in a passage of great beauty, a sort of prophetic description of what the Platform has very nearly brought the system of government to.

"I have," he wrote, "always maintained that under a representative government, where the great cities of the Empire must naturally have the power, each in its proportion, of reacting upon the capital and the councils of the nation in so conspicuous a way, there is a result waiting on the final improvements of the arts of travelling and of transmitting intelligence with velocity such as cannot be properly appreciated in the absence of all historical experience. Conceive a state of communication between the centre and the extremities of a great people, kept up with a uniformity of reciprocation so exquisite as to imitate the flowing and ebbing of the sea, or the systole and diastole of the human heart, day and night, waking and sleeping, not succeeding to each other with more absolute certainty than the acts of the metropolis and the controlling notice of the provinces, whether in the way of support or of resistance. Action and reaction from every point of the compass being thus perfect and instantaneous, we should then first begin to understand, in a practical sense, what is meant by the unity of a political body, and we should approach to a more adequate appreciation of the powers which are latent in organisation. For it must be considered that hitherto, under the most complex organisation, and that which has best attained its purposes, the national will has never been able to express itself upon one in a thousand of the public acts, simply because the national voice was lost in the distance, and could not collect itself through the time and the space rapidly enough to connect itself immediately with the evanescent measure of the moment. But as the system of intercourse is gradually expanding, these bars of space and time are in the same degree contracting, until finally we may expect them altogether to vanish; and then every part of the Empire will react upon the whole with the power, life, and effect of immediate conference amongst parties brought face to face. Then first will be seen a political system truly organic, *i.e.* in which each acts upon all, and all react upon each; and a new earth will arise from the indirect agency of this merely physical revolution."[1]

Important and useful though the functions of the Platform are, yet there are many persons who do not hesitate to deplore its existence. The words so familiar in the past—demagogues, harangues, or any other abusive epithet that was employed—still find an echo in their minds. It is useless, however, to deplore its existence. Parliament, long the sole permitted field for the discussion of political measures and events, became ever more and more inadequate for the public requirements in this respect. As the nation passed from childhood to youth, and from youth to manhood, other means had to be found for expressing its thoughts. One circumstance alone was sufficient to prove the insufficiency of Parliament—namely, that it sat for only a certain portion of the year. For, on an average, six or seven months in every year there was no Parliament. Crises so great as to evoke the feelings of the people, and to impel them to utterance, frequently arose during this period of Parliamentary inanition. The people would not, could not be expected to, remain in a state of silence under such circumstances, and yet, except by the Platform, they had no adequate means of expressing themselves. The Press, the other great organ of public opinion, though affording some vent for their feelings, was insufficient. Newspapers were dear; their circulation was not large; and furthermore, it was not every one who could obtain the opportunity of discussing subjects therein. Nor even if they could, would any newspaper discussions have sufficed for the public requirements. The views of the people would have failed to reach the ears of the Government in such volume as to impress the Government with their due weight.

If the need for the Platform was felt already a century or more ago, when England was just beginning to enlarge her borders, and to multiply her needs, how manifestly greater became the necessity for its functions as years went on, as the country doubled and trebled its population, and as the Government kept gradually passing from the hands of a limited feudal aristocracy into the hands of the people themselves. Moreover, the experience of its advantages and utility has

[1] De Quincey, *Autobiographic Sketches* (Travelling).

ingrained or interwoven it into the very fibre of the public life of the nation. Of the inevitability of the Platform, therefore, there can be no question. Whether we like it or deplore it, whether we approve or disapprove of it, whether we admire its power, or tremble at the dangers involved in its use, the Platform is an unavoidable, inevitable necessity. Just as language is necessary for individual intercourse, so is the Platform necessary for general political intercourse.

That there are dangers connected with it no reasonable person can doubt. It has been said that "the advantages of a free Press are innumerable. With these society must be content to take some concomitant evils."[1] The remark applies with equal force to the Platform. The advantages of the Platform are innumerable. With them society must be content to take some concomitant dangers. Those dangers have at all times formed the subject of the most impassioned language by all who were opposed to any increase of popular power. From the time that the electors of Middlesex met to protest against the House of Commons depriving them of the right of electing whom they pleased, no subject has afforded so much occasion for such outspoken hostility, from the Sovereign himself on the throne, and his Ministers, down through all the gradations of social or political rank, to the most contemptible and meanest of Tory hacks—all have united in a chorus of obloquy against the Platform. It suited the purpose of many to represent the Platform as a most dangerous institution leading by the directest road to revolution, and when revolution was mentioned it was always intended to suggest September massacres, wholesale guillotinings, the extermination of the aristocracy, and the decapitation of kings. Every prominent incident in the progress of the Platform, or any illegal actions which could be remotely attributed to it, were seized on as the text for invective against the people having the right of meeting and speaking. Thus the more timid were appalled or coerced into the quiescence necessary for the prolongation of the existence of abuses, and privileges, and monopolies which the upper classes were interested in maintaining.

But we should err much were we to accept as true the ex-

[1] *The Times*, 12th January 1831.

aggerated allegations of interested or indignant partisans. Fortunately, experience has over and over again proved how exaggerated they were, and has induced a saner and more rational mode of looking at great popular meetings.

Undoubtedly the Platform has dangers—great ones, it must be admitted—but there is no reason why they should be exaggerated. Summarised briefly, the dangers, I think, are—(1) the immediate danger of disturbance or violence incurred by bringing large masses of men together; (2) the slower danger of the people being misled by it into evil courses; and (3) the greatest danger that can be alleged against it—such a combination of the Platform and organisation as may lead to a subversion of the Government.

The first of these dangers, then, is the risk of disturbance or violence incurred by bringing large masses of men together. It is not, however, peculiar to the Platform, for people can gather without any intention of using the Platform. The danger has been forcibly described by Lord Chief-Justice Tindal in his charge to the Grand Jury on the occasion of the trials at Bristol of the rioters of 1831.

It is to be remembered that these riots were in no way the consequences of Platform action, and I only quote the passage as illustrating the danger in its extremest form. The "excitement" referred to by the Lord Chief Justice was the demonstration against the Recorder, Sir C. Wetherell, on his arrival at Bristol. "It may be safely concluded," said the Lord Chief-Justice, "that if the excitement which led to the defiance of the law at the earlier part of the day had never existed, the weightier crimes subsequently committed by the populace would not have taken place, and it is precisely for this reason that the law of England hath at all times held in the greatest abhorrence riotous and tumultuous assemblages of the people. No man can foresee at the commencement what course they will take, or what consequences will ensue. Though cases may occur in which the object of such assemblies is at first defined and moderate, they rapidly enlarge their power of mischief; and from the natural effect of the excitement and ferment inseparable from the collection of multitudes in one mass, the original design is quickly lost sight of, and men hurry on to the commission of crimes which, at their first meeting, they never contemplated. The beginning of tumult is like the letting out of water—if not stopped at first, it becomes difficult to do so afterwards; it rises and increases until it overwhelms the fairest and the most valuable works of man."[1]

It cannot of course be disputed that any great gatherings of the people are more or less liable to result in violence or disorder; but it may with confidence be asserted that where the Platform brings people together, there is far less risk of danger than where the people come together for some other reason. In the latter case when a crowd collects there is no course of procedure prescribed; no beginning, middle, or end to any sort of ceremony as it were; nothing to compensate in any way for the trouble of assembling, or to occupy or keep the people out of mischief. Whereas, in the former case, they are to a very considerable extent under the influence of leaders charged with a degree of responsibility, there is more or less occupation in listening to public speakers, and assenting to resolutions, and to have taken part in a Platform meeting is in itself a usually sufficient vent to public ill-humour without proceeding to acts of violence.

Place, who had a considerable experience of public meetings, writing about 1840, said: "There is not a single instance during the last thirty years where any public meeting held for any avowed specific purpose ever went beyond it."[2]

And with very few exceptions the same statement might be made as to public meetings since. As regards danger to the State from such assemblies, the danger is infinitesimal. Any disturbances that may arise from a public meeting are local, and the force for the suppression of local disturbances is overwhelming.

"The law of England hath, in proportion to the danger which it attaches to riotous and disorderly meetings of the people, made ample provision for preventing such offences, and for the prompt and effectual suppression of them whenever they arise."[3] Moreover, the laws against violence and outrage, robbery or incendiarism, are very definite and deterrent; and so intolerant are Englishmen of violence and disorder,

[1] See *State Trials*, New Series, vol. iii. p. 3. [2] Place, MSS., 27,797, p. 23.
[3] Lord Chief-Justice Tindal's charge, *State Trials*, New Series, vol. iii. p. 4.

that offenders, instead of receiving popular sympathy, arouse the most intense popular antipathy.

So conscious, in fact, have popular agitators been of the weakness or insufficiency of a local or isolated demonstration, no matter how huge or impressive it was, that in order to make the agitation more effective, the attempt has been made to hold a large number of simultaneous meetings throughout the country, and thus to strike awe into the governing classes. The Catholic Association in Ireland, it will be remembered, held simultaneous meetings in Ireland on a certain day, and the Chartist leaders endeavoured to do so too, but with far less effect.

Furthermore, it is to be borne in mind that the law, though happily widely tolerant of quiet and lawful meetings of the people, and giving the fullest freedom, that even an enthusiast for liberty could desire, is very hostile to them if they pass beyond well-defined limits.

Judge Bayley, at the trial of Henry Hunt, in March 1820 explained the law on the subject very clearly. In the course of the case he said: "I think that if a meeting assembles in such numbers and with such strength as to excite alarm in the minds of peaceable subjects, that meeting is illegal. If the purpose of a meeting be legal, it may become illegal, if illegal means be resorted to for obtaining that purpose. Even if the meeting be legal in its object, it may become illegal by the manner in which it is conducted, if that manner be such as to excite terror in ordinary minds."[1] And in his charge to the jury he went into the subject more fully. "I have," he said, "no difficulty in stating to you that it is not because a meeting consists of 60,000 men, women, and children—a mixed multitude—that it is, therefore, necessarily an unlawful assembly. That number may meet under such circumstances as by no means to raise public terror, or to raise fears and jealousies in the minds of the persons in the neighbourhood where they meet. But if, in an assembly so constituted, met for perfectly legal purposes, any men introduced themselves illegally to give to that meeting an undue direction which would produce terror to his Majesty's subjects, although 59,000 out of that meeting would be perfectly innocent, there might be twelve or twenty

[1] *State Trials*, New Series, vol. i. p. 231.

illegally assembled; and those twelve or twenty would be liable to be tried upon the ground of illegally assembling there, although the assembly be perfectly legal as to the bulk of the people who are there."[1]

This, however, was not all, for he added: "If any persons by plan amongst themselves contrive that there shall be such observations made to them, by harangues, by placards, or by any such means as are likely to give to that large body of persons that direction which will be likely to endanger the public peace, and strike terror into the minds of his Majesty's subjects, those persons will be liable to the conviction of the offence of illegal conspiracy."

It is easy to see from these statements, which practically are as true now as when spoken, the law not having been since changed, how very easily a public meeting can lay itself open to legal consequences, and how very jealous the law is to guard against any abuse of the great privilege of public meeting.

The ultimate decision in a case where a prosecution is instituted for a breach of the law rests with a jury; but the very fact that the penalties of the law can be so easily incurred imposes both on the leaders of any popular demonstration, and on the participators therein, such a sense of responsibility as induces considerable moderation and caution. Hence, where all are more or less anxious to avoid incurring any unpleasant consequences, the dangers of riot and disturbance incurred by bringing large masses of the people together are considerably diminished. It is, indeed, a remarkable testimony to the law-abiding character of the people, that in all the great popular demonstrations which have taken place within recent years, the utmost endeavours have been made by the demonstrators themselves, by the appointment of stewards and others specially for the purpose of enforcing order, to keep their proceedings free from the danger of riot, violence, or any disturbance.

The second class of dangers which may arise from the Platform are the dangers of the people being misled by bad or ignorant men into evil courses. These are genuine dangers, proved by sad demonstration, time after time.

[1] *State Trials*, New Series, vol. i. p. 436.

"Out of one foolish word may start a thousand daggers," it has been strikingly said; but how much greater is the probability of such a result when thousands of foolish speeches are poured into the ears of an ignorant and poverty-stricken people. Gale Jones, Orator Hunt, Stephens, Feargus O'Connor, need but be mentioned, and we see how, at successive periods of our history, the people have been led into unwise or evil courses. The serious riots in Birmingham in 1839 were the direct result of incitement to violence by the Chartist leaders and speakers there.

The outbreak or rising at Newport in the same year was a far more formidable display of what evil counsel from the Platform could do; the discontent, which resulted in that movement, having unquestionably been fostered into activity by the speeches of certain of the Chartist agitators. The great "turn-out" in 1842 afforded further proof of the danger of the Platform, when misused.

These are the extremest cases, and they illustrate conclusively how greatly the Platform can be misused. But here, again, it must be pointed out, that these consequences are only possible by distinct and easily-proved violations of the law, and by incurring the risk of severe punishment. They are guarded against by the existing legislation of the country—guarded against by the laws against criminal acts, from high treason down to misdemeanours, once an effort is made to carry into effect the violent counsel of speakers—once men pass from speech to action—guarded against before they reach this stage by the laws which impose on speakers certain restraints as regards the language they use. For great as is the liberty of public speech in this kingdom, there are limits beyond which it is not permitted, or rather, if those limits are passed, the transgressor lays himself open to heavy penalties.

The particulars already given as to the prosecutions of the leading Chartists obviate the necessity of any re-statement of the laws by which certain limits are set on public speech. But as half a century has elapsed since then certain additional remarks must be made.

The whole present position of the Platform as regards its legal limitations has been very clearly stated by Sir James Fitzjames Stephen in his *History of the Criminal Law of Eng-*

land.[1] He there points out how the laws against "seditious libels" have practically fallen into abeyance. "The change of public sentiment as to the free discussion of political affairs has," he says, "practically rendered the law as to political libels unimportant, inasmuch as it has practically restricted prosecutions for libel to cases in which a libel amounts either to a direct incitement to crime, or to false imputations upon an individual of disgraceful conduct in relation to either public or private affairs. . . . Since the Reform Bill of 1832 prosecutions for seditious libel have been in England so rare, that they may be said practically to have ceased."

This, however, is far from implying that wholesale license is given to Platform speeches. Very far from it. Sir James Stephen has thus stated the present law on the subject: "As I understand it," he says, "every one commits a misdemeanour who publishes verbally or otherwise any words with a seditious intention." And a seditious intention he defines as "an intention to bring into hatred or contempt, or to excite disaffection against the person of her Majesty, her heirs and successors, or the Government and Constitution of the United Kingdom, as by law established, or either House of Parliament, or the administration of justice, or to excite her Majesty's subjects to attempt otherwise than by lawful means the alteration of any matter in Church or State by law established, or to raise discontent or disaffection amongst her Majesty's subjects, or to promote feelings of ill-will and hostility between different classes of her Majesty's subjects."[2]

[1] Vol. ii. p. 301, etc.

[2] In recent years, instead of violent speakers being prosecuted for seditious libel, the prosecution has taken the form of a charge of "seditious conspiracy." After mentioning several well-known cases of this sort, Sir Fitzjames Stephen says: "These prosecutions, etc., all proceed on principles very similar to those on which seditious libels are tried. The charge commonly is that the defendants conspired together to effect some purpose inconsistent with the peace and good government of the country, and that they manifested that intention by speeches made, meetings held, and other steps taken in concert. The proof commonly is, that some sort of organisation was formed in which the defendants took part, and that things were written and said in consequence which were calculated to effect the objects in question."

And then, referring specially to the memorable trial of Daniel O'Connell, he says: "This decision shows how wide the legal notion of a seditious conspiracy is. It includes every sort of attempt, by violent language either spoken or written, or by a show of force calculated to produce fear, to effect any public object of an evil character, and no precise or complete definition has ever been given of objects which are to be regarded as evil."

Those even not versed in the intricacies of the language of the law can gather from these statements a clear idea as to how the law endeavours to defend the people from the dangers of being misled by bad or ignorant men, and what restrictions are imposed on the Platform by the law.

There is, however, a subtler danger to which reference must be made, as it also comes under this class—that of their being led by mistaken men—and this danger is very much enhanced when the person has rendered great public service already, and has given the people reasonable ground for believing that he is again leading them right. This danger is well illustrated in the person of Attwood. He had led, with great tact and judgment, large masses of the people to the brilliant and decisive victory of Parliamentary reform; he had placed his countrymen under the deepest obligation to him; naturally, therefore, when he went on to urge his schemes of a reform in the currency, and, still later, most of the six points of the Charter, he had a large number of believing followers. We see now that he was leading them astray, but the services he had rendered in previous years blinded the eyes of his followers, and induced them to follow him into courses leading to disaster. The danger is mainly the result of a want of independence of judgment. It is, nevertheless, a sufficiently real one, and cannot be omitted from an enumeration of the principal dangers of the Platform.

The third and the greatest or most formidable danger that can be alleged against the Platform is such a combination of the Platform and organisation as may threaten, if not actually lead to, a subversion of the Government.

So far, in the history of our country since the Platform became a political power, has this danger only once displayed itself—namely, at the time of the Reform agitation in 1830-32. Then, and very little more would have turned the scale, and altered the history of England to the end of time. A man must be cold-blooded, indeed, whose feelings are not stirred as he reads, and in imagination lives through, the doings of the Platform in that great crisis, as he takes in the import of the huge meetings throughout the land, as he realises the subdued but dogged determination embodied in the speeches, and in the resolutions passed with acclamation by the assembled masses, and as he sees depicted in the countenances of the people their impassioned earnestness. One holds one's breath absolutely as one witnesses the checks, the reverses, of the proposed measure of reform—the check in the House of Commons, the reverse in the House of Lords, and the final climax in the second check in the Upper House.

Would the patience of the people hold out? or would their endurance be stretched to breaking-point, and a great popular convulsion effect a forcible revolution in the State?

With a feeling of the most intense relief one reads of the final surmounting of all obstacles, and of the termination of the crisis. But there must ever rest on one's mind the deep impression of the narrowness of the escape England had from a violent, if not a bloody, revolution; and one must acknowledge as real the danger that the Platform and organisation combined could have led to an actual subversion of the Government.

The Chartist demonstration of 1848, formidable though it was, never for one moment approached the degree of danger of the Reform Act agitation.

Since then there has been no attempt made to set up a rival to the House of Commons. Indeed, it may, I think, be assumed that, with the enactment of the successive Reform Bills, the danger has passed away. The possibility of the Platform forcibly subverting Government was due to the fact that the representation of the people in Parliament was then entirely disproportioned to its proper claims, and that it was only by a display of force behind such representation as there was, that popular opinion could impose its behests on Parliament.

Now that the franchise has been extended to every householder in the country, and to a good many other people besides, the House of Commons can never for more than a very brief period come into collision with the Platform. The views expressed from the Platform, and the resolutions of the meetings, if those of the real majority of the country, must in the course of a short time find themselves represented by a majority in the House of Commons, and as that House is practically the governing authority in the country, the views of the majority of the people must soon be given effect to. If the views of the Platform are not those of the majority, there can be no danger of the Platform subverting the Government.

That the alarm which was felt against all sorts of associations or conventions of delegates has very considerably diminished from what it once was is evident by the indifference with which Parliament now views great party political associations, which in earlier times would not have been tolerated for a moment. Annually now there are meetings of large numbers of delegates, who discuss and arrange, and even settle, the programmes for their parties—Liberal Associations, Conservative Associations, Trades Associations. Experience has shown that Parliament has no need to fear a rival in any of these. More powerful associations than any of them have flourished and passed harmlessly away. The Political Unions of 1830–32, probably the most formidable of their kind, dissolved themselves or melted away. The Anti-Corn-Law League, powerful as it was, dissolved itself, having accomplished its object. The Chartist Convention, thinned by the punishments to which its members laid themselves open, and torn by internal dissensions, decayed away and died. Moreover, so readily now does Parliament submit to the impressions or determinations of public opinion, that there is little danger of any attempt to set up, by means of the Platform and associations, any formidable rival to the House of Commons; or, if it were set up, would it have much prospect of success when pitted against a majority in the House of Commons and the vast forces which that majority would represent?

It would appear then that of all the dangers of the Platform to which I have alluded, the only real and abiding danger is, that of the people being misled into evil counsels by bad and ignorant men. Against this danger the real, and, in fact, the only safeguard is, I believe, education, using the word in its fullest, broadest sense. It is no new empirical remedy; it is one which has been tried, and to the extent tried has been successful. There was a time when the political education of the people was held by some to be a danger to society, now it is our sheet-anchor against the worst dangers to which the cause of good order in any community can be exposed.

Writer after writer on political subjects, from the very earliest days of the Platform, has pressed for political education—knowledge was the one thing wanted. Burgh, in his *Political Disquisitions*, written more than a hundred years ago, insists on freedom of discussion as necessary for political education. Edmund Burke, in his celebrated *Thoughts on the Cause of the Present Discontents*, putting the highest ideal before himself, said: "It is our business carefully to cultivate in our minds, and to rear to the most perfect vigour and maturity every sort of generous and honest feeling that belongs to our nature—to bring the dispositions that are lovely in private life into the service and conduct of the commonwealth, so to be patriots as not to forget that we are gentlemen."

Some of the leaders of the first Platform agitation of the civic industrial population in 1792–95—Hardy, Place, and others—deplored the state of ignorance in which the people were, and the ease with which they were consequently misled. Cobbett groaned over their ignorance, and did his best to educate them, and to wean them from violent courses which could only end in disaster. The better among the Chartist leaders—Lovett, Collins, and some others—looked upon political education as the first necessity for the people—not as some men will at once say the education which would make them go wrong, but the education which would prevent them going wrong, which would prevent them following will-o'-the-wisp leaders, or foolish schemes which could only end in misery.

"What better course," says Lord Brougham in his essay *On the Advantages of Political Science*,—"what better course (than sound and fair instruction) can be devised against the efforts of violent and intriguing men? What more sure remedy against the arts of political empirics whose natural prey is, and ever will be, the ignorant vulgar, but who in vain display their wares before well-informed and reasoning men?"

Mr. Mackinnon, in his clever work on *Public Opinion*,[1] wrote: "Assemblies of men, and even communities, may be

[1] See *On the Rise and Present State of Public Opinion in Great Britain and other Parts of the World.*—Anon., but by G. A. Mackinnon, ex-M.P., 1838, p. 21.

and often are influenced by their passions, by their interest, by their enthusiasm; but the real and proper sentiment on any given question that ought to influence the greater part of the well-informed in any country, to be styled public opinion, must be founded on the basis of moral principle and general information. It was this moral principle, this general information, which education would teach."

Roebuck, who, during a long political career, was a sturdy advocate for the people, dwelt upon the same question in one of his pamphlets. He said: "The mere possession of power by the people is not sufficient to ensure a right employment of it; to that end, knowledge, and a sound morality, are necessary."

Opinions on this point need not, however, be multiplied. But there is just one other I wish to refer to, more recent than those just quoted, and that of a man whose opinion on constitutional matters is justly regarded with great respect—Walter Bagehot. One of the main ideas which runs through his work on *The English Constitution*, is the vital importance of instructing and educating the mass of the electorate. He wrote: "The mass of the English people are politically contented as well as politically deferential. . . . A deferential community, in which the bulk of the people are ignorant, is in a state of what is called in mechanics unstable equilibrium. If the equilibrium is once disturbed, there is no tendency to return to it, but rather to depart from it. In communities where the masses are ignorant, but respectful, if you once permit the ignorant class to begin to rule, you may bid farewell to deference for ever. Their demagogues will inculcate, their newspapers will recount, that the rule of the existing dynasty (the people) is better than the rule of the fallen dynasty (the aristocracy)."[1]

It was once remarked that "the correlative to universal suffrage should be universal intelligence;" and it is towards this goal we should approximate as near as possible.

"We have not," wrote Mr. Bagehot, shortly after the passing of the Reform Act of 1867, "enfranchised a class less needing to be guided by their betters than the old class; on the contrary, the new class need it more than the old;" and

[1] Bagehot's *English Constitution*, p. 270.

the statement applies with even greater truth to the Reform Act of 1885. It is, however, unnecessary to enforce this argument, for there are few now who will be prepared to dissent from it.

Everything, in fact, points to the desirability, to the necessity of the people, using that term in its widest sense, learning and understanding the grounds upon which the great principles of government are based. The more those grounds are discussed, the more clearly will their wisdom and truth be recognised, and the stability of society be fortified against wild doctrines, however plausible or enticing.

The task of thus politically educating the people can alone be undertaken successfully by the best men in the nation recognising their responsibility, and taking their proper position as leaders.

Quite in the early days of the Platform did Burke point out the natural result of the better men not taking their proper part. Writing to Lord Rockingham in December 1769, relative to one of the Petitions in connection with the Middlesex election, he said: "Bold men take the lead to which others are entitled, and they soon come to a power not natural to them, by the remissness of those who neither know how to be effectual friends or dangerous enemies, or active champions in a good cause." [1]

But it was not until the last decade of the last century, when the first stirrings and movements of the civic industrial population began to display themselves, that the necessity for the people having leaders, instead of misleaders, became so vitally urgent. It was most unfortunate when those who were their natural leaders joined the camp of the Minister of the day, when even "the Society of the Friends of the People" abandoned their cause, and let them fall into the hands of such men as Gale Jones and some of his friends. Fox saw the importance of the occasion, and did his best.

There is a letter of his, written in 1795, which sets forth his opinions shortly and clearly. He wrote: [2] "But among all the dangers of which we have the option, I have no doubt that

[1] Burke's *Works*, vol. i. p. 110.

[2] See letter to his nephew, Lord Holland, in 1795.—Grey's *Life of Lord Grey*, p. 10.

the right part of a man who means well to the country is to endeavour to rouse the people before it becomes too late to act by other means than those of force, by giving them leaders who mean well, to direct their efforts to such remedies to the present evils as are least likely to create confusion."

Time after time, in the period which has been under review, were deep lamentations expressed by the people themselves at their being left to their own resources, whilst those who should have been teaching them or helping them stood aloof. And on each fresh outburst of agitation, as the numbers of the people multiplied, and they became more formidable, did the necessity for good leadership become more and more imperative.

Carlyle, who had fathomed the deep of French revolution, and, with the knowledge derived therefrom, was witnessing the developments of Chartism, has most impressively expressed the need for teachers, for leaders. "What is the meaning of the 'five points,' if we will understand them? What are all popular commotions and maddest bellowings, from Peterloo to the Place de Grève itself? Bellowings, *in*articulate cries as of a dumb creature in rage and pain; to the ears of wisdom they are inarticulate prayers. 'Guide me, govern me! I am mad and miserable, and cannot guide myself!' Surely of all 'rights of man' this right of the ignorant man to be guided by the wiser, to be, gently or forcibly, held in the true course by him, is the indisputablest. Nature herself ordains it from the first; Society struggles towards perfection by enforcing and accomplishing it more and more. If Freedom have any meaning, it means enjoyment of this right, wherein all other rights are enjoyed. It is a sacred right and duty, on both sides, and the summary of all social duties whatsoever between the two. Why does the one toil with his hands, if the other be not to toil, still more unweariedly, with heart and head? The brawny craftsman finds it no child's play to mould his unpliant rugged masses; neither is guidance of men a dilettanteism; what it becomes when treated as a dilettanteism we may see!"[1]

Lord Brougham, in his essay *On the Advantages of Political Science,* puts the matter on somewhat different ground. He

[1] Carlyle, *Chartism,* chap. vi.

says: "The question is no longer left open to us whether the people shall be taught politics or not. Taught they must be, and the only question is, whether they shall be well taught, or ill instructed and misinformed. Do what you will, somebody will take the part of public instructor. It is an office that any man in a free country may assume, and it is one which almost every one thinks himself qualified to fill. If the people are not taught sound doctrine upon the subject by calm and tolerably impartial men, they will inevitably listen to guides of a far different description, and will fall a prey to the violent and more interested class of politicians, to the incentives of agitators, the arts of impostors, and the nostrums of quacks."

In the quite early stages of its existence the Platform had been in the hands of able men of more or less position, and, as may be remembered, it had been controlled by party leaders. Subsequently it fell into the hands of Gale Jones, Binns, and men of similar position and capacity. After that, for a while, Sir Francis Burdett and a few members of Parliament, holding popular views, did their best to lead the people. But they were shunned and despised by their contemporaries and fellow-members for so doing, and the most conspicuous Platform leaders were Orator Hunt and Cobbett. Lord Liverpool and his colleagues, with the notable and brilliant exception of Canning, naturally never condescended to a proceeding which they considered degrading, and as savouring of revolution. Even the Whigs were averse to Platforming. But by degrees they were forced to adopt it.

After the Peterloo Massacre of 1819 some of them began to take the lead again on the Platform, and we find Brougham corresponding with Lord Grey in 1820 as to the possibility of endeavouring to take the monopoly of the Platform out of Orator Hunt's hands, and then, some ten years or so later, the Whigs, as a body, giving their full strength to the Platform in the agitation for the Reform Act.

And it was a sign of still greater progress when the Tory party, who had shunned the Platform as they would have done the plague, found they could not—without too great detriment to themselves—leave so powerful an instrument exclusively in the hands of their opponents, and took to using it too. Once the Platform was adopted as an engine of party warfare, once it was employed for great party discussions, its position was for ever and aye secured. The Tories were slow in learning the use and power of the Platform. Canning had given them the lead, but it was not till years after his death, and after the first Reform Act had been passed, that another great Tory statesman, Sir Robert Peel, arose, who followed and improved upon Canning's example. From the issue of his Tamworth manifesto in 1834 Sir R. Peel showed the most thorough appreciation of the value of the Platform; he was a regular speaker in public meetings, and delivered some of his most important and eloquent speeches at them.[1]

And then, once more, the Platform sank down to the level of the dregs of Chartist agitators, and was an instrument of evil in the hands of many a bad and ignorant man—blind or wilful misleaders of the people. From this slough it was rescued by men whose names will live for ever in Platform history as shining lights—Cobden, Bright, Villiers, W. J. Fox, and many other members of the Anti-Corn-Law League who raised the Platform from the depths to which it had sunk. Marvellous was the impress which these men made on the Platform. By prodigious labour and self-sacrifice, by the constant reiteration of the highest and noblest truths of political morality, and by the high-toned example which they set, they weaned the rougher elements of society to constitutional courses; they instilled great political principles into their minds, and set them an example of what the Platform ought to be, and how, with it, to win an apparently hopeless cause. Attwood is given credit for the modifying, restraining influence which he exercised in the most critical and excited moments of the Reform agitation. The work of Cobden and Bright was even more memorable. They stayed the people in a career rushing to violence and bloodshed, and showed the world how an instrument which was being perverted to evil was, in reality, an instrument of boundless good.

Fortunately for the welfare of the State, from that time on,

[1] It is much to be regretted that no collection of Sir R. Peel's extra-Parliamentary speeches has ever been made or published. Such an omission is a commentary on the strange want of appreciation hitherto shown by historians of the importance of extra-Parliamentary speeches.

in ever increasing numbers, the best men of the nation have been coming forward utilising the Platform to mould and form public opinion, to educate and instruct the masses. Nor can the example be too widely followed. Those who are the leaders of thought, those who are qualified to instruct the people, and who are able to throw light on the multifarious problems and perplexities of the times, should take their full part in doing so. They can less afford to hold back now than at any former period of our history. In the great tasks of persevering in the political education of the people and of elevating the tone of political life there is one great encouragement—the vast and manifest improvement which such efforts have already produced. Place, writing in 1843, or thereabouts, said: "Political circumstances are much better understood than they were since I was a young man. . . . The truth is this: The people have greatly increased their stock of knowledge, and cannot be excited and put in motion as they used to be for objects they do not clearly comprehend. . . . If they are now expected to take any decided part in any measure, appeals must be made to their understandings. Appeals to their passions seldom fail to rouse them at the instant, but all such agitations are evanescent. This has been shown over and over again. The greatest agitator who ever for so long a period endeavoured to operate upon the common people was the late Henry Hunt. He caused repeated ebullitions among large numbers of them, but they were only ebullitions, and led to nothing—not even to any decided outrage." [1]

But to come to our own time. Contrast for one moment the mental and moral attitude of the people as represented by the Platform in 1839 with it in 1890, and one sees what a gulf separates them. The speeches received then with rapturous cheers of approval would now, in the vast majority of cases, be drowned by roars of angry or contemptuous disapproval. The people, with their growing power, have risen to their increased responsibilities; far wider knowledge is displayed at their meetings than formerly; a far higher moral tone is apparent; a more discriminating judgment; quicker intelligence; and one is struck by the cordial response which high and noble sentiments evoke from the hearers. The public

[1] Place, MSS., 27,827, pp. 219, 220.

assemblies of the present day, in fact, prove visibly and palpably the immeasurable improvement which has taken place. Just as the enormous addition to the wealth of the country within the present century has lifted vast numbers out of poverty and placed them in positions of prosperity, so the spread of knowledge and education has lifted the great body of the people out of the depths of ignorance and passion, and helped to qualify them for duties which, not long ago, they were utterly incompetent to perform.

It would be impossible to say what has been the share which the Platform can claim in this progress. Certainly a very great one, for the improvement is most marked within its own sphere. The long training and disciplining in public meetings has brought out the better qualities of the nation. Cobden once said, when he was nearing the end of his Anti-Corn-Law campaign: "There are men now brought out by this very agitation in every borough and large town that I have visited—new men, not the old hacks of party, but persons drawn out with a solemn and earnest conviction, with a craving after justice and truth in this matter, who are diligently at work in every part of the kingdom."[1] And so it has been with other agitations—even with mere electoral struggles.

The very grounds too on which the principal agitations have been conducted have been in themselves great educational, great improving forces. They have been struggles for liberty, for justice, for fair treatment; and the constant assertion from the Platform of these great principles has engrafted deeper and deeper in the public mind the truth, the goodness, of these great principles.

This effect has been well described by an American writer already referred to. He says: "The ends for which the Political Union, the Anti-Slavery Society, and the Anti-Corn-Law League laboured, and the triumphs they won, were of immeasurable value in themselves, but the educational means they employed in enlightening the mind of the masses, in teaching them to think, reflect, and compare, and observe for themselves, produced results of equal importance." And then applying these conclusions to a wider area, he adds: "Nor

[1] Cobden's *Speeches*, vol. i. p. 132, 1844.

was this organisation of the moral forces of the nation's mind limited in its benefits to England. Like the development and application of some new mechanical or natural force, it extended to other countries, where its operation is even more needed than it was in England. The Birmingham banner—'Peace, Law, and Order,' as Lamartine said of the tricolour—will yet make the tour of the world, sweeping away with its white folds all the red flags of brute force, and rallying aggrieved populations to the Platform instead of to the barricade."[1]

One fact is conspicuous at the present time, and that is the extreme popularity of the Platform. Nor is this unnatural, for there are many reasons why the people should like it. So far back as 1818[2] a writer in the *Edinburgh Review* gave a partial explanation of the charms of the Platform: "In numerous meetings (meetings of large numbers) every man catches animation from the feelings of his neighbour, and gathers courage from the strength of a multitude. Such assemblies, and they alone, with all their defects and errors, have the privilege of inspiring many human beings with a perfect, however transient, disinterestedness, and rendering the most ordinary men capable of foregoing interest and forgetting self in the enthusiasm of zeal for a common cause. Their vices are a corrective of the deliberating selfishness of their superiors. Their bad, as well as good qualities, render them the portion of society the most susceptible of impressions, and the most accessible to public feelings. They are fitted to produce that democratic spirit, which, tempered in its progress, through the various classes of the community becomes the vital principle of liberty."

But there are other reasons. As individuals people feel themselves of little consequence, but a public meeting begets a sense of power, and to some extent also a sense of responsibility; often too in the speeches from the Platform not alone does one hear one's own views put more powerfully and conclusively than one could put them one's self, but fresh information is gained, and new ideas are awakened. There is also, in affirming or rejecting a particular proposition, a sense

[1] See *Walks in the Black Country*, by Elihu Burritt.
[2] *Edinburgh Review*, vol. xxxi., "Universal Suffrage."

of participating in Government which is pleasing to men's self-esteem. The Platform is, in fact, the outward and visible sign of their possession of power.

Then there is another and likewise a potent reason of the popularity of the Platform—the personal acquaintance which it enables the people to make with their leaders, or the remarkable men of the nation. Men of whom they have heard much and read much are brought into personal contact with them.

"It is much to see and hear sentiments and opinions advocated by the most suitable exponents and champions. It is a great deal to be able to associate the words and the man, the speech and the personal career . . . the great majority of mankind do reasonably prefer to be a little acquainted with the man who pretends to instruct them."[1]

And one reason more may be added—and that is, the intense pleasure which comes from listening to a really great speaker, and many of the great men of the present century have been not merely great speakers but great orators.

The rivals of the Platform in the exercise of popular influence are Parliament and the Press. Roebuck, in a pamphlet written in 1835, has a very carefully stated summary of the influence of the Press. He said: "The powers and opportunities of a teacher of the people through the periodical Press is greater than those of any other class of teachers. He has an immense audience, and by constant repetition he is able to produce a certain and lasting effect. New ideas cannot be introduced by any sudden or singular effort, however powerful or well directed; it is the dropping of the water on the stone, the line upon line, the precept upon precept, that brings about important changes. The people can be effectually moved only by being constantly addressed." And in 1844 Mr. Bright paid a fine tribute to the Press. He said:[2] "There is nothing more glorious to my mind than the possession of an organ of the Press like a daily newspaper in this country, if it be managed with honesty and integrity. I do not think any man, however great his ambition, if he were to look narrowly into it, could wish a prouder position than one in which he would be enabled to pour forth every morning to 10,000 or 20,000 readers

[1] See *The Times*, 7th November 1868. [2] See *The League*, 1844, p. 666.

the reflections of an honest, honourable, and intelligent mind. Why, he is actually insinuating his own soul into the souls of the people among whom he lives! and, though he cannot trace precisely how much good he has done, yet he has the satisfaction of knowing that what he is publishing is a great truth; that it is a sublime idea which he has laid before the world; a great truth which he has developed; and the good seed which he has sown is going on vegetating from generation to generation, and until the end of all things the amount of good which he has done to his species shall never be told."

To compare the power of the Press and the Platform as political institutions of popular government, I think precedence must be given to the Platform, though, as must be fully and freely acknowledged, a very great deal of its power is dependent on the Press. The speaker on a Platform has as large an audience as any organ of the Press, often, indeed, a far larger, and by constant repetition, as the numerous Platform agitations have shown, is able to produce a definite and lasting effect. The articles in the Press are anonymous, and their merit or demerit cannot be weighed, so far as authorship is concerned. Speeches from the Platform are personal, and the speaker's identity adds to or detracts from the merits of his speech. Moreover, a speech which is received with the approval of a large assembly becomes practically the voice of that assembly, and is therefore of greater weight than any individual view. A powerful speech delivered by a leading statesman from the Platform has greater effect than a powerful article in the most influential organ of the Press. The Press may represent "public opinion"; the Platform represents "public opinion" plus physical force.

The other rival of the Platform is Parliament. It and the Platform are in some ways so closely connected that it is a little difficult to separate them so as to compare their influence. The great men in Parliament are now with but few exceptions great Platform speakers too; and members of Parliament figure in the double capacity of speakers in Parliament and speakers on the Platform. Still, I think, some approach at a comparison may be made.

There is an article in the *Edinburgh Review*[1] of 1826 on

[1] *Edinburgh Review*, vol. xliv. p. 458.

"Parliamentary History," which discusses the relative importance of Platform speeches, and of Parliamentary speeches, and which contains a valuable comparison of the power of the Platform, and of Parliamentary speeches, and of the Press at that period. The writer said: "A great sensation may, upon any question, be excited by pamphlets and newspapers; and public meetings may increase this materially. But it is in vain to deny that the community looks with far greater interest to the debates upon the same subject in Parliament; and we accordingly find that the meeting of this body deprives all other disquisitions of the attention which was bestowed upon them during the recess. . . .

"Reports of proceedings at public meetings approach nearest to those of Parliamentary debates; but they are left far behind, even in the extent of their publicity—still farther in the interest excited by them, and, consequently, in the impression they make. . . . But suppose even that the proceedings at any meeting were of a kind so interesting as to find their way to every reader, and excite the same attention with the most important Parliamentary debate, it is only once, and away. The impression is gone to-morrow; as it may be, indeed, with the debates in Parliament—that is, with any one debate. But the grand difference is, that the debates go on day after day—the subject is revived over and over again—the same persons renew their appeals to the same readers for weeks and months, in every variety of discussion—in speech and in reply—in good set phrase and interlocutory remark—in grave formal debate and in passing conversation—and the speakers at last become known to the readers almost as if they debated in their presence. Thus, whether they deserve it or not, the Parliamentary debaters, from belonging to the body which has in its hands the honour of making laws, and indeed directly or indirectly ruling the country, have by far the greatest weight in regulating the public opinion upon any given question, and the greatest influence in directing that opinion generally upon subjects connected with public affairs."

Doubtless, this was true at the time it was written, and the view is most valuable as enabling us to see how the objections made to the Platform then have not any existence now. The whole matter has undergone a vast, a complete change. It is no longer now, "only once and away" with subjects treated by the Platform. The subject of Platform agitation of the time being is rung through every key with a pertinacity to which Parliament cannot for one moment pretend. Where were the Bulgarian atrocities most discussed—in Parliament or on the Platform? Was it the speeches in the first and second Midlothian campaigns, and the Platform speeches of the leaders of the Liberal party, or the speeches in Parliament which most enlightened the people, or most influenced them at the polls in 1880? Where was the last Reform agitation against the Lords most discussed—in Parliament, or on the Platform? The answer to every one of these questions must, I think, be "the Platform."

The debates in Parliament, important as they are, influence and inform the members who hear them, and to a certain extent the leading political thinkers of the day; but they lack attractiveness for the general public, whom they reach usually in an abbreviated form—they are no longer the exclusive source of information or political instruction they once were. The Platform has, in some ways, usurped the place of or supplanted Parliament. The really great and vital discussions are now carried on outside Parliament, and, as a rule, are threshed out there and moulded into some more or less definite decision or conclusion before they reach Parliament for legislative or executive purposes. On the Platform there is no "closure" of debate. Subject to the laws of libel or seditious conspiracy or incitement to crime there is no restraint upon the Platform; there is no limitation to its times and seasons of speaking. So small has the United Kingdom become in these days of telegraphs, and almost instantaneous verbatim reports of the newspaper Press, that, practically, the discussions on great measures of home policy, and on great questions of external policy have become national, and not merely Parliamentary. Speaker answers speaker across the country just as member answers member across the floor of the House of Commons, and the nation stands by listening to and taking part in the debate; and then, in any really great crisis of the nation, instead of the division bell ringing, and the decision being taken within the four walls of a chamber, the tocsin of Parliament sounds, Parliament is dissolved, and the nation itself decides, the constituencies dropping their pebbles into the urn, to be counted up, when Parliament again meets, to record the result. There is something indisputably grand in this, that catches the imagination, that appeals to men's pride. It is, indeed, the acme of national self-government, the triumph of democracy.

So much, then, for the present and the past. But there is another sphere to which also many eyes are often and not unanxiously turned. What of the future? What benefit, after all, will result from the recognition of the right of public discussion, from the free exercise of the right of public meeting, and from the control over Parliament which these rights have given the people? A full reply cannot yet be given, but this much can be said now. First, that inasmuch as the government is, by means of the Platform, in the hands of the people themselves, they have the strongest possible motives towards a careful and wise course and system of government; for with them now, and not with an individual ruler, nor even a special or separate class, rest their destinies and those of this mighty empire. They hold their fate in their own hands. Bright, in one of his most eloquent perorations, in a speech delivered during the Reform agitation of 1866, said: "If a class has failed (to make an Eden), let us try the nation—that is our faith, that is our purpose, that is our cry—let us try the nation. This it is which has called together these countless numbers of the people to demand a change; and as I think of it, and of these gatherings, sublime in their vastness and in their resolution, I think I see, as it were, above the hilltops of time, the glimmerings of the dawn of a better and a nobler day for the country and for the people that I love so well."

But the dawn may be dimmed, and the day may be darkened by rash or hasty action on the part of the people themselves who now constitute the power of the nation. They have, therefore, the most powerful incentive to the acquisition of that education and knowledge, and the cultivation of those qualities and talents, which will best qualify them to acquit themselves wisely and faithfully of the fearful responsibility with which they are charged. That is one of the benefits which we can now assert springs from the Platform, and which cannot fail to influence beneficially the future.

And next, it may be said that all the discussion which has been rendered possible by the acquisition of the right of free public speech affords a process of sifting and seeking for the truer, better things, and is therefore beneficial. It is only so that truth can ever be assured, only so that foolish courses can be discovered and rejected, wise courses ascertained and followed. All true life, national as well as individual, is a striving for, a straining after a higher, better, nobler life, and an immense step has been gained in this direction when a nation has secured for itself the free, uncontrolled, untrammelled right of public discussion.

The Platform may, then, fairly claim that it has given the highest human incentive to the progress of political education and enlightenment among the people. It may fairly claim, too, that it has facilitated the way towards a higher national life. These are vast gains in the rough path of human progress, and though we now are unable to discover the secrets of the future, yet, when we bear these facts in mind, and when we consider the sterling character of the people, we may look forward with calm and hopeful confidence to the ultimate destinies of this great nation.

THE END

INDEX

A

C

Q

R